PROPERTIUS:
A HELLENISTIC POET ON
LOVE AND DEATH

PROPERTIUS:
A HELLENISTIC POET ON
LOVE AND DEATH

Theodore D. Papanghelis

LECTURER IN CLASSICS,
UNIVERSITY OF THESSALONIKI

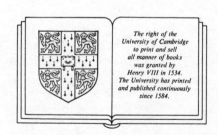

The right of the
University of Cambridge
to print and sell
all manner of books
was granted by
Henry VIII in 1534.
The University has printed
and published continuously
since 1584.

CAMBRIDGE UNIVERSITY PRESS

CAMBRIDGE

LONDON   NEW YORK   NEW ROCHELLE

MELBOURNE   SYDNEY

Published by the Press Syndicate of the University of Cambridge
The Pitt Building, Trumpington Street, Cambridge CB2 1RP
32 East 57th Street, New York, NY 10022, USA
10 Stamford Road, Oakleigh, Melbourne 3166, Australia

First published 1987

Printed in Great Britain by the University Press, Cambridge

British Library cataloguing in publication data
Papanghelis, Theodore D.
Propertius: a Hellenistic poet on love and death.
1. Propertius, Sextus–Criticism and interpretation
I. Title
874'.01   PA6646

Library of Congress cataloguing in publication data
Papanghelis, Theodore D.
Propertius: a Hellenistic poet on love and death.
Rev. and expanded version of thesis (Ph. D.)–
Cambridge University.
1. Propertius, Sextus–Criticism and interpretation.
2. Love in literature.   3. Death in literature.
I. Title.
PA6646.P37   1987   874'.01   86-14689

ISBN 0 521 32314 2

For Demetrios *and* Theodora

nec umquam
esse satis potero, praestem licet omnia, gratus

Ne méprisez la sensibilité de personne.
La sensibilité de chacun, c'est son génie.

Baudelaire, *Journaux intimes*

CONTENTS

PREFACE

Tristan rides the crest of an ecstatic and mystical passion, craving not so much Iseult as liberating Darkness and self-annihilation. Tristan and Iseult spurn the duality of physical love; the one-ness they seek can only be realised through and beyond death. It is this awesome, and distinctly European, secret of the medieval legend that unfolds over the three acts of Wagner's homonymous musical drama. Thus Denis de Rougemont in the celebrated and controversial *L'Amour et l'Occident.* He may be right or wrong, but there can be little doubt that what he deals with is – as the English rendering of the very beginning of J. Bedier's version of the legend would have it – 'a high tale of love and death'.

Before any reference can be safely made to the humble and scholarly tale of this book the pitch must be considerably lowered. Not because this tale is less distinctly European, nor yet because genuinely passionate and romantic love, as distinct from merry sensuality, was invented by the eleventh-century French Troubadours. When erudite men like C. S. Lewis in his *Allegory of love* and Denis de Rougemont in the above-mentioned work thus define the eras of European Love, they court disbelief – and on this point I firmly side with Niall Rudd (*Lines of enquiry*, ix). Why, having myself embarked upon the present study somewhat in the spirit of the Wagnerian *Liebestod* (I mean de Rougemont's interpretation of it, not the one that has Wagner glorifying sensual desire), I have then increasingly and for the most part felt the need to exorcise, or at least keep at bay, that spirit – this I trust the following pages to make clear.

I started thinking about Propertian love and death some six years ago, in Greece. Teachers and friends in the Classical Faculty of the University of Thessaloniki allowed me to try out some of my ideas on them. I thank them warmly. In 1981 the Greek State Scholarship Foundation wafted me to Cambridge where three years of unremitting largesse enabled me to enjoy a much-needed φιλόφρων ἡσυχία and a highly congenial academic environment. Thus my college – 'The Evangelist St John my Patron was' – found its own generosity, in the form of a Benefactor's Studentship, anticipated, but it was not slow to help when other emoluments were petering out. To both these foundations I am deeply grateful for the support and the honour.

This book presents the revised and expanded version of my Cambridge Ph.D. thesis, which has also been adapted in order to accommodate my view of Propertius 4.7. The long section on the latter poem did not form part of the doctoral enterprise which Professor E. J. Kenney, while allowing me my head, supervised with exhilarating interest, intellectual stimulation and heartening humour. I am aware of being indebted to him for much that goes beyond my work, not least for his courteous hospitality. Miss M. Hubbard and Mr I. M. Le M. DuQuesnay, my Ph.D. examiners, had many useful and thought-provoking comments to offer, as did Dr R. O. A. M. Lyne, to whom I am very grateful not only for his stimulating criticism of the thesis material but also for his enthusiastic encouragement. L. P. Wilkinson *vidi tantum*. The distinguished scholar invited me to his rooms in King's College for an urbane discussion on 4.7, a draft of which he had previously read 'with great interest and generally with assent'; it was the warmest day I ever experienced in the British January. Guy Lee has read with sensitive vigilance through successive drafts of the whole work; my very special debt to him is for many a valuable point on both style and content – but, above all, for his invaluable friendship. I basked in it during the whole of my stay in Cambridge and, back at home, I am still its beneficiary. He has made the task of giving English translations for the Propertian passages immensely easier for his Greek friend by providing him with his own versions of all relevant elegies from Books 1 and 2, and also of 4.7. A non-native wielder of English cannot be too grateful for this, though in my case the requirements of the argument abetted by a native stubbornness dictated divergences at a few places, namely, 1.13.21–2, 1.13.26–9, 2.26b.58, 2.28.56, 4.7.11–12 and 4.7.79–80. More hazardously, I have given my own translations of all other Propertian passages, and indeed of all other literary quotations, whether modern or ancient, which appear in the book *except for* Lucretius and Theocritus' *Idylls*, for which I have used the translations of C. Bailey and A. S. F. Gow respectively, Virgil's *Eclogues* and Tibullus, where Guy Lee kindly allowed me to quote from his translations, as did Professor Constantine A. Trypanis for the passages quoted from Musaeus' *Hero and Leander* (with a very slight alteration at ll. 341–2). And the translated passages from Balzac's *Le Père Goriot* on p. 168 are those of M. A. Crawford, Harmondsworth 1951.

The occasional cackling of the gander, especially where Propertian translations are concerned, may thus disconcert even the charitable reader. But the current, and quite reasonable, practice calls for translation of Greek and Latin passages; it was put to me that translation is a good discipline for the author himself and makes him reveal his hand by declaring what he thinks a given passage means; and I was enamoured enough of the English language to take up, partly and in a small way, a metaphrastic challenge which nowhere involved my natural idiom. I found the effort, some Flaubertian agony over the *mot juste* notwithstanding, quite rewarding; where I have not succeeded in clearly revealing my hand through my version, I hope for indulgence.

I am conscious of having learned from more books and articles than could be referred to or listed here. I hope that the introduction as well as the individual footnotes allow my salient creditors to be clearly identified. For the rest, I allow myself to take a leaf out of Miss Hubbard's Propertius and thank all those who recognise here their property but fail to find sufficient or explicit acknowledgement in the pages that follow. The opinions and obsessions that will be found in them are entirely my own, and so are the errors and infelicities.

This book owes a great deal to the combined operation of Pauline Hire and Susan Moore, of Cambridge University Press. To the former I am especially indebted for encouragement and advice, and to the latter for her tactful subeditorial skill. In thanking them both I cannot but think of the expertise applied to the production of the book by other members of the staff of C.U.P.

Dr N. Follett has kindly permitted me to refer to material of which she holds the copyright. Miss Catherine Arambatzis typed first the thesis and then the book with skill and tact; had she not been there for these last two hectic years, I would still be fumbling and mumbling over the keyboard.

T.D.P.

Thessaloniki
March 1986

ABBREVIATIONS

Note. In abbreviating the names of ancient authors and the titles of their works I have generally followed the conventions of the *Oxford classical dictionary*; in abbreviating periodical titles those of *L'Année philologique*.

Gow	A. S. F. Gow, *Theocritus.* 2 vols. 2nd edn Cambridge 1952.
Gow–Page	A. S. F. Gow and D. L. Page, *The Greek Anthology: Hellenistic epigrams.* 2 vols. Cambridge 1965.
van Groningen	B. A. van Groningen, *Euphorion.* Amsterdam 1977.
Kl. Pauly	*'Der Kleine Pauly' Lexicon der Antike.* K. Ziegler and W. Sontheimer (eds.). 5 vols. Stuttgart 1964–75.
Nisbet–Hubbard	R. G. M. Nisbet and M. Hubbard, *A commentary on Horace: Odes Book I.* Oxford 1970.
OLD	*Oxford Latin dictionary.* P. G. W. Glare (ed.). Oxford 1982.
Pfeiffer	R. Pfeiffer, *Callimachus.* 2 vols. Oxford 1949–53.
Powell	J. U. Powell, *Collectanea Alexandrina.* Oxford 1925.
RE	*Real-Encyclopädie der klassischen Altertumswissenschaft.* A. Pauly, G. Wissowa and W. Kroll (eds.). Stuttgart 1893– .
TLL	*Thesaurus linguae Latinae.* Leipzig 1900–
West, IEG	M. L. West, *Iambi et elegi Graeci ante Alexandrum cantati.* 2 vols. Oxford 1971–2.

1

INTRODUCTORY

To speak of love *and* death in the same breath is to speak of romantic passion *par excellence*. Classical antiquity knew such passion – and, as a rule, frowned upon it. Marriages of convenience and other practical considerations would normally take precedence over romance.[1] It was also in a practical spirit that people prodded themselves to timely sensuality in view of death's inevitable onset. The *carpe diem* mood is as unavoidable as human weakness. Catullus, Propertius and Tibullus shared with their contemporaries a sensitivity to it, but they could also fly in the face of their contemporaries' conception of love by endorsing, in varying degrees of seriousness, a type of lover consumed by the *morbus*, intent on the *militia* and wallowing in the *servitium amoris*. These are metaphors on which the idea of death will naturally thrive, although not in order to militate against, but rather in order to confirm the idea of love. 'Love until death' and 'death in the service, or because of the hardships of love' do not mark an antagonism (which lies at the root of the *carpe diem* mood) so much as a certain *rapprochement*. Such *rapprochement*, apt to be accounted a mere cliché of love poetry today, would have struck the contemporary reader of love elegy as part of an idiom that wanted, whether in jest or earnest, to sound unconventional. This idiom Propertius shared with his fellow elegists but in dealing with one of its cardinal topoi, namely, the rapport between elegiac love life and death, he also developed an 'idiolect' of his own. It is a central claim of the present book that this poet, chiefly in the course of his second poetic book, reached out towards modes of erotic expression which cannot be probed or adequately described simply in terms of 'love *until* death' or 'death *in* and *because of* love'; that the potential of the Propertian *amor* is fully realised and its quality best revealed within the frame of various death fantasies; and that the association of love and death in his work grows so radical as to shade off into various forms of identification, where the one comes to be envisaged in the pictorial and conceptual terms pertaining to the other.

Scholars freely acknowledge the frequency and intensity of Propertius' references to erotic death but their pronouncements on the subject do not

---

[1] Allen (1950) 258–64, Burck (1952) 163–82 and Sullivan (1976) 81–91 offer informative accounts, but a more recent and livelier picture is to be found in Lyne (1980) 1–18.

make it clear whether he differs from other love poets in kind as well as in degree. S. Commager, speaking of 'Propertius' peculiar linkage of love and death', 'quasi-sexual union in death' and the like, marks one of the exceptions. 'Radical association', the expression I have just used, is also his. He observes that the reasons behind it 'are problematic, and it is easier to trace their ramifications in his verse than to define their roots in his psyche'.[2] An age of Freudian experience may find it imperative to reach for 'psyche' wherever such primal forces as Eros and Thanatos seem to be involved; and no doubt there must be a path, however elusive and sinuous, that leads from verse back to those regions. But what the critic is more immediately exposed to, and a more competent judge of, can perhaps be better described as a certain brand of artistic sensibility and/or aesthetic thought; and for that (at least in the case of poets like Propertius where no explicit critical theory complements poetic practice) no more reliable evidence exists than the poet's own verse. I have, accordingly, tried to trace in a number of elegies the artistic sensibility and/or aesthetics that underlie the bond between love and death – a bond which has always and on all hands been recognised as typical of this poet.

Much of what I have to say on Propertius' sensibility has already been, in one way or another, outlined or touched upon by such scholars as P. Boucher and A. La Penna in their important books on the poet,[3] and the present book attempts to bring some of their insights, broadened and qualified wherever this seemed fit, and buttressed by fresh evidence, to bear more systematically – and, it may be, more obsessively – on the reading of some of the most stimulating and, as it happens, problematic elegies. It is, I hope, not churlish on the part of someone perfectly conscious of his debt to these scholars to complain that in their studies a critical assessment of any one elegy *as a whole* is hard to come by. If it is reasonable to point out that enterprises anxious to present a comprehensive, overall picture of the poet cannot accommodate detailed treatment of individual poems, it is, I believe, also fair to draw attention to the possible inadequacies of a method which normally entails arguing from the evidence of isolated passages and lines and within the requirements of a specific chapter, but seldom, if ever, with reference to the basic unit, that is, the poem with its particular structure and thought sequence. Attention to these – which, as I hope to show, is essential in the case of the poems to be discussed – is encouraged by a more restricted scope. Not that a restricted scope is an unmixed blessing, but it at least allows a sharper focus, and I have endeavoured to preserve one throughout.

<hr />

[2] Commager (1974) 20.   [3] Boucher (1965) and La Penna (1977).

2

Boucher studies Propertius' sensibility under four headings: 'Tempérament visuel', 'Le sentiment de la mort', 'La *fides*' and 'Le sens patriotique'.[4] It is my central assumption that it is the first of these which is of overriding significance, being, in my view, the chief reason for the prominence of the second and the monitor of the expression of the other two. Amid the controversy surrounding the 'patriotic' 4.6 scholars forget to ask themselves whether this poet could describe the events at Actium except by means of isolated, almost incoherent, visual effects. Boucher himself seems to have sensed as much, for he writes that Propertius' 'tempérament visuel' manifests itself not only in love but whenever his sensibility is set astir by his favourite themes: beauty of Cynthia, passion, beauty of works of art, death, love of Rome and awareness of her grandeur.[5] It had been my original plan to examine all those poems which are organised around the themes (or, perhaps, the complex of themes) specified here, save the last one. But I was apprised in good time that I would not be suffered to send the juggernaut of this project rumbling over the Ph.D. word-limit rules; and when, having transferred myself to the jurisdiction of the C.U.P. Syndics, I was mercifully allowed to extend the dissertation by the long section on 4.7, I needed no one to tell me that insistence on the original project was hardly making for an economical and εὐσύνοπτον book. Thus a number of pieces whose general drift seemed to me to promote not so much the pair love–death as a highly peculiar complex of beauty–art–death had eventually to be left out. However, 4.7 does partly belong with this group; the discussion of 4.7.51ff. on pp. 170ff., and especially 173, will go into some of the implications of the latter emphasis, and will adumbrate others. Both from this poem (on which more anon) and from 2.13 it will be clear that with Propertius the distinction I have just drawn is a very fragile one. I venture it not in the certainty that I can make a virtue of a technical necessity but in the hope that I shall be able to deal elsewhere with this other group of poems without undue spatial pressure and better prepared for the job.

Boucher was not the first to stress but was the first to attach such importance to Propertius' 'tempérament visuel' as to devote a whole chapter to it. This concept, however, can and must be broadened. Propertius gives pride of place to the eyes (*oculi sunt in amore duces* 2.15.12) in a poem where he responds to love with the full range of his senses. This is not visual temperament so much as sensuous temperament spearheaded by sight. Propertius obeys a human instinct that assumes all other senses active but subsumes them under the most obvious or, perhaps, valuable. Therefore, Boucher's chosen term need not be a misnomer and one should

---

[4] Boucher (1965) 41–159.   [5] Boucher (1965) 59–60.

not find it at all difficult to see it as a synonym for La Penna's felicitous 'esaltazione estetica della gioia dei sensi'.[6] Writers with a penchant for this, especially those of the nineteenth century, have often been called 'Aesthetes'.[7] I have not shunned this and other anachronisms, indeed I expect them to be condoned, at least by those who like to ponder Propertius' modernity. A modern literary critic tackling Donne, Keats or Baudelaire would not feel apologetic about harping on their sensuousness or, indeed, about writing a whole book on it. Classical critics, more puritanical as a rule, are apt to examine their chosen poet under general or local anaesthetic (a rule occasionally challenged by delightful exceptions). 'Sensuous' and its two, so to say, satellites, namely, the more neutral 'sensory' and, given our thematic area, 'sensual', will feature in the following pages with a frequency that may strike some as importunate. I confess to feeling only slightly apologetic about this, not only because these are keywords capturing what I take to be the keynotes of my subject but also because I think that Propertius is, along with Lucretius, the Roman poet most deserving to be 'sensitised'.

Poets whose main strength lies in their sensuousness should perhaps not be expected to excel in the serio-problematic treatment of moral, social and existential issues. In any event, I do not believe that Propertius delved into the moral and existential implications of *Liebestod*. But there are those who obviously think he did. 'For some time', writes G. Luck, 'it had been fashionable to read into Roman love poetry important statements on religious, philosophical and political issues.'[8] H. Drews is anxious to get to the bottom of Propertius' 'Todesangst' and to investigate his attitude to death.[9] U. Wenzel takes the frequency of the poet's references to death as evidence of preoccupation with a special problem.[10] I can see no *problem* here, though I think I can see the seriousness of Propertius' sensuousness. Neither Drews nor Wenzel have anything to say on this (in their studies I miss the word 'Sinnlichkeit' or the like), which should give the measure of my disagreement with these works. Nevertheless, Wenzel's is the more discriminating of the two in that she

[6] La Penna (1977) 213.

[7] The use of the term 'aesthetic' to refer to a definite, mainly nineteenth-century literary trend should not be confused with the rather neutral sense the word bears in philosophical discourse, where it refers to the general criteria by which art is appraised. Such confusion (often venial in view of the fact that some at least of the implications of the literary-critical use derive from the emphasis placed by Aesthetics on the 'beautiful') is observable in non-specialised discussions. The word, as is the way with such words, is apt to be abused.

For the various attempts to define the province of Aesthetics as a branch of philosophy see Osborne (1972) 1–24.   [8] See Luck, p. xx.

[9] Drews (1952) 78–145, esp. 108–20 and 136–45. On pp. 38–77 and 146–53 she asks the same questions in connexion with Tibullus and Ovid respectively.

[10] Wenzel (1969) 53.

4

repudiates the view, held also by W. Herz,[11] that in Propertius more often than not the theme of death is subordinate to the wooing of the elegiac lady – what German scholars often refer to as 'Werbung um die Geliebte'.[12] One should agree with Wenzel that in a number of poems the thought of death is so tenuously motivated by the erotic situation as to appear quite autonomous;[13] and, of course, there are poems like 3.7 and 3.18, where death's powerful imagery and atmosphere have nothing whatsoever to do with love. And yet even in such cases, and despite some superficial indications to the contrary in the poems themselves, I should rather start from Boucher's remarks as quoted on p. 3 than see these pieces, with Wenzel, as general statements on the nature of death.[14]

Neither the suffering nor the liberating experience of lofty poetry is to be sought in Propertius. La Penna, who instructed thus back in 1951, also denied the poet a world vision from which his work could be said to spring.[15] Propertius had no vision of the lover's destiny, any more than he had a vision of the world. Yet there is no dearth of attempts to follow in poem after poem, and with disproportionate scrupulousness, an arduous lover's progress.[16] Would it not be better 'to analyse the poems as artistic constructions, as though they were *paintings*, demonstrate their finer points and bring out their essential qualities...?'[17] My italics show what I feel to be a most important point in this suggestion.

'The usefulness of approaching Propertius without keeping one's eyes shut to painting'[18] is rather obvious nowadays. The pictorial quality of his mythology in particular is yet another open secret. In the following pages I have clung to the belief that Propertian mythology is more of an art gallery than a typological system of universal import; and that what it lends to the postures of the protagonists is form, colour and texture, not absolute and timeless significance.[19] This, however, is not to say that a simple relationship is assumed here between visual art as model and poetry as reproduction. When Théophile Gautier takes up a painter's subject he does not attempt a faithful verbal comment on what he sees. It is rather the case that the poet executes like a painter.[20] Keyssner understood this better than Birt;[21] and so did Hubbard: 'The imagination

---

[11] Herz (1955) 88, 131, 149 and *passim*.
[12] See Wenzel (1969) 57 n. 1 and 67 nn. 1 and 2. [13] Wenzel (1969) 64ff.
[14] Wenzel (1969) 95. [15] La Penna (1951) 124.
[16] Wiggers (1972) offers an example. See, for instance, her first chapter (pp. 10–35) and the summary on p. 36. [17] See Lee (1960) 519. [18] Hubbard (1974) 166.
[19] Allen (1962) 130 concludes that myth serves 'to raise the experience from an individual to a universal level'. Kölmel (1957) 49 had taken a similar view: through the use of myth the love poet 'becomes a type himself'. Contrast Lyne (1980) 84ff.
[20] See Snell (1982) 85–6.
[21] Keyssner (1975) 264–77, 284; Birt (1895) 31–65, 161–90. What is at issue here is the relation-

of Propertius is limited by the scope of the painter or sculptor.'[22] No one-to-one correspondence between a given mythological passage and a specific piece of visual art need be inferred from this. Kölmel warns against attempting to establish in each case which particular painting Propertius might have had in mind, unless genuine pictorial intentions can be ascertained; I should incline to agree with him, if I knew what exactly his 'echt "malerische" Absichten' means.[23]

There is little room within the limits of this work for mythological taxonomy; but what I have just said in the preceding paragraph should explain why on the whole I find it too abstract for my purposes. If this poet's sensibility fleshes itself as highly visual myth, to tear off, abstract and classify his mythology is, in one sense, to subscribe to the outdated view that it is ornamental and external rather than integral and intrinsic. And although it does not seem altogether unhelpful to draw a few broad distinctions by way of establishing a convenient framework for discussion, as R. Whitaker does for example,[24] La Penna's animadversions, first voiced in 1951, are, I believe, still topical: 'a separate analysis of [Propertius'] mythology is abstract and superfluous'[25] – and it calls to mind scholastic works of some time ago which were also apt to foster the impression of a poet whose frigid learning, especially in the form of mythological illustration, impaired the quality of his poetry. Since then a change of taste has combined with a more industrious scholarship to alert us to the possibility that *doctrina* may galvanise a poet's sensibility into highly original and deeply individual expression.

So in studying the themes of love and death in Propertius' poetry I have endeavoured to retrace, so far as I could, what Paolo Fedeli has aptly called his 'itinerario culturale'.[26] That this occasionally reached back through classical Greek literature to Homer is beyond question. But we can also be fairly certain that the terrain traversed is predominantly Hellenistic; and that the sightseeing is being done through Hellenistic eyes. There are notorious blind spots in the area and those frequenting it have by now learned to live with guesswork. I have felt confident enough to add some more – not by way of mere *Quellenforschung*, nor yet in order to single out a particular work as the main influence on any given elegy, but rather with a view to adumbrating the artistic quarters towards

ship of poetry to sculpture rather than to painting, nevertheless the objections Keyssner raises against Birt's simplistic view of Prop. 1.3.1ff. as an exact commentary on the plastic details of the Vatican Ariadne are relevant to any question concerning literature and visual art in general.

[22] Hubbard (1974) 164.   [23] Kölmel (1957) 47.
[24] Whitaker (1983) 88.
[25] La Penna (1951) 102; cf. *id.* (1977) 196–7.
[26] Fedeli (1977) 99 'perché questo significa interpretare la sua poesia'.

which Propertius must have felt drawn both by education and by innate sympathy of sensibility.

If Propertius brings a sensuous temperament to bear on the themes of love and death, and if he treats these themes as a Hellenistic poet, then Hellenistic erotic poetry can be expected to display a similar slant. And yet what, even today, is habitually publicised as the hallmark of this kind of poetry is its study of the psychological intricacies of erotic passion. True as this may be, it is but part of the story. The view E. Rohde reached quite a few years ago is more comprehensive inasmuch as it does not lose sight of the sensuous charm (*sinnlichen Reiz*), as distinct from the woes and delights, of erotic passion.[27] Sensuous, or sensory, charm is seldom innocent; the sinister, the morbid, the grotesque are of its essence. Scholars have used similar adjectives to capture the qualities of Hellenistic erotic material.[28] This is the 'Decadent' side of Hellenistic 'Romanticism'. The odd specimen from the modern literary field (of which I claim no specialist knowledge) has been rather fitfully brought in not only to vindicate the employment of the anachronisms but also to hint that Propertius as much looks forward to European modes of sensibility as he looks backward to the Alexandrian masters. If the same position can be predicated of other Roman poets as well – if, that is, some of them can be seen as intermediaries between ancient and modern – it is Propertius' unique distinction that by employing motifs destined to become topoi of Western culture he founded 'the uneasy and dialectical relationship between love and death'.[29] Indeed, those who do not fight shy of parallels which in some quarters are still thought too hazardous to be of any value are most likely to cherish the Propertian treatment of erotic death as one of the tokens of the unity of Western literature.

The axis of the discussion passes through Book 2, with Chapters 3, 4, 5 and 6 devoted to each of poems 1, 13, 26b and 8 respectively. Passages and poems germane to the issues raised by these central pieces are adduced from the entire corpus both as supporting evidence and in order to allow a clearer view of the developments and shifts in the poet's technique and emphases, especially in the course of the first two books. Clarifying Propertius by means of Propertius is, needless to say, as important as placing him in a broader literary context. All four poems just mentioned display, I think, a similar structural pattern which tends to assert itself, on a smaller or larger scale, in the majority of the elegies

[27] See Rohde (1914) 109.
[28] See, for instance, Clausen (1964) 190; Cairns (1979) 22 and Lyne (1980) 82.
[29] Paduano (1968) 27.

which bring together the themes of love and death. Attention to structure where a self-conscious craftsman is concerned needs hardly any justification, but in the case of Propertius it is all the more vital as it can afford valuable clues to the vexed questions of the unity and/or the boundaries of individual poems.

Chapter 7 takes a brief look at poems 9, 17, 20 and 24b of Book 2. These poems, although thematically and structurally akin to those of the previous group, have less marked structural patterns and display a less characteristic *Liebestod* in that the interpenetration between the two themes is 'conceptual' rather than 'sensuous'. They are important, however, as evidence of Propertius' engrossment, during the composition of Book 2, in a particular set of poetic ideas, and of his repeated variations upon a specific kind of structure as a vehicle of their expression. These two groups, together with poems 4, 15 and 27 (all of which are considered below), account for almost one-third of the total number of lines in Book 2 (approximately 430 out of 1,360 lines). Had the group of elegies referred to on p. 3 been allowed to contribute its evidence, the buzzing of the bee in the poet's bonnet would have come through louder and clearer. Scholars contract different kinds of obsessions. Voices have been recently raised to the effect that Book 2 has a discernible structure as a whole, with neat correspondences among its poems. At the end of Chapter 7 I have a word to say on this, and also on the question of the book's unity.

To flank Chapters 3–7 there are the discussions of two poems from each of Books 1 and 4. Chapter 2 seeks to find out what the *amor* of 1.19 is likely to mean in the face of death – or, rather, in view of the received ideas about this poem, what it is unlikely to mean. Chapter 8, which tackles 4.7, is the lengthiest one less because the poem itself is a massive composition than because it strikes me as a unique and self-conscious synthesis of themes and images which, though they always appeal to the poet's sensuous imagination, are nowhere else granted such bold coexistence within the boundaries of a single poem. Although the prophecy with which Cynthia's speech grinds to a halt in ll. 93–4 allies 4.7 with the love-and-death fantasies of Book 2, 'Hymne à la beauté' would perhaps give a better suggestion of its bias than 'La mort des amants', so discussion in this case calls for a slight readjustment of the critical focus; and since this poem is a fine, if comparatively idiosyncratic, specimen of Propertius' late manner, it also warrants some comment on the significance and achievement of his mature style, the surge of realism in particular. For this reason and also because of the 'readjustment' I have just spoken of, some readers may well feel that the approach to 4.7 causes them to stray from the track beaten in the rest of the book towards new regions which the title would never lead them to surmise. In point of fact, the differences in narrative technique, style and structure far from obscuring underscore in 4.7 the constant among the variants, namely, a peculiar aesthetic sensibility and the themes through which it preferably finds expression. Let me state here, more emphatically than I have done on p. 3, a case that takes this and, perhaps, yet another instalment to be fully argued on the basis of all the evidence available: between Propertius' 'love and death' and 'beauty and death' (and 4.7 looks different partly because in discussing it I have made much of the latter pair) there is a subtle distinction without a clear-cut difference. Re-readers who come back to, and bring a keener awareness of the poet's sensibility to bear on, the *amor* of 1.19 (which *amor*, I thought, demanded a whole preliminary chapter to itself) will no doubt procure themselves much more than an inkling of the profound affinity that binds together the Dead Beauties of 4.7 with the *Liebestod* of the other pieces.

Propertius can be witty and humorous. More often, however, he is deeply ironical. I have laid stress on a particular kind of irony that collaborates with sensuous pathos; this brand of irony, to use Ciceronian language, is not *peracutum et breve*[30] but works almost as a structural device; it eludes theorising, although it can be seen clearly at work in individual poems.

Finally, Chapter 9 draws some of the threads together and places some of the points made in the book in their wider context, but not without raising a couple of new ones, notably in respect of the historical–social backgrounds against which Propertius, his Hellenistic models and some of the nineteenth-century European poets, with whom his congeniality is suggested or implied, wrote their poetry.

[30] Cic. *De Or.* 2.218.

9

2
NOSTRIS PUER HAESIT OCELLIS: THE LESSONS OF 1.19

Tu sais avec quelle ardeur j'ai recherché la beauté physique, quelle importance j'attache à la forme extérieure, et de quel amour je me suis pris pour le monde visible.

Gautier, *Mademoiselle de Maupin*

ὅταν ξυπνᾶ τοῦ σώματος ἡ μνήμη,
κ' ἐπιθυμία παληά ξαναπερνᾶ στό αἷμα·
ὅταν τά χείλη καί τό δέρμα ἐνθυμοῦνται,
κ' αἰσθάνονται τά χέρια σάν ν' ἀγγίζουν πάλι.

Cavafy, ''Ἐπέστρεφε'

F. Jacoby and R. Reitzenstein were at daggers drawn over the question of where the point of 1.19 was to be found, but they obviously agreed that in the central part of the poem Propertius was propounding the notion of love outlasting life and living on in the hereafter.[1] None of the later critics quarrelled with this, and in view of the grand *traicit et fati litora magnus amor* 'Great love can cross even the shores of fate' in l. 12 it would certainly have seemed captious, to say the least, to do so. G. Williams is no exception here, but his penetrating discussion is of special interest in that it broaches an issue whose wider implications seem to me to affect the semantic scope of the word *amor* and thereby seriously to qualify the import of 12 and its immediate context. *fata*, he says, means 'death' but 'the reader must be conscious that *fatum/fata* can also have a concrete sense of "dead body"'.[2] He goes on to notice that *funus* (3), *exsequiis* (4) and *pulvis* (6) are subject to the same ambiguity; and elsewhere he explains that Propertius can alternate between striking visual effects and 'manipulation of words, without the interference of the mind's eye'.[3] But to my mind, he hits upon something far more vital when he sees in the poem 'deliberate juxtaposing of concrete and abstract'. In fact, the whole poem articulates with dense urgency a dialectics of the concrete and the abstract, caught up in which *amor* can hardly be as abstract as it has been

---

[1] Jacoby (1910) 29ff.; Reitzenstein (1912) 94ff.
[2] See Williams (1968) 766ff.   [3] Williams (1968) 393.

thought to be. 1.19 has attracted a good deal of scholarly discussion[4] so I feel at some liberty to offer a rapid and selective commentary on this aspect alone.

Legend had it that Protesilaus' Underworld furlough was granted out of regard for a deeply loving Laodamia.[5] The myth had an emotional appeal; by shifting the yearning on to Protesilaus' ghost Propertius gives it a very different kind of fascination. Lines 7–10 propound the intricate and intriguing paradox of a ghost's *sensory* nostalgia:

> illic Phylacides iucundae coniugis heros
> non potuit caecis immemor esse locis,
> sed cupidus falsis attingere gaudia palmis
> Thessalus antiquam venerat umbra domum.

> *There, in the unseen world, Phylácides the hero*
> *Could not forget his lovely wife,*
> *But eager to clutch delight with disappointed hands*
> *Came as a ghost to his old home Thessaly.*

Protesilaus yearns with senses he recalls rather than possesses. His memory is *visual* (the juxtaposition *caecis–immemor* promotes subliminally the idea) and *tactile*. More than the focus of his affection Laodamia is the epitome of the sensible world he misses. She is *iucundae* (7), a *mot juste* for the ripples of delicious sensation but not for the billows of deep emotion;[6] thus, her physical magnetism multiplied by metaphysical distance, she holds out the promise of *gaudia*. When the charms of a tender bride are at issue, *cupidus* should be a comment on the vigorous excitement of her partner; the unbowdlerised upshot of its implications here would have to be something of an erectile shade, and the impotent stretching of the exsanguinated hands is made to look very much like a corrective

---

[4] Apart from standard commentaries and the works referred to in the present discussion, see Boyle (1974), Falkner (1975) 9–31, Hodge and Buttimore (1977) 194–201. Unlike Otis (1965) 10–15, I can see no appreciable 'contradiction' or 'contrapuntal' difference between 1.19 and – on Otis's assumptions of symmetrical arrangement – its correspondent 1.1.

[5] See Fedeli's informative note on 1.19.7–10. Catull. 68.73–6 is evidence of the popularity of the myth in Roman neoteric poetry, and Prop. must have surely had this passage in mind. I find it equally likely, though nowhere suggested, that Prop. also remembered Virgil's Orpheus and Eurydice in *G.* 4.464ff. (see p. 19 n. 34 below). When she is *iam luce sub ipsa* (490) Orpheus looks back *immemor* (the adj. is prominent enough as the first word of 491 to have called forth the *immemor* of 1.19.8) and his wife sinks back into insubstantiality moaning: *invalidasque tibi tendens, heu non tua, palmas* 'stretching out to you, alas no longer yours, my impotent hands' (498 cf. 1.19.9 *falsis...palmis*).

On the versions and treatment of the Protesilaus myth in Greek and Roman literature see Lieberg (1962) 209ff.

[6] Williams (1968) 769 vindicates the status of the adj. against Axelson's perverse conception of it as a vulgarism, but his 'highly subjective, evaluative word' does not go far enough. See also *OLD s.v.* 3.

euphemism.[7] Line 9 plaits concrete and abstract, solid and insubstantial into infinite tantalising: *falsis* drives a wedge into a syntactic unit; *cupidus* and *attingere* look stranded on either side of it. *palmis* is juxtaposed to, but never reaches its objective, 'though winning near the goal', and the sombre nasality of the 'golden' pentameter with its suggestions of dark hollowness (appropriate both of the apparition and of the *ancient* household) signals a rather inauspicious setting for the desirous gesture. Protesilaus is both back from the Underworld and manacled to it.

Propertius is in a similar predicament. Having projected himself into a non-sentient existence, he then works out its paradox and its agony. Clearly, what he has pinned his hopes on is the possibility of sensuous perception; *forma* preys on his mind:

> illic *formosae* veniant chorus heroinae,
>   quas dedit Argivis Dardana praeda viris;
>   quarum nulla tua fuerit mihi, Cynthia, *forma*
>   gratior   (1.19.13–16)
>
> *There let them come in troops, the beautiful heroines*
> *Picked by Argives from the spoils of Troy,*
> *No beauty of theirs for me could match yours, Cynthia –*

When Propertius says *forma* he means nothing but what meets the eye; and, unlike Catullus, he contents himself with it. Nakayama has made the comparison with commendable discrimination.[8] Ostensibly, the heroines of the Underworld, ushered in with Alexandrian preciosity by l. 13,[9] advance and make advances to a staunchly uxorious Propertius. In point of fact, the wooing at the level of the dramatic situation is far less important than the contemplative mood suggested by the poem's aesthetics. These ladies are more passive than they seem, they are there to be gazed upon – and to be judged, on purely formal criteria, less attractive than Cynthia. The *amor* of 1.19 is not so much the result of emotional nostalgia as of sensuous obsession. If we cannot help bringing

[7] *cupidus, at-tingere, gaudia* are all dyed-in-grain 'eroticisers' as is clear from Pichon (1902) *s.vv.* Fedeli *ad loc.* contends that *attingere gaudia* signifies the vain attempt at embrace, 'non certo un approccio erotico crudamente realistico'; but there is certainly nothing crude about Protesilaus' illusory concupiscence.

[8] Nakayama (1963–4) 62–73. His paper is packed with printing errors and insights into Propertius' use of *forma, formosus* and the like. See esp. pp. 61–8 and his concluding remarks on p. 72 to the effect that whereas for Catullus *formosus* points to the spiritual/intellectual, Propertius uses the word with reference to external form only.

[9] *heroine*, a transcription of the Hellenistic ἡρωίνη (see Tränkle (1960) 60–1), is affected by Prop. alone. It brings 1.13.31 (*illa sit Inachiis et blandior heroinis*) and 2.2.9 (*qualis et Ischomache Lapithae genus heroine*) to a stately spondaic close and imparts a hypnotic (not to say narcotic) quality to 1.19.13. Apart from these three spondeiazontes Prop. has four others, namely 1.20.31, 2.28.49, 3.7.13 and 4.4.71. Tibullus, no *cantor Euphorionis* in this, as in other respects, has none. Cf. also Sullivan (1976) 128.

in the *idea* of love, we should at least recognise that in this piece it derives from, and takes second place to *form*.

We can now go back to ll. 3–4 (*sed ne forte tuo careat mihi funus amore | hic timor est ipsis durior exsequiis* 'But the fear that when dead I may lose your love | Is worse than the funeral itself') and to Williams: 'it [i.e. *funus*] could mean "death", "dead body", "funeral", "grave"; clearly all these meanings are appropriate but no single one to the exclusion of the rest, and the sense must be as abstract here as that of *amor* – will he be loved when he is dead?'[10] – but *amor* is far from being abstract and the question calls for drastic revision: will there be *amor* without *formal embodiment*? Can there be *amor* that cannot actually be *seen*? The query and its excruciation come naturally to the aesthete. 'If the slogan "de la forme naît l'idée"... became an Art for Art's Sake motto, it was one that Gautier was finally unable to reconcile with the fact of personal death; everything must cease with the failure of perception.'[11] Until he reconciles himself to the same fact, which will not start happening before 21ff., Propertius reacts, or overreacts, with sensory bigotry:

> non adeo leviter nostris puer haesit ocellis,
>   ut meus oblito pulvis amore vacet.   (1.19.5–6)

> *Not so lightly has Cupid clung to our eyes*
> *That with love forgotten my dust could rest.*

The prodigy, therefore, of the sentient dust has an intrinsic impetus, although Hubbard may well be right in suggesting that the *manes* of the Roman funerary cult have contributed to it.[12] The other thing to notice about this couplet is that in it *amore* gives away its visual slant. It will not do to object that ll. 5–6 are yet another variation on the age-old idea of love working its way through the eyes, for here the eyes themselves (and, one must infer, the other senses as well) are both its destination and abode. Lines 7ff. dramatise the personal dogma brandished at Demophoon in 2.22a.20: *numquam ad formosas, invide, caecus ero* 'I'll never be blind, my envious friend, to a beautiful girl'. '*Never*' encapsulates the kind of obstinacy compressed in *haesit* (5), displayed by Protesilaus in l. 8 and, I believe, by the poet himself in l. 12. Despite an alluring semblance of transcendence this pentameter does not ultimately escape the poem's sensory determinism. What it announces is an experimental lease of life for sensuousness as the poet knows it, not the prolongation of a spiritualised bond into eternity. 'esaltazione dell' amore eterno', 'ewige Liebe' and

---

[10] Williams (1968) 767.   [11] Snell (1982) 50.
[12] Hubbard (1974) 35–6.

the like[13] paraphrase misleadingly a proposition illustrated by a Protesilaus who is a bundle of sensations, and by a Propertius who is all eyes. These dear sweet eyes (*ocellis*) the poet does not seem prepared to change for a halo – which, in fact, he would be doing, if ll. 17–18 were 'genuine' enough.

I do not believe they are. The poet is here waiting patiently in his Underworld niche for Cynthia to make old bones and then join him. Lyne has seen that Propertius has very little to say about his own and Cynthia's ageing: 'One sees Propertius' point...Romantic aspiration needs the indulgence of a blind eye.' I should add that decrepitude is no sight for the eyes of the aesthete. It is a measure of Tibullus' different poetic treatment of love that, as Lyne again observes, he can accommodate the problem of senility.[14] Lines 19–20 hark back to 3–6:

> quae tu viva mea possis sentire favilla!
> tum mihi non ullo mors sit amara loco.

> *If only the living you could feel this for my ashes,*
> *Then death, wherever, for me would have no sting.*

If dust is amorous in 6, then so can be the embers in 19. In fact, 19–20 repeat the fears and assertions of 3–6 but in a subdued manner and without the striking conceit of 5. This makes for a smoother transition to the following thought paragraph.

The retreat is signalled by ll. 21–2:

> quam vereor, ne te *contempto*, Cynthia, *busto*
> abstrahat a *nostro pulvere* iniquus Amor

> *But, Cynthia, how I fear that love's iniquity*
> *Scorning the tomb may drag you from my dust*

At the level of the poem's fictional reality Cynthia enters upon a new love

[13] See Reitzenstein (1912) 93 and Fedeli's introd. note to 1.19. The most enthusiastic spiritualisation to date comes from Alfonsi (1945) 28: Propertius, he contends, knows that love can only be fully realised beyond the grave.

[14] Lyne (1980) 66–7. I shall be attempting brief comparisons, whenever this is germane to the main argument, between Prop. and Tib. in particular. It is beyond question that traffic of ideas did take place between the two elegists but it is not part of my intentions (nor does space allow) to go into the vexed problem of who is imitating whom. For our purposes it will suffice to see how sharply the two poets may differ in their treatment of love and death, especially when they exploit the same motifs. Let it be noted, however, that most, though not all, scholars would seem to agree that the Monobiblos was published before Tib. 1 and that Prop. 2 appeared after Tib. 1, but the arguments are largely inconclusive and the picture that emerges from the discussions is a pretty complicated one. On these and other questions of chronology and imitation see mainly Enk's ed. of Book 2, Part 1, 34–45; also Jacoby (1909) 601ff. and (1910) 22ff.; Reitzenstein (1912) 60ff.; La Penna (1950) 223–36 and (1951a) 55–62; Hubbard (1974) 44; Wimmel (1976) 93–111 and Fedeli's introd. to the edition of Book 1, p. 10.

affair; in our own terms of reading she snaps the sensory lifeline inaugurated in l. 5. It is clear that the life Propertius claims for his dust and embers is conditional on the presence of the perceiving woman. Gautier fell prey to the same fear. R. Snell produced revealing evidence of how he came to the conclusion 'that nothing exists except tangible matter, and that, in the absence of perceiving man, forms exist without issue and meaning'.[15] We shall be watching closely later on a fascinatingly similar development in 2.13.47ff. I only note here that l. 41 of that poem (*interea cave sis nos aspernata sepultos* 'Meanwhile beware of slighting us, the buried') echoes the concern of 1.19.21 but causes a complete *dégringolade* which 1.19 diverts to a drastic *carpe diem*:

> quare, dum licet, inter nos laetemur amantes:
> non satis est ullo tempore longus amor. (1.19.25–6)
>
> *So, while we may, let us delight in loving each other;*
> *No love is ever long enough.*

The couplet has the effect of blood rushing back to Protesilaus' palms. There never was any serious doubt at any turn within the poem as to the real roots of *amor*. Simply, the poet indulged the idea of transplanting them in the beyond, whence he now comes back perhaps a sadder, but certainly a more resolutely sensuous man.

To unfurl the sails of 1.19.12 without using the ballast of 1.19.25–6 is to throw caution to the winds. And caution is particularly desirable when Propertius is – quite legitimately, I believe – placed in the context of European poetry. An engaging article by W. Naumann draws attention to a sonnet by Francisco de Quevedo (1580–1645), very much a poet of love and death.[16] The theme is love's immortality and in the last two verses Propertius' 1.19 must have flashed, as Naumann suggests, through the Spaniard's mind, for here ashes and dust are endowed with residual feeling and amorousness: 'serán ceniza, mas tendrá sentido; | polvo serán, mas polvo enamorado.' Yet all similarity must end here. Despite an unmistakable breath of paganism in the imagery, the poem hinges upon the distinction soul–body (*alma–cuerpo*), its setting is austerely internalised, and its *amor* has very little to do with the sensorium. Naumann himself indirectly concedes as much when he says that instead of the human and earthly warmth of Propertius' images it betrays an inhuman solitude.[17]

---

[15] Snell (1982) 50–1.   [16] Naumann (1968) 157–68.
[17] Naumann (1968) 167. What he chooses to compare with 1.19 is perhaps the most famous of Quevedo's love sonnets (no. 471 in the edn of J. Manuel Blecua, Vol. 1, Barcelona 1963). But students of Quevedo's poetry may have noticed, or may be interested to know, that it is the octave

And what is inhuman solitude here if not absence of human form as an embodiment of love? This neither Propertius nor his mythological counterpart in 1.19 can bring themselves to countenance. The Roman elegist writes untrammelled by Platonic or Christian dualism and with sensuous devotion, which is more than can be said of Quevedo, and which – to take another major poet of love and death – is not quite John Donne's way either.

John Carey has recently suggested that Donne's love poems transcribe into erotic terms the crisis of his religious apostasy. Here is something to bear in mind.[18] Yet, for our purposes, the first thing to remember about Donne is his much-resented blindness to visible beauty. Let me quote the same critic:

> If Donne seems, much of the time, unconcerned with or immune to visual beauty, then visual beauty becomes an inadequate concept with which to approach his work... The shortage of visual beauties in Donne's poems is not felt as an emptiness, because it is the outcome of other and more intense pressures which have forced visual beauty out. Donne's persistent investigation of inner experience, and his corresponding scorn for 'he who colour loves, and skinne', are only the most obvious of these pressures.[19]

No wonder that this poet does not ache for female flesh. For these and other reasons[20] comparison with Propertius in respect of love and death demands cautious discrimination, and, whenever such a task is felt to be worth undertaking, their difference in 'tempérament visuel' should bulk large in the critic's mind. In a task of a similar kind La Penna has set an example of good sense.[21]

He warns against facile parallels between Propertius and Petrarch.[22]

of another sonnet, no. 478, that seems to reproduce very closely the 'it is not death itself I fear, but...' movement of the first two couplets of 1.19. The sonnet opens: 'No me aflige morir; no he rehusado | acabar de vivir...' 'Death gives me no pain; I have not refused an end to my life'; cf. the opening of 1.19, *non ego...tristis vereor...Manis,* | *nec moror extremo,* etc. It then continues in its second quatrain: 'Siento haber de dejar deshabitado | cuerpo que amante espíritu ha ceñido' 'but I regret having to leave uninhabited a body which has contained an amorous spirit'; cf. *sed ne...careat...funus amore* | *hic timor est.* But what strikes here is the formal similarity, for otherwise this sonnet is, as Olivares (1983) 119 remarks, about 'the essential conflict confronting the poet: the body and the spirit'. In his chapter on 'Love and Death' (113ff.) the same scholar argues that this conflict and the metaphysical anguish it implies are central to Quevedo's love poetry. Prop. 1.19 is a far cry from metaphysical baroque.

[18] Carey (1981) 37ff.   [19] Carey (1981) 131.

[20] Carey (1981) 131–66 defines admirably Donne's will to penetrate the outward in a bid to capture the body's organic life and the intricacies of its sedes. His medical training made him more sensitive to function than to form, and it is this sensitivity that he brings to love poetry as well. In this sense it is no exaggeration to say that Prop. belongs to an altogether different universe.

[21] See La Penna (1977) 250–99.   [22] La Penna (1977) 254–61.

Platonism and Christianity are the keys to an erotic poetry where, in N. Rudd's words, 'sexuality has been refined out of existence'.[23] La Penna makes an informative survey of Propertius' fortunes up to the seventeenth and eighteenth centuries, when the poet became the beneficiary of a new fascination with Greece, Alexandrian literature in particular,[24] and came to be valued mainly for his treatment of Greek myths, which he was thought to show in an intensely romantic light. La Penna further notes that poets and critics of this period, and some belonging to the nineteenth century, display something of that 'esaltazione estetica della gioia dei sensi' of which he holds Propertius eminently capable.[25] Gautier, whom I have thought fit to bring into the discussion of 1.19, belongs to this last group. He is a hero of 'Aestheticism', a movement which was the ultimate result of the Romantic cult of subjectivism and individual sensibility, and which overlaps with the Symbolist trend of the same period. G. Luck's view that Propertius would have found congenial spirits among the *Symbolistes* of nineteenth-century Paris is rather vague but perfectly understandable.[26] By the same token, it is legitimate to speak of Propertius' romanticism, only this term is now too diffuse for the critic to use without the necessary qualifications. All such labels tend to be approximative, and tend to proliferate.[27] Taken together, they mark off the broader area in which I have occasionally sought supportive evidence and illuminating contexts.[28] I have not done

---

[23] Rudd (1981) 142.   [24] La Penna (1977) 282–3.
[25] La Penna (1977) 213.   [26] Luck (1969) 121.

[27] One critic's 'Aesthete' is another's 'Decadent'. 'Decadents', 'Symbolists', 'Aesthetes' are all labels which identify tendencies of the latter part of the nineteenth century and refer to artists often collectively characterised as 'Last Romantics', a capacious area also associated with such currents as Pre-Raphaelitism, fin-de-siècle, art for art's sake, the *Yellow Book*, Parnassianism, poèsie pure and absolute Dichtung. Specialists in this area like R. Z. Temple (1974) can afford to be sarcastic about the truths and illusions of labels; the non-specialist must be content with noting that 'Aestheticism' has been often seen (cf. Temple, p. 209) as the most wide-ranging and comprehensive term of them all.

'Decadent' is used throughout this study without the ghost of a moral overtone. It was mainly on moralistic grounds that Désiré Nisard in his *Études de moeurs et de critique sur les poètes latins de la décadence* (2nd edn 1848) diagnosed decadence from Lucan onwards. And it was perhaps due to Nisard and others like him that the Aesthete–Decadent des Esseintes, the hero of Joris-Karl Huysmans's *À Rebours* (1884), found no room for Golden-Age Propertius on the shelves of his blue and orange study, in which Lucan, Petronius and Apuleius were prominent.

On the terminological problem, apart from Temple's article referred to above, see also Praz (1951) 1–16; Thornton (1970) 15–33; the Preface to Bradbury and Palmer (1979) and Thornton (1979) 15–29 with the bibliographical note on p. 14.

[28] Aesthetes and Decadents are, as a rule, endowed with 'tempérament visuel' and give abundant evidence of 'esaltazione estetica della gioia dei sensi'; they appeal to the senses more than to emotion and reason; most of them aspire to being 'story painters and picture writers' and, in fact, some, like D. G. Rossetti, were both poets and painters; they are given to contemplating love–beauty in the context of death; and, generally, they seek the Keatsian–Paterian condition of a quickened, multiplied awareness of the sensuous. The following

so on any simplistic assumption of complete symmetry between ancient and modern. The latter is unquestionably more complex and has more dimensions.[29] But of the usefulness of this kind of enterprise I am convinced. Some general thoughts on this subject will be set out in the last chapter when, as I hope, discussion of individual passages will have cast light on some of the problems, terminological and otherwise, involved. 1.19 has provided a good starting-point, and we may conclude this section by summarising the position reached through our study of that poem.

Jacoby sought the real message of 1.19 in ll. 21–6; Reitzenstein read it in the 'eternal love' proclaimed in l. 12: a pragmatic Propertius pitted against a romantic one. Fedeli inclines to the latter version;[30] Lyne wants to trace a downward movement 'from romantic to more prosaic belief' effected through deployment of what he styles 'myth believed – precariously', where romantic = 'belief...in the power of love to transcend death'.[31] This is a fairly broad and empirical use of the term 'romantic'; Lyne knows it to be so[32] and as such it would be unobjectionable, were it not that, at least in this poem, it is used to stress a contrast which ultimately falsifies the relationship between the forces of love and death by keeping them starkly antagonistic. Rather than operate with the obvious dichotomy, I have tried to follow the trajectory, as it were, of a piece of aesthetic speculation. From this perspective love and death seem to join forces.

This will not take us outside the limits of psychological plausibility. One resorts to the *carpe diem* advice because the prospect of death shows the good things of life to be all the more valuable. But the collective wisdom that sounds engagingly obvious on the lips of the man in the street leads a more complex form of life in the creative moments of those sensitive to form, colour and texture. 'One characteristic', writes Walter Pater, 'of the pagan spirit the aesthetic poetry has, which is on its surface – the continual suggestion, pensive or passionate, of the shortness

discussions should show in what sense and to what extent Prop. can be said to measure up to this picture.

On the subject of Aestheticism–Decadence I have profited chiefly from Praz (1951); Hough (1949); Carter (1958); Starkie (1962); Munro (1970); Gaunt (1975); Bradbury and Palmer (1979); Thornton (1983) and Warner and Hough (1983).

[29] Symbolist and quasi-religious yearnings for the apprehension of the invisible (mainly in France) are an obvious point of difference; the paroxysmic cult of the artificial in Huysmans's *À Rebours* is another. Cult of individual sensibility is a common feature, but the modern one, fed by the complexities of a modern society, is far more neurotic, even when only histrionically so.   [30] See Fedeli's introd. note, 439–40.

[31] Lyne (1980) 98ff.   [32] Lyne (1980) ix.

of life. This is contrasted with the bloom of the world, and gives new seduction to it – the sense of death and the desire of beauty: the desire of beauty quickened by the sense of death.'[33] Perhaps this is why Propertius gazes so avidly on the *dead beauties* of 1.19.13ff.; this is why those dead beauties will recur time and time again throughout his *oeuvre*. *forma* (that is, love itself) in 1.19 is the beneficiary of death, in death's own domain. Death enhances the sensuous not by threatening it so much as by being one of the possibilities in the poet's palette. 1.19 does much to sublimate the crude impulse which lies at the root of its concluding couplet. Thus if I forbear to speak of prosaic truth intruding upon a romantic dream, it is because I see a different kind of romanticism – the romanticism which underlies Pater's words and which considers sensuous beauty and excitement as the best part of love. It is of love *thus defined* that all the major elegies to be discussed in the following pages, in varying degrees of urgency and explicitness, seem to me to give evidence.

1.19 reveals the delights and limitations of the Propertian *Liebestod*. If, as on metrical grounds seems probable, it is of late composition within the Monobiblos,[34] it shows the poet already in the grip of a fascinating obsession to which much of Book 2 bears testimony. There we must now turn our attention.

---

[33] From the *Appreciations* (London and New York 1889), p. 227. The essay from which the quotation comes is entitled 'Aesthetic poetry'; Pater did not allow it to appear in subsequent editions of his work but extensive selections from it can be conveniently found in Warner and Hough (1983) II 59–63.

[34] It has only one non-disyllabic pentameter ending in 4, *exsequiis*. Cf. Platnauer (1951) 17. Virgil's *Georgics* was finished by 29 B.C. and read by the poet to Octavian in the summer of that year. Unless, therefore, Prop. had heard Virgil reciting sections of the poem before that date, the latter half of 29 B.C. must be seen as *terminus post quem* for the composition of 1.19, which, if I am right (p. 11 n. 5 above), shows knowledge of the Orpheus and Eurydice story in *G.* 4.464ff. 30 B.C. would, then, have to be ruled out as the year of the publication of the Monobiblos, the early part of 28 being perhaps the most probable date. This hypothesis (triggered off by a perceptive remark of Guy Lee) is in perfect tune with the metrical evidence for a late composition of 1.19.

3

IN AMORE MORI:
WITCHES AND LOVERS

Je t'apprendrai des choses terribles...des choses divines...tu
sauras enfin ce que c'est que l'amour! Je te promets que tu
descendras, avec moi, tout au fond du mystère de l'amour...et de
la mort!...L'amour est une chose grave, triste et profonde....
L'Amour et la Mort, c'est la même chose...
Octave Mirbeau, *Le Jardin des supplices*, quoted in Praz (1951) 278

Discussion of 2.1 has always centred upon the relationship between ll.
1–46 and 47–78: how does the rapturous troubadour of the first part
stand to the gloomy lover of the second? Lefèvre, keen as he is to look
on the bright side, runs out of material by l. 47.[1] Earlier critics found it
quite reasonable to question the poem's unity, and the history of their
bewilderment can be followed in Enk[2] and Wimmel.[3] Suffice it to say that
out of the MSS' 78 lines, two or three poems or several fragments have
been made. Arguments for unity have become more fashionable in recent
years, although no two scholars are in complete agreement as to what
brings it about. Enk, for instance, a repentant separatist, maintains that
the incongruity between the delightful girl of the opening and the *dura
puella* of the closing lines is meant to reflect Cynthia's fickleness in a
manner that is programmatic for the whole book. Kroll had earlier
argued along the same lines.[4] A different line is taken by Wimmel. He
views the second part as a *captatio misericordiae* calculated to counterbal-
ance the arrogance and complacency of the first by rousing sympathy for
the poet, mortally endangered because of his love life. This, however, is
no argument from psychological plausibility but an attempt on Wimmel's
part to show that 2.1 *as a whole* represents a large-scale literary apology
of the Callimachean type addressed to Maecenas; and as a full-blown
version of this type of poem, 2.1 provides the starting-point for an
extensive scrutiny of the Roman 'Apologetik'.[5]

Now it is true that ll. 17–46 leave little to be desired in the way of a
formal *recusatio*. Nor is it to be doubted that they were written with the
Callimachean *Aetia* prologue foremost in the poet's mind. And yet there

---

[1] Lefèvre (1966) 22–9. [2] Enk, II introd. note, 7ff.
[3] Wimmel (1960) 13ff. [4] Kroll (1924) 229 n. 11.
[5] Wimmel (1960) 14ff.

seems to be little justification for seeing this passage as a model for the thematic sequence of the poem as a whole rather than for one of its components. Wimmel is at pains to show that the idea of being close to death (*Todesnahe*) suggested by 2.1.47ff. is the counterpart to the old-age theme that appears in l. 33 of the prologue in order to sum up the poet's life and to still the bitter feelings roused by the preceding polemical part. But 2.1.1–46 are, strictly speaking, not polemical in the sense that Callimachus' prologue is; what is perhaps more important, the Alexandrian's references to old age suggest the idea of a literary rejuvenation rather than that of literal death. I do not see how analysis of the poem in terms of 'apologetische Form' can take this stumbling-block in its stride. To Wimmel's discussion we must briefly come back later on.

Kühn shares Wimmel's view that from l. 46 onwards Propertius seeks to rouse compassion. Alive as he is to the fact that the elegists are given to equivocal language when it comes to love poetry and love life, he none the less draws the line between the two at 46 and argues that up to that point Propertius had been talking about the thrills he gets out of love poetry, but thenceforward broods on the harassments of love life. The reason would be that Maecenas could put up with the harmless ravings of the poet but would hardly countenance anything of the sort from the actual lover. The result, according to Kühn, is a sharp difference in tone and mood between the two parts of 2.1.[6] Wenzel has no quarrel with either Wimmel or Kühn. She obviously regards their analyses as complementary and essential for the understanding of the poem's unity, which she would rather seek in a conflict within the poet's mind than in the form of the poem.[7] I shall be presently arguing that considerations of form can yield substantial proof of the poem's unity; and I hope that my reading of 47ff. in particular will show that talk of 'Konfliktsituation', self-pity, dejection and the like misrepresents the nature and tone of 2.1.

We must shuttle back to the Monobiblos and look at poems 6 and 7. In both Propertius declares inability or unwillingness to take up a different style of life or literary activity respectively. Now the Augustan elegists will often speak of their pursuits in life in terms that suggest their chosen genre, using deliberately ambiguous language to conflate apparently distinct activities. *nos, ut consuemus, nostros agitamus amores* 'We, as comes natural, agitate our love' (1.7.5) is typical of a convention that blends life and poetry, and the reader familiar with it would have been tempted to see the poems addressed to the soldier Tullus and to the poet Ponticus

[6] Kühn (1961) 88–98.   [7] Wenzel (1969) 19.

as two sides of the same coin. Once this complementary relationship is grasped, the parallelism of their thought sequence stands out clearly and, what is more important, invites comparison with the poem addressed to Maecenas.

1.6 begins with all those things Propertius would do to please Tullus (1–4), were his mistress not dominating his life in the way she does in 5–18; it goes on to congratulate Tullus on his noble aspirations (19–22) and then drifts towards the death theme of the closing lines. 2.1 opens with Cynthia's domination of his poetry (1–16) which makes it impossible for Propertius to write on subjects that would have pleased Maecenas (17–34), goes on to pay the latter a deferential compliment on his loyalty to Augustus (35–8), and after giving the reason for the refusal of epic (39–46) veers round to, and is dominated to its end by the death theme. 1.7 ushers in Ponticus, already embarked on his ambitious enterprise in the field of epic, for which he receives dubious wishes for success, and which is brought into contrast with Propertius' own elegiac tribulations (1–8). The elegist waxes self-confident in the course of weighing against each other the claims the two genres lay to immortality and practical success in love (9–20), fancies himself dead and famous (21–4) and, finally, delivers another brief caveat (25–6). Kühn remarks upon the instructive similarity of thought movement between 1.6 and 1.7,[8] but a brief glance at 2.1 will show that the *Gedankenbewegung* is much the same in all three poems. To put it generally: the poet declines an explicit or implicit invitation to a different life-style or literary genre, sets forth the reasons for his choice, assesses the values and prospects of the contrasting attitudes and declares resolution to stick to his own lot. We cannot fail to notice that thoughts of death are invariably involved in the process. In fact, it looks as if the latter, death-centred section of 2.1 is part and parcel of a certain structural pattern. This, however, may sound too formalistic to those vexed by the psychological anacoluthon that has Propertius leap out of the bed of 45–6 into the ever deepening trough of 47ff.; and it may also be pointed out with good reason that the refractory maid of 1.6 and 7 is the obvious cause of her lover's demise. The problem calls for a close-up view of the relevant passages.

G. Williams has seen that an outstanding characteristic of Propertius is that he can 'select a word which will create, by itself, a maximum appropriate effect in a given context'.[9] Such words are usually endowed with a wide range of associative potentialities so that their semantic scope

---

[8] Kühn (1961) 100.   [9] Williams (1968) 781.

is not conditioned solely by the immediate context. If any word qualifies for this distinction in l. 46, it is certainly *conterat*. Commentators quote expressions such as Cic. *Tusc.* 1.41 *quam quisque norit artem, in hac se exerceat* 'Let each man spend his energy on what he knows how to do well', and generally settle for the attenuated 'spend' or 'pass' the verb means in phrases like Cic. *Quinct.* 41 *frustra tempus contero* (see, for example, Enk and Camps). This is not good enough. When Propertius uses the verb in its simple form he aims at sharp, local, material effects: 4.7.16 *trita fenestra* (Cynthia's windowsill rubbed away), 4.7.10 *triverat ora liquor* (Cynthia's lips frayed by the Lethean waters). His imagination intrudes into the process of erosive penetration, as in 2.25.15–17:

> teritur robigine mucro
> ferreus et parvo saepe liquore silex:
> at nullo dominae teritur sub crimine amor

> *Steel blades are worn away*
> *By rust, and flint by dripping water.*
> *But love's not worn away by an accusing mistress*

where the figurative is chaperoned by the solidly literal. The verb is strong (Camps) *and* poignantly physical; and it is never more so than when it points to sexual activity. 'Verbs of this general semantic field', writes Adams in a section on words denoting 'rub, stimulate' and the like, 'are neither exclusively metonymies nor metaphors when applied to sexual acts. A verb meaning "rub away" is metaphorical if used of sexual intercourse, but "rubbing" can be interpreted as a concomitant of the sexual act.'[10] Propertius has much more than that. One need only remember the ghoulish lewdness of 4.7.94 *mixtis ossibus ossa teram* 'And bone on mingled bone I'll grind.' There is a somewhat gentler congress in 3.20.6 *forsitan ille alio pectus amore terat* 'perhaps he is being consumed by passion in another's embrace', but in the most devastating one-verse Augustan vilification of Cleopatra (*et famulos inter femina trita suos* 'a female pursuing her daily grind even among her slaves' 3.11.30) the passive participle 'grinds' the harlot-queen with a ferociousness one would hardly expect from a servile entourage. In all the above cases *terere* suggests either gradual material destruction or libidinous abrasion or, as in the last three instances, a mixture of both. As used by Propertius, *terere* is apt to have a potential at once deadly and erotic.[11]

---

[10] Adams (1982) 183.
[11] It is this blend that remains peculiar to Propertius; I can find no sign of it either in Catullus or Tibullus or in Ovid.

It is not, I think, otherwise with *conterat* in 2.1.46,[12] and a full view of
ll. 43–8 can help make this clearer:

> navita de ventis, de tauris narrat arator,
> enumerat miles vulnera, pastor ovis;
> nos contra angusto versantes proelia lecto:
> qua pote quisque, in ea conterat arte diem.
> laus in amore mori: laus altera, si datur uno
> posse frui: fruar o solus amore meo!

> *The sailor talks of squalls, the ploughman of his oxen;*
> *The soldier counts his wounds, the shepherd sheep:*
> *But we engage in battles on a narrow bed.*
> *We should all rub along in our own way.*
> *It's glorious to die for love, and glorious to be granted*
> *One to enjoy. O may none but I enjoy my love!*

Erotic death smoulders in the *militia amoris* metaphor in 44–5, is fanned
by *conterat* in 46 and blazes up in the *laus in amore mori* of the next line.
Furthermore, the references to Callimachean principles in 39–42 and the
fleeting 'Priamel' in 43–5 incubate the idea of elegiac *ars* as a chiefly
literary activity, and yet when it eventually hatches between *conterat* and
diem in 46, *ars* refers as much to life as it does to literature. The next
couplet then shifts the emphasis on to the former.

It begins to emerge that the transition from 46 to 47 is not as abrupt
as it seems at first sight. Elegiac death spans the alleged gap (*conterat–mori*);
so do, I think, the ideas of *ars* and *laus*. In the comparable *recusatio* of 3.9,
with Maecenas again as the addressee, Propertius appeals to the example
of famous artists who obeyed their natural talents: *gloria Lysippo est animosa
effingere signa* 'Lysippus' glory is to mould statues that seem to breathe'
(9), *in Veneris tabula summam sibi poscit Apelles* 'Apelles claims the highest
praise for his Venus painting' (11). These and others have deserved their
fame (8); to go against the grain and choose to do what you are not equal
to would be shameful (5). In other words, 3.9.5–20 invite us to fill in *laus*
in 2.1.41–6 and *ars* in 2.1.47–8: *in amore mori* is a laudable art on a par
with those listed in 43–4. It is worth noting that *conterat* with its load of
associations is in good company; the preceding hexameter is ambiguity
itself: *nos contra angusto versantes proelia lecto*. Surely, 'only the finest line,
or lines, stands between his going from bed to verse'.[13] This densely
suggestive couplet spills over into the next: *mors, amor, laus* and *ars*, all ride
astride the supposed rift. By now the fact should begin to dawn upon the

---

[12] As far as I am aware, Richardson is unique in commenting upon the erotic overtones of
conterat in this line: 'Both *tero* and *contero* can be used as sexual metaphor, so there is a ribald
overtone.'   [13] Commager (1974) 6.

reader that death is canonised rather than deprecated. That, in turn, would make the 'compassion' theory about 47ff. look less convincing. But this is a question that should not be raised until those lines have come under close examination. For the time being we must see what additional light poems 1.6 and 7 can cast on the lines we have just been discussing.

2.1.45 has a worthy precursor in 1.7.5 *nos, ut consuemus, nostros agitamus amores*. Similar reasoning, i.e. rejection of uncongenial pursuits, leads up to both statements. More importantly, similarly phrased arguments back up Propertius' stance in both poems. 1.7.9 *hic mihi conteritur vitae modus* 'Thus I grind out my life's measure', where *vitae modus* is to all intents and purposes a synonym for *diem*, gives a foretaste of 2.1.46. But does *conteritur* have the force of *conterat*? One thing that can be safely said is that, in view of the love life / love poetry ambiguity four lines earlier, *conteritur* implies energy spent on both love and poetry. I would also suggest that *conteritur* effects the transition here, just as *conterat* does in its own context, to considerations of death that culminate in 23–4. Clearly, what Propertius envisages in 11–22 is a *posthumous* recognition of his talent. There is here a projection into the future, and the elegist's forecast about the rough weather in store for the epic poet, should he fall in love, is invested, with slight but amusing exaggeration I think, with the indisputable authority of the *outre-tombe*: *maius ab exsequiis nomen in ora venit*. The movement from present rivalry to universal veneration of the elegist is neatly mirrored in the poem's temporal structure: present indicatives for the literary skirmish (1–8), via the significant *conteritur* and the bridging optatives (11–14) to the authoritative futures of 15–24. Unlike this poem, 1.6 feigns humbleness, but develops along parallel lines. It is in keeping with the tone adopted here that ll. 25–6, which can be seen as corresponding with 1.7.5 and 2.1.45, sound defeatist in the extreme:

> me sine, quem semper voluit fortuna iacere,
> hanc animam extremae reddere nequitiae.

> *Let me, whom Fortune wills among the fallen,*
> *Lay down my life in extreme misconduct.*

This leads to

> multi longinquo periere in amore libenter   (1.6.27)[14]

> *Many the willing casualties in love's long service*

a statement which by virtue of its position in the development of the argument and the aspiration it evokes reads very much like 1.7.9 and

---

[14] *libenter* in a 'humble' poem is a diplomatic substitute for something that is insidiously claimed through being disclaimed two lines later: *non ego sum laudi* (29).

2.1.46. In a poem geared to the soldiering-of-love metaphor, *longinquo* is not only happily topical (a literal *militia* being as a rule a long job), it is also suggestive of the welcome protractedness conjured up by *contero* in 1.7.9 and 2.1.46; better still: '"longinquo periere" suggests a very protracted dying, one which many people find desirable...the lover enjoys his "dying"'.[15] The sum and substance of all three lines can be checked against their wording: erotic dying (= *longinquo periere* 1.6.27, *conteritur* 1.7.9, *conterat* 2.1.46) is a glory-winning (= *libenter* 1.6.27, *fama* 1.7.9) art (= *arte* 2.1.46). We can see *laus in amore mori* in the making here, as we can see the conceptual mechanism that clasps together 2.1.1–46 and 2.1.47–78.

The evidence, then, of poems 1.6 and 7 is valuable on two counts. Not only do they provide verbal and conceptual parallels that confirm the forward-looking and unifying quality of 2.1.45–6, they also prefigure a thematic/structural pattern which the programmatic elegy of Book 2 reproduces on a larger scale. Two distinct movements can be generally descried: a rivalry between elegiac and un-elegiac modes resolves into a definitive erotic statement which involves thoughts of death. We shall see that a fair number of poems within this book are cast in a similar mould, those that will detain us longer more clearly so. If this is right then some new light can be shed on the question of the unity, or the limits, of individual poems. It is not by sheer chance that Book 2 is infested both by death and textual problems. Not all of the latter are related to the former; but some are, and in these cases the hypothesis of a recurrent structure as a vehicle for the Propertian *Liebestod* may put the discussion on a more promising basis. Otherwise one may find oneself arguing in a hand-to-mouth sort of way, as I think Wimmel does when he traces the death theme in 2.1.47ff. back to the Callimachean *Aetia* prologue. Regarding this section as an excusatory description of the poet's condition in life (i.e. the endangerment of his life through love) calculated to balance the arrogant rejection of epic, he wants to accommodate it to the poem's apologetic purposes; he further finds that such 'Stil-Apologien' display a distinctive pattern of their own in which Horace, Propertius and Persius allow the biographical element, whose function is excusatory, to become ever more evident towards the end of the 'apologetic' sequence.[16] Now one fact that emerges from his list on pp. 18–19 is that Horace, Ovid and Persius are all ringing the changes on the perfunctory excuses of *nequitia, paupertas* and slender inspiration as the driving forces behind, and limitations of their chosen type of poetry. Nowhere does the death theme receive mention, let alone extensive treatment. To say that Ovid, *Am.*

---

[15] Hodge and Buttimore (1977) 114.   [16] Wimmel (1960) 17.

1.1.22 (*legit in exitium spicula facta meum* 'he [i.e. Amor] picked out arrows made for my undoing') stands for (even if not meant in earnest) proximity to death, which warrants the preference of love poetry over epic (*legitimierende Todesnähe*), strains credulity. And even in Propertius, apart from 2.1, no other piece features the death theme (3.1.35ff. is irrelevant here). The conclusion seems inescapable that whatever else the biographical ingredient consists of, death is certainly not one of its characteristic topoi. Still less could Wimmel's theory account for the extent and the rich suggestiveness of the death-centred 2.1.47ff. In discussing the latter poem Wimmel has allowed the 'apologetische Form' to usurp the shaping power of Propertian love and death.

His emphasis on 'Form', however, is methodologically sound. Wenzel is unappreciative of the fact that Wimmel's arguments for unity are, in the last analysis, formalistic. This is because she believes that the poet is in the throes of an inner 'Konfliktsituation' (see p. 21 above). Whether this is so ll. 47ff. will show. One should attend to them as closely as possible.

Enk's paraphrase of *laus in amore mori* as 'laus est usque ad mortem amare' is something of a rallying-point for the critics, however different their tastes or various the views they take about the other issues raised by 2.1. That l. 47 appears to arise from 46 is noted, but *conterat* is taken for granted, while 1.6.27 and 1.7.9 are referred to as verbal and conceptual parallels which reinforce the idea of dying while a lover or that of love until death. To quote Enk again on ll. 51–6: 'whether I must drink magic potions or perish by witchcraft, I shall love Cynthia until death'. But the paraphrase reads more smoothly than the actual text and I do not know that Hartman's complaint about the oracular obscurity of the passage was just an exaggeration:[17]

> seu mihi sunt tangenda novercae pocula Phaedrae,
>   pocula privigno non nocitura suo,
> seu mihi Circaeo pereundum est gramine, sive
>   Colchis Iolciacis urat aena focis,
> una meos quoniam praedata est femina sensus,
>   ex hac ducentur funera nostra domo. (2.1.51–6)

> *Even if I had to touch stepmother Phaedra's potions,*
> *Potions unable to harm her stepson,*
> *Even if I had to perish by Circe's poisons, or*
> *The Colchic cauldron boiled me on Iolcan fires,*
> *As there's one only woman robbed me of my senses,*
> *It's out of her house I'll be carried feet first.*

[17] Hartman (1921) 342.

27

Commentators find it necessary to assume a deflection in the poet's thought: Propertius evidently illustrates his resolution to remain faithful to his one love by referring to Phaedra's ineffective love philtres, but then he goes on to mention Circe and Medea, who are nowhere said to have put their magic to amatory uses, and who are associated with either transformation or death and destruction. Shackleton Bailey posits a change in mid-course from 'no magic potion can make me unfaithful' to 'however I die, I shall die faithful'.[18] This is also what Williams's solution, stripped of its technicalities, amounts to.[19] The metamorphosis theme assumes central importance in other quarters. Rothstein, for instance, explains that exclusive devotion will defy love philtre (Phaedra), metamorphosis (Circe) and laceration *cum* rejuvenation (Medea), whereas Wimmel entertains the idea of a transformation attempted by Maecenas in the hope of ostracising Cynthia from Propertius' poetry and life.[20]

At the root of such reasoning lies a self-defeating pernicketiness which expects nothing less than a one-to-one correspondence between mythological example and contextual situation. This is misguided, never more so than when the myths themselves have their own moot points, as they do here. Phaedra administering love philtres is unattested outside Propertius; further, Medea's practices – τὰ μὲν ἐσθλά, τὰ δὲ ῥαιστήρια – affected Pelias in a very different way from Aeson, and it is as arbitrary to opt for the former rather than the latter incident (or vice versa) as it is unlikely to suppose that the poet intentionally allows both possibilities.[21] Ink is spilled on such problems as if Schöne had not convincingly illustrated three-quarters of a century ago the poet's habit of treating mythology in a loose and arbitrary manner.[22] Camps, as often, contributes a dash of pragmatism: 'they are cited here simply as typically powerful witches' – but there is a lot more to it than that.

Lines 51–4 present a brief mythological catalogue. Propertius likes to weave into his poems mythological material in the form of exempla series, and in such cases some 'Procrustean' practice is observable. A central effect is aimed at and the myths forgo such particulars as do not contribute to it, while the reader is invited to suspend irrelevant associations. The same habit will cause even an isolated example to appear dictated not by logic so much as by the requirements of an art

[18] Shackleton Bailey (1956) 63.   [19] Williams (1980) 170.

[20] Wimmel (1960) 23. Luck (1962) 38–9 sees in the mythological examples of 2.1.51–4 the ironical suggestion that all three women for all their proficiency in witchcraft failed to captivate their lovers; accordingly, he sets a powerful 'internal' magic, stemming from Cynthia's qualities, against an unavailing 'external' one. It will be evident below why I regard such a distinction as untenable.

[21] See Rothstein on 2.1.51; Wimmel (1960) 24 and n. 1; Tupet (1976) 354ff.

[22] Schöne (1911) 29–37.

that wants to be suggestive[23] or to create atmosphere – that quality of the 'Stimmungshafte' on which Kölmel has made some fine points.[24] Mythological female groups are mostly deployed to this effect. The heroines and goddesses of 1.2.15–20, 1.15.9–22, 2.2.7–14 or 2.28.51–4 are less individuals and case histories than they are collective embodiments of some 'moral' or aesthetic ideal. So when Tupet seeks to define the 'dénominateur commun' of the three examples in 2.1.51–4 she is on the right track.

One thing we can be reasonably certain about is that these Propertian *dames du temps jadis* are almost always thought of as beauties. But antiquity, or death for that matter, is a leveller as well as a beautifier.[25] In catalogues that tend to be aesthetically egalitarian and amoralistic Propertius rallies together heroines, courtesans, harlot-queens, goddesses – and witches. This, to be sure, does not include the creatures of 1.1.19–24. Some of the things said about 2.1.51–4 would never have been said, had the romantic and aesthetic potential of Medea and Circe been fully appreciated. These women, much like Phaedra, are conceived of as beautiful and *qua* beautiful as lovers to boot. There is an intrinsic logic here that makes diligent enquiries into the amorous associations of the two witches all but otiose,[26] although it is, of course, quite reasonable to assume that the lovesick Medea of Apollonius, for instance, or the eroticised versions lying behind Hor. *Epist.* 1.2.25 *sub domina meretrice* [i.e. Circe] *fuisset* [i.e. Ulysses] *turpis et excors* 'he would have grown ugly and senseless, in the power of a harlot mistress', provided a convenient background.[27] At any rate, after Tupet's discussion the literal-minded should be satisfied that *all three* figures in 2.1.51–4 are both great witches and great lovers. But then Tupet swerves into a line of argument that makes of *pocula* (51), *gramine* (53), and *aena* (54) love philtres devoid of deadly power; in her own words: 'Il n'est pas question ici de rites de destruction.'[28] She thus aligns herself with those who take the concoctions of 51–4 – destructive or not – as ineffective assaults on the poet's single-minded devotion to Cynthia, that is, as a *test* of his enduring love. It is my suggestion that what Propertius strives to convey here is not so much 'love of one woman *until* death' as 'love of one woman *as* death'.

In what relation does the woman of 55–6 stand to those of 51–4? The effect she has on her lover's constitution should give the answer: *una meos quoniam praedata est femina sensus* (55). Lesbia works likewise upon Catullus

[23] Boucher (1965) 254.   [24] Kölmel (1957) 108–11.
[25] Cf. Kölmel (1957) 64–5.
[26] See, for instance, Tupet (1976) 355–7.
[27] On Circe as a lover see Ov. *Rem. Am.* 263–88 and cf. Rohde (1914) 111 with n. 1.
[28] Tupet (1976) 357.

in 51.6 *eripit sensus*, and the result is the kind of sensory devastation one would naturally associate with the practices of 51–4, the more so since Propertius opted for the far more drastic *praedata*. Phaedra, Circe and Medea have done nothing if not wrought havoc in people's physical condition, and here they are mythological substitutes for Cynthia.[29] Lines 55–6 are the 'real-life' apodosis of a mythological protasis (51–4). At the literal level there can be felt an alluring tension between the grammatical structure and the drift of thought, as the conditional mood is counteracted by the urgency inherent in the gerundives (*sunt tangenda, pereundum est*); the *quoniam* clause is a bit Janus-faced, looking as it does backwards in sense but forward, to the apodosis proper, in grammar. The overall effect is, I think, not so much one of orthodox condition as of tentative statement – a statement of the type: 'this is how I feel my love' rather than 'this is how I am prepared to prove it'. This is not unlike Propertius. 'A Propertian sentence may be clear enough, but just not mean what it says; or it may be wilfully irrational; or its rational content may be almost negligible.'[30] Whether the distinctions are tenable or not, Quinn makes an important point and puts his finger on those complex pressures that here cause the sense to transcend the construction. In the process the conventional range of the witchcraft/poison associations has been transcended as well.

A stir in the direction of 2.1.51ff. can be traced as early as 1.5. Gallus is warned to keep clear of Cynthia lest he should find himself treading on fire or drinking the poisons of Thessaly, *et bibere e tota toxica Thessalia* (6). But *Thessalia* has none of the suggestiveness and evocative power of our mythological trio, through which Propertius contrives to establish the feeling of a stealthy and deadly eros. The cup, the herbs and the cauldron do spell death and destruction; and they do not put love to the test but reveal its, so to say, *chemical* composition.[31] I want to underline yet again

---

[29] Wiggers (1972) 32 recognises that Propertius 'places Cynthia in a class with the witch-women' but she sees in 55 a feeble 'one woman has stolen my senses' and in the whole passage little else beyond a proof of constancy in love.

[30] Quinn (1963) 130.

[31] There are some useful observations in Follett's (1973) 7–67 chapter 'Magic in Propertius', especially on the different treatment of the topos by Prop. and Tib. She argues, rightly to my mind, that whereas in the latter magic does not play a part 'in the clarification of his condition as a lover' (p. 29), in Prop. 'magic is one of the major means by which Propertius delineates the nature and the depth of his love'. But Follett labours the implications of a witchy Cynthia: she can be both benign and malign; like Phaedra and Circe she may not eventually prevail on her lover (cf. Luck's theory, p. 28 n. 20 above); and 'in trying to retain his devotion by unscrupulous methods, she may work her own downfall' (pp. 25ff.). Thus, it seems to me, a great deal is read into 2.1.51ff. which can hardly be there, the Propertian construct of a 'deadly and romantic enchantress' is all but dismantled and, what is more important, the sensuousness of the poet's response to witchcraft (see below) is missed.

a sensory thrust which, filtered through the material of 51–6, comes across as some kind of sinister sensuousness. There is more to be said on this later on.

To sum up so far. As far as ll. 51ff. are concerned we need not postulate a movement from *love* philtres in the case of Phaedra to merely *destructive* witchcraft in the next couplet, nor do we have to assume any deflection in the poet's thought, for, as has been seen, by l. 46 the possibility of the deadly/destructive blending with the erotic is well established. It is in the wake of the complex of associations roused by *conterat* in particular that the mythological figures of 51ff. follow.[32] Their common denominator is their being enchanting and deadly at the same time – like Cynthia and like love itself.

Those who have been reading these lines otherwise will probably have sympathy for Camps's note on 57ff.: 'The thought of fidelity until death to a single love (56) suggests the somewhat different thought of love as an incurable complaint'. But Ribbeck had gone so far as to start a new poem here and Wimmel's brief conspectus shows others to have taken exception to the transition as well.[33] Most of the ground has, I hope, already been cut from under their feet. For the rest, it seems to me worth reminding ourselves that antiquity was liable to look upon medicine as magic of some kind and that, therefore, the doctors of 59ff. are contiguous to the witches of 51ff.[34] Yet even so, by comparison with the potent blend of the latter passage the notion of love as incurable disease might seem a retrograde and conventional step. This initial impression will not survive a close reading of the mythological illustrations in 59–70. Propertius marshals two groups of exempla, balancing a bunch of celebrated physicians (59–64) against a series of adynata (66–70). Both groups hinge on the challenge of l. 65 (*hoc si quis vitium poterit mihi demere* 'Were there a man could rid me of this vice of mine') and are meant to bear out the proposition of 57–8:

> omnis humanos sanat medicina dolores:
> solus amor morbi non amat artificem.

> *Medicine can heal all merely human ailments;*
> *Love alone hates the pathologist.*

But in the process of doing so they modify the traditional ideas that sustain it.

[32] For what it is worth, let it also be noted that *(con)tero* appears to be something of a technical term in the (chiefly magical) potion and herb industry; see, for instance, Prop. 2.17.14, Virg. G. 4.63, Ov. *Ars Am.* 3.465, Ov. *Met.* 4.504 and 14.44.
[33] Wimmel (1960) 24.   [34] Cf. Eitrem (1941) 40–1.

G. Williams has seen that of the four myths in 59–64 that of Androgeos goes beyond the others and 'resonates beyond its immediate context' in that it features the death theme prominent until 56 and to be taken up again in 71–8.[35] That may be so, but first and foremost its implications reverberate throughout its immediate context. It occupies the central position in its own group and at the same time, by virtue of Androgeos' experience of both worlds, it preempts the framework of the Underworld myths adduced in 65ff. The chief function of his story is to work a specific slant into the other examples of 59–64, namely to impart mortuary overtones to what would otherwise have remained within the area of a comprehensible, even if intractable, medical complaint. Thus the poet intensifies his initial statement, *omnis humanos sanat medicina dolores* (57), in the direction of 'even death can be cured'. The idea of death once drawn in has never ceased to hang over the poem and it is reasonable to suppose that it has also influenced the choice of the adynata in 66ff. We have no doubt about the traditional habitat of Tantalus and the Danaids but it is noteworthy that the irrevocability of Prometheus' affliction makes *Caucasia* (69) look merely formulaic – possibly another instance of integration due to the pervasiveness of the idea of death.

What is, then, the cumulative effect of 59–70? I think that through the sustained hyperbole of his mythological language the poet is insinuating the conceit of love as the one irreversible kind of death. In this way he not only reassesses the more or less familiar proposition of 57–8 but also compounds the message of 55–6: not only love as a kind of death but love as irreversible death – or, perhaps, love as a kind of irrevocable infernal adventure. Both in 47ff. and 57ff. the oblique mythological discourse works subtle changes on an initial statement by modulating its tone, redefining the relations between its concepts, extending its scope. The impression is hard to escape that these passages, especially 57ff., represent a more radical version of the erotic manifesto 1.1 has given voice to. For in that poem Propertius rehearses the received image of the lover as a helpless madman in prostration before an unresponsive mistress, but he can still appeal to his friends for help (26) and consider, albeit distrustfully, possible remedies ranging from downright surgery to therapeutic trips (25–30). If such expedients are out of the question in the revised programme of 2.1.47ff., it is, I think, because the poet has moved on to the more idiomatic definition of exclusive love as an experience of death. It is not a point on which I wish to dwell here, but I think that the treatment of the witchcraft (19–24) and medicine themes (27–8) in the

---

[35] Williams (1980) 171.

first Monobiblos poem gives the measure of its difference from its opposite number in Book 2. The enchantresses of 2.1.51ff. announce thraldom to a venomous and deadly charm that goes beyond the vociferous slavery of 1.1 as well as beyond the understanding of the physicians. Two other poems of Book 2 that incorporate episodes of this intoxication can contribute essential information both on symptoms and causes.

2.4 is one of them, and it is beset by two problems. The first concerns its limits. Barber's Oxford edition adopts those of the MSS, but controversy arose when Schrader and Lachmann transferred the last five couplets of 2.3 to form the beginning of the next elegy. This question, however, does not affect our discussion;[36] the second can perhaps be helped by it. Birt transposed 15–16 to follow 8, whereas Enk placed 9–10 after 14.[37] Camps, who does neither, has a lucid note on the premiss of the first of these two proposals: 'The connexion [i.e. of ll. 9–10] with what has gone before is puzzling at first, since magic (lines 7–8) is not usually spoken of by the elegists as protecting against love...but as expelling it, or as forcing the person loved to reciprocate.' One might get the impression that Camps shares the conviction of other commentators that mythological witches are invariably brought into poetry with regard to their precise speciality and function (see p. 28 above), but he goes on to show that he surmises better than that: 'I think, however, that Propertius in this passage is not concerned with the precise functions of witches' magic...and that the idea in his mind is a general one.' What this general idea is like can be asked in the light of 2.1.47ff.

2.4.7–8

> non hic herba valet, non hic nocturna Cytaeis,
> non Perimedaeae gramina cocta manus

> *No herbs can help you here, no midnight sorceress,*
> *No simples mixed by Perimede*

may be seen as a compression *cum* variation of 2.1.51–4. *Cytaeis*, which embodies an abstruse geographical allusion and contains the exotic upsilon sound, replaces *Colchis* (2.1.54). The unusually long and sonorous *Perimedaeae* rounds off the mystery as well as the learning. We should next notice that the arch-sorceresses of 2.1.51–4 precipitate the *funera* of 56, while those of 2.4.7–8 bridge the gap between the foppish antics of 5–6 and the ominous remarks of 9–12, which in their turn lead up to the funeral of 13, *ambulat – et subito mirantur funus amici!* 'He's up, and

---

[36] On this see esp. Shackleton Bailey (1956) 67–8 and Enk, introd. note to his 2.4.

[37] Barber, Giardina and Fedeli (1984) transpose after Birt; no transposition in Rothstein, Luck, Richardson, Hanslik.

suddenly friends marvel at a corpse!' The incurability theme, shrunk to one couplet (2.4.11–12), is also there. Finally, the sequence in 2.4.7–14, witchcraft–incurability–*funus*, does not differ from that of 2.1.51–78. The parallelism is unmistakable and although it cannot guarantee, it certainly suggests the possibility that the mythological figures of 2.4.7–8 are not considered so different from those of 2.1.51–4 as to be credited with an unambiguously benevolent function, whether preventive or repressive, in matters of love. Whatever he may have thought of witches on other occasions, Propertius draws them in here because they are uniquely apt to call up, just as in 2.1.51ff., the ideas of stealthiness and deadliness, which are of the essence of love. Again he speaks of love in terms of *herba* and *gramina*, that is, in terms of an insidious poison. Now if there is one couplet in this poem that rises by the most natural of associations from 7–8, it is the one that follows immediately after these lines:

> quippe ubi nec causas nec apertos cernimus ictus,
> unde tamen veniant tot mala caeca via est (2.4.9–10)

> *For we can find no cause and no visible wound;*
> *Whence such troubles come is a mystery*

For how does poison work if not through a *caeca via*? And what kind of death would an era of pre-scientific toxicology have felt to be more insidious and inscrutable than that caused by poison? The poet who lets the dark channels of 9–10 follow hard upon the banes of 7–8 gives himself away in the mighty curiosity to scan the intravenous course of the viper's venom:

> bracchia spectavi sacris admorsa colubris,
> et trahere occultum membra soporis iter. (3.11.53–4)

> *With my own eyes I saw her arms bitten by the sacred snakes and her limbs*
> *channel the stealthy course of slumber.*

The pentameter is about Cleopatra's lethal poisoning, and yet, but for *soporis*, it would be appropriate of lethal loving too: *ardet amans Dido traxitque per ossa furorem* 'Dido is burning with love and has absorbed the madness into the marrow of her bones' (*Aen.* 4.101). Propertius' pictorial and verbal response to either plight is the same. He is obviously thrilled by the 'impenetrable' even as he attempts to penetrate it. *nec apertos* and *caeca via* in 2.4.9–10 result from the occult practices of *nocturna Cytaeis* and scheming Perimede. The continuity, however, is not immediately perceptible and the same tensions arise as in 2.1.51–6. Thought in 7–8 seems to shoot out towards 'the witches' concoctions are powerless where love is concerned' but then it recoils in 9–10 as if the poet had suddenly realised that the implications of witchcraft/poison were the *ne plus ultra* for the definition of love: love is more potent than poison – but works exactly like it. Thought never quite crystallises in 7–10, one might even say it is abortive; but its power resides in this very abortiveness. No need to resort to the possibility of a Propertian 'para-rational statement' (does not mean what it says? wilfully irrational? rational content negligible?),[38] although one may try, with Camps, a number of plausible question marks ('the movement in 7–10 being "do not suppose that magic can *help* you (? to get your way, ? to regulate your desire)"...') The last thing one should do is transpose. There seems to be no logical gap in the order of the lines as presented by the MSS. After the definition of love in 2.4.7–10, the despair of 11–12 comes as no surprise. Even more fitting is the collapse of 13; victims of poisoning may waste away but more often than not one prefers to think of them as dropping dead. *incautum* in the next line sums up 9–10 and provides a perfect motivation for the following couplet.[39]

We may canvass 2.27 for another clue. Some scholars have taken a rather dim view of this poem, with Butler–Barber complaining of jerkiness and faulty construction and Quinn regarding it as little more than a fragile 'scaffolding of clichés', even if an ingenious one at times.[40] Despite the admittedly staccato manner in the poem's movement, I believe that such criticisms are rather unfair. The elegy lists in a rapid, quasi-Priamel fashion the classical short cuts to doom, whose unpredictability harasses the general run of men and throws into relief the mystery of the lover's demise; and it is arguably written in much the same vein as 2.4, as salient verbal and conceptual links show. The first two couplets recall 2.4.15, with the divinatory role here assigned to astrology. *funeris* (1), *qua sit mors aditura via* (2), and *caeca pericla viae* (6) signal preoccupations which are central to 2.4. Death's *caeca via* in 2.27 stretches across land and

---

[38] See Quinn (1963) 130–3, esp. 130, and cf. p. 30 above.

[39] Of the two transpositions mentioned above Birt's finds some palaeographical support in the homoeoteleuton *manus* (8) – *anus* (16), which might have caused 15–16 to be omitted after 7–8, and perhaps also in the fact that the sequence 7–8–15–16 unites, as we shall presently see, two Theocritean reminiscences. Perhaps, one should bear in mind that Latin is not all that rich in iambic words (11.2% according to some statistics, see Platnauer (1951) 16), that most of them were badly needed as pentameter endings and that as a result homoeoteleuta are more likely to occur here than anywhere else. The reminiscences, however, come from different points of Theocritus' poem (*Id.* 2.15–16 and 91) and they are likely to have been kept apart by Propertius himself.

[40] Quinn (1963) 182–7. His view that *periturus* in 2.27.11 is of a piece with the conventional use of *pereo* to mean 'I am suffering the anguish of unrequited love' has been convincingly refuted by Baker (1970) 670–4. Literal death must always be reckoned with in Prop. erotic statements. Thus Wenzel (1969) 85–7 observes rightly that the death of ll. 11–16 is meant as literally as that of ll. 1–10. Nevertheless, she is not innocent of metaphysical considerations apropos of 2.27.11ff., although not nearly as guilty as Birt, whom she quotes (p. 86 n. 2) as waxing enthusiastic over bodily resurrection envisaged by a prophetic and mystical poet.

sea (5–6), passes through uncertain civil strife (7–8) and urban accidents (9). Line 10 crowns the list of such hazards: *neu subeant labris pocula nigra tuis* 'Lest black potions pass your lips'. There is a movement in ll. 5ff. from the outward and morally acceptable (war against external enemies) towards the inward and most insidious (*subeant*). This can hardly be accidental. Propertius concludes with a kind of death whose motives are normally to be found in the intimate field of human relationships because the next casualty belongs to this sphere: *solus amans novit, quando periturus et a qua | morte* 'Only the lover knows when he will die and by what | Death' (11–12). The reader will tend to measure this death against the last-listed and more contiguous item, and may infer that the lover's death is 'esotericised' beyond the awesome deadliness that *pocula nigra* strike into the heart of ordinary *mortales*. But given the analogies, verbal and conceptual, between 2.27 and 2.4, one may also legitimately suspect that a game of associations is played out here similar to that in 2.4.7ff. What obscures this affinity is the fact that in 2.27 Propertius instead of dwelling on the symptoms of erotic poisoning goes for a conceit that makes the lover's death and resurrection dependent on the whims of his mistress. But lines 13–16 do not promote the notion of the lover's immunity so much as they afford the poet an opportunity to indulge an aesthetic obsession which is to be discussed in connexion with 2.26b (see pp. 91–2 below).

Symptoms may lead back to at least some of the causes. 2.4 provides a good starting-point. References to magic are so widespread in ancient poets that we could hardly relate ll. 7–8 of this poem to any specific text, were it not that the arcane *Perimedaeae* combines with 15–16 to suggest that it is Theocritus' μήτε τι Μηδείας μήτε ξανθᾶς Περιμήδας (16) and...καὶ ἐς τίνος οὐκ ἐπέρασα, | ἢ ποίας ἔλιπον γραίας δόμον ἅτις ἐπῇδεν; 'And to whose house did I not go, what hag's did I pass over, of those that had skill in charms?' (90–1), both from *Idyll* 2, that Propertius had in mind. On the basis of this (by no means unnoticed) fact further possibilities may be explored. Simaetha in the Theocritean poem resorts to magic in order to win back her reluctant lover, as is clear from her refrain throughout the first sixty-three lines. She addresses herself to Selene and Hecate, asking for φάρμακα worthy of Circe and the other two witches mentioned above. Now Hecate was often associated with witchcraft and is here, as Gow *ad loc.* suggests, invoked in two of her three capacities, namely as Luna (10–11) and Proserpina (12). The whole passage is pregnant with an almost murderous occultism out of proportion to Simaetha's avowed purpose. In fact, the object of ll. 26, 53–6 and 62 is the destruction rather than the repossession of the lover. This is most probably because, as Gow remarks, love is coupled with desire for revenge in the woman's mind; but if so Simaetha needs no special effort to bring out the purely deathly, as distinct from the miraculous, aspect of such demonic ensembles, for whenever they are invoked by lovers 'magie d'amour et magie destructive s'entrelacent'.[41] This particular combination appealed to Propertius and, as has been argued, he made a new and potent blend of it. I think that he did so with eyes fixed on Theocritus. Commentaries may give the impression that the influence of the Greek poet on the elegist amounts to no more than a couple of verbal reminiscences. This is not surprising but it is wrong. The φαρμακεύτρια of the second *Idyll* had already been spirited away into a prominent role in Virgil's eighth *Eclogue*, but then Virgil, unquestionably fascinated as he was with his model, was to a considerable extent engaged in generic emulation. Propertius' encounter with the Theocritean poem led to less obvious, because more radical, results. This is a claim that can only be substantiated through close analysis of 2.28 and, especially, 4.7,[42] but 2.1 and 4 also give food for some speculation. 2.1.53–4 and 2.4.7–8 list between them and in similar contexts all three witches mentioned in *Id.* 2.14–16:

> χαῖρ', Ἑκάτα δασπλῆτι, καὶ ἐς τέλος ἄμμιν ὀπάδει,
> φάρμακα ταῦτ' ἔρδοισα χερείονα μήτε τι Κίρκας
> μήτε τι Μηδείας μήτε ξανθᾶς Περιμήδας.

Hail, grim Hecate, and to the end attend me, and make these drugs of mine as potent as those of Circe or Medea or golden-haired Perimede.

If Propertius is thus drawing attention to a source already made famous by Virgil's *Eclogue*,[43] alert readers would have been certain to notice that Theocritus' all-important Σελάνα–Ἑκάτα was the conspicuous absentee in this reunion. But was she? Simaetha calls upon a goddess who, being *triformis*, could also manifest herself as Ἄρτεμις, the Roman Diana also known as Cynthia. Whatever the reasons behind this divine merger, E. N. O'Neil has made it clear that this last epithet came to be used of *Luna* as well, and went on to present a case for an intimate connexion between Propertius' mistress and the moon.[44] Not all the passages he adduces seem to me conclusive but 1.1.19–24, both because of its studied obscurity and by its position in a programmatic poem, is a very cogent

---

[41] Eitrem (1941) 62 with regard to Dido's magical practices in *Aen.* 4.

[42] On 4.7 see below pp. 156ff.

[43] Perhaps in some measure by Catullus as well, if Wiseman (1985) 193–4 is right about a lost poem (mime?) of the latter modelled on Φαρμακεύτρια. For other possible influences of *Id.* 2 on Catullus see Wiseman (1985) 198 with n. 68.

[44] O'Neil (1958) 1–8. The Apollonian–poetic associations of Cynthia need not be impaired; the name is versatile. Cf. Boyancé (1956) 172–5.

instance.[45] May one also entertain the suspicion that in the programmatic poem of the next book the most deadly and versatile among Theocritus' figures lives on in ll. 55–6, giving her lover hell worthy of Ἑκάτα under a name that calls up Σελάνα?

Interest in magic was vigorously awakened in Late Republican Rome to persist as vigorously for the next hundred years or so.[46] The social and anthropological roots of the phenomenon are the province of comprehensive studies like Tupet's. Some remarks made by La Penna in a brief section on 'la magia fra letteratura e realtà' are more relevant to our purposes. He finds that in their attitude to witchcraft the Augustan poets combine *lusus* with a taste for the macabre; and that they are also receptive to the aesthetic fascination of the horrible ('anche l'orrido ha il suo fascino estetico'), especially when it is not taken too seriously.[47] When passages like 2.1.51ff. and 2.4.7ff. are simply pronounced gloomy one feels that these possibilities have been hardly reckoned with. But *Cytaeis* (2.4.7), more even than recondite geographical lore, is a dash of euphonious exoticism.[48] Kölmel comments on the tension (*Spannung*) that can already be felt between myth and the present in ancient Greek lyric poetry.[49] A concomitant tension, which concerns mainly the Roman, operates at the phonological level: Περιμήδας did not engage the Greek reader in the way *Perimedaeae* engaged his Roman counterpart, and not only because the concentration of the vowels helps broaden the sonority

---

[45] Cf. Commager (1974) 33–6. Were it certain that Prop. Book 1 contains 354 couplets calculated, as Habinek (1982) 589–96 suggests, to call to mind the lunar year, then Cynthia–Luna would have been a certainty and Habinek would have upstaged the Monobiblos numerologists at a stroke.

[46] For possible socio-historical reasons see Tupet (1976) 149–50.

[47] La Penna (1977) 192–5.

[48] 'l'origine di Medea da Κύταια...è creazione degli Alessandrini' notes Fedeli on Prop. 1.1.24., where the MSS have played havoc with the woman from Κύταια. The adj. smacks of neoteric mannerism anxious to dodge the banality of the mere proper name by means of a geographical designation; and it is obscure enough to be worthy of Euphorion. Propertian commentators miss, so far as I know, the fact that this poet used it at least once: ὅσσ' ἐδάη Πολύδαμνα, Κυτηϊὰς ἢ ὅσα Μήδη (fr. 14 Powell = fr. 15 van Groningen, where see notes). Apollonius Rhodius, to be sure, says Κυταιέος Αἰήταο of Medea's father (*Argon.* 3.228), but is quite likely that the geographical epithet was applied to Medea herself either by the tragedian Lycophron (τὸν μελλόνυμφον εὐνέτην Κυταϊκῆς 174) or, if *Alexandra* is the work of a later poet, by the other σκοτεινός of Chalcis, Euphorion. Further, if Gallus 'can be seen clearly behind each section of Propertius' first elegy' (Ross (1975) 62ff., esp. 69), then 1.1.24 (which I would be inclined to read with Hertzberg: *posse Cytaeines ducere carminibus*) may well be taking up by way of allusion a Euphorionic form first transcribed into Latin by Gallus. Be that as it may, 2.4.7–8 present us with a prime example of a poetic tradition whose 'learned', 'derivative', 'obliquely allusive' and 'interlocking' character Kenney (1983) 44–59 has most recently illustrated in connexion with Virgil's second and eighth *Eclogues*. (In 2.4 Theocritus and Euphorion–Gallus are also joined, as I shall be arguing, by Lucretius.) Apart from Fedeli's note on 1.1.24, see also van Groningen on Euphorion, fr. 15.3 and *RE* xvi (1931) 30–1.

[49] Kölmel (1957) 30.

of the latter word. *Colchis Iolciacis* (2.1.54) telescopes *more Hellenistico* a mythological sequence which straddles two continents. This is what Baudelaire would probably have called 'sorcellerie évocatoire'. Hellenistic Tibullus cannot be said to have excelled in it; consider, for instance, 2.4.55–6:

> quidquid habet Circe, quidquid Medea veneni,
> quidquid et herbarum Thessala terra gerit

> *All Circe's magic potions, all Medea's drugs*
> *and all the herbs that sprout in Thessaly*

The names seem to lack perspective; no sound effect accentuates suggestive prolongations. But then Tibullus was less of an aesthete than Propertius was, especially when it came to the sinister and the macabre.

Whether the latter genuinely believed in the supernatural is not, strictly speaking, our concern, but if 2.1.51ff. were the only evidence available I think that the answer should be: No. What supernatural there is in this passage is firmly rooted in sensation. The poet moves from the touched vessel (*tangenda...pocula*) through the more specific herbs to the effervescent cauldron, thereby escalating the concreteness and physical threat of the magical utensils until these absorb the visual imagination as prominent features of a *tableau vivant*. Thus strong physical suggestion is an integral part of any *ideas* that may be evoked. Line 55 with its fierce *praedata...sensus* is, as I have already argued, a sharp reminder that what is at stake in the preceding couplets is the physical rather than the metaphysical. When Propertius comes back from the temple of Apollo on the Palatine he is replete with the luminous beauty of the marbles, and the poem he writes on the occasion is 'l'expression d'une sensibilité esthétique sans aucune expression religieuse'.[50] One need not consult Tupet or read J. G. Frazer to learn that magic and religion stem from the same human need, or that the ancient world did not distinguish sharply between the two. Propertius would probably not have cared to. I think that he was able to view the sinister aspect of witchcraft as just an incitement to write sensuously about puissant love.

In doing so he not only reflected contemporary fashions and preoccupations but also turned to his own purposes a favourite theme of Hellenistic genres. In composing *Id.* 2, Theocritus is widely believed to have drawn upon one of Sophron's mimes which had magic as its subject;[51] of course the idyll itself, together with *Idd.* 14 and 15, is to all

---

[50] Boucher (1974) 93.
[51] See Gow's preface to the poem, 33ff.

intents and purposes an urban mime which has nothing to do with the pastoral world. Erotic enchantments, magic potions and the like also seem to have featured heavily in the plots of New Comedy and, in imitation of it, later erotic literature. Since a number of the themes of Latin elegy can also be traced back to New Comedy, some of the similarities in respect of erotic magic between Lucian, for instance, and the elegists are most probably a matter of common literary sources.[52] Callimachus and the Hellenistic epigrammatists, on the other hand, do not seem to have developed a similar taste to any appreciable degree,[53] but there always was Apollonius Rhodius' monumental witch-lover who, as it is not irrelevant to remember, was Circe's niece as well as Hecate's priestess.[54] Sub-literary genres, anecdotes and story-telling in Hellenistic society laid prurient emphasis on similar topics; as P. G. Walsh remarks, 'the dominant type of anecdote reflected the seamier sexual proclivities of humankind, reinforced by spooky accounts of sorcery and witchcraft'.[55] We are moving here in the world of Greek love romance and picaresque novel, of Petronius' *Satyricon* and Apuleius' *Metamorphoses*. Both of these novels have more than their fair share of gruesomeness, but it is in the second Book of the latter that the hero, Lucius, seeks knowledge of witchcraft by way of a sexual adventure which is enacted in the abode of a fearsome witch.[56] Apuleius' clear implication is that Lucius' transformation into an ass is the wages of the combined sins of unbridled sensuality and sorcery.[57] If he is thus taking up a particular fusion of magic–love–metamorphosis in an older source, we should perhaps for a moment reconsider the transformation element in 2.1.51ff., though, of course, from an altogether different angle.

The theme of magic was not unknown in pre-Hellenistic literature, nor was the taste for it confined to the lower classes; it is rather the case that, curbed by the religiosity of the heroic and decried by the philosophical thought and rationalism of the classical age, it came into its own during the Hellenistic period.[58] What caused it to flourish during this last period is not beyond speculation. Apart from reasons related to ingrained human superstition, an important factor must be seen in that quintessentially Hellenistic curiosity about, and interest in, technical subjects and rituals of all kinds. Since in this case the theme of love is also involved, Hellenistic romanticism must have found promising material in erotically

[52] See Day (1938) 96–8.
[53] Cf. Tupet (1976) 153–4, 162–3.
[54] *Argon.* 3.310–11 and 251–2.
[55] Walsh (1970) 10–11.
[56] *Met.* 2.6ff., cf. also 3.15ff.
[57] This is clear from the words the priest of Isis addresses to Lucius after he has regained human form in *Met.* 11.15. Cf. Walsh (1970) 176–7.
[58] Tupet (1976) 164.

disposed witches and witchcraft-associated seductresses. Romantic colouring, however, should not blind one to a very wide streak of realism. This was a concomitant of the Hellenistic littérateurs' newly-acquired interest in the everyday life of ordinary people, and magic, especially love magic, seems to have formed part of it. Low and ugly realism holds its own fascination, but it is not until Book 4 that Propertius proves himself a master of it.

Hellenistic romanticism cannot easily be separated from *doctrina*. Sapient allusiveness, evocative use of mythological shorthand and verbal poetry appeal to and make up both. There is, however, a drier, even if brilliant, side to Hellenistic learning which reflects the systematic linguistic pre-occupations of the pioneering Alexandrian philologists. This is etymology and semantics. In discussing them one has to bear in mind that although they are patently unscientific and, as a rule, inaccurate, their intellectual appeal was relatively high among the ancients. Cairns, who has recently made a convincing case for Tibullus' Hellenistic verbal learning, aptly remarks that even when they border on mere verbal association and assonance one should remember that they formed part and parcel of a respected rhetorical education.[59] The pitfall for the modern reader lies, of course, in the fact that he unconsciously takes for granted what for a pre-Saussurean era could be a matter for dispute, namely, the arbitrariness of the linguistic sign. Besides recognising its conventional nature, the Greeks and Romans could earnestly speculate on the intrinsic relationship between *verba* and *res*; Isidore of Seville's *omnis enim rei inspectio etymologia cognita planior est* (*Etym.* 1.19) echoes a conviction that remained unchallenged to his own day and, as Curtius reminds us, very much alive beyond it.[60] I want to suggest that the word play *amore mori* in 2.1.47 relies on the same conviction for its effectiveness.

For an etymological point to be made the relevant words would often be brought into significant propinquity.[61] Propertius chooses adjacency. *amore* and *mori* sound like each other and, as he will go on to show in this and other poems, can actually be spoken of as being very much like each other.[62] With assonant economy we are apprised that death is written into

[59] Cairns (1979) 87–110, esp. 90–9. [60] Curtius (1948) 495–500.
[61] Cf. Cairns (1979) 93.
[62] Isidore would have considered this 'etymology' similar to that whereby *homo* is derived from *humus*. This is etymology 'ex origine', the other two being 'ex causa' (*rex* from *regere*) and 'ex contrariis' (the famous *lucus a non lucendo*). See Curtius (1948) 44.
   The difference of quantity in *amore–mori* is neither here nor there. Varro is anything but fussy about it, his theory (*Lingu.* 5.6) being in perfect harmony with his practice: *Lingu.* 5.22 *poetae appellarunt summa terrae quae sōla teri possunt, 'sōla terrae'* 'the poets have called the earth's surface, which alone can be trod, "the soil of the earth"'; 5.23 *hūmor* from *hŭmus*; 5.25 *Pŭteoli* (the town)

love. I believe Ovid's *alterius dicor amore mori* (*Am.* 2.7.10) shows the juxtaposition to have sounded rather catchy; I also believe that Lucr. 4.1045ff. strongly suggest a *deliberate* and *pointed* juxtaposition in 2.1.47 but I expect the likelihood of this to come more clearly into view when the case for substantial links between 2.1.47ff. and the related – as we have seen – 2.4.7ff. on the one hand and the Lucretian passage on the other will have been fully argued.

Lucretius, perhaps more than any other Roman poet, was fascinated with the expressiveness of sounds; moreover, it has long been observed that some of his undoubtedly deliberate jingles aim at getting across the comparison he makes between letters in words and atoms in things. C. Bailey, for instance, notes that 'the syllable *ign* occurs both in *ligna* and *ignis*, *ter* in *mater* and *terra*, who is the mother of all things, *mor* in *umor* and *amor*, whose physical expression involves the moisture of the seed'.[63] The latter pair comes from Book 4 of the *D.R.N.*, which contains the well-known fulminations against the conception of love as a romantic passion. Lucretius ridicules the whole idea by a demonstration of the purely physical origins of love. In ll. 1037–57 romance boils down to mere sex impulse, all the lover seeks to communicate is the seed, the *umor* that swells his limbs: *et iacere umorem in corpus de corpore ductum.* | *namque voluptatem praesagit muta cupido* 'to cast forth the moisture drawn from one body into the other; for an unspoken desire foretells the pleasure to come' (1056–7). Line 1058 then reads: *haec Venus est nobis; hinc autemst nomen amoris.* Some scholars think that *nomen amoris* picks up the *cupido* of l. 1057. Rather than that, as Friedländer has pointed out, it means the 'name *amor*'.[64] The phrase *hinc est nomen Amoris* 'hence the name of Love' points to *umor* (1051, 1056), and it is surely intended as an explanation of the etymology and, we are to infer, of the nature of *Amor*.[65] Is it, then, the case that Propertius

from *pŭtei* (wells), or perhaps from *pŭtor* (foul smell), as the area is often *pŭtidus* with smells of sulphur and alum. These will do.

[63] Bailey (1947) I 159; cf. also p. 128 below.

In respect of etymologising assonances and jingles, Lucretius is undoubtedly *hors concours* but not for this reason irrelevant. Propertius, by no means an *aficionado* of this particular game, 'etymologises' in *this* particular context (see below) precisely *because* the poet it puts the reader in mind of indulges so conspicuously in this sort of etymologising; need one also say that, whatever Lucretius may have thought of or attempted to do through it, Propertius is obviously welcoming an opportunity for a witty allusion which, as it happens, points with elegant incisiveness to the preoccupations of Book 2? It is not in a linguistic sense that Prop. is serious about the etymology and semantics of *Liebestod*.

[64] Friedländer (1941) 18; cf. West (1969) 95–6 and Snyder's (1980) 90–108, esp. 94–5 helpful observations on Lucretius' use of *paronomasia* to convey natural association between 'signifieds' whose 'signifiers' present acoustic resemblances.

[65] Wiggers (1972) 31–2 rightly remarks that '*in amore mori* seems to warn us visually and aurally that death is a part of love', but she does not discuss the expression in terms of conscious poetic etymologising.

is delivering an etymological repartee? And if Kenney is right in arguing that in his diatribe against love Lucretius uses weapons stolen from the armoury of those who in their writings propounded a romantic and sentimental notion of love, is it not possible to think of Propertius as availing himself of the selfsame device?[66] One does not have to assume that the elegist had been poring over Lucretius' volume; the gist of the latter's theory was too well known among the literati of the time. On the other hand, there is reason to believe that it was not only by word of mouth that Propertius came to be familiar with some of the points made in *D.R.N.* 4.1037ff.

After the 'etymology' of l. 1058 Lucretius offers a most vivid image:

> hinc illaec primum Veneris dulcedinis in cor
> stillavit gutta et successit frigida cura.   (4.1059–60)

from it first of all that drop of Venus' sweetness has trickled into our heart and chilly care has followed after.

It has been suggested that the nature of the image may have been prompted by the idea of *umor* in the preceding lines. Indeed, ll. 1037–57 ebb and flow in a sublime colour-contrast between life and death, and their 'liquidity' may well have given rise, by association, to 1059–60. The actual wording, on the other hand, of the image is, as commentators note, reminiscent of Euripides, *Hipp.* 525–6 ἔρως, ἔρως, ὃ κατ' ὀμμάτων | στάζεις πόθον 'Eros, Eros, you that instil desire into the eyes' – a fine and, it would seem, bandied-about erotic metaphor which, in respect of imagery at least, would have been very much to Lucretius' taste. *illaec*, as Kenney again suggests, points to the same conclusion: Venus' drop sounds like a quotation.[67] If Euripides is, in fact, its source (and Propertius would no doubt have been better placed than we are to know) it is tempting to suppose that the Lucretian reminiscences now to be discussed had also something to do with Phaedra's joining the company of 2.1.51ff.[68] As a preliminary to this discussion, it is perhaps worth

[66] Kenney (1970) 380.

[67] See Kenney (1970) 385 '...does not "that drop of Venus' sweetness" mean the drop that is notorious because we have heard about it in the poets?'

[68] *D.R.N.* 4.1059–60 do point to the extant *Hippolytus* 525–6, yet the possibility cannot be ruled out that the lost Ἱππόλυτος Καλυπτόμενος contained a similar image. But whatever may have been in Lucretius' mind, it seems very likely that Propertius' was very much preoccupied with the lost play when 2.1.51ff. were being written. If, as it seems more than probable, the witches of this passage hail from Simaetha's moonlight incantation in Theoc. *Id.* 2, the Schol. of l. 10 (p. 271 Wendel) of this poem is quite revealing: 'it is usual for women in love to invoke the Moon, like Phaedra in Euripides' *Veiled Hippolytus*'. This is as good a confirmation as one can get in such matters that the Phaedra of 2.1.51f. comes from the lost *Hippolytus*, and the problem of 2.1.52 (in the extant play Phaedra does not administer love philtres) should be seen in this light. The ancient scholiast is valuable in another respect too, for if Prop. recalls the Theocritean Simaetha

pointing out that both Lucretius' image and the mention of Phaedra in 2.1.51 follow hard upon the rival etymologies of *amor*.

2.1.59–70 warrant further speculation. Lucretius goes on to warn against the folly of pledging oneself to one single woman:

> ulcus enim vivescit et inveterascit alendo
> inque dies gliscit furor atque aerumna gravescit

(4.1068–9)

For the sore gains strength and festers by feeding, and day by day the madness grows, and the misery becomes heavier

If we count out a couple of topical details (*alendo, furor*) we are left with a love-smitten 'Philoctetes'; for his was an ἕλκος *par excellence*. It is, of course, the idea of 'festering' that begins and concludes the Propertian list of miraculously cured diseases, and Philoctetes' story is the first to be adduced. Does the Lucretian nosography have something to do with this? We have good reason to reckon with this possibility, for it looks as though *solus amor morbi non amat artificem* (58) embroiders upon the *amore mori* of 47 which, it has been suggested, may look askance at the Lucretian thesis. Given the Procrustean improvisations of ancient etymologising in far more unlikely cases, the intimate relationship between *mors* and *morbus* must have gone without saying – at any rate for Lucretius, who brings the words into meaningful propinquity or juxtaposition in no fewer than six passages throughout Book 6, namely, 771–2, 1095, 1144, 1232, 1250–1 and 1255.[69] And besides, Catullus had clinched the case in poem 76. The facts speak for themselves. Half-way through (l. 13) he admits: *difficile est longum subito deponere amorem* 'It is hard suddenly to get rid of a long-lived passion'; and he begins the culminating prayer (25–6) with: *ipse valere opto et taetrum hunc deponere morbum* 'I wish to be well myself and to get rid of this vile disease'. Does, then, *artificem* in 58 recommend another oblique glance at the Epicurean?[70] Is Propertius, by implying the failure of far better qualified doctors in 59ff., poking fun at the philosophical prescription? Certainty is unattainable here but 2.1.47–8 make emphatically a point which is central in Lucretius' case against love: one should strike at the root of passion and suppress recollection of the beloved one

and the Euripidean Phaedra invoking the moon, Cynthia–Luna (see pp. 37–8 above) gains plausibility.

[69] Cf. Snyder (1980) 100.

[70] In a fit of undue fastidiousness Shackleton Bailey (1956) 63–4 suggests *auxilium* for the MSS *artificem* in 2.1.58. None of his objections is fatal and one of them, namely that Prop. could not have echoed 1.2.8 (*nudus Amor formae non amat artificem*) so closely, has been adequately met by Ross (1975) 67–8. The latter scholar believes that in both these lines Prop. echoes Gallus, which is possible. If he does, he answers Lucretius on behalf of a fellow craftsman as well.

> atque alio convertere mentem
> et iacere umorem collectum in corpora quaeque
> nec retinere, semel conversum unius amore,
> et servare sibi curam certumque dolorem.　　　(4.1064–7)

and to turn your mind some other way, and vent your passion on other objects,
and not to keep it, set once for all on the love of one, and thereby store up
for yourself care and certain pain.

Against the expediency of *vulgivaga Venus* Propertius sets perseverance in one love; what Lucretius reviles, the elegist revels in:

> laus in amore mori:[71] laus altera si datur uno
> posse frui: fruar o solus amore meo!

Lucretius is, so to say, made to stand on his head: (a) it is *amor–mors* not *amor–umor*, (b) it is a matter for praise, not censure, (c) it has to be experienced exclusively, not to be showered indiscriminately. I think that this focal couplet gains much point if it is seen as a piece of allusively ironical polemic.

2.4, which, as we have seen, claims kindred with 2.1, seems to me to lend further support to the view that Propertius' redefinition of love's essence is targeted against Lucretian 'reductionism'. The enigma of the lover's death forms the core of 2.4:

> quippe ubi nec causas nec apertos cernimus ictus,
> unde tamen veniant tot mala caeca via est　　　(9–10)

For we can find no cause and no visible wound;
Whence such troubles come is a mystery

There is no way the lover can tell from which direction the blows come. Lucretius thought he could, and wanted to communicate his knowledge through yet another image; *umor*, moisture, seeks out that body from which the mind has received the wound of love; for, as a rule, all men fall in the direction of the wound, our blood spurting out in that direction from which the blow comes:

> idque petit corpus, mens unde est saucia amore.
> namque omnes plerumque cadunt in vulnus et illam
> emicat in partem sanguis unde icimur ictu　　　(4.1048–50)

Typically Lucretian visual immediacy and rather apocryphal hydrodynamics must have earned the simile considerable distinction. It turns

---

[71] Unlike Kühn (1961) 93 and Lefèvre (1966) 28–9 I do not think that *laus in amore mori* plays upon pious expectations for something more like *dulce et decorum est pro patria mori*. It may instead owe something to jingles of which *mortis amor* in Ov. *Tr.* 1.5.6 and Lucan 6.246 may also be echoes. Cf. La Penna (1977) 50.

upon a favourite Lucretian noun, *ictus*, which is commended to our attention by assonance and etymologising juxtaposition in 1050, and appears again in its figurative sense in 1052, both times as the last word of the hexameter.[72] This is its *sedes* in the Propertian hexameter too. Although position may be accidental, the use of the word itself by Propertius is less likely to be so.[73] Admittedly, its full flavour might have been lost on someone who – if one may presume with some plausibility – had not bothered to read the *D.R.N.* from cover to cover, but still it carries the weight of Lucretius' simile and would, therefore, have seemed most suitable to spearhead and tag Propertius' retort. What Propertius seems to take ironical and witty exception to is Lucretius' pretensions to omniscience in matters erotic. The Epicurean offers his reader an aphrodisiac chart; the love poet rejoins that it is simply not feasible to steer clear of love's black hole. The expression *caeli tempus* (12) could turn out to be additional evidence of Lucretian presence in 2.4 (see below), and one may also wonder whether the speculations on the advantages of homosexual and disadvantages of heterosexual love that conclude the poem (17–22) could not have received an impulse from *D.R.N.* 4.1053–4, where both boys and women are credited with sex appeal.

K. Quinn winds up an eloquent reminder of Lucretius' poetic and intellectual prestige during the Augustan period with an overestimation of the chastening effects his attack on love had on subsequent amatory verse.[74] But Catullus, as Quinn himself grants, did not take this attack to heart, and even Horace's detached Epicureanism need not have sprung from any source but his own intellectual and emotional constitution. Quinn wants to make a different case for Propertius, for he sees him as responding to Lucretius by trying, especially in Book 2, new erotic themes, novel fantasies and a more complex, intellectual manner of handling them.[75] Although much of what is said in pp. 162–97 is undeniably enlightening and brilliant comment, it seems to me that what is happening in Propertius Book 2 does not represent a response to some external pressure but the result of the poet's having reached a more learned, colourful and enterprising stage in the 'itinerario culturale' that

[72] Lucretius can use *ictus* as a synonym for *plaga* to describe the central atomist concept of the clash of atoms falling downward in the void (see, for instance, *D.R.N.* 2.225–50 and compare ll. 227 and 241). Roberts's (1968) concordance of the poet records forty-five instances of the use of the noun. It is instructive to compare the similar number of Ovidian instances – gleaned, of course, from a far more extensive corpus. One may also note that Prop. used the noun only twice, its other occurrence being 3.2.24.

[73] Richardson is the only commentator to remark upon the 'Lucretian ring' of 2.4.9–10.

[74] Quinn (1963) 144–8.   [75] Quinn (1963) 162ff.

starts from the Monobiblos. This, I hope, will become clear as we go along. 2.1 and 2.4, on the other hand, show that the elegist was not writing in blissful oblivion of the most withering and perhaps most famous assault on his literary fare. We have seen that 2.1 in particular incorporates a *prise de position*, phrased with elegant allusiveness and wittily barbed with Lucretian notions-in-reverse. Propertius brings no philosophical earnestness to match that of Lucretius. The reader should find sufficient delight in the incongruity that arises when a love poet operating with the conceits of amorous passion 'corrects' a philosopher-poet bent on rationalising love out of existence.[76]

This brings up the question of tone and mood for 2.4 as well as for 2.1. One may start from the lesser poem by calling attention to its blend of mystique, cool matter-of-factness and sustained literary allusiveness. Side by side with the remote enchantresses of Theocritus we read in ll. 11–12 the professional verdict of a puzzled physician:

> non eget hic medicis, non lectis mollibus aeger,
> huic nullum caeli tempus et aura nocet   (2.4.11–12)

> *This patient needs no doctor and no soft bed to lie on;*
> *It's not the season or the air that harms him.*

No wizards with a superhuman record of medical feats, nor cavalier treatment of the disease but rational scientific weighing of possibilities; metaphysics and superstition are carefully kept out. No approach could be more Lucretian, and Shackleton Bailey spots another Lucretian element in 2.4 when he explains *caeli tempus* (12) as 'time of year' on the basis of *D.R.N.* 1.1066 and 5.231.[77] This should strengthen our suspicions about the Lucretian connexions of 9–10. What happens in the next hexameter is a very down-to-earth incident given in a very down-to-earth style: *ambulat – et subito mirantur funus amici. funus* is a hopelessly fluid word in Propertius. To realise how many things it may stand for – (a) funeral ceremony, (b) funeral procession, (c) corpse, (d) death, destruction – is to get, even if for a moment, the impression that the poet is issuing a gleeful warning that his readers (which should include classical scholars) are bound to marvel at the apparent unpredictability of the funeral factor in some of the poems to come. However that may be, it is hard to see why

---

[76] Propertius' love is also, philosophically speaking, 'sensationalist', and to that extent 'Epicurean'. But erotic sensationalism is part and parcel of his aesthetic vision, and it never comes as a raw tip from a cynical sensualist, which Lucretius strives to be in *D.R.N.* 4 and which does not come unnaturally to Horace either. But Propertius' position *vis-à-vis* Lucretius, not only in 2.1 and 2.4 but, I think, in other elegies as well, is a very interesting subject which perhaps demands a study to itself. See also pp. 208–9 below.   [77] Shackleton Bailey (1956) 68.

one should call this a 'curiously bleak' piece, full of 'unrelieved pessimism', 'the outgrowth of a cruel humiliation'.[78]

And it is equally hard to see why one should use similar expressions of 2.1. One scholar who takes a more promising line here is Steidle, who argues that 2.1.47ff. are by no means gloomy, since Propertius is not concerned with the misery attendant upon unfulfilled passion but with describing 'love as destiny'.[79] Indeed, the fact that the poet may entertain thoughts of death irrespective of his amatory fortunes (Steidle rightly draws attention to 1.6) should warn us against always reconstructing a background contretemps from such catchwords as *dolor, lacrimae, dura* etc. Nor is the addressee of 71ff. invited to shed earnest tears over a *fatum* endorsed with unreserved enthusiasm in 47–70 and caused by the delightful creature of 1–16. Wretchedness (*misero* 78), fate (*fatum* 78) and a cruel mistress (*dura puella* 78) constitute the motto of the elegiac family and in this programmatic elegy Maecenas is seasonably apprised that Propertius is a conscientious member thereof.

To sum up and conclude. 2.1 seems at first to present a complex movement. Read, however, in conjunction with 1.6 and 7 it turns out to be a rehandling on a larger scale of a structural pattern which asserts itself for the first time in these poems. Love and death are the main thematic ingredients here. Through the implications, associations and practices of the mythological witches of 2.1.51ff. the two themes are allowed to interact upon each other in a way that suggests a definition of love as a kind of witchcraft/poison-induced death. This is supported by the evidence of poems 2.4 and 2.27. While it is historically certain that magic was very much in the mind of Propertius' contemporaries, unmistakable verbal reminiscences in poems 2.1 and 4 permit an outlook over the Hellenistic literary predilection for the theme of love magic that motivated Propertius' far more radical version. Keywords and turns of expression both in 2.1 and other poems strongly suggest the conflation of the ideas of love and death by 2.1.46, thereby vindicating the organic continuity of 1.1–46 with what follows. What follows has, as a rule, been taken to betray dejection and pessimism. Yet one is far more likely to feel the tone by paying close attention to the technique the poet employs in order to bring together love and death: verbal wit and 'revised' etymology, light-hearted *prise de position* and sustained 'polemical' allusion to the revered Roman poet-philosopher, learned and evocative mythological abbreviation – all testify that the spirit of creative euphoria, artistic

[78] See Richardson's introd. note, 222.   [79] Steidle (1962) 130–3.

self-consciousness and, indeed, complacency which informs 1–16 has by no means given way to despondency in 47ff. In contrast to the introductory elegy of the Monobiblos, which builds up its masochistic bravado on the conventional – and Lucretian – conception of love as disease or madness, 2.1 announces a different kind of *Liebestod*. Here death imagery is conspicuously eroticised and death language becomes the most authentic instrument for the analysis of love. 2.1 lays a highly original and thoroughly Hellenistic emphasis on love and death. So do the poems to be discussed next.

4

IN AMORE MORI: THE FUNERAL

for when our love-sick queen did weep
Over his waned corse, the tremulous shower
Heal'd up the wound, and, with a balmy power,
Medicined death to a lengthened drowsiness:
The which she fills with visions, and doth dress
In all this quiet luxury

Keats, *Endymion*

L'amoureux pantelant incliné sur sa belle
A l'air d'un moribond caressant son tombeau.

Baudelaire, 'Hymne à la Beauté'

There is, as far as I know, only one editor who would not take Propertius'
melancholy in 2.13 'entirely seriously'.[1] Most would object to Butler and
Barber's division (after Broekhuysen) of the elegy into two separate pieces
(1–16 and 17–58), but few would completely reject the editors' main
reason for doing so: 'But the inconsistency of tone which exists between
them, the one full of thoughts of life, the other written in deep dejection
and permeated with brooding anticipation of death, precludes their
union...'[2] If, on the other hand, there is a reason that links the parts
together, it has never been made quite clear. Rothstein's explanation is
too fanciful to be true; besides taking the *spicula* of l. 2 more seriously than
usual, one would have to suppose that the poet bleeds all the way down
to 16.[3] Both La Penna and Enk gloss over the problem by means of
speciously neat summaries.[4] Wimmel takes no special interest in the poem
but in a note remarks that 2.13 is the counterpart to 2.1, and the question
of its unity should therefore be decided as in that poem.[5] L. P. Wilkinson

[1] Richardson, introd. note, 248.

[2] Butler and Barber, introd. note to their 2.13b, 212.

[3] See Rothstein's note on 2.13.17: 'The attentive reader, who keeps in mind what has been
said in the first couplet and has seen clearly what the situation is in the last one, can hardly be
surprised by the fact that the poet is thinking of death.'

[4] See Enk's introd. note to 2.13, pp. 179–80. White's (1958) 103–4 'In lines 11–16 Prop.
sketches the manner of life which he considers ideal for himself, that of a love poet successful in
love. Is it not possible that out of lines 11–16 there arises in the poet's mind the notion that this
modus vivendi is to last until death?' marks no advance over the views of La Penna and Enk.

[5] Wimmel (1960) 41 n. 1.

in what is by far the most articulate defence of the poem's unity has successfully hunted down throughout the poem the Callimachean catchwords and has made it clear that the symbolism of λεπτότης persists beyond l. 16 into the instructions concerning the funeral. Yet death crops up in his paper as unexpectedly as it does in the poem: 'So much for the first part, 1–16. The poet now turns abruptly to his favourite theme: imagining what will happen after his death.'[6] Perhaps 'favourite' hints at one reason (I suppose the one also suggested by Camps in his introduction to the poem) but in this particular context the word begs the question. Wilkinson advances cogent arguments in favour of unity but does not explain why Propertius should declare his artistic allegiance in funerary images. G. Williams has tried to face the problem by suggesting that 'the immediate connexion is that the hostility of Juppiter suggests, by metonymy, the poet's death'.[7] But one may well hesitate to believe that the single expression *inimicitias Iovis* in 16 provides an adequate motivation for what follows. Wenzel alone admits to finding the 'Todesvision' motiveless and unnecessary.[8] Yet it should be possible to produce reliable evidence, both formal and pictorial, for the poem's unity.[9]

In terms of thematic structure at least, Wimmel is right. The *recusatio* section apart, 2.1 offers conspicuous analogies to 2.13. The first section of the former poem, that is, the sixteen lines before the apostrophe to Maecenas, celebrate the *puella* as the sole inspiration and subject of Propertius' poetry. Similarly, in the first verse paragraph of 2.13, which also consists of sixteen lines, the poet declares his loyalty to the slender Muses of love poetry, the sole aim of which is to please the girl's cultivated ear. We do not need to enter into the details of the first lines. They are obviously connected with Virg. *Ecl.* 6, and R. Reitzenstein argues that Linus is here regarded as the originator of epic poetry.[10] Be that as it may, the opposition between poetry aiming at powerful and spectacular effects on the one hand and Propertius' own modest love Muse on the other is sufficiently clear. There is a noticeable shift of emphasis from physical

---

[6] Wilkinson (1966a) 141–4, esp. 143.   [7] Williams (1980) 126.

[8] Wenzel (1969) 67–8.

[9] If proof were needed that the continuity between 2.13.1–16 and 17ff. is *still* worth defending, Fedeli (1984) provides it. In his critical apparatus he sympathises with Wilkinson ('elegiam unam esse censet Wilkinson ClR 80 (1966) 141–144, non minimi momenti argumentis nisus'), but in the text he divides with Broekhuysen.

[10] Reitzenstein (1896) 194–6. But see also Ross (1975) 21–3, 35–6 who argues that Propertius' as well as Virgil's Linus derive from a common source in Gallus who, after Callimachus, had promoted this figure, in a *pastoral* capacity, to a place of importance.

beauty in 2.1 to *doctrina* and culture in 2.13, to which the poet may be drawing attention in 2.13.9 *non ego sum formae tantum mirator honestae* 'I am no mere admirer of distinguished looks'; but otherwise both flaunt a distinctly Callimachean snub of the grandiose; and both exhibit the characteristically Roman eroticisation of the Callimachean credo by giving pride of place to the elegiac mistress. 2.13.1–16 are more obsessively studded with standard terminology (*Ascraeum, doctae, puris, populi* and probably *graciles* as an equivalent of λεπτός) but this is only because in 2.1 the technicalities are reserved for the *recusatio*. The latter and by far the larger section in both poems is then devoted to the death theme. The movement of thought is rather more complex in 2.13.17ff. but we should notice that in one respect at least it is the sequel to 2.1.47ff., as it takes up and expatiates upon the topos of the poet's funeral and tomb. In fact, Propertius draws attention to this by means of the poem's structural and thematic analogies – perhaps also by means of an unmistakable verbal echo, since 2.13.17 *quandocumque igitur nostros mors claudet ocellos* 'Whenever therefore death shall close my eyelids' will almost certainly recall 2.1.71 *quandocumque igitur vitam mea fata reposcent* 'Therefore whenever Fate calls in my loan of life'. At any rate, it is clear that the poems move along similar lines from the choice of slender Muse and elegiac life-style as against more pretentious genres towards the death theme. At least as far as formal unity is concerned, such considerations should put the onus of proof on those who divide. Those who do not may follow up the argument from the form with one from the imagery.

One form of co-operation Propertius often demands from his reader is sharp visualisation. 2.13 is particularly instructive in that it shows the interpretative advantages of keeping a firm grip on the visual thread throughout. A posture is established in ll. 11–12:

> me iuvet in gremio doctae legisse puellae,
> auribus et puris scripta probasse mea.

> *I'd like to read my work in the lap of a clever girl*
> *And have it approved by faultless ears.*

Enk, very appositely I think, compares the well-known scene from the prologue of the *D.R.N.* which features Mars reclining in Venus' bosom (1.31ff.). Lucretius has a knack for dwelling lovingly on what he professes to dislike or not care about. I shall argue below that a similar manoeuvre is the mainstay of Propertian irony. For our present purposes it may be noted that it is Venus' *gremium* (33) that deflects the arch-warrior from the more ambitious pursuits: *in gremio maxima bella gerit*. The noun's more

intimate overtones[11] need not be operative where Propertius is anxious
to present the bluestocking as well as the mistress, but the juxtaposition
gremio doctae is a most graphic illustration of the converging amatory and
literary ideals. What we have here can best be described as a visual motif
on which painters and sculptors had probably been the first to ring the
changes. Its central feature is a reclining, normally love-lorn, male (like
Lucretius' Ares), but one that more often than not drifts towards or muses
upon death.[12] Daphnis in Theoc. *Id.* 1 fits this pattern and Tibullus'
dream in 1.1 offers another, more cogent, parallel. What he has in mind
when he says to Delia: 'if only I'm with you' *tecum | dum modo sim* (57–8)
is clear from the embrace he envisages in ll. 45–6:

> quam iuvat immites ventos audire cubantem
> et dominam tenero continuisse sinu!

> *How pleasant lying there at night to listen to wild winds*
> *and contain a mistress in tender embrace!*

But tender idleness in Delia's lap shades off into thoughts of death:

>   tecum
> dum modo sim, quaeso segnis inersque vocer.
> te spectem, suprema mihi cum venerit hora,
> et teneam moriens deficiente manu.   (1.1.57–60)

> *They can call me*
> *slack and ineffective, if only I'm with you.*
> *O let me gaze at you, when my last hour comes –*
> *hold you, as I die, in my failing grasp!*

I do not know that D. Bright makes a fanciful comment: 'She [i.e. Delia]
is in many ways an angel of death for Tibullus, providing the enclosed,
secure, tomblike setting for which he had longed earlier.'[13] Death here
is a nuance of amorous immobility, and this also applies to the lover of
2.13. Nothing but the closing of eyelids stands between 2.13.1–16 and
17ff., but this is part of a visual motif, itself a lover's ideal, that modern
critics have missed. Pillowed upon the breast of his beloved, Keats longs

> Still, still to hear her tender-taken breath,
> And so live ever – or else swoon to death.[14]

[11] See, e.g., Adams (1982) 92.
[12] C. Bailey (1947) on *D.R.N.* 1.33 considers (after Giussani) the possibility of a sculptural
group behind Lucretius' description. Dionysus is depicted reclining in Ariadne's lap in the great
picture sequence of the Villa of the Mysteries at Pompeii (cf. Maiuri (1953) 62). On another
characteristic posture (that of 2.28.45–6 where Cynthia is depicted as sitting at Jupiter's feet)
which is indebted to literary and, possibly, visual precedents, see Hubbard (1974) 56.
[13] Bright (1978) 130; cf. Wimmel (1976) 56–61 on the Tibullan 'Todesthema'.
[14] From the 'Bright Star' sonnet (Garrod, 372). The posture is romantic and engenders a

Few would feel compelled to commiserate with this poet for having been 'half in love with easeful Death' and it seems rather strange that one should do so with Propertius, who anticipates a demise equally easeful and more luxurious. This visual continuity between 2.13.1–16 and 17ff. must reflect a no less even tenor of mood. But visual continuity is no more than an indication. The key to the poem's mood and tone lies, I think, in construing the pretensions to Callimachean ideals as broadly as possible, which, in turn, involves putting the Callimachean claims to modesty to a rigorous test.

The literary self-description of the Augustans was particularly prone to what V. Pöschl has termed 'Vorbilddenken'.[15] It is as idle to dwell on this well-known fact as it is worth stressing that the habit often creates a gap between poetic self-description (*Selbstdarstellung*) and the nature (*Wesen*) of the poetry actually produced.[16] There is, as we are going to see, such a gap in 2.13. The problem, however, is not that of Propertius, who does *not* see the Hellenistic quality of his poem as solely a function of Callimachean modesty (supposed to pervade and bring into harmony his life, literary activity and death), but of the critics, who take it for granted that he does. The poet stands four-square within a broad tradition of Alexandrian writing by virtue of a number of characteristics, some of which, neither eminently nor exclusively Callimachean, seem to have been more intensely cultivated by later Hellenistic generations. We may sample some of these characteristics in ll. 17–24.

very aesthetic–decadent wish. In 'For Annie' (Mabbot, 1 458–9) E. A. Poe hovers voluptuously between erotic slumber and death:

> She tenderly kissed me,
> She fondly caressed,
> And then I fell gently
> To sleep on her breast –
> Deeply to sleep
> From the heaven of her breast.

But sleep modulates into death in the next two stanzas.

Ernest Dowson in the Propertius-sanctioned 'Cease smiling, Dear! A little while be sad' (see pp. 209–10 below) brings nothing new:

> What sweets had life to me sweeter than this
> Swift dying on thy breast?

Instances could easily be multiplied.

[15] Pöschl (1956) 89: 'It should be clear that the Romans *wish* to appeal to models.'

[16] Making 'Callimachean noises', as Lyne (1980) 147 put it, does not mean that one is saturated with Callimachus. 'Sacred Books' pay the price for 'sacredness' by being superficially quoted more often than they are profoundly studied. In a sense, throughout Books 1–3 Prop. takes Callimachus' name in vain; and the way he atones for this in Book 4 leaves much to be desired. But the (apparently paradoxical) point I want to make (see below) is that he is being Hellenistic all the time. Cf. Boucher (1965) 161–226 on Propertius' relationship to Callimachus and Philetas.

Here Cynthia is instructed to dispense with the ostentatious luxuries of a stately funeral. The passage is worth quoting in full:

> quandocumque igitur nostros mors claudet ocellos,
>   accipe quae serves funeris acta mei.
> nec mea tunc longa spatietur imagine pompa,
>   nec tuba sit fati vana querela mei;
> nec mihi tunc fulcro sternatur lectus eburno,
>   nec sit in Attalico mors mea nixa toro.
> desit odoriferis ordo mihi lancibus, adsint
>   plebei parvae funeris exsequiae.

> *Whenever therefore death shall close my eyelids*
> *Let this be the order of my funeral:*
> *No long cortège bearing ancestral images,*
> *No trumpet vainly bewailing my fate,*
> *No couch with ivory fittings to carry me,*
> *Spread for my death with cloth of gold,*
> *No line of incense-bearing platters, but the small-scale*
> *Rites of a plebeian funeral.*

The sudden projection into the future; the teasing vagueness of *igitur*;[17] the repetition combined with polyptoton: *nec mea*...(19), *nec*...*mei* (20), *nec mihi* (21), *nec*...*mea* (22); the variety of grammatical subjects which is accentuated by the invariability of their third person singular jussive subjunctive (broken only by the plural *adsint* in 23 as if to underline the sole positive injunction); the bold but highly expressive *longa*...*imagine* (19); the uncommon grandiosity of *mors mea* (22); the ceremonial sadness of the nasals in 19; the configuration of the five-syllable (the longest word in the passage) *odoriferis* and the assonance with the juxtaposed *ordo* (23), which seem to follow the long line of mourners; the sensory – visual, aural and olfactory – bias in the lines that tell of the trumpet's wailing rising amid the suffocation of perfumes and incense; the dazzling contrast of ivory (*eburno* 21) and gold (*Attalico* 22) – every single touch betrays the care lavished on the passage. Propertius shows a unique flair for looking on the bright and aesthetic side of the funeral ritual, and we would not be far from the truth if we argued that this voluptuously lugubrious set piece is brought in for its own sake and is meant to be appreciated in its own right. This is a *tour de force* of dense writing in the best traditions of a technique recently discussed and conveniently summarised by F. Cairns in connexion with Hellenistic Tibullus: anticipation of the future,

[17] *igitur* implies, according to Butler and Barber, 'a melancholy past all healing'. This is one extreme; the other is to want to pin down (as other commentators do) its precise logical connexion.

suppression of strictly logical links between verse paragraphs (or triviality of such links), syntactical variation and sensory emphasis lie close to its heart;[18] and they are also in evidence in 2.13.17–24. Taken individually, such features are, of course, hardly peculiar to the Hellenistic school; yet a major concentration of them is often symptomatic, and sensory emphasis is perhaps the most symptomatic of them all. There is in 2.13.17–23 the kind of 'éclat, solidité, couleur' that must appeal to the aesthete, and Hellenistic poets achieve it more often than anyone else before them. To this important point we shall, and must, keep coming back.

Propertius, of course, lingers over the luscious cortège only to dismiss it as incompatible with his plebeian contentedness (23ff.). But we must be on our guard here. On 3.2.11ff., a less ornate case, Hubbard writes: 'He [i.e. Propertius] lacks, he says, the delights of a fine Roman house and villa (described, as so often, in an affectionate detail that reveals a taste for what it condemns: no columns of *verde antico*, no coffered ceiling of gold and ivory).'[19] 3.2.12 *nec camera auratas inter eburna trabes* 'nor [do I have] a vault of ivory set among gilded beams' is lit up by the same colour contrast as 2.13.21–2, (see pp. 67–8 below); clearly, the mind's eye is caught by an effect to which the poet declares himself indifferent by using the same conjunction in both passages: *nec*. This is Propertian irony, and 3.2.11–14 is an instance thereof, though on a small scale. Differing in degree, not in kind, but controlling the movement of the whole poem, the irony in 2.3 comes closer to that in 2.13. Attempting the anatomy of his infatuation Propertius unfolds in four superbly pictorial and characteristically Alexandrian couplets the figure of his mistress:

> nec me tam facies, quamvis sit candida, cepit
> (lilia non domina sint magis alba mea;
> ut Maeotica nix minio si certet Hibero,
> utque rosae puro lacte natant folia),
> nec de more comae per levia colla fluentes,
> non oculi, geminae, sidera nostra, faces,
> nec si qua Arabio lucet bombyce puella
> (non sum de nihilo blandus amator ego)   (2.3.9–16)[20]

It's not so much the face, fair as it is, that caught me
(Lilies are no whiter than my mistress;

---

[18] Cairns (1979) 111ff.   [19] Hubbard (1974) 78.

[20] Such hymns to female beauty, especially when Jupiter is involved as a lover (as he is implicitly in 2.2.3ff. and explicitly here, ll. 30–1), have been shown by Alfonsi (1960) 254–5 to be characteristically Alexandrian in inspiration. On the milk-and-roses complexion as another typically Alexandrian theme imitated by the Romans see André (1949) 324–6.

Picture Maeotian snow vying with Spain's vermilion,
And rose petals floating on pure milk);
Nor the well-groomed hair rippling over that smooth neck,
Nor the eyes, those twin flares, my stars,
Nor when she shimmers in Arabian silk
(No, as a lover I'm hard to please)

It is not, he says, *this* that enthralls him so much as (*quantum quod* 17) her *spiritual* and artistic accomplishments, which he then describes in three couplets (17–22) that lag behind in colour and plasticity. If the poem ended here it would perhaps be arbitrary to challenge that order of preference, but when it goes on to reveal Helen of Troy as the girl's legendary counterpart, it becomes difficult to acquiesce. The hub of the matter is conspicuously female *forma* and *facies*, exemplified to perfection first by Helen, now by the girl: *post Helenam haec terris forma secunda redit* 'Helen's beauty here returns to the world' (2.3.32). Nor is it difficult to see that the aspiring painter of 41–2

> si quis vult fama tabulas anteire vetustas,
> hic dominam exemplo ponat in arte meam

> *Should any painter seek fame greater than the old masters',*
> *Let him take my mistress as his model.*

is far more likely to derive inspiration from 9–16 than from 17–22; in fact, in the parenthetic 10–12 he might even recognise the colourist's stock technique and technical jargon.[21] The elegy aspires to the condition of painting with an urgency that must call in question the correctness of the *nec...tam* (9) *quantum quod* (17) evaluation. But if irony can be felt as a gentle quiver throughout most of 2.3, in 2.13 it sharpens into a ruse of dissimulation and insinuation worthy of the Ciceronian description according to which *insinuatio est oratio quadam dissimulatione et circumitione obscure subiens auditoris animum* 'insinuation is a kind of discourse which circuitously and as it were by false pretences steals imperceptibly into the mind of the listener' (*Inv. Rhet.* 1.15.20). 2.13.17–24 strike me as a fine instance of *dum dissimulas in hoc ipso petis*. Ancient rhetoricians speak in such cases of *praeteritio*, which they know to be often combined with ἐνάργεια.[22] To this all three instances quoted from Propertius bear

---

[21] André (1949) 292, 400 notes that *minium* and *miniaceus* belonged to the technical vocabulary of the professional painter.

[22] The poet offends against truth but, in Aristotelian terms, he does so as an εἴρων who pretends to claim very little or nothing at all, not as an ἀλαζών who claims far too much. *Praeteritio* (παράλειψις), which often gives expression to this kind of irony, may be underscored by *evidentia* (ἐνάργεια) – that is, high visual quality sometimes due (as it is in our passage) to detailed description (λεπτολογία) of what is ostensibly being disavowed, declined, supposed to

witness; in none of these is the poet upon oath, and the same goes, I think, for 2.13.17–24.

Here the pictorial resonance tends to emancipate the *Todesphantasie* from the repeated negations and thus to obscure the line between the unpretentiousness of the preferred and the extravagance of the repudiated ritual. It is not the case that we enjoy the vivid images without caring whether the poet has actually seen or simply imagined these things;[23] it is rather that we are enticed to see through the disingenuousness and appreciate the opportunities it offers the poet. But the claim to modesty that sounds false in 17–24 rings hollow in 25ff. as well. The ritualistic punctiliousness with which Cynthia is urged to discharge her funerary duties is matched only by the obsessively egocentric demands for extreme display of grief. And no sooner is one allowed to put these down to mere melodrama than the rising undercurrent of sensuality in 27ff. alerts to less innocent possibilities. These must be explored.

The lover is incinerated by the agency of a highly ambiguous element: *deinde, ubi suppositus cinerem me fecerit ardor* 'Then, when the heat below has turned me into ashes' (2.13.31). *ardor* goads Gallus in his mighty passion for the woman of 1.13 – a different kind of *ardor*, we should think, yet one that is brought about in much the same fashion:

> nam tibi non tepidas subdidit illa faces,
> nec tibi praeteritos passa est succedere fastus,
> nec sinet abduci: te tuus ardor aget.   (1.13.26–8)

> *So fierce the fire she kindled in you:*
> *Nor did she let your previous arrogance return.*
> *There's no escape. Passion will drive you on.*

One feels tempted to favour a literal flame in 2.13.31, a figurative one here, but the temptation should be resisted. Propertius' eager sensuousness gets exacerbated when it comes to love and death. Again he seems to 'hand over sensations bodily'.[24] In 1.13.26–8 we cannot settle for a simply metaphorical fire, seeing that the poet himself does not. For how else are

be irrelevant or of no immediate interest. See Lausberg (1960) 436–7: 'the irony becomes even clearer when the enumeration, which is only meant to be a *percursio*, is decked with vivid attributes...' For other examples and quotations from ancient works on rhetoric see also Lausberg 160–1 (§§ 280–1) on *insinuatio*; 339–407 (§§ 810–19) on *evidentia*; 436–7 (§§ 882–6) on *praeteritio*; and 446–50 (§§ 902–4) on *ironia*.

[23] See Boucher (1965) 62–3.

[24] The phrase comes from T. E. Hulme's essay on 'Romanticism and classicism' (see *Speculations. Essays on humanism and the philosophy of art*, ed. by H. Read, 2nd edn. London 1936, p. 134), where he speaks of poetry as 'a compromise for a language of intuition which would hand over sensations bodily. It always endeavours to arrest you, and to make you continuously see a physical thing, to prevent you from gliding through an abstract process.'

we to account for the material, concrete obtrusiveness of *non tepidas...faces*? What is virtually a dead (extinct, rather) metaphor comes alive here with such sensory urgency that it no more operates as pure metaphor. Erotic passion is depicted so as to feel, in a *bodily-physical* sense, like fire. For this reason, and also because *sup-positus...ardor* is only an imperceptible pictorial and verbal variation on *sub-didit faces* which follows hard upon the loving gestures of 2.13.27–30, the *ardor* of 2.13.31 can hardly escape erotic overtones. The same powerful alchemy can be seen again at work in the brief but strongly evocative legend that precedes 1.13.26–8:

> nec sic caelestem flagrans amor Herculis Heben
> sensit in Oetaeis gaudia prima iugis.   (1.13.23–4)

Amorous Hercules burned less when, aflame with heavenly Hebe, he first possessed her on Oeta's heights.

sensit and *gaudia* are as strongly carnal and tactile here as they were in 2.1.55 and 1.19.9 respectively.[25] With this the *abstractum pro concreto* (*amor Herculis*) might be thought to be at variance. In point of fact, there is very little that is abstract in this couplet. Commentaries do not spell out but commonly assume that allusion to Hercules' death on Mount Oeta is only made in the pentameter, with *flagrans...Heben* in 23 patterned on such expressions as Virg. *Ecl.* 2.1 *Corydon ardebat Alexin.*[26] It is then promptly noted that this is the unique instance of *flagrare* with accus. in the metaphorical sense 'to be in love with someone'. I think that the couplet implies a single setting and a single event with a double significance. Where Oeta is specified, to keep *flagrans amor Herculis* apart from *flagrans rogus Herculis* would be to go against the grain. Propertius does not. By turning to account a traditional 'Herculean' construction he retrieves the substantive (*amor*) from the concept of *Hercules amans*;[27] and by qualifying the *amor* as *flagrans* he subtly calls up the central element of a well-known mythological incident, that is, the Oetean *pyre* on which Hercules ended his life on earth. The *amor/rogus* blazes too real for *flagrans* to be simply figurative, and too purposefully to dispense with a direct object; hence *Heben*. It is a tribute to the poet's suggestive powers that the most recent editor of his first book misses *rogus* so much that he is driven to change, after Schrader, the unanimously attested *iugis* into *rogis*. Quite unnecessarily, for if we read with our sensory antennae on the alert we know by the end of the hexameter that Hercules has achieved euthanasia and Hebe's devirgination (*gaudia prima*) amid the flames of one and the same

---

[25] See the discussion on pp. 11 and 29–30 above.
[26] See Butler and Barber and Fedeli *ad loc.*
[27] Cf. 1.20.15–16 *error...Herculis*; it goes back to Hes. *Theog.* 951 ἷς Ἡρακλῆος.

fire.[28] The material vehicle for Neptune's erotic passion in the immediately preceding couplet is, naturally enough, water. The two examples are complementary:

> non sic Haemonio Salmonida mixtus Enipeo
> Taenarius facili pressit amore deus   (1.13.21–2)

> *With love less supple Neptune confluent with Enipeus overwhelmed Salmoneus' daughter.*

facili…amore in 22 for *flagrans amor* in 23, liquescent fondling for incandescent penetration.[29] The natural phenomenon with its inevitable materiality encroaches forcefully upon the domain of metaphor – and also upon that of mythology. Commentators cavil about details: in every account Hebe's union with Hercules took place on Olympus, whence she should not have been dragged down (by Propertius or inadvertent scribes) to be incorrectly married off on Oeta.[30] 'Oeta spells death, not wedlock', object Butler and Barber. No, it spells death, therefore wedlock. Propertius regards the letter of mythology well lost for the spirit of his poetry, which wants Hercules consumed by fire while consummating his marriage. Hercules burns exactly as Gallus does but in the nuptial context of 23–4 his flames may have a more technical dimension as well. The fires of death and the fires of wedding mark just one of several emblematic analogies between the two rituals, and the idea of making poetical capital out of them did not originate with Propertius.

One impulse must surely have come from those sentimental vignettes of the *Greek Anthology* where death dogs the heels of Hymenaeus and the epigrammatists harp on the οὐ γάμος ἀλλ' Ἀίδας, οὐχ Ὑμέναιος ἀλλὰ γόοι theme. *A.P.* 7.182 (= Gow–Page 4680–7) by Meleager is fairly representative of this type of epigram:

> Οὐ γάμον ἀλλ' Ἀίδαν ἐπινυμφίδιον Κλεαρίστα
> δέξατο παρθενίας ἄμματα λυομένα.
> ἄρτι γὰρ ἑσπέριοι νύμφας ἐπὶ δικλίσιν ἄχευν
> λωτοί, καὶ θαλάμων ἐπλαταγεῦντο θύραι.

---

[28] See the brief but penetrating comments of Commager (1974) 14. Cf. also Wiggers (1972) 122, Richardson's note on ll. 23–4 and Whitaker (1983) 126–7.

[29] *facili amore* is almost 'watery love', a stroke of the sensuous imagination guaranteed by 1.20.47 *facili…liquore*. Camps's 'love that met a sweet response' and Fedeli's 'perché Tiro…non oppose alcuna resistenza a Nettuno' are dry as dust.

[30] Hence Scaliger's *ab Oetaeis* (= after Oeta). Schrader combined this with his own *rogis* and is followed by Luck and Fedeli. On *ab Oetaeis rogis* one could do worse than refer to Rothstein (Anhang, 468) who protests that as well as ruining the erotic message of *gaudia prima* this reading impairs the vidid poetic quality of the couplet.

The MSS reading in 1.13.24 eventually displeased Luck but not before it led him (in his note on l. 23) to the interesting thought that Hebe becoming Hercules' spouse on the funeral pyre is a scene one would like to think of as a subject of Hellenistic painting.

ἠῷοι δ' ὀλολυγμὸν ἀνέκραγον, ἐκ δ' Ὑμέναιος
σιγαθεὶς γοερὸν φθέγμα μεθαρμόσατο.
αἱ δ' αὐταὶ καὶ φέγγος ἐδᾳδούχουν περὶ παστῷ
πεῦκαι καὶ φθιμένᾳ νέρθεν ἔφαινον ὁδόν.

*No bridegroom but Death awaited Clearista on her bridal night as she
unfastened the girdle of her maidenhood; for but a while ago at evening the
sound of the flutes could be heard at the bride's door and there was plenty of
knocking on the door of her bridal chamber, but at dawn there rose a shrill
lament, the wedding song was silenced and changed to a mournful tune. The
very same torches that had burnt bright around her bridal bed showed her in
death the way to the nether regions.*

Similar motifs may be found in *A.P.* 7.711 by Antipater, 7.712 by Erinna
and 7.298 anon. (= Gow–Page 548–55, 1789–96 and 3864–9,
respectively). The last-named is more poignantly interesting in that it
features a young couple who meet with simultaneous death when their
bridal chamber collapses on their very wedding night. Despite the fact
that, in the best specimens at least, a genuine aura of romantic melancholy
overrules the indigenous wit, and although the aesthetic potential of the
togetherness-in-death image in 7.298 is almost breaking through the
heavily emotional surface, the risk in such pieces *alla piccola maniera* is that
the torch Death snatches from Hymenaeus can rapidly degenerate into
frigid conceit, and the pointed paradox of similar emblems pointing to
diametrically opposed emotional situations can easily be worked to
death.[31] Similar devices that help bring into line with each other the
furniture of death and wedding have found their way into the Cornelia
elegy. L. Curran in a perceptive discussion has observed that 'Cornelia
constantly refers to one ceremony in terms that suggest the other. The
torch of the funeral pyre (10) is picked up by those of the marriage
procession (33). She uses *lectus* both of the new marriage Paullus may
make (85) and of her own funeral bier (10)...'[32] He goes on to point out
a number of other hints as well. One may also notice that the intricate
association of the two events is summed up with forceful economy in l. 46
viximus insignes inter utramque facem 'between the torches [i.e. of marriage
and death] we led a prominent life'. Cornelia's personal account is served
well by the analogical thinking of the impersonal epigrammatist. She
manipulates the heraldry of her life and death with more neatness than
emotion. Propertius may have thought it fit to keep her at the semiological,
as it were, level, since it was predominantly at this level that her life in

---

[31] The gongorism of the epigrammatists presupposes such classical specimens of Death and
Wedding interplay as Soph. *Ant.* 810ff., a famous play which Propertius probably knew in the
original.　　　　　[32] Curran (1968) 134–9, esp. 138.

a noble Roman household had been conducted. It is interesting to see
how, when the subject matter did not impose its own restraints, more
supple and suggestive poetry could be made out of the same stylistic
repertory. 3.13.15–22 are a case in point.

These lines represent a full-blown version of what we have already seen
in 1.13.23ff. At the heart of this poem lies a paradox which, whether
accidental or not, seems to have eluded the critics. Propertius attributes
the venality and promiscuity of Roman women to the luxuries imported
from the East at the same time as he represents Eastern wives as the
paragons of marital fidelity. Lines 15–22 are jammed among moralistic
and oracular platitudes:

> felix Eois lex funeris una maritis,
>   quos Aurora suis rubra colorat equis!
> namque ubi mortifero iacta est fax ultima lecto,
>   uxorum fusis stat pia turba comis,
> et certamen habent leti, quae viva sequatur
>   coniugium: pudor est non licuisse mori.
> ardent victrices et flammae pectora praebent,
>   imponuntque suis ora perusta viris.

*How delightful and unique the funeral custom enjoyed by Eastern husbands,
whose complexion crimson Dawn darkens when rising with her steeds. When
the last torch has been cast on the dead husband's couch, the bevy of faithful
wives, their hair let loose, engage in a mortal competition for the honour of
burning alive in the husband's funeral pyre; it is a shame not to be allowed
to die thus. The winners are aflame, offer their breasts to the fire and press
scorched lips against their husbands.*

The first couplet contrives to place at a quasi-legendary distance a
practice which in itself must have sounded weird and exotic in the first
century B.C., as it still did in the eighteenth century of our era. Julius,
in F. Schlegel's *Lucinde* (1799), seizes on it while raving about his ideal
kind of marital relationship. If such projection outside the familiar world
into the fabulous Orient argues Schlegel to be a Romantic, it makes sense,
in this particular case, to think of Propertius as a romantic too. There
are differences, of course. Julius flatters himself: 'Ich weiss, auch du
würdest mich nicht überleben wollen, du würdest dem voreiligen Gemahle
auch im Sarge folgen, und aus Lust und Liebe in den flammenden
Abgrund steigen...'[33] What, goaded by *Lust* and *Liebe*, the suttees did
on the pyre Schlegel never specifies. But then his marriage comes straight

[33] Behler, v 11. 'I know, you wouldn't want to survive me either, you too would follow your
rash husband into the grave and through desire and love you would step into the flaming abyss.'

from the *Frühromantik* and has a strong idealistic side, whereas that of Propertius points to the more 'fleshly school of poetry'. The distinction seems to me important, for Propertius has too often been credited with the wrong kind of romanticism to be then, by way of reaction, denied romanticism altogether. And yet the quoted passage achieves an intensity of vision and invites considerations which are normally thought of as lying outside the range of classical love poetry.

Are the suttees comrades-in-death or brides-to-be? Is this a cremation or a wedding-night? Is the torch destined for the bier setting fire to the wedding bed? Commager is brief and trenchant: 'the word used for "pyre", *lectus*, is that also used for "bed"...*ardent* (21), equivocally "burn with love" or "burn in fact"'.[34] The wives are in the heat, they offer their breasts to the flames and kiss, with charred faces, their husbands; gestures are rife with eroticism, words are subject to ambiguity and overtone. The ceremonies of death and wedding blend here as they do in the epigrams, but the poetry that conveys the blend lies outside the scope of the epigram. The couplet that follows 15–22 does, in fact, suggest the contribution of more pretentious genres:

> hoc genus infidum nuptarum, hic nulla puella
> nec fida Evadne nec pia Penelope.   (3.13.23–4)

> *Our brides are fickle; here no girl is faithful like Evadne, devoted like Penelope.*

Penelope is a byword for fidelity but also, I think, a bit of a padding here. It is Evadne that matters, for she is the mythological type of the suttee. She first appears in this role in 1.15.21–2 to reinforce another diatribe against the vanity and infidelity of Cynthia in particular:

> coniugis Evadne miseros elata[35] per ignis
> occidit, Argivae fama pudicitiae.

> *Evadne, proud to burn on her poor husband's pyre,*
> *Died a paragon of Argive purity.*

P. Fedeli has made a good case for seeing behind this mythological shorthand the loving wife of Eur. *Supp.*, esp. ll. 1014–20.[36] One may agree with him while also bearing in mind that Evadne's gesture was spectacular and sensational enough to have appealed to more than one post-Euripidean specialist in erotic melodrama.

---

[34] Commager (1974) 20.
[35] On this reading, preferred to Barber's *delata*, see esp. Fedeli's note *ad loc.*
[36] Fedeli (1977) 93–6.

We can now cast an even more prejudiced eye on 2.13.27–30. The first thing to be noticed here is the kind of mourning gestures enjoined on Cynthia and the order in which they are expected:

> tu vero nudum pectus lacerata sequeris   (27)
>
> *But you must follow, tearing your naked breasts*
>
> osculaque in gelidis pones suprema labellis   (29)
>
> *You must press the last kisses on my frozen lips*

This runs parallel to 3.13.21–2. To visualise the scene is to wonder whether it is not 'more appropriate to a lover's winning his mistress' consent in bed than her tears at his death'. I borrow again a phrase from D. Bright's comments on Tibullus 1.1.61–4 (p. 130) but I believe that it suits Propertius in a way that it does not suit Tibullus. The latter desires death larded with sentimentality; for this he needs a single bed and Delia's lachrymose bedside manner. Note the emotional straightforwardness of Tib. 1.1.62 *tristibus et lacrimis oscula mixta dabis* 'and you will give me kisses mixed with bitter tears'; and put alongside this the sensory sophistication of 2.13.29: the endearing warmth of the diminutive *labellis* marked by the stark *gelidis*, the last kiss lending warmth for one fleeting moment. There is here the same craving for intercourse of sensations as in Olive Custance's quintessentially Aesthetic–Decadent: '...I yearn | To press warm lips against your cold white mouth! '[37] But of all that Tibullus is quite innocent. Propertius yearns for an erotic death, for death as love. The aspiration sounds laudable as well as desirable: *laus in amore mori*. Failure to do so is neatly formulated in 3.13.20: *pudor est non licuisse mori*.

One may think (and most do) that the substitution of three slim volumes (25–6) and one mourner for the pomp and ceremony of the patrician cortège is unalloyed modesty. In reality 17–23 and 27–30 differ in degree, not in kind. Sensual plenitude in death granted through the offices of Cynthia is a phenomenon of the same order as the sensory radiance of the preceding lines. The visual, the aural and the olfactory are by no means given up (cf. ll. 28 and 30) but there is a change of emphasis as the glow of colours and sheens in the first ceremony gives way to more tactile images in the second. What is more important is that both are at odds with the trumpeted unpretentiousness. And this is tantamount to saying that, at the deep level of intent, the two funerals merge and complement each other. In fact, if I am right about one particular strand

[37] From 'The White Statue' (1897); see Thornton (1970) 45.

that went into the making of 2.13, it may well be that Propertius found the ingredients for each of his two funerals in one single tableau. The question is whether the poem entitled Ἐπιτάφιος Ἀδώνιδος and attributed to Bion has influenced the shape and quality of the Propertian *Todesphantasie*. I believe the answer can be returned with reasonable certainty.

At this point it helps to bring again into focus the poem's central image: Propertius dying or dead, reclining so as to receive Cynthia's attentions. Daphnis', Gallus' (although no female soothes their plight) and Tibullus' precedents may have been influential, but Adonis may have been more so. The details of his death hour were well known and regularly re-enacted at the Adonia. What Dioscorides made of this religious festival is too charming to be missed:

> Ἡ πιθανή μ' ἔτρωσεν Ἀριστονόη, φίλ' Ἄδωνι,
> κοψαμένη τῇ σῇ στήθεα πὰρ καλύβῃ.
> εἰ δώσει ταύτην καὶ ἐμοὶ χάριν, ἢν ἀποπνεύσω,
> μὴ πρόφασις, σύμπλουν σύμ με λαβὼν ἀπάγου.
>
> (*A.P.* 5.53 = Gow–Page 1475–8)[38]

Aristonoe beat her breasts at your funeral, dear Adonis, and I was smitten by her charms. If she is prepared to oblige me in the same fashion, when I die, do not hesitate to take me with you as a companion on your voyage.

Nor is Propertius likely to have missed it. That Dioscorides/Adonis and Aristonoe/Venus may have been a prod on the way to Propertius/Adonis and Cynthia/Venus is not an irreverent guess, for 2.13 too abuses the same mythological/ritual posture, albeit in a more serious vein than that in which the roguish epigrammatist jumps into Adonis' shoes. But if one of the stimuli came from this source, the continuous spell was most probably due to Bion. It is as part of the business of citing parallels that commentators note one or two verbal similarities between Bion's poem and 2.13: 2.13.30 *Syrio munere* cf. Bion 1.77 ῥαῖνε δέ νιν Συρίοισιν ἀλείφασι; 2.13.53 *niveum* cf. Bion 1.9–10 χιονέας κατὰ σαρκός; 2.13.56 *diceris effusa, tu, Venus, isse coma* cf. Bion 1.19–20 ἁ δ' Ἀφροδίτα | λυσαμένα πλοκαμῖδας ἀνὰ δρυμὼς ἀλάληται.[39] As far as I know, no further inferences have been drawn from the above and, in fact, none can be drawn unless a more profound affinity of poetic intention is perceived.

Wilamowitz read this lament for Adonis with appreciation. Apart from drawing attention to its general sensory bias he also stressed the specifically pictorial quality, which is of particular interest as it ties in with our

---

[38] See Gow–Page, introd. note to this epigram for its relationship to the almost identical *A.P.* 5.193 (= Gow–Page 1479–82). [39] See, for instance, Enk's notes.

hypothesis that visual art may have given poets their lead by representing postures similar to that adopted by the protagonists of 2.13: Bion's Adonis, he remarks, suffices to prove that during the Hellenistic period poetry was no less modern, pictorial, romantic and 'atmospheric' (*romantische Stimmungspoesie*) than painting.[40] Wilamowitz leaves one to gather that when he says 'romantische' something along the lines of Goethe's 'unhealthy Romanticism' is very much in his mind. 'And health in art – what is that?', asked Oscar Wilde in a lecture, just after referring to Keats's 'sensuous life of verse' and with Adonis' *beautiful agony* in mind.[41] It makes, I think, excellent sense to suppose that the aesthete was thinking here of Bion's Adonis, if of Shelley's *Adonais* as well. The whole poem is, so to say, a symphony of colours and fragrances, but it relies for its impact mainly on the sublime contrast between Adonis' snow-white skin and the blood gushing from his wound.[42] This chromatic bravura marks one of the chief articles of the Alexandrian aesthetic credo. In a revealing piece of statistics André says that χιόνεος is attested *only* for Bion, and that *niveus*, also a poetic word, was coined in imitation of that adjective.[43] If so, *niveum...Adonem* in 2.13.53 (an instance André missed) speaks for itself. The verbal similarities listed above can now be seen in perspective; and some others can also be advanced as indications of dependence. 2.13.29 may echo Bion 1.45 ἔγρεο τυτθόν, Ἄδωνι, τὸ δ' αὖ πύματόν με φίλησον 'Wake for one moment, Adonis, kiss me for the last time.' The last-kiss motif is prominent and treated with climactic pathos by Bion. Propertius has compressed it into one line; he has created, as if in compensation, a suggestive verbal tension by putting in proximity *oscula*, the warm kiss of the living, and *gelidis* (see also above); and he has taken care to allude to the crucial πύματον. In the Greek poem, Venus is urged to beat her breast (πλατάγησον στήθεα, ll. 4–5) and keeps calling Adonis' name throughout; this is exactly what Cynthia is expected to do in 2.13.27–8. The accumulating evidence also suggests that the mention of Persephone in 2.13.26 has something to do with Bion 1.54 λάμβανε, Περσεφόνα, τὸν ἐμὸν πόσιν 'Persephone, take my husband.' But there may be more than leaps to the eye.

Stately Roman funerals would have certainly displayed the furniture

[40] Wilamowitz (1900) 17–18; he knows that Théophile Gautier and Swinburne read the poem with appreciation – a very interesting piece of information indeed!

[41] See Ross, vol. entitled 'Miscellanies', p. 262.

[42] See André (1949) 324–6 and 345–51 for colour contrasts in Roman poets in general. The dry, technical ring of this book's title belies the fact that after consulting it *in extenso* one is better placed to appreciate the *color poeticus* of many a Latin passage.

[43] André (1949) 375, 39 ('création poétique à l'imitation de l'hellénistique χιόνεος (Bion, I, 10; II, 19)...'); see also some interesting points on colour symbolism, 260–3.

described in 2.13.21–2. It is nonetheless quite possible that life and literature have made here, as so often, complementary and inextricable contributions, for Bion 1.70ff. read:

λέκτρον ἔχοι, Κυθέρεια, τὸ σὸν νῦν νεκρὸς Ἄδωνις·
καὶ νέκυς ὢν καλός ἐστι, καλὸς νέκυς, οἷα καθεύδων.
κάτθεό νιν μαλακοῖς ἐνὶ φάρεσιν οἷς ἐνίαυεν
ὡς μετὰ τεῦς ἀνὰ νύκτα τὸν ἱερὸν ὕπνον ἐμόχθει·
παγχρυσέῳ κλιντῆρι πόθες

Cytherea, let now dead Adonis have your couch; he is beautiful even in death, in death he is beautiful, as though he were sleeping. Rest him on the soft coverlets, where he used to spend the night when he shared with you the ritual slumber; lay him on your couch of solid gold

Whether Propertius was peering over Bion's head at the couch of the Theocritean Adonis in *Id.* 15.123ff. is impossible to assert, yet the chromatic explosion in this passage is one of those that haunt the mind's eye:

ὢ ἔβενος, ὢ χρυσός, ὢ ἐκ λευκῶ ἐλέφαντος
αἰετοὶ οἰνοχόον Κρονίδᾳ Διὶ παῖδα φέροντες,
πορφύρεοι δὲ τάπητες ἄνω μαλακώτεροι ὕπνω

(123–5)

O ebony, O gold, O eagles of white ivory that bear to Zeus the son of Cronos a boy to pour his wine. And crimson coverlets above, as soft as sleep.

Catullus 64.47–9 shows analogous ambitions:

pulvinar vero divae geniale locatur
sedibus in mediis, Indo quod dente politum
tincta tegit roseo conchyli purpura fuco.[44]

But the magnificent marriage-couch of the goddess is set in the midst of the palace, exquisitely wrought in Indian tusk, covered with purple which the rosy shell had stained.

Whatever their relationship, these passages are distinguished by that kind of sensory energy that Alexandrian poets especially knew how to transmute into feats of ἔκφρασις. In a sense, 2.13.17–23 are also an ἔκφρασις, though one brought in not by digression but by dissimulation. Ivory (*eburno*) may

---

[44] 'For my own part, I confess that I cannot understand how anyone who reads lines 43–9 aloud to himself, and reads them in context with the forty-two lines that precede them, can fail to see that Catullus is revelling in the sensuous luxury of what he describes.' Thus Jenkyns (1982) 91 against critics who postulate a moralising Catullus inveighing against luxury as a stern good old Roman. Jenkyns seeks the sensuous excellence rather than the moral message of 64 and is alive to the 'aesthetic', as distinct from the 'moral', aspect of the 'decadent'. When I first set (pleasantly surprised) eyes on his work, my own had already got to an advanced stage.

have vied with gold (*Attalico*) in a first-class Roman cortège, but it most certainly did so in Hellenistic poetry. One feels tempted to contend that the catafalque of the Roman magnate in 2.13.21–2 was bound to be infected by the colours and texture of Adonis' couch.

Vantage ground has thus been reached from which ll. 51–6 may be viewed as a confirmation of our suspicions. When Propertius renews his plea for tears in line 51, he advances Venus as the model of the grieving mistress. That amounts to showing his hand,[45] and it would be tempting to suppose that he does so with a wink at the *docta puella* and through her at the knowledgeable audience on whom he has pinned – so he has said in 11ff. – all his literary hopes.[46] They might have noticed that in 1.19.11ff. his Underworld existence was a personal extension of the Protesilaus myth, and if so, they may have been interested to find that it was now the myth that trailed behind a far more spacious and intense personal vision. As a result, 2.13 is made to look like some kind of *poème à clef*, with the mythological 'keys' withheld until the very end of the elegy. Strictly speaking, this is not quite the kind of information-retention technique that Cairns illustrates in connexion with Tibullus; it is nevertheless to be noticed that what such retention has maximum effect

---

[45] 'Propertius *is* now the dead Adonis, Cynthia *is* Venus' remarks Kölmel (1957) 121, thus emphasising an identification whose retrospective validity he never surmises.

[46] A knowledgeable contemporary reader would also have grasped subtleties which we can at best only grope after. Gallus' presence, for instance, can be sensed behind 2.13.1–8, but could he have something to do with the Adonis story as well? Speculation starts from Prop. 2.34.91–2: *et modo formosa quam multa Lycoride Gallus | mortuus inferna vulnera lavit aqua* 'And lately Gallus, killed by beautiful Lycoris, | Bathed how many wounds in the water below'. Hertzberg saw first that this couplet may well be a variation on an expression used by Gallus himself in one of his poems (this allusive process being like that followed by Virgil in *Ecl.* 10); here Euphorion's ghost looms into view too, for it is supposed that the Gallan expression on which 2.34.91–2 was moulded had itself been patterned on Euphorion's Κώκυτος μοῦνος ἀφ' ἕλκεα νίψεν Ἄδωνιν 'Cocytus alone washed away Adonis' wounds' (fr. 43 Powell = fr. 47 van Groningen, where see notes). This fragment comes from a poem entitled Ὑάκινθος and it is an old hypothesis of Scheidweiller (see fr. 40 Powell) that the story of the comely youth whom Apollo's disc accidentally struck down was linked with the premature deaths of other *formosi* such as Adonis. Gallus would have either translated the poem or simply taken over Adonis' example in one of his own compositions, which makes Gallan reminiscence persist far beyond Prop. 2.13.1–8. (See, for instance, Boucher (1965) 310, 318–19.) This is plausibility itself, but if the Euphorionic–Gallan Adonis was no more than a brief reference occurring in a series of exempla, it will hardly account for the *sustained* 'impersonation' of 2.13. This will be better explained by the ampler scope and rich material of Bion's *Adonis*. (Cf. above the discussion of χιόνεος–*niveus*.) Need one say that the paramount attractions of a particular precedent do not preclude multiple and overlapping reminiscence? An imperfect analogy, but one difficult to resist, is presented by Shelley's *Adonais*. Bion is here again the chief inspiration for a poem compact with echoes from, among others, Theocritus, Virgil, Dante, Spenser, Milton and Keats.

If, finally, Gallus is to be brought in, as most probably he should, I suggest that Hermesianax must be reckoned with too. The first Book of his *Leontion* seems to have been about the loves of shepherds (cf. frr. 1, 2 Powell and Day (1938) 20–1), and it will be remembered that *et formonsus ovis ad flumina pavit Adonis*.

on is proper names.[47] We need not step on to controversial ground by calling this technique peculiarly Hellenistic, but it is at least clear that its deployment betrays an inclination to complex and sophisticated narrative modes promptly associated with the more self-conscious craftsmanship of that period. We are, I think, on firmer ground if we bring Propertius' acting out of a mythological incident in a private fantasy within the scope of the Hellenistic humanisation of myth.[48] Again his readers could have been reminded of 1.18, where he seems to cast himself in the role of the Callimachean Acontius (frr. 67–75 Pfeiffer).[49] This, so to speak, wholesale mythological plagiarism cannot be discussed simply in terms of technical experimentation; it reflects the needs of an increasingly assertive and individual sensibility.[50] How this sensibility works within and shapes 2.13 we shall probably be better attuned to judge once the quality of Bion's influential precedent is brought into focus.

Wilamowitz, as has been mentioned, diagnosed a rather morbid Hellenistic romanticism. The poem is cloyed with a luxurious sadness which, as T. B. L. Webster saw, one can rightfully associate with the Hellenistic spirit without having to postulate an Oriental streak.[51] Yet the most enterprising and searching account seems to me that of G. Bonelli.[52] Bion's Adonis image is brought here into direct line of descent from Theocritus' Daphnis; emotional content is banned from this type of bucolic sensibility; what really matters is 'the sensuous contemplation of form'. It is a similar idea that is expressed as 'sentimentalismo estetizzante', and there is practically nothing to choose between this and the 'sensuous life of verse' (see p. 66 above). The gist of Bonelli's discussion is that 'love' and 'death' dominate the Ἐπιτάφιος Ἀδώνιδος not as pointers to tragic suffering and pessimism but in order to effect a purely physical, carnal counterpoint (*contrappunto carnale*) which alone sustains the imagery. The 'romanticism' of the lament has nothing to do with emotion; it is totally Alexandrian and to that extent aesthetic–decadent.[53] It comes as something of a surprise to find the same scholar maintaining in his next chapter that extant Roman love elegies are incapable of this kind of Alexandrian aestheticism.[54] To dismiss this possibility in the

[47] Cairns (1979) 144ff., esp. 156: 'This practice [i.e. the withholding of proper names] goes back to early Greek lyric. A succession of clues is given to the identity of the person under discussion, but the actual name is only revealed after the clues.'

[48] On this see Fraser (1972) I 640–1; Cairns (1979) 9; and see also pp. 203–4 below.

[49] See La Penna (1951) 167ff. – a discussion that escaped Cairns (1969) 131–4.

[50] Cf. some good remarks on the increasing importance of myth in Book 2 as 'an index' to Propertius' sensibility in Verstraete (1980) 259–68.

[51] Webster (1964) 203. [52] Bonelli (1979) 35–42.
[53] Bonelli (1979) 38–9. [54] Bonelli (1979) 44–54.

course of no more than ten pages one needs a number of false assumptions and sweeping statements, and Bonelli has both: 'contenuto umano' applied far and wide and the bandying about of the 'subjective-emotional' character of Roman love elegy are not promising tools.[55] Cornelius Gallus, says Bonelli, having been closer to Euphorion and Parthenius, could have written a more 'alessandriniggiante' kind of poetry. One is driven to ask at this juncture with G. Luck: 'But are the erotic adventures of Propertius, Tibullus and Ovid really so different from those of a mythological character in Hermesianax, say, or Phanocles?',[56] but that would be to overreact, generalise, and probably miss the point – which is that the personal framework of 2.13, far from spelling the doom of the aesthetic attitude, gives it a more complex sounding-board in the form of a private fantasy with all its vibrations of irony, moments of self-absorption, sensuous enthusiasm, and finally, as we shall see, with its doubts. Bion's objective framework, on the other hand, makes for a linear aesthetic meditation, the sensuous enactment of a ritual that lacks the tonal suppleness of individual life. A difference of emphasis between the two poems must find its explanation here. 'Love (although love predominantly sensuous) and Death' is true of 2.13, as 'Beauty (although beauty tinged with emotion) and Death' is true of Bion's poem. But the distinctions would become meaningless if pressed, and when everything has been said, it is clear that what has been quoted above from Bonelli would be equally at home in the analysis of 2.13. This would also imply that the pessimism and tragic suffering that are kept at bay in the Greek poem do not burden the vision of 2.13 either. A man irked by luxury and a man prone to melancholy are somewhat contiguous ideas. Understandably enough, those who swallow the protestations of modesty in an undiluted form also tend to make an issue of the dejection in 2.13. And as a matter of fact, ll. 31ff., where the spotlight moves to the tomb, seem to bear them out. But do they?

---

[55] Bonelli takes a simplistic view of Roman elegy as primarily an expansion of the epigram, and holds that, unlike Hellenistic narrative elegy, bucolic and epyllion, it serves as the vehicle of personal passion and suffering. It must be conceded to him that Catullus' brief compositions cannot play host to aesthetic yearnings (but poem 64 can); nor can he be wide of the mark when he misses in Tibullus the pastoral aestheticism which he finds, rightly I think, in Theoc. *Idd.* 1 (see pp. 30–3) and 7 (pp. 27–9). Ovid is almost irrelevant in his amatory poetry with its particular *Kunstwollen* (he is not, however, irrelevant in his *Metamorphoses*). But Propertius? What about such early pieces as 1.19, 1.20 and 1.3? Bonelli has approached his poetry with preconceived notions, otherwise he could not have missed the affinity between 2.13 and Bion's poem, to which he responds with such brilliant sensitivity. But Bonelli partly torpedoes his own thesis when he admits (p. 47) that Roman elegy took over the 'erudizione tipica dell' elegia alessandrina' after having argued, rightly to my mind, that the aesthetic detachment of the Alexandrians is achieved by means of this very erudition (pp. 9–12).

[56] Luck (1969) 42.

The small clay pot (*parvula*) of 32 and the narrow grave (*exiguo*) of 33 are probably meant to have an air of 'Callimachean' modesty; but it is hard to see what chance they stand against 37–8:

> nec minus haec nostri notescet fama sepulcri,
> quam fuerant Pthii busta cruenta viri.

> *And this my tomb will grow to be as famous*
> *As the Phthian hero's bloody sepulchre.*

To hope to surpass the fame of Achilles' tomb is nothing if not great expectations, and to have such expectations tacked on to ll. 31–6 is a small-scale tactical move that should recall ll. 3–8 of the same poem, where the limitations imposed by *Amor* on Propertius' poetry lead up to the not-so-modest *tunc ego sim Inachio notior arte Lino* 'Then I'd be better known than Argive Linus' (2.13.8).[57] In both places Propertius does not set modesty against pride, but proposes an alternative pride: the elegist eventually outshines the epic poet, the lover the epic warrior. The disingenuous slant given by Callimachus to the 'small' and the 'out-of-the-way' is operative, and very self-consciously so, in Roman contexts. But an out-of-the-way tomb need not always point to the literary manifesto; it may be more an image in its own right than a symbol of something else. This is made clear by another Propertian fantasy.

In 3.16 the poet receives a note from his mistress inviting him to Tibur at midnight. He weighs the danger against the woman's anger, and after entertaining the idea of the lover's immunity for a while he anticipates death and burial:

> afferet haec unguenta mihi sertisque sepulcrum
> ornabit custos ad mea busta sedens.
> di faciant, mea ne terra locet ossa frequenti,
> qua facit assiduo tramite vulgus iter! –
> post mortem tumuli sic infamantur amantum.
> me tegat arborea devia terra coma,
> aut humer ignotae cumulis vallatus harenae:
> non iuvat in media nomen habere via.   (3.16.23–30)

> *She will bring me perfumes and deck my tombstone with garlands of flowers*
> *and keep vigil over my tomb. I pray to the gods that she may not consign my*
> *bones to some busy place where the crowds keep moving to and fro all the time;*
> *for it is thus that dead lovers' tombs are desecrated. Let me rest in a solitary*

---

[57] Wright (1983) 113 notes that Virgil's claims to Callimachean λεπτότης in the *Eclogues* do not preclude aspirations to greatness. He also remarks (p. 150 n. 39) in regard to 2.13 on the poem's 'central theme of the paradox of the "slender Muses" (3) whose poetry will rival even the might of Homeric epic (37–8)'.

spot under the shadow of some leafy tree, or let me be hemmed in by heaps
of unknown sand. I hate to have my name read by those travelling on the
highway.

terra frequenti, vulgus, media via can all be anathema to a devout Callimachean, but not in a poem where literary programmes are not at issue. In
the context of 3.16 these terms are inert as polemical jargon and point,
by contrast, towards an idyllic landscape, a kind of funereal *locus amoenus*.
How exactly the poet pictures it may again have been determined by
pictorial sources. 3.16.28 is the most telling touch; a lonely tomb
shadowed by the foliage of some tree, unnamed here but tendentiously
specified in 2.13.33-4:

> et sit in exiguo laurus super addita busto,
> quae tegat exstincti funeris umbra locum

> *And above it plant a bay-tree on the narrow grave*
> *To shade the site of my burnt-out pyre*

'Certain Pompeian landscape paintings', comments Richardson on
2.13.33, 'show what must be tombs with various trees growing about
them, so P. is probably not eccentric in his request.' Eccentric, no;
romantic, yes.[58] Goethe's love-lorn Werther, with suicide in mind, sets his
heart on a similar décor: 'Auf dem Kirchhofe sind zwei Lindenbäume,
hinten in der Ecke nach dem Felde zu; dort wünsche ich zu ruhen.' He
cannot help bringing into this sequestered, tranquil spot his beloved
Lotte: '...blicke nach dem Kirchhofe hinüber, nach meinem Grabe, wie
der Wind das hohe Gras im Scheine der sinkenden Sonne hin- und
herwiegt';[59] and all that in the twilight of a summer evening. Religious
and erotic ardour blend in this novel with a thoroughness a pre-Christian
love poet could hardly have dreamed of, and this should make the
'Religion of Love', which has been discussed by some critics in connexion
with Tibullus and Propertius, and on which a couple of points will be

[58] Romantic landscapes were favoured by the Pompeian artists from the Second Style
onwards; 'the landscape', writes Maiuri (1953) 117, 'is pastoral or idyllic...and the painters
tend to use such familiar...motifs as little rustic shrines sheltering under big, leafy trees with
domestic animals grazing all around, and wayfarers contemplating the holy place in attitudes
of humble reverence'. For a characteristic *sacred-idyllic* landscape featuring a hallowed precinct
with a sacred tree in its middle see pp. 121-2 and Maiuri's comments on the picture produced
there.
   Dawson (1944) 62-79 argues that real landscape-painting owed very little to Greek
precedents, being almost entirely the creation of the Romano-Campanian painters. Cf. also
Lyne (1980) 85.
[59] Beutler, IV 508-9 and 489. 'In the churchyard, at the corner that looks towards the fields,
there are two lime-trees; there I wish to rest'; 'look towards the churchyard where my grave
is and notice how in the light of the setting sun the wind waves the high grass'.

made below, appear in its cooler, mundane light. Werther's 'I now pray but to her' presupposes Christianity, the portrayal of his tomb is simply romantic; and so is Propertius', with one or two more touches that call for further comment.

What Propertius expects in 3.16.23–4 is tantamount to a cult of his grave. From the study of epitaphs it would seem that the Romans were more generous than the Greeks with flower offerings.[60] It is not certain whether this had any religious significance or, as Lattimore thinks, whether it was purely decorative; the notion nonetheless of a grave-temple in which occasional offerings are made is not alien to antiquity.[61] I think it asserts itself in ll. 23–4 too, only here 'sitting by my tomb' (*ad mea busta sedens*), a unique, as far as I know, image in such contexts, reaches vaguely forward to the rather exceptional ideal of sepulchral cohabitation – which makes one forget for a moment the Corpus of Graeco-Roman epitaphs and recall Poe's 'Annabel Lee' instead. Is it, then, the case that Propertius is toying with the idea of a shrine solely accessible to a mistress-priestess? We need only glance at ll. 11 ff., where the lover bears a charmed life, to realise that such a view of ll. 23ff. would, in fact, extend the claims to divinity beyond, or rather around the grave. Viewed in this light the lonely tomb envisaged in 3.16.23ff. with its resident guardian angel is anything but humble; what it loses in outward magnificence it gains in sanctity. At what tonal level is all that placed?

One verdict that 3.16 does not warrant comes from Rothstein: 'gloomy in mood'.[62] Lefèvre's 'gespielte Furcht', on the other hand, is an important contribution:[63] 'simulated fear' should put us in mind of the simulated modesty in 2.13, especially as both stances play midwife to visions of death. Death thus *engineered* (see also the discussions of 2.26b and 2.8, pp. 84ff. and 116–17 below) is less than gloomy. The ironist who shows through the gap left between the poem's flippant dramatic occasion and the elevation of the ensuing speculations does not cancel out, nor is he cancelled out by the voluptuary of the death fantasy.[64] 3.16, like other major poems that come under discussion in this book, is designed to gravitate towards the death theme. Nothing is allowed to intercept this career, not even the sacrosanct-lover guarantee, which Tibullus expounds in 1.2.25–34 without so much as a hint at a possible breakdown. F. Solmsen (with whom one may agree that these lines of

---

[60] Lattimore (1962) 129–30.

[61] Lattimore (1962) 131–2 adduces Greek and Latin inscriptions that suggest a genuine cult of the grave, which is sometimes characterised as βωμός, *ara*, and, in Latin inscriptions only, as a temple (*templum*).

[62] See Rothstein's introd. note to the poem. [63] Lefèvre (1966) 47–50.

[64] Cf. Lefèvre (1966) 48.

Tibullus and, possibly, Horace's *Integer vitae*, had their impact on Propertius' imagination) observes that in 3.16 Venus' power is less in evidence than in Tib. 1.2; as for 3.16.19–20 (*sanguine tam parvo quis enim spargatur amantis | improbus? exclusis fit comes ipsa Venus* 'For who could be so shameless as to bespatter himself with a lover's exiguous blood? Venus in person becomes the companion of lovers left out in the cold'), 'the thought of this couplet flies in the face of Tibullus' conception'.[65] Quite so, and for good reasons. Unlike Tibullus, Propertius is not interested in demonstrating the lover's invulnerability so much as he is looking forward to the sepulchral romance his eventual downfall will open the door to. Unlike Tibullus, Propertius is ironically willing to win an idyllic monument at the cost of a well-worn motif: *quod si certa meos sequerentur funera casus, | talis mors pretio vel sit emenda mihi* 'But if certain death were the result of my venture, I should welcome such a death and even pay a price for it' (21–2). *quod si* is consistently used by Propertius to usher in those parts of his death fantasies that would have to be jettisoned if the gods intervened to rescue the lover(s); they are never thought of as definitely doing so, for they would then ruin the poem. *quod si* is an ironical signal-particle, in which capacity we shall see it clearly and in more detail when 2.26b.57 presents us with a very characteristic instance.[66] Here it introduces the end (21–30) to which 11–20, despite their relative elaboration, are only the means.[67]

Another comment of Solmsen's on 3.16.11–20 is of some interest to our discussion. He maintains that 'In these verses thought and style cannot be separated from one another. Hellenistic critics would have branded the ideas as well as the language of the passage as *kakozelon*; they would have found them lacking in restraint and hopelessly at variance with the λεπτόν.'[68] It is not easy to see why any Hellenistic critic would have responded thus to these lines,[69] but it is less difficult to see why Solmsen

---

[65] Solmsen (1961) 277–81.

[66] See pp. 90–1 below and cf. the remarks on pp. 131–2.

[67] Lefèvre (1966) 49 observes that 1–10 and 11–20 contain some humour, but he obviously assumes a darkening of tone in the third part of the poem, namely ll. 21–30, with its description of the elegiac lover's death. This, however, belies his own view of 21–30 as not gloomy and betrays his general tendency to mark off humorous/ironic from more serious passages within a single poem, as he does for example with 2.1 (pp. 22ff.). Apart from problems arising from his definition (or, indeed, his lack of clear definition) of Propertian humour and irony, the possibility can be lost sight of here that irony and a certain degree of pathos can sit easily, and with mutual benefit, together. Propertius' use of *quod si*, here as elsewhere, ensures a continuity both of irony and of pathos (i.e. Propertius' kind of pathos), and to separate these two elements or see a particular passage as dominated by either of them is very difficult indeed.

[68] Solmsen (1961) 279.

[69] What is *ipse Amor accensas percutit ante faces* 'Love himself leads the way shaking the lighted torch ablaze' (16) if not Hellenistic rococo?

should think so. He finds solemnity and religious fervour in Tib. 1.2.25–40 and believes that Prop. 3.16.11–20, although 'toned down', also partake of Tibullus' *hypsos* and *enthousiasmos*. That, he asserts, is un-Hellenistic, not λεπτόν. But, for one thing, a Religion of Love with anything approaching spiritual elevation is hard to come by until the twelfth-century *amour courtois*, and here Christianity makes all the difference; in this sense *hypsos* and *enthousiasmos* are no such things. For another, did not λεπτόν come to be identified, especially in Rome, with erotic poetry in, sometimes polemical, contradistinction to the traditional epic line? If Callimachus was a byword for non-epic or downright erotic, so were the catchwords traditionally associated with him. The words he first launched outlived the precise spirit of their original context. Solmsen exemplifies a (not always conscious) tendency to see Hellenistic as coterminous with Callimachean, and Callimachean as coterminous with the implications of the *Aetia* prologue. But some poems and some passages are only 'Callimachean' by some kind of terminological inertia and others look deceptively so when in fact their Callimachean shibboleths have been revalued and turned to other purposes. This, we have seen, is the case with *terra...frequenti* (25), *vulgus* (26) and *media via* (30) in 3.16, but Solmsen thinks otherwise, for when he writes that Propertius 'leads us from the proud words of 11–18 to the more intimate and tender thoughts of 21–30' he obviously believes that these expressions are there not as pointers to romantic self-indulgence but in order to signal a genuine desire for modesty and unpretentiousness of the Callimachean type. What difficulties are bound to arise from such determination to cling on to the Callimachean factor we will immediately learn if we go back to 2.13 and read ll. 39ff.

Wilkinson's reaction is eloquent enough. Noting 'a more pronounced switch' at 38 he writes: 'Leaving the Callimachean theme, Propertius develops the funeral thoughts that were an application of it.'[70] But to say that Propertius abruptly suspended at l. 39 a sustained symbolism of λεπτόν and then moved on to indulge in unrestrained grief is an expedient one should be slow to resort to. In other words: if Propertius in prescribing his funeral puts into practice, up to 39, a Callimachean ideal, whereas from 39 onwards his funeral images convey a 'self-pitying appeal' to Cynthia, he has certainly fallen short of his normal standards of *internal* cohesion. His elegies – and this is a point that must be taken up on another occasion – may occasionally seem jerky and desultory, but

[70] Wilkinson (1966a) 143.

75

they are so in terms of formal presentation, not in terms of mood and tone. These also may undulate, but sharp turns, as that of 2.13.39 would be, they hardly ever take. A major modulation does occur at 39 but it calls for a different explanation, and one that can be smoothly brought into line with our approach to 2.13 so far.

If we have been scanning the poem's visual line, we will find that, disturbed in 31–8, it can by no means extend beyond 39:

> tu quoque si quando venies ad fata, memento,
>   hoc iter ad lapides cana veni memores.
> interea cave sis nos aspernata sepultos:
>   non nihil ad verum conscia terra sapit.   (2.13.39–42)

> *You also, when white-haired you come to die, remember*
> *To come this way to the recording stone.*
> *Meanwhile beware of slighting us, the buried;*
> *Dust is conscious and can sense the truth.*

A tangible, even if about to be incinerated, body and a picturesque tomb are more than cold comfort. But in these lines the monument has been reduced to mere *lapides* – a calculated touch, I think – and the body has been irrevocably removed from view. This is hammered home by *sepultos*, *terra* and also, in the mythological story of 46–50, by *cinis* (46) and *humari* (49). The visual line fractures but the result is not so much despondency as banality. Propertius 'apprehends the world in which he moves primarily through his senses'.[71] As long as death is perceptible by the senses (in the form of an opulent, erotic funeral, in the form of a beautiful dead body, or even in that of a scenic tomb), he can make exquisite and thrilling poetry of it; his poetry thrives on concrete form. As soon as death becomes an idea with time-honoured moral-philosophical implications instead of some formal embodiment, he is apt to slump into vapidity. Consider the cento of ready-made wisdom on life's vanity in 43–4:

> atque utinam primis animam me ponere cunis
>   iussisset quaevis de Tribus una Soror!

> *If only one of the Three Sisters had decreed*
> *That I lay down my life in the cradle!*

This sounds very much like the homely reflections in *A.P.* 9.359.9–10 (= Gow–Page 3188–9) ἦν ἄρα τοῖν δοιοῖν ἑνὸς αἵρεσις, ἢ τὸ γενέσθαι | μηδέποτ' ἢ τὸ θανεῖν αὐτίκα τικτόμενον 'The choice, then, is between two things, either never to be born or to die soon after.' Lier reminds us that this piece of wisdom had grown stale among the Greeks *iam antiquissimis*

[71] Michels (1955) 179.

temporibus, and from his examples it is evident that it was no less hackneyed in Latin sepulchral inscriptions;[72] the same goes for the next three couplets, where another topos exposes the negative aspects of Nestor's longevity: 'Gravissimus est luctus, si liberi vivis parentibus de vita decedunt', or 'Why should parents outlive their children?'[73] Such things smother the sensuous life of the verse. We may regret the conceptual shadow they cast over 17ff., but we should realise that what we are faced with is primarily a failure of aesthetic vision, not one of emotional nerve. The distinction is essential and, as I have suggested, asserts itself as early as 1.19. There Propertius made it clear that the one thing he refuses to contemplate is the failure of sensuous perception. Death as such is an irrelevant abstraction (*non...vereor, nec moror*), love that cannot be seen or touched is as good as myth – so let us enjoy *now*...What the poet despairs of in 19–24 is not Cynthia's loyalty after his death, but the posthumous function of his senses (see pp. 12ff. above). And what engenders this despair is the fact that he is projecting himself beyond the grave as something bodiless and non-sentient, be it dust or bones (ll. 5–6 are a conceit of sensuous agony, not a conviction). 2.13.39–58 re-enact the same drama: again Propertius dead and buried (this time his bodily detritus is described as *terra*), again Cynthia enjoined not to turn her back on his grave, again a fleeting self-delusion of lingering sentience in 41–2. The scene is set for the *quare, dum licet...*, but Propertius chooses to dwell a bit longer on the burial–annihilation theme. The important words are *cinis* in 46 and *humari* in 49, with the nipping-in-the-bud theme of 43–4 thrown in for good measure. The Nestor example introduces a slight emotional deflection (parental sorrow) which is neither here nor there. Lines 51–2 hark back to 39–42 but also usher in a key passage that looks back over the whole poem. The expectation of a 'cheer-up' is never fulfilled. Instead of rushing back to solid flesh, the last couplet moves even further down the scale of decomposition: *crumbling* bones (*ossa minuta*). I do not pretend to understand exactly why, but I still believe that dejection, gloom, melancholy – in the sense that most critics use these words in connexion with 2.13 – have very little to do with it. However, if I were pressed for a possible explanation, I would quote these last thoughts of A. K. Michels's important article:

> Because of the acuteness of his sensuous perceptions, he thinks of death, not as the extinction of his personality, but as the loss of his body by which he has communicated with life. Naturally then he represents it in physical terms. This is no morbidity but an expression of his intense vitality.[74]

[72] See Lier (1903) 465–6.   [73] Lier (1903) 456–60.   [74] Michels (1955) 179.

77

To sum up and conclude. Lines 17–38 form the core of 2.13. They are visually continuous with the preceding section, indeed they transpose very smoothly the posture of 11ff. into a 'lengthened drowsiness', in the course of which the luxuries of death and love shade off into each other. Although visual art may have combined with well-known pieces of literature to give shape to this Cynthia–Propertius complex, it seems reasonably certain that Bion's *Lament for Adonis* held Propertius' imaginative sensibility spellbound during the composition of the elegy. Yet the Roman transfused the essence of the Greek poem into a sustained personal meditation on love and death, built upon significant ambiguities and propelled by an unobtrusive ironical mechanism. This mechanism, which can be seen at work in other elegies too, integrates into the poem's aesthetic will lines 19–23. It is quite possible that the sensuousness of this passage, for all its recognisable real-life ingredients, has been winnowed from the lavish *mise-en-scène* of Bion's poem. If Callimachus' restrained and slender muse never aspired to the Hellenistic, 'estetico-decadente' romanticism of Bion's Ἐπιτάφιος Ἀδώνιδος, then Propertius' poem is cosmetically Callimachean while being profoundly Hellenistic.[75] The strictly limited purpose of what must ultimately be a false distinction will be evident to those who find it more dangerously false to read all Hellenistic poetry in the narrow perspective of Callimachus' literary manifesto. It is only when this has been understood that one can safely skate on the thin ice of G. Williams's: 'The language is as Alexandrian as the ideas: avoidance of the grand and epic, emphasis on technique, and the adoption of Hesiod as a symbol. But the purpose is not Alexandrian: Cynthia is to be struck dumb by his poetry.'[76] If Cynthia was as appreciative as she is made out to be she may well have been struck dumb, but if she also was *au courant* with the relevant literature she must have known that the purpose was no less Alexandrian. The purpose itself I would rather call 'dazzle' (*stupefiat*), and the whole effect 'breathtaking'; these are more likely words when one is exposed to colours, sheens and sensations rather than to thoughts. There is, I believe, no genuine *cri de coeur* in 2.13, no crude *Todesangst*. Far from being overpowered by death, Propertius is deftly manipulating its pictorial equivalents to orchestrate a luscious ritual impregnated with eros; death

[75] Cf. Lesky (1966) 727 on Bion's poem: 'The subject matter evokes a lofty fervour which stands in strong contrast to Callimachean control and is typical for this epoch of the Hellenistic era. Latin poetry followed this trend in a large measure.' Cf. also Lyne's (1978) 182 remarks on the tactics of 'later or more extreme Callimacheans'. Scholarly discussions forget or blur the distinction at their peril.   [76] Williams (1980) 128.

affords him an erotic triumph. Nor is this in any sense, however refined and qualified, a *Gebrauchselegie* or *werbende Dichtung*, for no attempt is made, or needs to be made, to sway the woman's feelings towards sympathy or pity.[77] This cortège, these funeral scenes are calculated to have an impact that Tibullus could never have aspired to. Much of their subtle fascination eludes description; and what the following curio from M. Praz's *Romantic Agony* may communicate is only part of the fascination:

> One evening in Florence Berlioz came upon the funeral procession of a young woman who had died in giving birth to her first child. One knows what a sinister effect is produced by Florentine funerals even to-day, as they move along in the evening by the smoky light of torches, with files of hooded brethren of the Misericordia. Imagine what an impression it must have made on a Romantic with his head full of the gloomy fancies of the 'tales of terror'. Berlioz, at the sight of the procession, 'présent des sensations'. It seems that he succeeded in getting the coffin opened and in remaining close to the corpse in order to abandon himself to a delicious flow of gloomy meditations. He stooped over the dead woman and took her hand: 'Si j'avais été seul je l'aurais embrassée!'[78]

[77] Thus rightly Wenzel (1969) 69–70 against Rothstein. Falkner (1975) 47, 61 has got firm hold of the wrong end of the stick: 'Propertius' true concern is not with his own funeral, but with the emotions of Cynthia'; 'in 2.13 death becomes a way of punishing her'.

[78] Praz (1951) 123.

5

IN AMORE MORI: THE SHIPWRECK

...Ν' ἀγαπηθεῖ ἀκόμη περισσότερον
ἡ ἡδονή πού νοσηρῶς καί μέ φθορά ἀποκτᾶται·
σπάνια τό σῶμα βρίσκοντας πού αἰσθάνεται ὅπως θέλει αὐτή –
πού νοσηρῶς καί μέ φθορά, παρέχει
μιάν ἔντασιν ἐρωτική, πού δέν γνωρίζει ἡ ὑγεία...

Cavafy, '῎Ιμενος'

The editor who would take Barber's II.xxvia, xxvib and xxvii as one
single elegy may appeal to the evidence of some *deteriores* which indicate
no break between 2.26b and 2.27 as well as to the fact that no MS, with
the exception of the Neapolitanus which makes a new poem begin at
2.26b.29, indicates any break between 2.26a and 2.26b. If, however, such
a concatenation has rarely been advocated[1] one may suspect that it is
because of the complexity of the thought movement that it would involve
rather than of the length, which is by no means unparalleled in
Propertius. Rothstein makes one poem out of 2.26b and 27. Camps and
Giardina, while accepting the independence of 2.26a, follow the
Neapolitanus in taking ll. 29–58 as a separate poem and make another
one of 21–8. Enk is in complete agreement with Barber; that is, he accepts
J. D. van Lennep's division into two poems (1–20 and 21–58) of what our
best manuscripts present as a single piece, and regards 2.27 as a separate
elegy; so does R. Hanslik. The most recent voices raised in defence of the
unity of 2.26.1–58 are those of C. W. Macleod,[2] L. Richardson,[3]
E. Lefèvre,[4] G. Williams[5] and N. Wiggers.[6] It is obvious that recent
editors accept the independence of 2.27; their comments make it equally
clear that unlike 2.1 and 2.13, where unity, although not the reasons

---

[1] E.g. by White (1958) 152ff.   [2] Macleod (1976) 131–6.
[3] Richardson, introd. note, 286. He also regards 2.27 as a fragment of a separate poem.
[4] Like Richardson, Lefèvre (1977) 47–51 sees a strong indication of unity in the fact that both
parts are made up of visions; on this see a little below. His other argument is based upon the
idea of a 'concatenation of states of mind' in the course of a 'monologo interno' characterised
by a relatively free thought movement. This is a valid viewpoint as long as it does not entice
one into acquiescing in formlessness. The line has to be drawn somewhere and, as I shall be
arguing, there are other Propertian visions which afford a clue as to where it is to be drawn
in this case.
[5] Williams (1980) 129–31.   [6] Wiggers (1980) 121–8.

behind it, is generally agreed upon, it is more difficult to reach any consensus about 2.26.1–58.

As might be expected, those who argue for unity build upon the fact that both ll. 1–20 and 29–58 tell of shipwreck and drowning. Thus G. Williams maintains that the dream related in the first part anticipates thematically and 'legitimates' the imagined adventure of the second part.[7] C. W. Macleod contends that the dream presages the possible outcome of the sea voyage Cynthia is about to undertake and, on this account, it can be seen as the equivalent of a schetliastic propempticon which in l. 21 turns out to have been successful.[8] But Macleod never makes clear what the relation between the dream of the first and the fantasy of the second part is – nor does Richardson in his brief introductory note. Shipwreck and death are indeed contemplated in both parts but the simple fact must not be lost sight of that in one case they are the subject of a dream, in the other of a fantasy. Can a dream featuring a beauty in danger of beatification through graceful drowning have much to do with the couple of 21ff.? Such a juxtaposition of such unrealities is, to my mind, inherently improbable, although, admittedly, this would be highly inconclusive as an argument against the unity of 2.26.1–58. It is, I believe, consideration of the formal patterning and thematic structure of ll. 21–58 that may cast more serious doubts on continuity with 1–20.

Reitzenstein was the first to emphasise that Propertius, even in narrative poems, is not primarily concerned with depicting the outer reality (*Wirklichkeitsbild*) as such, but rather as an indicator of the poem's emotional movement.[9] Nevertheless, in poems with narrative content (and it is on those that Reitzenstein's monograph concentrates), between outer drama and inner response an interaction is still possible which is hard to trace in 2.26b, and indeed in all major elegies of Book 2 that come under discussion in these pages. Of these poems it would be more true to say, with Reitzenstein again, that 'a compressed report on a certain incident or situation at the beginning of the poem provides the starting-point for subsequent emotional developments'.[10] This is a good descrip-

---

[7] Williams (1980) 129.

[8] Macleod (1976) 131 compares 1.8. But 1.8.1–26 are conspicuously propemptic (cf. Cairns (1972) 148ff.) and 27–46 confirm the effectiveness of the σχετλιασμός. By contrast, 2.26.21–58 celebrate a prospect which a successful propempticon should have nipped in the bud. At any rate, the argument from oneirology is bound to be shaky. White (1958) 153–63 interpreted 2.26.1–20 differently (namely, to the effect that the poet's dream of a faithful Cynthia comes true in ll. 26ff.); Artemidorus might have opined otherwise, and so might we. This is why Fedeli's (1984) certainty in his crit. app. ('carmen unum esse ostendit Macleod') looks to me like such stuff as dreams are made on.   [9] Reitzenstein (1936) 38.

[10] Reitzenstein (1936) 35.

tion of 2.26b (where ll. 21–8 would represent the compressed report), but not good enough. 2.26b.21–8 are not an abbreviation of a dramatic event so much as the abstract of a contest between different styles of life and genres of literature. The choice between affluent philistinism (perhaps of the military type) and cultured αὐτάρκεια in love, where recital of poetry is instrumental in bringing about the girl's conversion, is only a variation on the rivalry between elegiac and other modes, also embroidered upon, as we have already seen, in 2.1.1–16 and 2.13.1–16.[11] 2.1.14 (*Iliadas*), 2.13.5–6 (*non ut Pieriae quercus mea verba sequantur,* | *aut possim Ismaria ducere valle feras* 'Not that Pierian oaks should follow my words | Or that I draw beasts from Ismarus vale') and 2.26b.25 (*beatos*) all hint at the antagonism; and in all three the elegiac coalition of eros and poetry is pitted against and prevails over epic or financial projects. When this is fully understood 2.26b.21–8 will slide into place and appear in its true light – not as a separate piece nor yet as the aftermath of the dream narrated in 2.26a, but as the formal equivalent of the introductory paragraphs of 2.1 and 2.13. Another noteworthy parallelism will then become clearer.

Discounting the inset *recusatio* in 2.1.17–46, all three elegies right after their opening verse paragraphs veer to, and conclude with, a long section dominated by the death theme. Moreover, arithmetical symmetries, not of course to be pressed too far in themselves, may suggest a conscious care for proportion: to the first paragraph 2.1 devotes sixteen lines; so does 2.13. 2.26b has exactly half that number, a reduction of volume perfectly understandable in the light of the exhaustive cataloguing of the girl's physical charms and intellectual accomplishments in 2.1.1–16 and 2.13.1–16. To the death theme 2.13 gives twenty-one couplets, of which six are taken up with the 'non-visual' digression on the vanity of human life; 2.1 gives sixteen and so, I think, does 2.26b. Here most editors suppose a lacuna after 28, the reason being that *seu* in the beginning of the next line can hardly stand without a correlative *seu* or *sive*. Camps has a lucid note *ad loc.* but he adopts the emendation *heu* on the assumption that 29–58 is a self-contained piece.[12] On the whole, I would agree with those who argue that an alternative reference to travel by land is missing before 29.[13] Such a reference need not occupy more than one couplet since, as will become evident, it is on the sea voyage that

---

[11] La Penna (1977) 139ff. makes the attractive suggestion that in such cases Prop. may be deliberately substituting the *autarkeia* of the lover for that of the wise man, a theme to be found in poets of Epicurean convictions such as Lucretius and Horace as well as in diatribe.

[12] See also Enk *ad loc.*

[13] Thus Housman, Rothstein and Butler and Barber – the first, though, with a complication on which see below.

Propertius is keen to expatiate here. This would make the death-centred section of the poem consist of sixteen couplets, an exact equivalent of 2.1.47–78; and it would add another item to the list of analogies which, viewed in their totality, make a good prima facie case for the unity and/or independence of 2.26b.21–58. This rather formal approach to the question can be complemented by a closer examination of ll. 29ff. whereby we must try to assess the tone and scope of the shipwreck-and-death themes.

The pioneers of ship-building and navigation often come under fire from classical writers.[14] But if the accusations of impious temerity sound ever more like a rhetorical topos, the danger of death at sea and consequent exposure of the untended corpse on unknown shores was only too real. This particular horror has a long literary pedigree that goes back to Homer, and is also responsible for a host of epigrams in Book 7 of the *Anthology* which dwell on every conceivable aspect of a sea tragedy.[15] Seen against this background, Prop. 3.7 on the death of Paetus reads like an expanded epigram[16] but, in contrast with the generic and impersonal quality of the experience communicated by the latter, the traditional details are integrated in the elegy with the personal history and pathetic gestures of a fully sketched individual to heighten the agony of his drowning.[17] This poem has its fair share of textual problems and its ostensibly rhetorical nature has even cast doubts upon the poet's genuineness of sympathy for the ill-fated Paetus.[18] Its general outline, however, is quite clear and the gruesome realism that informs the account of the protagonist's death places it in a class of its own. One need only look at such lines as 8 *et nova longinquis piscibus esca natat* 'and drifts bizarre food for fishes in distant seas' (cf. *A.P.* 7.273.5–6 by Leonidas = Gow–Page 2349–50, with their note on line 2347 κἀγὼ μὲν πόντῳ δινεύμενος ἰχθύσι κύρμα | οἴχημαι... 'I'm gone, swirled in the eddies of the sea, a prey to fishes'); 11 *sed tua nunc volucres astant super ossa marinae* 'But now the seabirds perch on your bones' (cf. *A.P.* 7.652.5–6 by Leonidas = Gow–Page 2044–5 χὼ μέν που καύηξιν ἢ ἰχθυβόροις λαρίδεσσι | τεθρήνητ' ἄπνους εὑρεῖ ἐν αἰγιαλῷ 'He lies lifeless on some stretch of beach

---

[14] For an extensive list of relevant passages see Smith (1913) on Tib. 1.3.37–40; also Nisbet–Hubbard, introd. note to Hor. *Carm.* 1.3.

[15] For the evidence of epitaphs see Lattimore (1962) 199ff.

[16] Apart from the commentaries, see Schulz-Vanheyden (1969) 58–66 and Hubbard (1974) 82ff.

[17] Cf. Schulz-Vanheyden (1969) 66–9 for a useful discussion of the differences between 3.7 and the epigrams drawn upon.

[18] See, for example, Camps's and Richardson's introd. notes.

lamented by seabirds and fish-eating gulls'); 51–2 *huic fluctus vivo radicitus abstulit unguis,* | *et miser invisam traxit hiatus aquam* 'His fingernails were completely torn off by the waves while he was yet alive, and his miserably gaping mouth drank down the hateful water', where the hexameter strikes a weirdly ghastly note.[19] Yet, however gripping, 3.7 remains perfectly in line with contemporary feeling. This feeling Propertius understands and conveys with vigour. It seems that he can also count on it to throw into relief a more deviant stance in 2.26b.

Enk's summary of 2.26b.29–58 makes the eventuality of shipwreck and death into a touchstone of Propertius' devotion, just as, according to the received ideas about 2.1.51ff., the dangers of witchcraft are there contemplated as an ultimate test of faithfulness. By and large, all the interpretations of 2.26b that I know of move along these lines. Those who bring themselves to pay a passing tribute to the unusual sentiment or the arresting imagery of, for instance, ll. 57–8 do not fail to point out the orthodoxy of 45–56, where hopes for uneventful sailing are pinned on the tutelage of sympathetic deities, clement monsters and weather.[20] But it is also worth pointing out that the mythological examples of Neptune and Boreas are not free of a certain incongruity, featuring as they do the two deities in erotic rather than rescuing activities. One reason for that is not far to seek: those lords of the sea have learned through their own *amours* to have a soft spot for lovers that run mortal risks within the boundaries of their jurisdiction; *non ignari amoris amantibus succurrere discunt*. But then the question should be asked: how did these lovers find themselves in such an emergency in the first place? Perhaps also: how horrified do they seem to be at the prospect of the disaster? The answer is to be sought in ll. 29ff.

Propertius' mistress will not be content with hugging the coast: *seu mare per longum mea cogitet ire puella* 'Or if my girl plans a sea-voyage' (29). The adjective serves to hint at the scale of the undertaking and at the same time prepares the reader for the perilous seas of 35ff. But it is a precarious vessel that is envisaged in the next five lines (30–4):

> hanc sequar et fidos una aget aura duos.
> unum litus erit sopitis unaque tecto
>   arbor, et ex una saepe bibemus aqua;
> et tabula una duos poterit componere amantis,
>   prora cubile mihi seu mihi puppis erit.

> *I'll follow her*
> *And the same breeze will drive a faithful pair.*

[19] One may single out here Robertson's (1969) 382 'a disturbing pre-Raphaelite vividness', for it shows well how a Propertian pictorial effect may compel recourse to the modern parallel.
[20] See, for example, Rothstein, Camps, Richardson.

We'll sleep on the same beach with the same tree for shelter
And drink of the same water;
And the same plank can bring together two lovers,
Whether my quarters are fore or aft.

Indeed it is only at 34 that a definite shape with prow and stern emerges, and even then both *prora* and *puppis* are put to unexpected uses – a ghostly ship with indifferent mariners whose only equipment seems to be an inextricable embrace: *idem navigium, navitae, vectores*. This schema is hammered home by anaphora and polyptoton: *una...aura* (30), *unum litus* (31), *una...arbor* (31–2), *ex una...aqua* (32), *tabula una* (33). To much the same effect contribute: the rhymes at mid-point and end of ll. 30 (*fidos...duos*) and 32 (*una...aqua*); the juxtaposition *una duos* in 33; the *apo koinou* construction of the shared *cubile* and, perhaps, the chiastic arrangement in 34, *prora cubile mihi seu mihi puppis erit*. A long (*longum* 29) sea voyage calls for active seamanship; it is an amalgam of erotic effusions that Propertius offers instead. Between the tenderness of the lovers' closed world and the potential cruelty of the open sea there is a tension which forebodes, and is resolved by, the storm. This breaks out in 35ff. but it is just possible that the themes of shipwreck and death already glimmer in the images of 31–3. For what can 31–2 possibly suggest? Housman, who thought that a couplet containing a reference to an alternative route by land was lost after 28, transposed 31–2 before 29, taking them as a reference to the necessary intermissions during the wayfaring.[21] On this interpretation *litus*, which in the nautical environment of 29–34 can only mean 'coast' or 'shore', remains unexplained.[22] It would be more reasonable to suppose with Rothstein that the stopover is made during the sea voyage, when the couple would step ashore for the night, although the imagery hardly speaks for a scheduled event. In fact, it seems to me that shipwreck is at the back of the poet's mind; and so is death. In 1.17.1–8 it is a comparable setting that evokes persistent considerations of death; and if we were right about the romantic potential of 3.16.28 (*me tegat arborea devia terra coma* 'let me rest in a solitary spot under the shadow of some leafy tree'), the lonely tree that crops up on the coast here (ll. 31–2) should mark out a *locus amoenus* no less redolent of erotic

[21] Housman (1888) 7 (= *Classical Papers* I 33). He also read *unum litus erit positis torus unaque tecto*.

[22] Cf. Enk *ad loc*. Housman transposed 'ingeniously, but without due cause' as Butler and Barber put it, but also, I think, with some detriment to the connexion of the ideas, since *et tabula una duos poterit...*(33), which follows smoothly on *et ex una saepe bibemus...*(32), with *et* linking particularities of the same order (*aqua – tabula*), would be somewhat awkward and abrupt after 30, where *et* adds a general feature which is, strictly speaking, independent of the lover's will.

death than is that of 3.16.[23] It is perhaps hazardous to credit *sopitis* (31) and *componere* (33) with mortuary undertones,[24] but the *tabula* in this context is almost certain to conjure up the shipwrecked's expedient before it is revealed as a couch *faute de mieux*. Something of M. W. Edwards's 'intensification of meaning' and/or Pound's 'logopoeia' plays over ll. 31–4 ('the straightforward effect of a word is enhanced by conscious-ness of another meaning');[25] as a result the imagery of sailing and reciprocal love appears shot through with intimations of impending 'tragedy'.

The lovers' embrace can be assumed in the euphoric 21–8 and actually seen throughout the defiant 29–42. This is the poem's visual nucleus and, as in 2.13, one is well-advised to keep it present to the mind's eye; again, as in 2.13, the amorous posture is struck in life and persists into death (l. 44, *me licet unda ferat, te modo terra tegat* 'The waves can have me if only earth covers you', is no more than a pious flash in the pan):

<blockquote>

certe isdem nudi pariter iactabimur oris (43)

At least we shall be tossed together naked on one shore

</blockquote>

This is a striking image and one that ll. 29ff. have been subtly leading up to. To put it otherwise, it represents the double climax of nautical foolhardiness and physical inextricability that 29 inaugurates. *isdem . . . oris* as well as consummating the simultaneity-and-unity theme of these lines directs specifically back to *unum litus* (31) – we are encouraged to read backwards as well as forwards. Waiting for the weathercock to revolve in 35ff. before the possibility of shipwreck and death on the shore is allowed means missing a good deal of the vigorous irony that tosses the lovers towards the final stage of their vision. Propertius does something more than merely brave the dangers. Within the framework of the fantasy he is actually courting the disaster and relishes its outcome – and he flouts time-honoured feelings to which he pays full allegiance in 3.7. The contrast between the two poems is underlined by a number of un-mistakable verbal similarities: 2.26b.37–8 *quicumque et venti miserum vexastis Ulixem,* | *et Danaum Euboico litore mille ratis*; cf. 3.7.39–42 *saxa triumphalis fregere Capharea puppis,* | *naufraga cum vasto Graecia tracta salo est.* | *paulatim socium iacturam flevit Ulixes,* | *in mare cui soliti non valuere doli*; 2.26b.51

---

[23] See pp. 71ff. above. *ex una bibemus aqua* implies search for water on the coast, not, we must suppose, always an unalloyed pleasure for ancient sailors but sometimes an occasion for pure romance in ancient poets, as the popularity of Hylas' story suggests. Richardson's note is worth quoting: 'The picture of P. and his mistress hunting a spring together in a wild landscape is a romantic one.'

[24] Which, of course, they are perfectly capable of; see *OLD s.vv.* 1 and 4c respectively.

[25] See Edwards (1961) 137.

crudelem et Borean rapta Orithyia negavit; cf. 3.7.13 *infelix Aquilo, raptae timor Orithyiae.*

Line 43 offers an impressive crescendo: *cert(e)* (1), *isdem* (2), *nudi* (2), *pariter* (3), *iactabimur* (4 syllables). *iactabimur* is far more vivid than φέρεται in an analogous Callimachean context (cf. *A.P.* 7.271.3 = Gow–Page 1247 νῦν δ' ὁ μὲν εἰν ἁλί που φέρεται νέκυς... 'now he drifts dead somewhere in the sea'). It is, however, more probable that it was, among others, *A.P.* 7.501 (= Gow–Page 2871–4) by Perses that Propertius had in mind. If so, we should perhaps read the epigram's first couplet with Hecker as Εὔρου χειμέριαί σε καταιγίδες ἐξεκύλισαν, | Φίλλι, πολυκλύστῳ [MSS πολυκλαύτῳ] γυμνὸν ἐπ' ἠιόνι[26] 'The wintry squalls of Eurus cast you up, Phillis, naked on the surfy shore' on the assumption that the elegist, by the right of the greater genius, brought out the implications of a quasi-formulaic adjective in the powerful image of the tossing bodies. The slow spondees before the main caesura in the third foot seem to keep the naked bodies immobile for the few seconds that the surf ebbs, while the flow that pitches them on the shore again is conveyed by the accelerated rhythm of the rest of the hexameter – perhaps by the prominent *r*-sound as well. Although almost every word here can be paralleled in the various descriptions of shipwreck, l. 43 is more sharply visual and sensual because it represents the acme of an intensely erotic sequence. This is not the inhospitable shore of the epigrams; nakedness is not merely the standard attribute of the drowned; 'ordinary and erotic connotations are sometimes interwoven', remarks Edwards apropos of, among other words, *nudi* in 2.26b.43, without, however, canvassing the frequentative *iactabimur* for more poignant sexual overtones.[27] 'To be tossed by the waves of passion' is a common metaphor;[28] *iacto* is also *mot juste* for the febrile restlessness the bed of sick or love-sick persons witnesses:[29] Propertius, it would seem, does not wish us to visualise 'corpses tossed by the waves' without being distracted by the thought of 'bodies tossed by erotic passion'. Cynthia would have found it less easy to deny here, as she denies in 2.29b.36, that there are signs of two having rolled together – *signa volutantis...iacuisse duos*. Even *pariter* may have more weight than it seems at first sight. *isdem oris* appoints the place, *pariter* prescribes synchronised movement. If this is an assignation we might do well to remember Ovid's obsession with harmonious sexual activity and simultaneous orgasm: *Am.* 1.10.35–6 *cur mihi sit damno, tibi sit lucrosa voluptas, | quam socio motu femina virque ferunt?* 'Why should sexual

---

[26] See Gow–Page *ad loc.*   [27] Edwards (1961) 138.
[28] See, for example, Catull. 64.97–8 and Prop. 2.12.7.
[29] See *TLL s.v.* 53.22ff.

pleasure, which requires co-ordinate movements from both partners, be a cause of loss to me, of gain to you?'; *Ars Am.* 2.727–8 *ad metam properate simul: tum plena voluptas, | cum pariter victi femina virque iacent* 'hasten to the goal together; it is the peak of pleasure when the partners collapse simultaneously'; *ibid.* 3.800 *quo pariter debent femina virque frui* 'which man and woman should equally enjoy'. Was *pariter*, then, a recognisable item of the sexual jargon?[30] We cannot be certain; adverbs are less likely than nouns to acquire a technical sense. The poem's final couplet, however, seems to pick up and put the finishing touches to the innuendos of l. 43:

> quod mihi si ponenda tuo sit corpore vita,
> exitus hic nobis non inhonestus erit.　　　　(2.26b.57–8)

> *And if I must lay down my life upon your body*
> *A decorous finale this will be.*

Heavy weather has sometimes been made of *tuo corpore*. Such free use of a simple locative ablative, though not very frequent, can be readily paralleled,[31] and yet it is remarkable that the Propertian passages adduced should not include a very close parallel from a comparable context. Propertius sees Gallus clinging feverishly to the body of his mistress

> et cupere optatis animam deponere labris,[32]
> et quae deinde meus celat, amice, pudor.　　　(1.13.17–18)

> *Eager to lay down your life on longed-for lips –*
> *The rest my friendly modesty conceals.*

The most inveterate voyeur could hardly hope for more. Despite the *de rigueur* aposiopesis in 18, Propertius contrives to insinuate in l. 17 that he has in fact witnessed the peak of the erotic play between Gallus and his girl.[33] 'to breathe forth the soul on the beloved's lips' is, I submit, the elegiac, 'idealised' version of the orgasmic moment,[34] described by Lucretius with uninhibited realism in *D.R.N.* 4.1106–9:

[30] The second of the Ovidian passages just quoted suggests that such a use of *pariter* might have something to do with the frequency of the race imagery as a metaphor for love-making. Cf. Adams (1982) 207–8.

[31] Cf., for example, 1.14.1 *abiectus Tiberina...unda*; 2.13.55 *iacuisse paludibus*. See also Shackleton Bailey (1956) 117–18.

[32] The MSS offer *verbis*, not *labris*, and Camps, like Rothstein and Richardson, defends their reading. The weight of the evidence, however, in Fedeli's ample note *ad loc.* indicates that *labris* must be preferred as bringing the idea expressed into line with the widespread topos that has the lovers' soul trafficking between their lips. If I am right about one particular passage behind 1.13.17 (see below), *labris* becomes almost irresistible.

[33] So Lyne (1980) 112: 'Propertius actually saw Gallus in the act.'

[34] That Gallus' 'expiration' should not be bowdlerised Apuleius, *Met.* 2.17 shows well. Apuleius rounds off the description of a sinewy κελητισμός with '*simul ambo corruimus inter mutuos amplexus animas anhelantes*' – a last-minute pruderie for which Dioscorides' (*A.P.* 5.55.7–8 = Gow-

iam cum praesagit gaudia corpus
atque in eost Venus ut muliebria conserat arva,
adfigunt avide corpus iunguntque salivas
oris et inspirant pressantes dentibus ora

*when the body has a foretaste of its joy and passion is on the point of sowing
the woman's furrows, eagerly they clasp and mingle the moisture of their
mouths, and pressing lip on lip breathe deeply.*

This version is at two removes from the ejaculations of 1.10.1ff. but it
seems to have commended itself to the elegist when Gallus became more
intimate with the girl two poems later. After what has already been
discussed in connexion with 2.1.47ff., the case for first-hand knowledge
of Lucretius need not be laboured. And though this in itself will not
guarantee the Lucretian connexion of 1.13.17–18, consider the sexual
vocabulary of this poem: *languescere* (15), *complexus* (19), *furor* (20),
gaudia (24), *ardor* (28); and compare *D.R.N.* 4: *tabescunt* (1120), *compagibus*
(1113), *furor* (1117), *gaudia* (1106) and *ardoris* (1116) respectively. Gallus'
erotic career gives another clue. This man, formerly a devotee of
Lucretius' *vulgivaga Venus*, stands to become a convert to the Propertian
creed of a single *inamorata* (cf. 11–12); worse still, whereas in the past he
would not countenance *in...amore moram* (6) he is now faced with *in amore
mori* (cf. especially 23ff.). If the come-uppance of a Lucretian lover can
be announced with a Lucretian aside, so much the better. Gallus' drama
of conversion previews the manifesto of 2.1.47ff. But it is the climactic
point of this drama that concerns me here, and I shuttle back to 2.26b.57
with the suggestion that the death it envisages cannot be much different
from the 'death' craved by Gallus in 1.13.17. To read *quod mihi si ponenda
tuo sit corpore vita* literally in the face of *animam deponere labris* is unnecessarily
restrictive, to say the least of it.[35]

So 2.26b.57–8 record the climactic breath as well as the last one – an
eminent instance of *laus in amore mori*, of love *as* death. Set from the very
beginning in the key of exultation, 2.26b depicts, through a series of visual
strokes supported by verbal artistry, the physical togetherness of the
lovers as increasingly threatened by the most dreaded of fates, releases the

Page 1489–90) frank (and stylish) counterpart is: μέχρις ἀπεσπείσθη λευκὸν μένος ἀμφοτέροισιν
| καὶ Δωρὶς παρέτοις ἐξεχύθη μέλεσι. We are ineluctably reminded of the just-quoted *Ars Am.*
2.727–8.

[35] *corpore* is neither vaguer nor more euphemistic than *labris*; in fact, this noun panders to *risqué*
intimations, as Ov. *Am.* 2.14.34 *figere sollicita corpora vestra manu* (to Corinna, the self-abortionist)
and 3.7.28 (of the male counterpart) confirm. *exitus*, moreover, in 58 may be another 'dark horse'.
Arnobius, *Adv. Nat.* 4.7 tells of the goddess Perfica under whose auspices sexual pleasures move
happily *ad exitum*. Either this noun or *finis* may have been occasionally used of such consummation
(*exitus* may denote both 'exit' and the 'final outcome' of an action; for *finis* referring to
consummatio libidinis see *TLL s.v.* 792.35 and cf. Adams (1982) 143 n. 1, 144).

anticipated catastrophe – and transfers the climax from universal horror to private sensuality by defamiliarising and revaluing the funereal details of a standard theme. We may notice that unlike 2.1.47–78, which prefix the programmatic proposition, 2.26b.29–58 culminate in it: *exitus hic nobis non inhonestus erit*. And if we are right in assuming that 2.26b has lost not more than one couplet before 29, it is perhaps worth remarking that both passages inculcate their *Liebestod* in the course of thirty-two lines.

2.26b.45–56 may seem a bow to conventional feelings about death at sea. But this would not be without problems. For one thing, they are hemmed in by the climactic stages of the erotic adventure. The poem's last couplet harks back to 43 with a single-mindedness that discredits the optative mood of the intervening lines. To understand 57–8 as 'should the worst come to the worst such death will be honourable for us' is to fail to realise that l. 43 represents what the poet has set his heart on ever since he launched himself and the girl into the voyage. This formal engulfment of a seemingly disruptive paragraph combines with another aspect of Propertian irony, namely, the appeal to the gods to ward off an eventuality which is in fact dwelt upon and patently savoured as the poem unfolds. This device, whose affinity with the *praeteritio* of 2.13 is not hard to see, seems to me to provide the key to 2.26a and 2.28. Pressure of space forbids me to expatiate upon what would have been a very instructive comparison, yet a poem which has already claimed our attention will prove no less illuminating. In 3.16.11–20 divine protection of the lover is taken for granted rather than confidently forecast as is the case with 2.26b.45–56, but this is a superficial difference and it is otherwise obvious that both passages have the same function within the death fantasy of which they form part (see pp. 73–4 above). *And both are immediately followed by a* quod si *which marks a relapse into ordinary vulnerability*; thought vaults over an interlude of inviolability back to its starting-point. This is the arch Propertius, 'prepared' for the better but hoping for the worse. So too in 2.28: Cynthia is critically ill (1–14); but things will turn out all right in the end; witness Io etc. (15–24); *quod si forte tibi properarint fata quietem* 'But if so be that Fate should hasten your repose' (25ff.), and the door is opened to the cherished vision of the Underworld heroines. This use of *quod si*, with its mild adversative force, captures a subtle convulsion of irony, which in 2.26b is the more effective for occurring at the poem's very last couplet.[36] Through it Propertius

---

[36] There can be no general account of the tonal message emitted by this particle, and one must watch out for subtle differences in its several uses. Williams (1968) 760 observes that as used by Horace in *Carm.* 3.1.41 it 'brings the ode to a halt at its climax to introduce the poet's own point of view in his own voice', and Woodman (1984) 83–6, for all his different views about the poem's significance, assigns it a similar role as is clear from his stanza-grouping and re-

picks up that strand of his fantasy in which he is genuinely interested; this, in the case of 2.26b no less than in 3.16, is not divine intervention. La Penna asserts that the poet cannot bring himself to believe that the gods could be anything but favourable towards this couple;[37] the answer must be that 45–56 cannot escape the combined effect of formal bracketing and irony. And besides, 45–56 themselves are more than a prayer for safety.

Aqua figures in Delatte's list of Propertian keywords, its frequency as well as that of semantically kindred words being due to a tendency to associate the dominant themes with water imagery; 'whether in connection with love, literature, the beyond, the poet's future or his past, water-imagery appears everywhere as a leit-motif'.[38] Delatte has usefully quantified a vital trait of the poet's sensibility but he has, in my view, given inadequate attention to the highly peculiar *complex* of love–water–death as we can see it for instance in 1.20.23–48 (where, incidentally, Zetes and Calais, *Aquilonia proles* and *genus Orithyiae*, seem no less intent on rape than their father is in 2.26b.51), 2.26a, 2.27.13–16 and 2.28.39–40. This certainly looks like a succulent morsel for psychoanalysts. For our purposes less enterprising speculation will suffice. Ovid has a similar penchant for watery landscapes, often accentuated by desirable human form, as for instance in *Met.* 3.407ff. (Narcissus), 5.585ff. (Arethusa and Alpheus) and 11.229ff. (Thetis).[39] The *dolce fresche e chiare acque* of Sulmone must be partly responsible here. This is Wilkinson's plausible suggestion, but note the difference between *Am.* 2.16.1–10, which he adduces in its support, and Prop. 4.1.123–4:

> qua nebulosa cavo rorat Mevania campo,
> et lacus aestivis intepet Umber aquis

> *Where misty Mevania deposits its dew on the hollow plain and the waters*
> *of Umbria's lake steam on hot summer days*

construction of Horace's argument. As used by Virgil in speeches 'it...produces', again according to Williams, 'a contrast which is accompanied by a change in the speaking voice'. An equally interesting point is touched upon by the same scholar on p. 775: 'The technique of closing a poem with a more or less generalizing distich, which often looks back over the whole poem, is very characteristic of Propertius' technique of composition, and these distichs are often introduced by a particle which slows and changes the tone of voice: so *quod si* in 1.1.37; ii.14.31; 26.57; 32.61; iii.14.33.' Whatever may be true of other passages, my argument is that such change in 3.16.21 and 2.26b.57 lays bare the poem's ironical mechanism at the same time as it exposes the seriousness of the poet's obsession. But more detailed discussion of the last-distich timing remarked upon by Williams must wait until we come to 2.8.39–40 (see pp. 131–2 below). [37] La Penna (1977) 145.

[38] Delatte (1967) 36, 52. But my views do not in general coincide with those Delatte puts forward in pp. 51–6 and I differ from him especially on 2.26b.

[39] Wilkinson (1955) 180–1: 'There are a dozen extended descriptions of natural scenery in the poem, and practically all of them centre round water, cool, calm and shaded.'

This could be the lake the lovers sail in 2.27.13–16 and 2.28.39–40; and the atmospheric effect is certainly that of 3.18.1–2, where Marcellus meets death no less insidious than untimely. Propertius' watery spots can be sombre in a way that Ovid's cannot; and, sombre or not, they can be *intrinsically* deadly whereas Ovid's are not.[40] 1.20.33–50 are a case in point. The ἔκφρασις of 33–8 adumbrates the quality of Hylas' downfall: *prolapsum leviter facili traxere liquore* 'And lightly drew him down head first in yielding water' (47) – a deadly and sensual liquidity with a distinct Alexandrian flavour.

Water–love–death, then, in the sense defined above, is a legitimate heading under which to read 2.26b as a whole. At this level ll. 45–56 are not situated outside the aesthetic continuum of 2.26b any more than 2.13.17–23 depart from the aesthetic line of that poem. In other words, the Neptune example is there in order to validate the aquatic setting and the concupiscence of 43 and 57–8, and *not* in order to provide a background of divine kindness against which the lovers can afford some bravado: therefore, it does not impair the death theme. In the dense account of Amymone's union with Neptune the fusion of the aquatic (*latices, palus, urna, profudit, aquas*) with the erotic (*compressa, amplexu*) is irrepressibly suggestive.[41] A parallel deserves to be once again emphatically drawn here: water is to the story of Neptune and Amymone what fire is to that of Hercules and Hebe in 1.13.23–4 (or to 3.13.17–22 for that matter) – the flaming copulation matched by the intercourse of lissom bodies. In fact, 1.13.21–4 juxtapose, as we have seen (p. 60 above), the two elements in a way that shows Propertius acutely aware of, and sharply sensitised by the parallel. At opposite ends of the sensory scale, fire and water both encompass and exhaust the sensuous potential of his *amor*.

Boreas and Orithyia are no more than a pendant to the Neptune example.[42] They serve to increase the volume of the mythological parallels, but the two stories also have the air of belonging closely together and a possible reason for this will be advanced later on. Scylla

[40] Ovid's landscape is not *intrinsically* deadly; this is not to say that its idyllic and serene beauty cannot act as a foil to the violence and death of which it often is the scene. See Segal (1969) 15ff.

[41] The association of water imagery and sexual energy has not escaped Wiggers (1972) 128–9. For the association of water with sexuality in Ovid see Segal (1969) 10, 24ff.

[42] Whitaker (1983) 99 believes that ancient readers were bound to think of Neptune and Boreas both as individuals–lovers and as antonomasiae whereby they stood for 'sea' and 'wind' respectively. A mild split of this sort would perhaps enrich the conceptual texture of the examples but in the last analysis the mind's eye, encouraged by visual representation of the myths, will not have 'squinted', and a gap such as to require skilful disguising by the poet (Whitaker thinks Prop. succeeded in disguising it) will scarcely have opened.

and Charybdis in the next couplet (53–4) assert unequivocally the 'safe conduct' theme, but the clear star-spangled skies of 55–6 promise safety while bringing to mind Catullus 7.7–8 *aut quam sidera multa, cum tacet nox,* |*furtivos hominum vident amores* 'or as many [i.e. kisses] as are the stars which in the silence of night witness people's furtive loves', where cosmic connivance enhances the undisturbed privacy of the erotic play. I take the destination of the voyage in 2.26b to be the shore of 43 – and the engagement of the naked bodies on it. La Penna, a pioneering explorer of Propertian irony and wit, has twice over read into 2.26b the uncompromising loftiness of a remote, luminous world with angelic inhabitants and chaste mistresses.[43] I believe that he unduly spiritualises a poem which is organised to a fleshly end.

Before attempting a foray into the literary background of 2.26b it will be rewarding first to set the poem within its Propertian context, for read in conjunction with elegies which draw upon the same set of motifs and ideas it will help to bring into sharper focus some changes in emphasis and technique in Book 2. The brief comparison with 3.7 will have shown how this poem by appropriating the pictorial content of the (normally) horrific death at sea projects an erotic-sensual adventurism; by design, as it were, 2.26b cashes in and plays on conventional response and its literary reflection. Even more interesting is a comparison with 1.8, an erotic piece and one with strong thematic affinities. It appears in most editions as two poems, 8a (1–26) and 8b (27–46), yet however one chooses to print these lines it is quite clear that they refer to the stages of one single dramatic episode.[44] Briefly: Cynthia is about to put to sea in the company of a rival when, rather unexpectedly, she heeds Propertius' plaintive muse, stays and gives him cause for rapture. Thematic similarities between 1.8.27–46 and 2.26b.21–8 leap to the eye. Looked at from a different angle, 2.26b as a whole is equal to 1.8.27–46 plus the voyage-and-death theme. And since the first part of 1.8 (1–26) is all about a prospective sea voyage, the overall relation between the two poems will admit further schematisation: 2.26b represents an enrichment of the thematic structure of 1.8 in the direction of *Liebestod*; or, to be more particular, Propertius substitutes celebratory *Liebestod* for the *nunc mihi summa licet contingere sidera plantis* 'Today I walk in heaven, among the stars' (43) or the more down-to-earth *ista meam norit gloria canitiem* 'That glory shall my grey hairs know' (46). Identical emotional situations authorise different, in terms both of quantity and quality, extravaganzas,

---

[43] See La Penna (1977) 146 and cf. *id.* (1951) 66.
[44] 'A problem for the editor rather than the interpreter', remarks Stroh (1971) 35 n. 78.

and it is here, if anywhere, that one may appreciate the new bearings in Book 2.

1.8 permits the reconstruction of a specific dramatic incident unfolding over the time. The poet does not deign to draw a clear picture of his rival (*quicumque est* 3) but the atmosphere definitely suggests an instance of military or mercantile acquisitiveness. The topographical indications are fairly accurate, Cynthia proposing to sail from an Italian port (*Tyrrhena* 11) across the Adriatic to *Oricos* (20) on the coast of Epirus, but then deciding to stay in Rome (31). 2.26b presupposes a similar situation but has curtailed, almost suppressed, dramatic externals. The girl's wavering loyalties are not dramatised, although *nunc*, the poem's opening word, introduces an emotional stage which implies a resolved crisis. Compared with 1.8.27ff., 2.26b.21–8 have a distancing effect. In the former poem the girl is thrice identified as Cynthia (8, 30, 42), but is never named in the latter; a conspiracy of envy comes to light in 1.8.27 *rumpantur iniqui!* 'go hang, the spiteful!' and 29 *falsa licet cupidus deponat gaudia livor* 'Eager envy can drop its glad illusions'; in 2.26b it is just hinted at by the impetuous *nunc admirentur* 'Now let them marvel' (1); *si Cambysae redeant et flumina Croesi* 'Even if Croesus' and Cambyses' streams returned' (2.26b.23) sounds more precious than Hippodamia's kingdom (1.8.35) and the wealth of Elis (1.8.36), just as the direct speech in 2.26b.24 *De nostro surge, poeta, toro* 'Rise, poet, from our couch' sounds more stiff than 1.8.33–4 *illa vel angusto mecum requiescere lecto |...maluit* 'Prefers to rest with me, though in a narrow bed'; and *dicit se odisse beatos* 'she says she hates the rich' (2.26b.25) is fairly formal when the corresponding comment in 1.8.38 *non...illa meos fugit avara sinus* 'Not being greedy, she prefers my assets' almost certainly incorporates a pun on *sinus*.[45] 1.8.27–46 are the enactment of an averted scandal in the congenial milieu of the capital, a slice of a drama that comes alive. 2.26b.21–8, on the other hand, are only prefixed to set the fantasy of the following lines moving; they have all the appearances of being a formal prop – and one that, in my view, the poet is not anxious to disguise at all.

What happens here can be succinctly described as a shift from drama to fantasy. Attention to this or similar developments in Book 2 has been drawn by the great majority of scholars, although often in a vague way and never, so far as I know, as a result of detailed comparisons between

---

[45] I do not find this suggested in the commentaries, but I think that *avara sinus* woos the ambiguity 'embrace–pocket'. 2.16, where the same or a very similar rival reappears, explains what Cynthia had in mind when fleeing Propertius' unpromising *sinus: semper amatorum ponderat una sinus* (12).

Another pun may lurk behind *redeant* at 2.26b.23. Camps (he reads dubitantly *munera* instead of *flumina*), who does not consider this possibility, favours the sense 'come in as income' over 'come back again'.

poems of the first two books. Back in 1930 Abel offered the first systematic account of a progression from genuine exhortation in Book 1 to the reflection-dominated Book 2.[46] Imaginative projection into, and anticipation of the future is one form such reflection can take.[47] Certainly this is the case with 2.13 and 2.26b. Editorial behaviour, if nothing else, *vis-à-vis* these poems (especially the first) suggests that somewhere along the line the poet–lover is felt to fly off at a tangent. Well, in a sense he does; and he can do so unfettered by the restrictions of the neat dramatic vignettes of the Monobiblos with their 'composition simple' and real-life addressees.[48] Boucher has argued with elegance that Propertius started his poetic career enmeshed in a real-life complex of friendship–literature–love. There is in Book 1 a coterie, a panel, as it were, of acquaintances whose actions interfere with the adventure of the protagonists; here the poems tend to be a sustained response to an external dramatic stimulus.[49] By contrast, the vast majority of the addressees in Book 2 appear shadowy, unidentifiable or generic,[50] the address being deployed as a pseudo-dramatic peg on which to hang egocentric fantasies and reflections that are not meant to be communicated – in any dramatic sense of the word, at least.[51] No poem shows this better than 2.8 (on which see pp. 113ff. below), but I think it is not previous to say that both 2.13.17ff. and 2.26b.29ff., so far from being characterised by the 'dialogic' (*Dialogischen*) and 'volitional' (*Voluntaristischen*) (which R. Heinze felt to be characteristic of Horace's lyric poetry, and which is much in evidence in the Propertian Monobiblos too),[52] come very close to achieving what F. Klingner described as 'pure expression of the inner self without any further purpose' and found best realised in Latin elegy.[53] It is, of course, undesirable to generalise; some poems in Book 2 can be more obtrusively 'volitional' than, say, 1.19. But I am making this point in conscious contrast to Stroh who does generalise and who has made of the volitional element, in the form of erotic wooing (*Werbung*) or usefulness (*Nützlichkeit*), an interpretative panacea. There may be some truth, he concedes, in Heinze's setting of the 'volitional' of Horace's lyric poetry against the 'subjective' of elegy, 'yet from the point of view of the elegists' literary

---

[46] Abel (1930) 3–51.

[47] Luck's (1969) 120 'Unlike Catullus' poems, those of Propertius are not really poems of love, but poems about love...exercises in new manners of celebrating it' is, I think, especially true of Book 2.

[48] See Boucher (1965) 354–5. He finds 'composition simple' in most poems of the Monobiblos (he excepts 1, 20, 21 and 22); 'ce type d'élégie se définit par l'unité d'un sujet'.

[49] Boucher (1977) 53–71; cf. Rothstein, introd., 12 and see also Lyne (1980) 102–20.

[50] Cf. La Penna (1977) 63–4 and Richardson, introd., 9–10.

[51] Cf. Lyne (1980) 125 and Warden (1980) 90–1.

[52] Heinze (1938) 187–204.   [53] Klingner (1956) 51–60, esp. 58ff.

self-description, what has been said of lyric is even more true of love elegy'.[54] But in 2.13 it is self-description that can lead one up the garden path and far from the true nature of the actual poem. Stroh is not unaware of this problem, as his remarks in pp. 186–96 would seem to suggest, but in his abundantly documented pages one gets the impression that a *façon de parler* gets more than its fair share of critical attention. It is in this vein that, generalising on the difference between Books 1 and 2, he sees an 'Orpheus' who seeks to work upon Cynthia's feelings in the former, and a 'Homer' intent on celebrating her in the latter[55] – too neat to be true and too narrow to be of real interpretative value. It is not easy to put Propertius' artistic development in a nutshell, and it is hazardous to see it in terms of the fortunes of the *Nützlichkeitstopik*. It is, I believe, comparison of thematically kindred pieces that affords the most reliable means of appreciating it. When 2.26b is thus compared to 1.8 it can be seen to have jettisoned 'dramaturgical immediacy'[56] in order to venture a more radical assertion of erotic euphoria. Cynical as it may sound, for this purpose any female will do. The poem has severed its links with life to organise itself as a vision wrung with a convulsion, so to speak, out of the dramatic blue.

To linger a little longer over 1.8. It would be otiose to rehearse here the well-known piece of literary history that brings together ll. 7–8, Virg. *Ecl.* 10.47–9 and, on the strength of Servius' comment there, the poet Gallus.[57] Now even if Virgil, for his own purposes, was culling motifs and turns of expression from a number of Gallus' erotic poems, Propertius in 1.8 is more likely to have had in mind a single poem, or perhaps a couple of poems, on a subject similar to his own in 1.8, namely, the desertion of Gallus by Lycoris for the sake of a military officer (cf. *Ecl.* 10.22–3). Should that be the case, some interesting possibilities arise. Are we to assume on the evidence of the Virgilian poem, which depicts Gallus in unrelieved despondency, that the latter's poetry failed either to dissuade his mistress from going away or to win her back once gone? If so, Prop. 1.8 might be meant as an optimistic variation on his predecessor's theme. Moreover, if Apollo's words to Gallus in *Ecl.* 10.22–3 ('*Galle, quid insanis?' inquit. 'tua cura Lycoris | perque nives alium perque horrida castra secuta est.*' '"Gallus, you're mad" he cries. "Lycoris your beloved | Pursues another man through snows and horrid camps"') echo a complaint in one of the latter's poems that the god proved slow to help the lover in his hour of

---

[54] Stroh (1971) 5.   [55] Stroh (1971) 54–66, esp. 64.

[56] Lyne's (1980) 131 phrase from a comparable discussion.

[57] Virg. *Ecl.* 10.47–9 constitute one of several elegiac themes that F. Skutsch (1901) 2ff. was the first to observe in the *Eclogue*. See also Boucher (1966) 97 and Ross (1975) 85–6.

need, it is quite possible that 1.8.41–2 (*sunt igitur Musae, neque amanti tardus Apollo,* | *quis ego fretus amo: Cynthia rara mea est!* 'So the Muse exists and Apollo makes haste to help the lover; | In that faith I love, for peerless Cynthia's mine') is a pointed rehabilitation of Apollo's reputation as much as it is a traditional compliment.[58] Unlike Pasoli, who has put forward a similar hypothesis, I would be inclined to see here playful rather than polemical allusiveness.[59] Yet this is by the way; my reason for going back to Gallus is that the assumption of a poem on Lycoris' walkout, which Propertius will have imitated with variations in 1.8 before branching out to 2.26b, would be a fine case of imitation followed up with self-imitation *cum* variation. It is, therefore, quite legitimate to give an account of 2.26b in terms of a recognised literary technique favoured by Hellenistic poets and their followers and dictated, in part at least, by the comparatively restricted thematic range available to love poets. As well as being legitimate this approach has a chastening effect on our perceptions of the form of a Propertian poem; this is not *organic*, in the Romantic sense of a spontaneous growth, but self-consciously designed in a way that betrays distancing rather than passionate involvement. I shall take up this point at a more appropriate place, when the structural pattern of a larger number of poems will have been surveyed, yet it is not anticipatory to observe here that two of the poems discussed so far in detail, viz. 2.13 and 2.26b, look very much like variations on the theme of *Liebestod*, their one essential difference being due to their pictorial purveyors, namely, the funeral and the shipwreck respectively. To grasp this is to grasp the essential unity of both pieces, and thus to put all subsequent discussion on a more secure basis – which in view of the uncertainties, imaginary and real, of the Propertian tradition is of the utmost importance.

If comparison between 1.8 and 2.26b reveals a shift of emphasis from erotic drama to erotic fantasy, comparison with 1.17 will show a shift of sense and sensibility in the deployment of the theme of death as part of a traditional poetic idea. 1.17 may be about separation and loneliness, 2.26b about fulfilment, but in both the sea voyage and its concomitant risks serve as an index of amatory fortunes. Now the sea and its condition, with their associations of danger and unpredictability, have inspired some of the world's oldest metaphors, among which the Ship of State[60]

---

[58] Gallus' pose in *Ecl.* 10 is modelled on that of Daphnis in Theoc. *Id.* 1, which does not feature Apollo. Although there is no dearth of reasons for the appearance of the god in the *Eclogue* (see R. Coleman (1977) on *Ecl.* 10.21) it is just possible that a reference to Apollo in Gallus was Virgil's very specific motive.

[59] See Pasoli (1977) 107–9. Wider implications were claimed for the *tardus Apollo* in 1.8.41 by M. Parca (1982) 587–8.

[60] See, for example, Nisbet–Hubbard's introd. to Hor. *Carm.* 1.14.

and the Ship of Love are perhaps best-known. And of these it is, it seems, the latter that has the longest pedigree and the most variegated history, since it encompasses a host of nuances (sea–woman, sea–passion, ship–love-affair etc.),[61] giving ample scope for imagery, wit and concetto. When it entered the repertory of the Greek epigrammatists, every item of the nautical gear proved valuable: Κύπρις ἐμοὶ ναύκληρος, Ἔρως δ' οἴακα φυλάσσει | ἄκρον ἔχων ψυχῆς ἐν χερὶ πηδάλιον 'Cypris is my captain and Love is in charge of the tiller, holding in his hand the end of my soul's rudder' (Meleager, *A.P.* 12.157.1–2 = Gow–Page 4642–3); and the whole gamut of navigational vicissitudes was turned to account as, for instance, in *A.P.* 12.156 = Gow–Page 3738–45. The lover may be a storm-tossed sailor yearning for the security of the haven: χειμαίνει δὲ βαρὺς πνεύσας Πόθος· ἀλλά μ' ἐς ὅρμον | δέξαι τὸν ναύτην Κύπριδος ἐν πελάγει 'And I'm buffeted by tempestuous Desire; but receive me, a sailor on the sea of Cypris, into your haven' (Meleager, *A.P.* 12.167.3–4 = Gow–Page 4570–1); or he may already be shipwrecked, albeit on land: Εἰ τοὺς ἐν πελάγει σώζεις, Κύπρι, κἀμὲ τὸν ἐν γᾷ | ναυαγόν, φιλίη, σῶσον ἀπολλύμενον 'Cypris, if you save those out at sea, come to my rescue too, dear goddess, for shipwreck on land is my own plight' (*A.P.* 5.11). Of course, none of these pieces claims to be more than a concatenation of *ben trovatos* that implicate the reader in a flippant oscillation between the literal and the metaphorical. Nor is this breezy ἐρωτοπλοεῖν alien to Propertius himself, as is evident from 2.4.19–20, 2.14.29–30 and, especially, 3.24.15–16:

> ecce coronatae portum tetigere carinae,
> traiectae Syrtes, ancora iacta mihi est.

But see, my garlanded ship has reached the harbour, the Syrtes have been safely sailed through and the anchor is cast.

A similar metaphor takes up the best part of Hor. *Carm.* 1.5 and it is, I think, the very transparency of the device that underscores the poet's detachment and compounds both the 'wit' and the 'astringent charm' that Hubbard and Nisbet emphasise, rightly I think, as against more sentimental interpretations of the ode.[62] It is in the nature of the figure to convey chiefly the dangerous aspects of love, but Ovid valued it more for its implications of technical, rational control: *Tiphys et Automedon dicar Amoris ego* (*Ars Am.* 1.8). This is the spirit of the epigram in the service of *arte regendus Amor*.[63]

[61] See Nisbet–Hubbard, introd. to Hor. *Carm.* 1.5 and notes on ll. 6–13. On sailing as a metaphor for love cf. also La Penna (1951b) 202–5 and Wiggers (1972) 116 n. 1.

[62] Nisbet–Hubbard, introd. note, 73.

[63] P. Green (1982) has a good note on *Ars Am.* 2.337–52.

In all the above cases, however, the metaphor, when not coextensive with a concisely phrased epigram, is grafted on, or inserted into the poem in order to establish a more or less transient analogy. This is not the case with 1.17, since here the poetic idea of love as a sea voyage provides an elaborate and consistent pictorial framework for the whole poem. What we have here is not merely original use or revitalisation of an overworked figure but transmutation of such a figure into an autonomous dramatic incident with a specific visual and emotional content. Imaginative pursuit of the pictorial implications of an effete metaphor – one of Propertius' strong points, as we first learned from 1.13.26–9 – tends to obscure in this case, as it never does in the other passages I have quoted, the line between the metaphorical and the literal. However, I need not elaborate the case for a basically metaphorical or symbolical, as against a biographical, reading of the poem since the essential points here have already been made by F. Solmsen,[64] E. W. Leach[65] and E. Lefèvre.[66] Still, I do feel that in one respect at least the record has not been set absolutely straight. What Solmsen sees as particularly original in 1.17 is the *mise-en-scène*, the fact that the lover is presented stranded on a deserted shore, which is a feature that cannot be paralleled in the general run of sea metaphors.[67] But would it not be better to invite the reader to appreciate the whole picture as an evolution from figurative contraptions penetrable by the naked eye? Whatever may be new in the configuration of the dramatic space, the essential originality of 1.17 resides in its promotion of a static and fanciful trope to the status of an imaginative and dynamic whole. To put it otherwise: it dramatises a metaphor.

It dramatises it, but without interfering with the accepted symbolism of its imagery. The bleak, inhospitable landscape of ll. 1–18 purports to be a projection of a mental landscape devastated by an erotic *contretemps*. The night (*nox*) and the treacherous shoals (*iniqua vada*) of l. 10 as well as the threatened shipwreck and drowning (1–8) suggest that the crisis in the relationship with Cynthia is rapidly coming to a head. Even such an original touch as the virtual identification of the mistress's mood with the storm in 5–6 *quin etiam absenti prosunt tibi, Cynthia, venti: | aspice, quam saevas increpat aura minas* 'Why, Cynthia, in your absence the winds take your part! | Look how the gale howls cruel threats!' may be a development of the personified desire in, for instance, *A.P.* 12.167.3 χειμαίνει δὲ βαρὺς πνεύσας Πόθος 'I am buffeted by tempestuous Desire'. Whatever variables the larger scale of the Propertian elegy entails, it is none the less clear that it shares with the other passages quoted above the emotional constant

---

[64] Solmsen (1962).   [65] Leach (1966).   [66] Lefèvre (1977) 33–5.
[67] Solmsen (1962) 79.

of the universally dreaded sea tragedy. This pet aversion of antiquity makes the frequency of the metaphor meaningful; and it is this that both the Propertian poem and the other passages artistically transcribe. What the epigrammatists play upon, or Horace congratulates himself about, or Ovid trifles with is the unchallengeable, if often latent, assumption that a love débâcle can be as dreadful as death at sea. 1.17 does not challenge this assumption.

The result is an all too familiar grievance (*haecine parva meum funus harena teget?* 'Will that patch of sand cover my corpse?' 8), a ritual swipe at the πρῶτος εὑρετής (*a pereat, quicumque ratis et vela paravit | primus* ... 'Ah perish whoever first constructed hull and sail' 13–14) and two outbursts of self-pity in 11–12 and 19–24. The latter passage records standard funeral scenes; in fact, it depicts 'a bourgeois funeral with all the trimmings, with Cynthia behaving like any conventional and affectionate mortal'.[68] This is the *tu mihi sola domus, tu, Cynthia, sola parentes* mood; for Cynthia read Delia as well and consider Tibullus 1.3.5ff. Like Propertius, Tibullus is in danger far from home and fears that in the event of his death he might have to forgo funeral attentions from his family and Delia. There is little to choose between the two elegists here but it seems to me that should Prop. 1.17.19–24 be quoted to 'a connoisseur who has not read the elegists for some time', she or he would most probably be tempted to pronounce it Tibullan.[69] We have come to associate such domesticated sentimentality with the Tibullan version of the death theme, probably because it is Book 2 which is seen as the *locus classicus* of the Propertian version. It is, therefore, instructive to spot an 'uncharacteristic' *Todesgedanke* in the Monobiblos, if only because it allows a clearer view of what is novel in Book 2. To sum up, 1.17.19–24 is a conventional funeral because what Propertius feels throughout the poem is the traditional *Todesangst* inspired by the nautical emergency.[70] Are we entitled to infer

---

[68] Hubbard (1974) 34.

[69] The phrase as well as the 'test' derive from G. Lee (1962) 149–50.

[70] When Propertius envisages in 1.17.19–24 a would-have-been funeral he is echoing, in an elegiac context, the complaint of the storm-tossed epic hero. Hom. *Od.* 5.306ff., 12.403ff. and Virg. *Aen.* 1.34ff. seem to have laid down some of the rules for all subsequent sea-storm descriptions. W.-H. Friedrich (1956) 77–87 reaches the interesting conclusion that, in contrast to the Homeric, Silver Latin epic allows a constant interaction between the depicted storm and the hero's emotional situation, between the outer and inner landscape. H. O. Kröner (1970) 388–408 made a further contribution in an article which undertakes to assess the differences between the *episches* and *elegisches Unwetter*. On the evidence of Ov. *Tr.* 1.2, *Fast.* 3.585–600 and Prop. 1.17 he concludes that, in contrast to epic, elegiac sea-storm descriptions are geared to the speaking poet-lover, the natural phenomenon itself being dwelt upon only in so far as it sets *his* feelings and fantasies in motion; and that as a result it is not vividness of description that is achieved but the depiction of the shifts and turns of the lover's emotional state (p. 405). This is, I think, basically sound and in Ovid's case, where we can compare an essentially epic treatment of the *Seesturm* in *Met.* 11.410–748 with his other elegiac versions, Kröner's remarks are

that the lover to whom a lonely shore suggests thoughts of a 'bourgeois' funeral is not yet prepared to suffer an 'aesthetic–decadent' death on a lonely shore? I think we are. This unconventional type of lover will not come into his own until Book 2, so the differences in dramatic detail and emotional state between 1.17 and 2.26b (loneliness and dejection vs. partnership and exultation) can be safely belittled. 2.26b revalues the metaphor out of which 1.17 grows; thus it is at two removes from the figure of the epigrammatists or, for that matter, of Ovid.

I have by now attempted to assess the nature of 2.26b both in terms of its formal structure and of its reversal and/or revaluation of a traditional figure for love; in fact, as it has been argued, the structure, by privileging the fantasy of 29ff., alerts us to the possibility of different sense and sensibility. We deal with familiar items but rearranged to create unfamiliar tensions, revealed as such by 43 and 57–8. These lines, 57–8 in particular, represent a comprehensive climax and advance an erotic vision whose shape is hard to parallel in classical literature. Whether it is this poet's property we shall probably never be able to affirm, yet a brief survey and some conjectures are in order.

That venue of shipwrecked bodies, the *Greek Anthology*, normally pictures solitary victims, nowhere an amorous couple. Classical Greek poetry offers such arresting descriptions of shipwreck as Archilochus, fr. 79a.2–5 Diehl, κύ[μασι] πλα[ζόμ]ενος. | κἀν Σαλμυδ[ησσ]ῶι γυμνὸν εὐφρονέσ[τατα] | Θρήικες ἀκρό[κ]ομοι | λάβοιεν...[71] 'drifting on the waves. And I hope the Thracians, who shave all but the top of their head, are kind to him when he turns up naked on the shore of Salmydessus', but nothing that might suggest, even in its general outline, a comparable situation; nor is classical dramatic poetry likely to have provided inspiration of any kind. We enter more promising areas when we come to the legendary erotic pairs of Hellenistic and later times. Here the great majority of sea disasters will have affected lovers, not merchants. This is, in effect, what we find in Ovid's Ceyx and Alcyone (*Met.* 11.410–748). Here the body of the shipwrecked and drowned lover drifts towards the coast but the catastrophe is alleviated by the subsequent transformation. The treatment of the story, like much else in the *Metamorphoses*, bears the unmistakable stamp of the absorbing and romantic pathos that the

illuminating. But still I am not quite sure that 1.17, with its tantalisingly vague, almost nondescript, setting (recognised as such by Kröner himself, 406), profits much from this comparison. 2.26b is more directly reminiscent of the epic storm (the ubiquitous winds (35–6); *quicumque et venti miserum vexastis Ulixem* (37); and Zeus' thunderbolt (43)) but Kröner has not considered it.

[71] West, *IEG* I 150, follows Blass in attributing this piece to Hipponax.

Greeks had managed to keep out of their literature until about Euripides' arrival on the scene. Like the Ovidian story, 2.26b presupposes this reformation of taste but it also implies an emancipation of sensibility that Ovid's erotic verse seems never to have taken advantage of.

It is the kind of sensibility that will not deny the attractiveness of a corpse washed ashore. Propertius is not pioneering here; take the following passage:

ἔνθα δὴ τὸν Θυμοίτην μετ' οὐ πολὺν χρόνον ἐπιτυχεῖν γυναικὶ μάλα καλῇ τὴν ὄψιν ὑπὸ τῶν κυμάτων ἐκβεβλημένη καὶ αὐτῆς εἰς ἐπιθυμίαν ἐλθόντα συνεῖναι· ὡς δὲ ἤδη ἐνεδίδου τὸ σῶμα διὰ μῆκος χρόνου, χῶσαι αὐτῇ μέγαν τάφον, καὶ οὕτως μὴ ἀνιέμενον ⟨ὑπὸ⟩ τοῦ πάθους, ἐπικατασφάξαι αὐτόν.

A short time after that Thymoetes chanced upon the body of an extremely beautiful woman which had been washed ashore by the waves, and he was assailed by a desire for her. However, a long time had passed since her death, and corruption was already setting in, so he made a grave mound for her; yet, as even so passion refused to loosen its grip, he killed himself beside the tomb.

This sounds like *roman charogne* but is in fact part of a story tucked away in Parthenius' Ἐρωτικὰ Παθήματα (31); It is, to borrow a triad of inevitable terms used by W. Clausen in analogous circumstances, 'erotic, morbid, grotesque'.[72] Parthenius and his manual were not available to Cornelius Gallus only. 'It is becoming clear', wrote Sullivan in 1976, 'that the influence of Parthenius...was considerable.'[73] In terms of subject matter his influence on Propertius may have been indirect but since we know almost nothing of his poetic practice it is arbitrary to say more than that.[74] If, for instance, he had himself embroidered upon Thymoetes' story in one of his lost poems, just as he had done with the legend of Caunus and Byblis, we could do with knowing what he made of that intriguing εἰς ἐπιθυμίαν ἐλθόντα συνεῖναι. In any event, the passage just quoted shows death and sensuality in flagrant harmony. One is tempted to posit, at the risk of oversimplification, a development from a 'healthy' classical dissociation through sentimentalisation and sensationalism towards various forms of *rapprochement*. Full documentation is of course impossible, but what documents we possess and the conjectural

---

[72] Clausen (1964) 190.   [73] Sullivan (1976) 118.

[74] See Crump (1931) 102ff.; Boucher (1965) 261; Sullivan (1976) 119 n. 12; and Crowther (1976) 65–71 for a survey of Parthenius' data and a sober assessment of his place on the Roman literary scene of the first century B.C.

combinations they warrant at least do not run counter to this schema.[75] The assortment of love and lust and death and self-destruction commended to Gallus confronts us with a *Zeitgeist*, not with the tastes of an eccentric individual. Parthenius was one of the last exponents (some say the last) of a tradition of Hellenistic poetry within whose periphery evidence must now be sought that in composing 2.26b Propertius kept his mind on a celebrated yarn of love and drowning.

To put it thus is to leave oneself with no other choice than the legend of Hero and Leander. When Virgil alludes to it in *G*. 3.258–63 he does not bother to name the protagonists and we may infer that by his time it was well known.[76] There has been a long debate on its origins and first artistic formulation but we need only mention here the two principal theories. According to some scholars the story received its first poetic treatment in those literary circles of Rome that in the second half of the first century B.C. comprised such Greeks as Parthenius, Antipater of Thessalonica and Dionysius of Halicarnassus. Others suggest an earlier Hellenistic poem, even by Callimachus himself, and argue that it was this that served as a common model for the two most extensive treatments that we possess, namely, Ovid, *Her*. 18 and 19 and a Greek epyllion entitled Τὰ καθ’ Ἡρὼ καὶ Λέανδρον, composed by Musaeus probably in the second half of the fifth century A.D.[77] The next move was an attempt to reconstruct the Hellenistic model on the basis of the similarities between the Roman and the Greek poem – a move that would probably have been less hazardous, even superfluous, had an Hermoupolis papyrus (Pap. Berol. 21249) been better preserved. As it is, some 50 mutilated hexameters dangle before our eyes the detritus of a scenario which featured a seascape, an intrepid lover, very significantly a tower (πύργον) and probably a tell-tale lamp, all prominent ingredients in our

[75] E. Rohde's (1914) 12–177 chapter on 'Die erotische Erzählung der hellenistischen Dichter' still affords the, to my mind, best panorama of this particular field. Whatever objections some individual hypotheses and points of interpretation may give rise to, the alert reader is certain to discern in the vast store of information and in the survey of the treatment of erotic subjects in Greek literature from the archaic period onwards some of the parameters of an evolution which put erotic passion in itself at a premium and inaugurated modes of erotic expression which the 'subjective' framework of Roman love elegy showed to advantage.

[76] To the same conclusion points Servius' comment on l. 258: *quia cognita erat fabula*.

[77] These questions have been discussed with a thoroughness and frequency that cannot be fully recorded here. Rohde (1914) 142ff. made some influential points; K. Kost's (1971) 15ff. introduction to a grand edition of Musaeus' poem will shepherd the reader through the main issues, as will T. Gelzer (1975) 302ff.

Although the question of authorship is not, strictly speaking, crucial to my discussion, in the following I shall be assuming, as most though not all scholars do, that *Heroides* 18 and 19 are by Ovid's hand.

extant poetic versions;[78] as E. J. Kenney put it in a 1980 Jackson lecture: 'if this is not part of a poem about Leander, coincidence has been putting in overtime'.[79] Whether, as Maehler and Lloyd-Jones and Parsons incline to believe; it is that Leander poem which, written around the middle of the first century B.C., created the *frisson* we can infer both from Virgil's brief mention and Ovid's emulation, is less certain.[80] Another woeful fragment of ten lines preserved on a Rylands papyrus (P. Ryl. III 486)[81] shows, if nothing else, that for a spell all and sundry tried their hands at this fascinating story – which of course would again confirm the hypothesis, made long before the papyri added their evidence, of the one successful and widely influential poem. With this, so to say, background reassurance we may now fall back on the certainties of Ovid and Musaeus.

The most salient similarity concerns the description of the storm that seals Leander's fate. Unlike Lord Byron, the youth commits himself to the currents of Hellespont on a stormy night. Since Ovid's presentation is refracted in order to meet the exigencies of the letter form, let me quote first from Musaeus' straightforward exposition:

> Ζεφύρῳ δ' ἀντέπνεεν Εὖρος
> καὶ Νότος εἰς Βορέην μεγάλας ἐφέηκεν ἀπειλάς·
> καὶ κτύπος ἦν ἀλίαστος ἐρισμαράγοιο θαλάσσης.
> αἰνοπαθὴς δὲ Λέανδρος ἀκηλήτοις ἐνὶ δίναις
> πολλάκι μὲν λιτάνευε θαλασσαίην Ἀφροδίτην,
> πολλάκι δ' αὐτὸν ἄνακτα Ποσειδάωνα θαλάσσης,
> Ἀτθίδος οὐ Βορέην ἀμνήμονα κάλλιπε νύμφης   (316–22)

Eurus, the east wind, blew against Zephyrus, the west, Notus, the south, wildly threatened Boreas, the north; and endless was the crashing of the loud-thundering sea. Leander, suffering dreadfully in the inexorable swirl, prayed many times to Aphrodite of the sea, many times to Poseidon himself and reminded Boreas of his Athenian bride.

In the Ovidian epistle (18.25ff.) Leander complains that the raging storm has thrice thwarted his attempts to cross the straits. Boreas is singled out for reproach:

---

[78] See Lloyd-Jones and Parsons (1983) 402, no. 901A. The *editio princeps* of the papyrus by H. Maehler in *MPhL* 6 (1982) was not available to me.

[79] To the unpublished text of this lecture Professor Kenney kindly allowed me access.

[80] See Lloyd-Jones and Parsons (1983) 402: 'haec fortasse isti aetatis hellenisticae carmini esse tribuenda, quod in manibus habuisse Vergilium, Strabonem, Ovidium...crediderunt viri docti.'

[81] See Lloyd-Jones and Parsons (1983) 453, no. 951: 'omnia incerta, sed nos quidem poetastro haec Aegyptiaco tribuamus, non poetae illustri et imitando.'

At tu, de rapidis immansuetissime ventis,
  quid mecum certa proelia mente geris?
in me, si nescis, Borea, non aequora saevis!
  quid faceres, esset ni tibi notus amor?
tam gelidus quod sis, num te tamen, improbe, quondam
  ignibus Actaeis incaluisse negas?   (*Her.* 18.37–42)

But you, most cruel of the violent winds, why are you waging war against
me with such obstinacy. If you don't know it, it is me you rage against, Boreas,
not the sea. What would you be doing if you hadn't known what it is like
to be in love? For chilly as you are, could you deny, you shameless wind, that
there was a time when you warmed to an Athenian love?

Hero in her own letter (19.121ff.) matches these grievances but blames
the storm mainly on Neptune:

at tibi flammarum memori, Neptune, tuarum
  nullus erat ventis impediendus amor:
si neque Amymone, nec   (*Her.* 19.129–31)

But you, Neptune, should remember your own affairs and not put winds in
the way of love: if neither Amymone, nor

and she goes on to list more of the god's *amours*. Kost's (1971) note on
Musaeus 320–2 says all that needs to be said on the quoted lines, namely,
that Leander's prayers to Poseidon and Boreas in Ovid are conclusive
evidence that both the latter poet and Musaeus found them in their
Hellenistic source, though Ovid, turning to account the limitations of the
letter form, divided up the prayers between the two lovers to emphasise
the identity of their feelings and wishes. What Kost's note does not say
is that the storm in Prop. 2.26b.35ff. is also the result of the same natural
causes, and itself the cause of similar prayers to the same gods on similar
grounds, in almost the same order, and with, as the poem's final couplet
clearly suggests, practically the same results: *saevus licet urgeat Eurus,* |
velaque in incertum frigidus Auster agat 'though savage Eurus blows | And
freezing Auster fills the sails at random' (35–6); *sed non Neptunus tanto*
crudelis amori 'But Neptune will not be cruel to so great a love' (45)
...*testis Amymone* 'witness Amymone' (47); *crudelem et Borean rapta Orithyia*
negavit 'Even Orithyia, forced by Boreas, never called him | Cruel' (51).
The last mythological story is also referred to in Ov. *Am.* 1.6.53 *si satis*
es raptae, Borea, memor Orithyiae and Stat. *Theb.* 12.630 *raptae qui conscius*
Orithyiae, where *memor* and *conscius* are much closer to Musaeus' ἀμνήμονα;
'obviously, echoes of an expression in a famous Greek poem', says Kost

on these verbal similarities.[82] A well-known Hellenistic poem would, in fact, best account for the allusiveness in Virgil as well as for the parallels between Ovid and Musaeus. I suggest that 2.26b.35ff. were written with the same poem in mind and that the sequence: invocation of contesting winds – invocation of Neptune – Boreas, being the same as in Musaeus' passage, most probably reproduces the sequence in their source. To dismiss the whole thing as pure coincidence on the grounds that the description of the storm is a widely used set piece and the myths quite common is to fly in the face of three facts: (a) that these items are simultaneously present and, in the case of Propertius and Musaeus, similarly arranged; (b) that Ovid, who could not present the storm as actually taking place, took special care to preserve, symmetrically apportion and duly emphasise the invocations, thereby acknowledging and underlining their prominence in his model; (c) that the theme, not all that frequent, of Prop. 2.26b is drowning and love, although of a different order.

A less obvious fact lends, I think, further support to this reconstruction. Combined reference to the North Wind as Orithyia's seducer and to Neptune occurs again in Prop. 3.7.13–15:

> infelix Aquilo, raptae timor Orithyiae,
> quae spolia ex illo tanta fuere tibi?
> aut quidnam fracta gaudes, Neptune, carina?[83]

Ah ill-omened North Wind, dreaded by the raped Orithyia, what rich spoils could you ever hope to win from him? Neptune, why do you gloat over the wreck of a ship?

Now it has already been remarked that the verbal parallels between this poem and 2.26b, besides making the contrast between their respective treatments of a sea disaster all the more poignant, indeed because of this contrast, suggest a more or less conscious link. Of this we would be more confident if it were possible to detect in 3.7 traces of the Hellenistic poem on Hero and Leander. Presumably, what the poem must have had in

[82] See Kost (1971) on Mus. 322.

Ovid soars to the solemn invocation from a snivelling context, only to plummet into a paraclausithyric banality in the following pentameter: *huc ades et surdas flamine tunde foris* 'come here and batter the deaf door with your blasts'. There is bathos here, and those who could recall the hexameter's original milieu would have surely better appreciated it. I can see no reason to suppose, as K. Morgan (1977) 43 does, that Ovid is here sending up Propertius 3.7.11–14 in particular.

[83] Sandwiched between 11–12 and 17–18 the apostrophe to Aquilo and Neptune has struck some as less than elegant. Transposition seems to me unnecessary, though not out of the question, but the following discussion should make it clear that the idea of a reader scribbling ll. 13–16 on the margin (no sooner mentioned than dismissed by Hubbard (1974) 84 n. 2) is not to be entertained at all.

common with 3.7 is the description of the agony of the drowning protagonist. If whenever Ovid's epistles and Musaeus' epyllion and, as my suggestion is, 2.26b present strong similarities, we can claim to have caught glimpses of their common model, it should be possible to draw a similar conclusion on the strength of substantial points of contact between Musaeus and 3.7. Leander is finally overpowered by the waves:

> πολλὴ δ' αὐτομάτη χύσις ὕδατος ἔρρεε λαιμῷ,
> καὶ ποτὸν ἀχρήιστον ἀμαιμακέτου πίεν ἅλμης.
> καὶ δὴ λύχνον ἄπιστον ἀπέσβεσε πικρὸς ἀήτης
> καὶ ψυχὴν καὶ ἔρωτα πολυτλήτοιο Λεάνδρου.   (327–30)

Of its own force much water poured down his throat, and he swallowed the useless drink of the irresistible sea. And the bitter wind put out the faithless lamp, and the life and the love of long-suffering Leander.

Paetus does not fare better:

> et miser invisam traxit hiatus aquam   (3.7.52)

and his miserably gaping mouth drank down the hateful water

> subtrahit haec fantem torta vertigine fluctus;
> ultima quae Paeto voxque diesque fuit.   (3.7.65–6)

As he spoke thus the waves caught him in a downward eddy; for Paetus those were the last words and the last day.

It is important to make a distinction between the comparatively high frequency of the idea and the distinctive expression it is given here. Homer has ὣς ὁ μὲν ἔνθ' ἀπόλωλεν, ἐπεὶ πίεν ἁλμυρὸν ὕδωρ 'so he perished there having drunk salty water' (*Od.* 4.511) – as predictable and literal as some of the other passages Kost adduces in his notes on Musaeus 327–8.[84] But *invisam* strikes the reader much as ἀχρήιστον does; and the

---

[84] Kost's (1971) *ad loc.* fine array of parallels includes Prop. 3.7.52 and 3.7.65–6, but he does not suggest any special link. Another parallel listed by Kost is Euphorion's... ζωὴν δὲ μεθ' ὕδατος ἔκβαλε πᾶσαν | χεῖρας ὑπερπλάζων ἅλμη δ' ἔκλυσσεν ὀδόντας (fr. 44.4–5 Powell = fr. 48 van Groningen). That the Hellenistic poet was indebted to this for the description of Leander's drowning I find quite likely; that Prop. also had Euphorion in mind I find even more so. Line 2 of the same fragment καὶ οἱ πήχεες ἄκρον ὑπερφαίνοντο ταθέντες (of the drowning Iphimachus) is a fine touch turned to account in 2.26a.11 *at tu vix primas extollens gurgite palmas* (of the drowning Cynthia), and, as far as death at sea is concerned, Euphorion may have strongly commended himself to Prop. at least twice if τῆς οὐδ' αἴθυιαι οὐδὲ κρυεροὶ καύηκες (fr. 130 Powell = fr. 131 van Groningen, where see commentary; the fragment comes from a poem whose remains on a first-century B.C. – or possibly A.D. – papyrus suggest a rapid change of images, but 'il est pratiquement impossible de déterminer le sujet principal') represents a salvage from another sea disaster; cf. *A.P.* 7.652.5–6 χὡ μέν που καύηξιν ἢ ἰχθυβόροις λαρίδεσσι | τεθρήνητ' ἄπνους εὑρεῖ ἐν αἰγιαλῷ; *A.P.* 7.374.3–4 ἀλλά με δαίμων | ἄπνουν αἰθυίαις θῆκεν ὁμορρόθιον and *A.P.* 7.277 (= Gow–Page 1265–8, where see note on αἴθυίη).

rhetorical pathos of both 330 and 66 resides in their quasi-zeugmatic quality. One would like to surmise a common source for both descriptions. Of course Leander perishes for love, Paetus for money; but once at sea they are in the same boat and so liable to the same treatment.

The description of the central event of drowning, the unavailing reproach of unresponsive gods and perhaps Paetus' wish that his corpse may be returned by the waves to his mother (3.7.63–4, cf. *Her.* 18.197–8) are strong indications that 3.7, no less than 2.26b, was composed under the spell of the pictorial and verbal felicities of an acclaimed Greek poem. Their testimony, therefore, should be added to those of Musaeus' epyllion and Ovid's epistles. It should surprise no one if the story of Ceyx and Alcyone (*Met.* 11.410–748), probably written not much later than the epistles, showed comparable 'symptoms'.[85] In view of Ceyx's determination to sail to Claros Alcyone asks to be allowed at least to share the risks of the voyage:

> me quoque tolle simul. certe iactabimur una,
> nec, nisi quae patiar, metuam; pariterque feremus,
> quidquid erit, pariter super aequora lata feremur. (*Met.* 11.441–3)

> *Take me with you too; at least we shall be tossed by the waves together, nor shall I fear anything beyond what I am going to suffer along with you; whatever is in store for us, we shall face together, and together we shall roam the wide oceans.*

In no other story of the *Metamorphoses*, comments F. Bömer, is *una* so frequently emphasised as in this one; 'likewise Prop. 2.26.29ff.'[86] I believe one should not hesitate to speak of an intentional echo, the more so since the Ovidian passage seems to embroider upon the magisterial 2.26b.43 *certe isdem nudi pariter iactabimur oris.* This vision of togetherness must have come straight from Propertius, but another similarity opens up a vista of more intricate relations. Ceyx is drowning: *Ceycis in ore | nulla nisi Alcyone est* 'none but Alcyone is on the lips of Ceyx' (*Met.* 11.544–5); *sed plurima nantis in ore est | Alcyone coniunx* 'but as he swims he keeps calling the name of Alcyone, his wife' (*ibid.* 562–3). Similarly, in a pathetic apostrophe to Paetus:... *quid cara natanti | mater in ore tibi est?* 'why is your dear mother's name on your lips, as you swim?' (3.7.17–18). Bömer's cautionary note on 544–5 ('The topos "nomen in ore"...is so widespread that any

---

[85] The relationship between the epistles and *Met.* 11.410ff. seems to go quite deep. Ceyx is wrecked by a storm (478–569) which must owe some of its details to the description of the heavy sea that must have figured prominently in Ovid's source for Hero and Leander and which *Her.* 18 and 19 had to miss out on. Cf. Kenney (1979) 417 n. 73.

[86] Bömer (1980) *ad loc.*

attempt to find out Ovid's immediate models (Propertius or Euphorion, for instance) is doomed to failure') can perhaps be qualified in the sense that we may eliminate all other possibilities except 3.7 and the lost Greek poem. This is still hazardous, but where a tangible pattern of affiliations emerges, as I believe it does here, one should be able to afford less compunction than usual. A further clue must not be overlooked. Ceyx in the same breath calls Alcyone's name and prays that the waves may cast his body ashore where she can see it: *illius ante oculos ut agant sua corpora fluctus,* | *optat...* (*Met.* 11.564–5). Paetus, as we have just seen, has a similar wish in 3.7.63–4 and so does Leander in *Her.* 18.197ff. Musaeus has nothing of the sort but ll. 338–9 (...παρὰ κρηπῖδα δὲ πύργου | δρυ-πτόμενον σπιλάδεσσιν ὅτ' ἔδρακε νεκρὸν ἀκοίτην 'And when she saw her lover dead by the base of the tower, his body torn by the rocks') may suggest an outcome that, in his model, the drowning Leander had prayed for. Perhaps one should trace the wish back to the Hellenistic Leander.

The discussion in the previous pages has aimed at pointing up a cluster of poems and poetic passages which, in varying degrees and in accordance with their generic conventions or thematic needs, are all indebted to a famous Hellenistic treatment of the Hero and Leander legend. Apart from the Ovidian epistles and Musaeus' poem, which rehandle the same legend, it is Propertius 2.26b which we can claim to have consciously taken over the greatest number of recognisable details.[87] If these questions have been discussed at greater length than seems relevant to the main issue, it is because this is a valid way to establish with as much certainty as the gaps in our knowledge allow a fact of the utmost importance for the conception and import of 2.26b. If in composing this poem Propertius drew on a poetic formulation of Leander's adventure, and if no other model can be traced for the simultaneous drowning fantasy, then it is more probable than not that the shape of the culminating vision of this composition is quite unprecedented. If Leander's prayer in *Her.* 18.197ff. had figured, as I have suggested, in Ovid's model, this may have prompted the image of 2.26b.43; again, the phrasing of this line is strongly reminiscent of similar descriptions in the Greek epigrams. But to locate the matrix of the Propertian death fantasy one need not look further than the finale of the famous story. Musaeus' version does not seem to have altered its essentials:

[87] It is worth noting that if, as is here suggested, 2.26b assimilates details from the Hellenistic poem on Leander's adventure, the ineffectiveness of the deities of ll. 45ff. (which, as I have argued above, pp. 90–1, Propertius insinuates by a battery of ironical devices) acquires a basis in the poem's literary background. Within this literary framework the reintroduction of this particular rescue team can hardly have struck the reader as a good omen and the possibility suggests itself that Propertius may be capitalising on just this 'mistrust'.

παρὰ κρηπῖδα δὲ πύργου
δρυπτόμενον σπιλάδεσσιν ὅτ' ἔδρακε νεκρὸν ἀκοίτην,
δαιδαλέον ῥήξασα περὶ στήθεσσι χιτῶνα
ῥοιζηδὸν προκάρηνος ἀπ' ἠλιβάτου πέσε πύργου.
καδδ' Ἡρὼ τέθνηκε σὺν ὀλλυμένῳ παρακοίτῃ,
ἀλλήλων δ' ἀπόναντο καὶ ἐν πυμάτῳ περ ὀλέθρῳ.   (338–43)

*And when she saw her lover dead by the base of the tower, his body torn by
the rocks, she ripped the finely wrought mantle from around her breasts and
rushed to plunge headlong from the steep tower. Hero died with her dead lover
and so even in the final disaster they had joy of one another.*

Hero falls to her death beside or upon Leander's corpse, at any rate close
enough to be able to enjoy with him love in death. That this is what
happened in Musaeus' model is clear from Virg. *G.* 3.263 *nec moritura super
crudeli funere virgo.* The outcome of Hero's suicidal leap brings the two
pairs visually in line. ἀλλήλων δ' ἀπόναντο goes with this posture and
it is a fair guess that it was not Musaeus who first struck this sharply erotic
note.[88] Propertius must have been confronted with a considerably
'advanced' erotic vision but what he made of it is something of a quite
different order: out of the lover's morally commendable ἐπαποθνήσκειν
there grows the aspiration for the lovers' sensual συναποθνήσκειν.[89] One
would like to believe that such leaven as Parthenius 31 contains
contributed to the transformation.

Ovid was not the only one to be smitten by this vision. Propertian
commentators like to compare Petronius 114.8–12, where Encolpius and
Giton, threatened with shipwreck, lash themselves together to make their
embrace immune to the waves and to ensure that their corpses drift
together at sea or are cast up on the same shore: *si nihil aliud, certe diutius,
inquit,* [i.e. Giton] *iuncta nos mors feret, vel si voluerit misericors ad idem litus
expellere*...It is a tribute to Petronius' *doctrina* that scholars have traced
in this and the next chapter echoes of Propertius and Ovid.[90] In fact, a
close reading of the two chapters will disclose a joint contribution by
Prop. 2.26b and 3.7 as well as by the Ceyx and Alcyone episode. In laying
under contribution this particular set of passages the author of the

---

[88] Cf. Kost (1971) on 342–3.

[89] The idea of a lover's praiseworthy ὑπεραποθανεῖν or ἐπαποθανεῖν was quite common. It
was clearly articulated by Plato, *Symp.* 179e: ἐτόλμησεν [i.e. Achilles] ἑλέσθαι, βοηθήσας τῷ
ἐραστῇ Πατρόκλῳ καὶ τιμωρήσας, οὐ μόνον ὑπεραποθανεῖν ἀλλὰ καὶ ἐπαποθανεῖν τετελευτηκότι
'He bravely chose to help his lover Patroclus and avenge him, and not only died for his sake
but also *joined* him in death.' Cf. also *id. Phd.* 68a and see Kost (1971) on Mus. 343.

[90] S. Lundström (1967–8) 68–97 shows that this is not the only place where Petronius displays
knowledge of the elegists. It is perhaps not irrelevant to remember that the author of the *Satyricon*
betrays a distinct penchant for the funerary, as W. Arrowsmith (1966) 304–31 well showed.

Satyricon may have known for sure that they had in common something which we can only recapture through laborious reconstruction.

Yet the last kiss, the *ultimum gaudium* (114.9) that Encolpius solicits from Giton falls short of the climax reached in 2.26b; their homosexual effusions have more than a whiff of the burlesque; nor has the Greek love romance anything more compelling to offer.[91] Quest of symmetry in vision and sensibility would take one further afield. On a couple of occasions I have used the term 'aesthetic–decadent', not least because I had A. C. Swinburne in mind. I would like to think that the Oxford undergraduate who could correct Benjamin Jowett on matters of classical literature had not neglected his Propertius. In 'Les Noyades', a poem from *Poems and ballads* (1866), a young supporter of the French *ancien régime* is condemned to death together with a beautiful maiden whom he has loved 'his whole life long':

> And the judge bade strip and ship them, and bind
> Bosom to bosom, to drown and die.

He lingers voluptuously over the lot that awaits their naked corpses:

> For the Loire would have driven us down to the sea,
> And the sea would have pitched us from shoal to shoal;
> And I should have held you, and you held me,
> As flesh holds flesh, and the soul the soul.

> Could I change you, help you to love me, sweet,
> Could I give you the love that would sweeten death,
> We should yield, go down, locked hands and feet,
> Die, drown together, and breath catch breath.[92]

Familiar sights: the corpses naked and interlocked; pitched by the waves on the sandy shore; and the recording of the ultimate breath. Whether this is to our taste or not, our Romantic–Decadent heritage counsels acquiescence when a scholar, by way of comment on this poem, writes: 'the young man exults in this consummation through death'.[93] I have endeavoured to show that Propertius has conceived, shaped and endowed the vision of 2.26b in a way that entitles the classical scholar to articulate a similar reaction without being hissed out of court.

[91] Whether apart from the Latin passages Lundström (1967–8) 77ff. and E. Courtney (1962) 86ff. adduce, Petronius was also casting a parodying eye on Greek love romance is not easy to decide. To be sure, shipwreck incidents were almost a set piece in this genre (see Courtney, p. 98 and the passages he quotes from Achilles Tatius and Xenophon of Ephesus, but cf. Lundström, p. 72) but the only such scene that antedates Petronius is one in the fragmentary Ninus romance (Courtney, pp. 92–3), where the dramatic situation is quite different from that in Petronius 114–15. On the date of the Ninus romance and the relevant fragment see B. E. Perry (1967) 153ff. [92] Gosse and Wise, 1 182–4. [93] I. Fletcher (1973) 26.

6

IN AMORE MORI:
CRIME PASSIONNEL

> Le meurtre passionnel nous paraît avant tout *un procédé de recon-*
> *quête*... Il a bien des apparences de la haine, mais cette haine diffère
> de la haine 'en général', comme le meurtre passionnel se distingue
> de la catégorie commune du crime...
>
> Georges Gargam, *L'Amour et la Mort*

Some of those who have grappled with the incoherent despair ostensibly portrayed in 2.8 ended up by contracting the very distemper they were anxious to explain. O. L. Richmond, Butler and Barber, Damon and Helmbold,[1] all carved up, with varying degrees of inhibition, the forty lines that our MSS invariably transmit as a unity. Those who came to the poem's rescue (chiefly Rothstein, Abel, La Penna, Enk)[2] have had the better cause, and more recent editions confirm that no recidivist activity has since taken place.[3] One suspects that this consensus has been reached not so much on the basis of Enk's vague 'si carmen psychologice interpretamur'[4] as because of the kind of arguments that T. A. Suits has advanced – namely, that the elegy exhibits a recognisable, well-balanced formal structure.[5] That this structure has been employed to accommodate what on the evidence of most interpreters must be a wellnigh unbalanced lover should be seen as one of the strengths of the poem. To a certain extent our response to 2.8 must be conditioned by an awareness of the

---

[1] Damon and Helmbold (1952) 228–9.

[2] Abel (1930) 46–50; La Penna (1951) 34–6; Enk, introd. note, 119–20; see also Enk (1956) 181–5.

[3] For example, Barber, Luck, Camps, Giardina, Richardson, Hanslik, Fedeli (1984).

[4] See Enk on 2.8.11–16. He tends to fall back on this remedy without much ado; cf. his note on 2.9.41–8.

[5] Suits (1965) 427–37. He has drawn attention to the pattern of changing addressees in the poem:

A1	1–12	(12 lines)	to the friend
B1	13–16	(4 lines)	to Cynthia
C	17–24	(8 lines)	to himself
B2	25–28	(4 lines)	to Cynthia
A2	29–40	(12 lines)	to the friend

This might well be an intentional formal polish, it would provide an additional argument for the poem's unity and would by no means be incompatible with the idea of a principal (and crucial to the poem's reading) division-point which, as we shall see, occurs after l. 16.

tension between formal neatness and turbid emotional content; in fact, this much can be extrapolated from such analyses as, for instance, Suits, in the above-mentioned article, and D. P. Harmon offer.[6] Yet this is only part of the story. What these and other critics have failed to do is to bring a functional awareness of the wider Propertian context to bear on the structural and other challenges posed by 2.8, which they have instead read as a self-sufficient and self-validating piece. To realise the limitations of this approach one has only to follow the agonised attempts, in successive interpretations, to establish the curve of passion and to indicate at which points on it murder, suicide and mythological illustration must be located. It is perhaps a comment on the arduousness of the task when the thought sequence of 2.8 is pronounced uniquely complex. But is it really so?

It is first of all important to sound the dramatic depth of ll. 1–16. With the *ex abrupto* beginning of the poem raising hopes of tangible drama, a 'friend' was inferred from the *amice* of l. 2 to whom 7–10 could then be assigned,[7] and whose disappearance thereafter led Boucher to describe the poem as either a dialogue that takes place within the poet's mind or a tragic monologue where passion clashes with reason.[8] In the same vein La Penna finds little difference between soliloquy and dialogue with an imaginary interlocutor,[9] and a similar view is also taken by Lefèvre, who sees Propertius' compositional technique in 2.8 as the kind of 'monologo interno' for which no model can be traced in Greek literature and which must, therefore, have been evolved by the Roman poets; since the first such monologue is that of Ariadne in Catullus 64.132–201, her creator is credited with a technique which was also used, according to Lefèvre, in the poem addressed to Allius and which was subsequently imitated by Virgil in *Eclogue* 10 to be brought to perfection some ten years later by Propertius. This sounds more schematic than in Lefèvre's actual exposition, which seems to me to make a considerable contribution to the understanding of the technique and unity of 2.8.[10] But whereas Lefèvre went beyond previous scholars in putting this poem in a broader and more illuminating context, like them he overlooked the significance of the Propertian context itself. To take account of it is by no means to refute or seriously modify his arguments. It is rather that his 'monologo interno' can be easily subsumed under our hypothesis of a structural pattern to which 2.1, 2.13 and 2.26b can arguably be seen to conform.

---

[6] Harmon (1975) 417–24.
[7] See mainly Abel (1930) 46–7 and Suits (1965) 432–3.
[8] Boucher (1965) 390.   [9] La Penna (1977) 64.
[10] Lefèvre (1977) 25–31.

2.8.1–16 deal in fairly familiar motifs: the girl is being lost to a rival (1–6); the wheel of love (7–10); the ineffectiveness of poetry (11–12); the *servitium amoris* (13–16). Compare 2.26b.21–8: the girl won back (21–2), through poetry (23–6), from a rival (27–8). Compare also 2.24b.17–32: the girl is being unfaithful (17–20); poetry proves unavailing (21–2); the rival is challenged (23–8); the wheel of love will turn again (30–2). In such passages there is no dramatic specificity to suggest episodes from a love affair, whether fictional, real or idealised, and Cynthia, or whoever the woman involved may be, could not have less individuality. If Propertius is dramatising something here, this is the familiar theorem of love and love poetry as threatened by, or triumphant over, different emotional and artistic ideals. Therefore, further comparison with the first movements of 2.1 and 2.13 suggests itself. At the risk of being unduly repetitive but in the hope of making the resultant 'isomorphism' as clear as possible, let me add another piece of statistics to the picture of pp. 82–3. In 2.1, 2.13, 2.24b (on which see also pp. 140ff. below) and 2.8, all first verse-paragraphs consist of sixteen lines, the sole exception being 2.26b, where the corresponding section has exactly half that number. What seems to me to redeem this from being a mere numerical accident is the fact that in all these cases (and allowing for the apostrophe to Maecenas in 2.1.17–46) Propertius invariably follows up the first paragraph with versions of *Liebestod*. I believe that these versions constitute the real *differentia* in this particular species of elegies. In their economy the first paragraphs can claim to be little more than formal preludes devoid of real dramatic substance. So if in 2.8.1–16 Propertius does not create 'the illusion of himself uttering on an occasion outside literature, in life'[11] it is because he is not interested in doing so.

It is, therefore, gratuitous to object that 1–10 ill sort with 11–12 and that '7–10 are a little out of harmony with 1–6';[12] unnecessary to give 7–10 to a friend; not particularly illuminating to suppose that in the same lines the poet is parroting his friend's inapplicable wisdom;[13] rather exaggerated to claim with Abel that 2.8 marks the high point of the Propertian 'Dialogtechnik'.[14] Further, it is important to realise that arguments from the psychological state purportedly depicted by one particular poem can be profitably tempered with arguments from the poet's compositional habits. It is quite likely that these habits owe

[11] See Lyne (1980) 125. 'The poem', he also remarks, 'is still in a sense dramatic. But its dramaturgical unity, its impression *of being itself a drama*, goes...Abandoning dramatic unity, he has abandoned the illusion of the poem being in itself a drama in life.'

[12] See Butler and Barber, introd. note, 203–4.

[13] Suits (1965) 433.   [14] Abel (1930) 49–50.

something to the 'monologo interno'. It certainly seems to be so in 2.8, for although this poem exemplifies a unique and ubiquitous Propertian propensity to what Tränkle calls 'lebendige Wechselrede',[15] its peculiarly vehement change of addresses strongly recalls one prominent feature of that technique, namely, the rapid succession of changing apostrophes.[16] Its use brings about marked tonal differences, especially in the first sixteen lines. Tears of rage and grief over the loss of the *puella* (1–6) give place to attempted self-consolation (7–10) and retrospective realisation of misplaced, poetic and otherwise, donations (11–12); this, in turn, releases a savage indictment of the tyranny imposed by her and endured by him:

> ergo iam multos nimium temerarius annos,
> improba, qui tulerim teque tuamque domum?
> ecquandone tibi liber sum visus? an usque
> in nostrum iacies verba superba caput? (2.8.13–16)

> *Was I really fool enough, over so many years*
> *To put up, selfish girl, with you and yours?*
> *Have you ever thought of me as free, or will you always*
> *Hurl at my head arrogant words?*

Content here is matched by style; 'outside this passage, *ecquandone* is only attested by Velleius and Apuleius. It is certainly an emphatic form of the colloquial language.' Furthermore, *ec-* is used to introduce urgent questions, and *-ne* after interrogative pronouns marks an emphasis in conversational style.[17] Lefèvre would, I suppose, see here a dialectics of passion;[18] the poem is certainly designed to suggest something of the sort. But neither he nor Boucher, who speaks of a *tragic* monologue featuring passion vs. reason,[19] seems appreciative of the transparent artifice of passion and its purposiveness in 2.8. So by way of introduction to a reading of this elegy which departs from the received opinion about these lines, let me simply say that the first section of the poem up to l. 17 is a redeployment of a set of literary motifs in such a way as to impress on readers a heightened sense of the lover's victimisation and thus prepare

---

[15] Tränkle (1960) 143ff.

[16] See Lefèvre (1977) 28–31. Tränkle (1960) 147, who classifies this as one of the forms the Propertian 'lebendige Wechselrede' tends to take, notes that this poet uses apostrophe ever more frequently than other Roman poets in general.
Mr I. M. Le M. DuQuesnay reminds me that the technique of the mime (a genre whose relations with elegy are now being widely recognised; see pp. 163–4 below) in Propertius' day, often one of frequent changes of scene and variety of emotional response on the part of the mime actor, may not be irrelevant to 2.8.1–16. Cf. esp. Hubbard (1974) 52–3.

[17] Tränkle (1960) 156.

[18] See Lefèvre (1977) 43. The phrase is F. Klingner's and he used it of Ariadne's monologue in Catull. 64.   [19] Boucher (1965) 390.

them for the proceedings of 17ff. It will be noted that Propertius perpetrates the glaring inconsistency of presenting his beloved first as a passive victim of abduction (*eripitur...cara puella* 1) and then as a hardened sadist. Those who assume solid drama behind these lines usually explain such things away as understandable symptoms of a distraught mind. I would instead suggest that we inaugurate here an ironical understanding with the poet roughly along the lines of Nietzsche's *aperçu* that there is no greater liar than an indignant man.

Yet indignation is necessary if the woman of 1–16 is to be plausibly induced into the role of *agent provocateur* that she assumes after the main thought punctuation at l. 16.

> sic igitur prima moriere aetate, Properti?
>   sed morere; interitu gaudeat illa tuo!
> exagitet nostros Manis, sectetur et umbras,
>   insultetque rogis, calcet et ossa mea!   (2.8.17–20)

> *And so, Propertius, will you die in your first youth?*
> *Die then. Let her revel in your ruin.*
> *Let her torment my spirit, persecute my shade,*
> *Jump on my pyre and trample on my bones.*

There has been speculation as to whether the first couplet betokens purpose (that is, suicidal intentions) or despair (that is, wasting away from unrequited love).[20] This is a question of how the mistress disposes and what the poet-*lover* proposes, but one to be asked, if it is worth asking at all, after due emphasis has been placed on the fact that it is the *poet*-lover who disposes and his heroine who proposes. Savagery is the order of the day and the elegiac coquette has foisted upon her a grotesquely exaggerated *Schadenfreude*. Lines 17–20 offer a crescendo of irreverence from her getting a kick out of his death towards kicking his relics. The staccato of the five third-person-singular present subjunctives, no less than the rigidity of the syntactical parallelism in 19–20, seems to reflect the crude straightforwardness of the archaic code of honour from which Propertius borrows the gestures of l. 20.[21] The corresponding decrescendo of psychological plausibility makes the whole thing sound like a study in disproportion, an impression which one cannot help applying retrospectively to the outburst of 13–16. The subjunctives of 18–20 provide yet another clue to the tenor of the passage: they are intrinsically similar to

[20] See, for instance, Suits (1965) 430: 'But there is nothing in 17–18 to indicate that the poet envisions a death that is anything more than a wasting away from unrequited love; *sed morere* (18) betokens despair, not purpose.' My own argument turns on the idea of purposeful despair.
[21] Cf. Hom. *Il.* 4.177 τύμβῳ ἐπιθρῴσκων Μενελάου κυδαλίμοιο 'leaping upon the tomb of glorious Menelaus', and see Enk on 2.8.20.

those of 2.26b.35 (*licet urgeat*), 36 (*agat*) and 42 (*incendat...licet*) in that either set of subjunctives acts as the catalyst for a sequence of emotional or natural movements that culminate in the lovers' death. The moods the poet uses are a reliable guide to the mood he is in.

Loss of one's mistress to a rival, musing on love's vicissitudes, amatory use of poetry, the idea of a household (*domum* 14), the verbal indignities suffered by the lover, his enslavement (15–16) – the composite picture that emerges belongs to the *Alltäglichkeiten* of elegiac existence; indeed, in its schematic way it contains all the essential ingredients of a low-life scene such as one may come across in Lucian, an urban mime or a New Comedy play. Only when this is fully realised can the, so to say, generic transposition that takes place in 17ff. be fully appreciated. Propertius measures his experience first by what seems to be a tragic (17–28), then by an epic yardstick (29–40). That this sequence is not accidental can be seen from l. 10: *et Thebae steterunt* [steterant Barber] *altaque Troia fuit* 'Thebes was a power once and Troy a city.' Thebes and Troy as well as being the respective settings of Haemon's and Achilles' love affairs are bywords for tragedy and epic, and the passages they herald have been carefully apportioned twelve lines each.[22] The articulation of the poem makes it a fair guess that Propertius aggrandises passion to make it commensurate with the generic atmosphere rather than seizing, on the spur of the moment, upon famous examples in order to illustrate the unfolding of a given emotional crisis. Here is a clue for the critic, who may find it more rewarding to follow the dramatic gestures of the pair along the generic axis of elegy–tragedy–epic than to attempt the intriguing task of indicating which thought carries which association within a mind that professes to have run riot. What this means in practice we shall learn when we come to ll. 21ff. First we must consider what kind of tragic and epic Propertius is likely to have had in mind and, if necessary, introduce some qualifications.

It is easy to miss the fact that 2.8.37–8

> at postquam sera captiva est reddita poena,
>   fortem illum Haemoniis Hectora traxit equis.

> *But after late amends restored the captive to him,*
> *He dragged brave Hector behind Thessalian steeds.*

presupposes a version of the story with an un-Homeric emphasis. A good reminder is due to Rothstein: in the *Iliad* the return of Briseis is not enough to bring Achilles back on the battlefield nor is her return a

[22] Cf. Williams (1980) 95.

condition for the latter's reconciliation with Agamemnon. She becomes a bit less shadowy later in the poem but not in a sense that might account for her prominence in 2.8.[23] Now it is always possible to think of Propertius as giving a sentimental inflection to the Homeric incident in order to bring it within the compass of his interests. By the same token he could be held responsible for the pathetic twist in Briseis' equally un-Homeric lament in 2.9.9–16, were it not that an analogous scene in Quintus Smyrnaeus 3.551ff. alerts us, as Rohde was first to argue, to the possibility of a common Hellenistic source.[24] Food for speculation of this sort is also provided by 1.15.9–14, where Calypso weeps over Ulysses' departure in the very Hellenistic posture of a *fanciulla abbandonata*. Here we are faced with three possibilities: Rohde's theory that the incident was treated by Philetas in *Hermes*, an epyllion which told of Ulysses' adventures in a modern-romantic vein;[25] Heinze's view that one need not assume a Hellenistic model for 1.15.11ff;[26] and Fedeli's hypothesis of an epyllion, presumably later than that of Philetas, followed by Propertius here and Ovid in *Ars Am.* 2.123ff. and featuring Calypso in the situation of the forsaken Ariadne in Catull. 64 or Dido in the *Aeneid*.[27] As long as the Hellenistic factor (postulated in one form or another by all three scholars), is kept present to the mind, favouring any one of these options is the last thing that really matters. Fedeli, however, goes deeper into the question in that he makes an essential allowance for the role of visual art in shaping Propertius' example. Pliny's report in *HN* 35.132 that a Hellenistic painter, Nicias of Athens, was credited with, among other paintings, a *Calypso sedens* should add some colour to Propertius' *multos illa dies incomptis maesta capillis | sederat* 'For many days in mourning, hair unkempt, | She sat' (1.15.11–12). Hellenistic sensibility and/or model and pictorial quality come to mind again apropos of 2.9.9–16 and 2.8.31ff.[28]

If these two passages betoken an amorous Achilles so does much of the post-Homeric evidence. That of all Homeric heroes he had to bear the brunt of Hellenistic sentimentalisation is hardly surprising. Indeed, so pervasive was the *Zeitgeist* that turned the hardy warriors of the heroic saga into tender gallants that even such an unlikely fellow as Hercules had eventually to toe the line.[29] Rohde remarks on the tendency to dilate

---

[23] See Rothstein on 2.8.37.
[24] See Rohde (1914) 110 n. 1; he believed, without elaborating, that ll. 9–18 did not belong to 2.9. Cf. also Enk on 2.9.10.   [25] Rohde (1914) 80, 111.
[26] Heinze (1914) 118 n. 1.   [27] Fedeli (1977) 90–2.
[28] On the pictorial quality of 2.8.33–4 and 2.9.9–16 see Boucher (1965) 265.
[29] See Rohde (1914) 44, 111ff.

upon any suggestion of *amour* in the original versions of mythological stories, and one often gets the feeling that in this respect the post-classical author has made a mile out of the inch he was offered.[30] As far as Achilles is concerned, the later melodrama echoed by Propertius and Quintus Smyrnaeus may be seen in embryo already in *Il.* 9.342–3 ὡς καὶ ἐγὼ τὴν | ἐκ θυμοῦ φίλεον, δουρικτητήν περ ἐοῦσαν 'as I loved her with all my heart, though she was booty won by my spear'. What kind of poem this may have given rise to must remain a guess. An epyllion expatiating on a sentimental interlude of the hero's expedition would have shown affinity of conception with those hexameter compositions that sang, *ad nauseam* it seems, of the Hylas-addict Hercules. His untimely end, on the other hand, could have inspired a later tragedian. There seems to have existed a close link between post-Euripidean tragedy and erotic poetry of the period, and it is quite possible that some stories of gloomy and destructive passion became subjects of erotic poetry after they had been given a full-scale dramatisation.[31] It may be that Propertius' reading of the Homeric texts themselves was, as a participant put it in a recent *colloquium*, 'précise, profonde, constante'; but it is good to see the same scholar being aware that when it comes to Propertius' imitation of Homer one should exercise prudence in view of the numerous intermediaries that are likely to have been active between them.[32] 2.8.21–8 have put such prudence to the test and found it wanting.

> quid? non Antigonae tumulo Boeotius Haemon
>   corruit ipse suo saucius ense latus,
> et sua cum miserae permiscuit ossa puellae,
>   qua sine Thebanam noluit ire domum?
> sed non effugies: mecum moriaris oportet;
>   hoc eodem ferro stillet uterque cruor.
> quamvis ista mihi mors est inhonesta futura:
>   mors inhonesta quidem, tu moriere tamen.   (2.8.21–8)

At Antigone's tomb did not Boeotian Haemon
Fall dead, wounded by his own sword,
And mix his bones with those of the poor girl
Without whom he would not go home to Thebes?
But you shall not escape; you have to die with me.
The blood of both shall drip from this same blade.
Though such a death for me will be dishonourable,
I'll die dishonoured – to make sure you die.

---

[30] Rohde (1914) 109; cf. Lyne (1978) 182.
[31] Cf. Rohde (1914) 107–8 and see p. 123 below.
[32] J. F. Berthet (1980) 153, 149.

Butler and Barber make no bones about it: 21–4 are 'peculiarly inept. Antigone was no faithless mistress; in all forms of the legend it is in grief for her death that Haemon slew himself. The inappropriateness is intensified by the lines which follow (25–8), in which the poet threatens to murder Cynthia.'[33] Enk sees no difficulty: 'Propertius does not compare Cynthia with Antigone, but he compares himself with Haemon, who could not live without Antigone.'[34] It is always possible to claim that the vast incongruity between paradigm and contextual situation in our passage is a deliberate attempt to convey the incoherence of the distraught lover's thoughts.[35] But the temptation to penetrate the incoherent is strong and some scholars set about registering the coruscations and scintillations of a free-association process in the poet's mind. Suits, for example, argues that the vision of a sacrilegious Cynthia calls up by contrast the image of the pious Antigone risking her life to bury Polynices, which in turn evokes, this time by association, other details of her story that Propertius finds relevant to his own situation; he concludes: '...the example is not adduced to justify suicide but itself suggests suicide. The thought of Antigone has led to that of Haemon, which only then leads to that of suicide.'[36] One wonders whether when these lines were written l. 10 was still in the author's mind, for otherwise he seems to be clearly conscious not only of the significance of l. 10 but also of a number of thematic and verbal links that Propertius has forged between 29–40 and 1–12. A. W. Allen's, D. P. Harmon's and R. Whitaker's solutions are by and large those of Suits,[37] while Kölmel takes a different line inasmuch as he sees the significance of the example exclusively in the 'subjective feeling' it implies for Haemon, namely the lover's despair. By identifying himself with a mythological lover who has reached the peak of such despair Propertius achieves a moment of complete parallelism between mythological past and 'real life' present.[38] Here is ingenuity of the empathetic (all this is achieved by an act of 'Hineinfühlen', writes Kölmel) rather than of the reasoning kind, but it seems to me that in this particular case even a reader deficient in both will be able to find his way provided that he has the will to look further than Sophocles; for it is the common assumption of all the above scholars that the couple of 21–4 come straight from his *Antigone*[39] – which is by no means a settled

---

[33] Butler and Barber, introd. note, 204.   [34] Enk (1956) 184.
[35] See, for instance, Camps on 2.8.21–2.
[36] Suits (1965) 431; cf. Williams (1980) 86.
[37] Allen (1962) 137–8; Harmon (1975) 420–1; Whitaker (1983) 119ff.
[38] Kölmel (1957) 118.
[39] Suits (1965) 431 n. 13 indicates awareness of a further possibility – fleetingly and in a way that has no bearing on his argument.

question. Rothstein's undeservedly neglected note on 21ff. says as much, but also passes over vital evidence.

One may start from Sophocles himself. On the basis of ll. 1228–9 of his *Antigone* and taking up a clue from S. M. Adams, W. M. Calder III has suggested that Sophocles knew of a version of the story in which Antigone was murdered by Haemon but as he 'did not consider such a murder to be compatible with his characterisation of the heroine' he 'chose...to *imply* a suicide but carefully used ambiguous language that never *literally* contradicted a murder'.[40] If this is so, Hyginus' *Haemon se et Antigonam coniugem interfecit* 'Haemon killed himself and his wife Antigone' in the story summarised in *fab.* 72 may well be an echo of the version to which Sophocles made his slight bow. Now since Hyginus gives a course of events far removed from that in Sophocles, and since his narrative obviously derives from a drama, it is quite likely that at least one other dramatist either chose to be explicit, if Sophocles was indeed ambiguous, or simply exploited different possibilities of an already diversified myth. Despite Welcker and a few other scholars that followed him,[41] this cannot have been Euripides, for Aristophanes of Byzantium, in the hypothesis of the Sophoclean *Antigone*, reports a happy outcome for his homonymous and, but for some forty-odd verses, lost play.[42] However, this is less important than the fact that love is in evidence in these surviving fragments in a way that it is not in the whole of Sophocles' play. It is a natural inference from Aristophanes' πλὴν ἐκεῖ [i.e. in Euripides] φωρα-θεῖσα [i.e. Antigone] μετὰ τοῦ Αἵμονος... 'there, however, she was caught in the act together with Haemon' that, unlike Ismene, Haemon did help Antigone bury her brother, which means, as Wecklein saw a long time ago, that the play showed the lover's ἔρως being stronger than sisterly affection.[43] But in Sophocles it is not eros that brings about the heroine's

[40] Calder (1960) 31–5.

Ant. 1228–9 read: ὦ τλῆμον, οἷον ἔργον εἴργασαι· τίνα | νοῦν ἔσχες; ἐν τῷ συμφορᾶς διεφθάρης; 'O my luckless boy, what have you done? What was the purpose of this, what misfortune made you lose your mind?' Creon addresses these words to Haemon when he finds him beside Antigone's hanged body. Calder argues that if ἔργον does not refer to Haemon's entrance into Antigone's tomb (as only Jebb among the commentators seems to think), then it must refer to the *hanging*. But if so, Kreon's words make no sense – since this is precisely what he would have liked to see, and he should have been grateful for Antigone's initiative. So why τλῆμον and διεφθάρης? The verb, says Calder, indicates that 'Kreon fears the boy deranged. This is plausible if he believes that Haimon has murdered his betrothed, but is nonsense otherwise.' If Creon is wrong, it is remarkable that he is nowhere contradicted in the play as we have it.

[41] See Welcker (1839–41) II 563ff., III 1588–9 and cf. Paton (1901) 267 n. 1.

[42] See Rothstein on 2.8.21; Enk on 2.8.24; and Paton (1901) 267ff.

[43] Wecklein (1878) 191–2; cf. the conclusions of Paton (1901) 275 concerning the Euripidean *Antigone*; see also *RE* I (1894) 2402–3 and *Kl. Pauly* I 379.

downfall nor is her fiancé's suicide unalloyed erotic despair, as attention to ll. 1220ff. will make sufficiently clear; and perhaps the ode to Eros in 781ff. is so famous because it stands out as the only sustained comment on emotion in a play otherwise dominated by moral concerns. These may not have been absent from the Euripidean version, but the one certainty that tempers speculations as to its plot concerns the prominence of the love theme. Given by no less than Euripides, the sentimental twist to the story will have been as influential as it was congenial to post-classical tastes. Two consequences can plausibly be envisaged. The one is that in retrospect Sophocles' heroine was also seen in a more sentimental light.

J. M. Paton suggests the other: 'With such a play [i.e. Euripides' *Antigone*] as a basis and a desire to give the story again a tragic ending, without imitation of Sophocles, it is easy to see how the dramatic original of Hyginus...arose.'[44] Paton's own choice falls on what is to us a mere name, viz. the dramatist Astydamas, whom *C.I.A.* II.973 shows to have been the first in 341 B.C. with the trilogy *Achilles*, *Athamas* and *Antigone*.[45] A few years earlier Wecklein had opted for Theodectes,[46] a contemporary of Astydamas, whose surviving lines, according to T. B. L. Webster, 'are pleasantly written with Euripidean echoes'.[47] But one may prefer to fall back on Heydemann's more liberal concept of a post-Euripidean Antigone,[48] for it leaves room for considerations that can take us into the vicinity of Propertius. To read Hyginus, *fab.* 72 with its terse *Haemon se et Antigonam coniugem interfecit* at its conclusion is to breathe the very air of the love romances Parthenius abstracted for the use of Cornelius Gallus. The Greek poet had a notable penchant for ἐρωτικὰ παθήματα whose *dénouement* stipulated more often than not violent death in the course of sentimental paroxysm. The formulas do not vary much: πολλὰ κατολοφυραμένη διεχρήσατο ἑαυτήν 'after long lamentations she killed herself' (Parthenius 4.7); ἔπειτα δὲ πολλὰ ἀποδυρόμενος τὴν παῖδα διεχρήσατο ἑαυτόν 'then, having much wept over the young woman, he killed himself' (10.4); καιομένη σφοδρῷ ἔρωτι τοῦ παιδὸς ἀναρτᾷ ἑαυτήν 'burning with a mad passion for the lad she hangs herself' (14.4); λαθοῦσα τὰς θεραπαινίδας ἀπό τινος δένδρου ἀνήρτησεν ⟨ἑαυτήν⟩ 'she slipped the attention of her maids and hanged herself from a tree' (28.2); ὡς ἔννοιαν ἔλαβε τῶν συμφορῶν, διαχρῆται ἑαυτόν 'when the disasters came home to him he killed himself' (13.4). The last but one is associated

---

[44] Paton (1901) 275.
[45] See Webster (1954) 304–5; *Kl. Pauly* I 379.   [46] Wecklein (1878) 190–1.
[47] Webster (1954) 303; see also pp. 302–8 for a discussion of the facts concerning Astydamas and Theodectes.
[48] Quoted by Wecklein (1878) 190; I have not been able to consult this book.

with Euphorion and the last actually comes from his *Thrax*. Other luminaries such as Philetas and Hermesianax are laid under contribution too, and it is a fair guess that they supplied material to more than one mythological handbook. Is it not possible that one of these poets took up in a poem a less well-known but more bloody and sensational variant of the Haemon–Antigone story which had been previously treated by a dramatist of the Euripidean persuasion?[49] We should keep present to the mind that later tragedy was laid under contribution by Hellenistic poets and raconteurs, especially when it portrayed the violent and tragic outcome of unbridled erotic passion.[50] If this particular story was culled for an anthology or mythological handbook one is tempted to translate Hyginus back into something like κατακτὰς τὴν Ἀντιγόνην διεχρήσατο (or, perhaps, ἐπικατέσφαξεν) ἑαυτόν. Whether Propertius worked out his own précis or went for a ready-made one need rouse no controversy.

The 'tragic couple', therefore, of 2.8.21ff., no less than the epic one of 29ff., is at one remove, at least, from the world in which the modern reader is conditioned to locate it. To be sure, the bloodshed still takes place in a very Sophoclean tomb (*tumulo* 21), but this is partly due to technical considerations to be presently examined, and besides, the point of the preceding discussion has not been to disprove Sophoclean reminiscence altogether – this would be perverse since, after all, Sophocles was the first to give the story a dramatic shape with which Roman audiences became thoroughly familiar through Accius' emulation –[51] but to widen and modify, so far as it is necessary, the literary experience that is normally brought to bear on the assessment of the example. In this sense

[49] It is not necessary to suppose that the story had a whole poem dedicated to itself. It may have occurred as one in a series of exempla, but in which poem it would be difficult to decide. PSI 1390 preserves two brief and obscure fragments of Euphorion, the only certainty about which is, according to Bartoletti (1965) 167, that they treated stories of exceptional violence, incestuous intrigues and conjugal atrocities. If they belong, as the same scholar believes, to the *Thrax* (which seems to have been taken up with a series of ἀραί) then this poem may be thought of as a candidate. It is well worth remembering that Euphorion was particularly fond of the less well-known variants of legends, that in his stories 'souvent le dénouement est triste' and also that 'Eros et Aphrodite... souvent invitaient à des actions criminelles'. See van Groningen, pp. 256–8.

No one who has read the byzantine and sanguinary tale of Leucippus in Parthenius 5 will regard its source, Hermesianax, as a less likely candidate, especially if, as Day (1938) 21 suggests, in the second book of the *Leontion* this poet transferred the scene from the countryside (see p. 68 n. 46 above) to the palaces of kings in order ' to continue the idea that no one, king or shepherd, can escape the tragic cruelty of love'. As for Philetas, on our flimsy evidence he appears, I think, less likely than both.　　　　[50] See Rohde (1914) 107–8.

[51] One may agree with Alfonsi (1973) 303 that Prop. was familiar with Roman tragedy but if, as Sconocchia (1972) 273–82 argues, Accius' *Antigona* (of which some ten lines are preserved) was, with one or two minor changes, faithfully modelled on Sophocles' *Antigone*, there seems to be no reason to believe that 2.8.21–4 were indebted to the Roman any more than to the Greek play.

the case for Sophocles in 2.8 raises the same range of problems as that for Homer, and demands the same alertness and discrimination. Surely, Propertius was not the first to attract Troy and Thebes into the orbit of erotic verse, and the critic cannot go about the task of interpreting 2.8 as if he actually was.[52] This poem compasses highlights from tragedy and epic but reproduces them on a preponderantly Hellenistic scale.

I would, then, suggest that 2.8.25–6 are by no means an afterthought sparked off by the preceding mythological example but represent the fulfilment of a pattern of the legend that has been uppermost in the poet's mind from the very outset; they are the dramatic, 'real-life' replica of a mythological (and un-Sophoclean) *crime passionnel*, just as 2.13.51–2, by summing up the procedures prescribed in 2.13.17ff., are revealed as the replica of a mythological death scene. The belief that in 21–4 Haemon does away with himself because Antigone has already done so rests on instinctive reaction rather than on textual evidence. If *tumulo* is a Sophoclean reminiscence (cf. *Ant.* 885–6 κατηρεφεῖ τύμβῳ), it is also a precarious one, for 24 *qua sine Thebanam noluit ire domum?* points resolutely away from Sophocles.[53] Nor is it any good soliciting l. 23 (*et sua cum miserae permiscuit ossa puellae*) for help, since, apart from reasons to be given below, Propertian practice with funerary words is, as 1.19 especially has shown, uniquely fluid, and *ossa* is no exception; it covers a wide range from 'hard bones' to what in the context of 1.19.18 can scarcely be more substantial than 'ghost' or 'shade';[54] here it can certainly point to a midway condition, viz. corpse, and I can see nothing in the passage that forbids us to put the corpse on Haemon's criminal record. *sed non effugies* in l. 25 does not mark a break with the preceding vision. Propertius does not readjust to the reality of his present situation because the asymmetry between what Antigone did to herself and what he proposes to do to

---

[52] The Hellenistic industry of treating *sub specie amoris* material originally belonging to other spheres was, it seems, too thorough and extensive to allow a first-century B.C. love poet appreciable initiatives of his own. Some room for manoeuvre was left, but not much. Sound as it is in principle, Schöne's (1911) 36 warning against postulating a lost treatment of a mythological story followed by Propertius, whenever he seems to depart from the common version, is seldom vindicated by a scrupulous study of the evidence. To simply say with Verstraete (1980) 263 that Prop. 'is capable of adapting epic material to the perspective of his love poetry', or with Dalzell (1980) 30 that 'he read Greek epic with the eyes of a Roman elegist, picking out what was best suited to his purpose', is all too often to risk conspiring with Fortune against the unknown Hellenistic eroticiser.

[53] See Rothstein on 2.8.21.

[54] That this can happen here does not detract from the general truth of Hubbard's (1974) 35–6 remarks (on which cf. also p. 187 below); but referring to the doctrine of Propertian editors that the poet says 'bones' when he means 'shade' and vice versa she says: 'This is quite false' – which, I believe, leaves no room for the play of imagination.

Cynthia flashes through his mind. At what purports to be the boiling-point of his fervour he cannot be expected to start l. 25 with *quare tu quoque non*... This is histrionics of form calculated to present a 'pre-meditated crime' as 'manslaughter without malice aforethought'. But the case for premeditation is far too strong, as the craftsmanship of 21ff. attests.

Line 21 *quid? non Antigonae tumulo Boeotius Haemon* shows verbal music and meaning, sound and sense in indissoluble harmony. Its long syllables embody something of Quintilian's *grave, sublime* and *ornatum* (*Inst.* 9.4.130–1). It also seems to me to offer a metaphor from sound values less open to the charge of mere subjectivity. Socrates' (Pl. *Cra.* 426c–427c) word-coiner associates *o* with rotundity; *u* has often been associated with obscurity.[55] The mind's eye is encouraged to see Antigone's κατηρεφεῖ τύμβῳ (Soph. *Ant.* 885–6), the inward ear to hear the reverberation of mournful sounds in the *o*'s, no less than in the diphthongal sequence *ae...oe...ae*: Poesque sounds in a Poesque vault, conveyed by a hexa-meter which has a claim on our attention by sheer concentration of Greek names. *et sua cum miserae permiscuit ossa puellae* (23) is a 'golden' line (ab verb AB); what matters here is word arrangement rather than sound: bones piled up on either side of the verb are evenly mingled. If l. 25 is a conscious refashioning of Naevius' *numquam hodie effugies, quin mea moriaris manu* (fr. 15 Ribbeck) it would be tempting to conjecture that Propertius saw fit to assign to the pair of Roman lovers a distinguished native tragic utterance.[56] The word patterning of the next hexameter (aA verb bB) courts attention and, like 23, vouches for the simultaneity of the contem-plated demise. Finally, 27–8 round off, through the expressive repetition of freely admitted guilt, the process of calculating resoluteness introduced by l. 17. This is surely Murder as one of the Fine Arts; and probably it is murder with a sexual motive. To establish this, an enquiry into its location and manner of execution must now be launched.

An important clue will emerge if we care to recall the case of 2.26b, for both poems propound a coveted isochronism of the lovers' death, although by different procedures. If, as the facts and figures on pp. 113–14 suggest, in the economy of 2.8 lines 1–16 have a function comparable to that of ll. 21–8 in 2.26b, the relation between the two passages must be seen as one of designed counterpoint: a schematised amatory situation in the one is reversed, almost motif by motif, in the other. Because 2.8 posits a recalcitrant mistress, 2.26b a reciprocating

---

[55] On this and related phenomena see L. P. Wilkinson's (1966) 46–85 fascinating chapter on 'Expressiveness', esp. 46 and 64 on the expressive value of certain letters.
[56] Cf. Shackleton-Bailey (1956) *ad loc.*

one, what is achieved through the felicitous complicity of storm and embrace in one poem must be enforced by murder in the other. The affinity of mood in the subjunctives of 2.8.17–20 and 2.26b.35–42 has been commented upon (see above p. 116). The obsessive reiteration of the bilaterally accepted emblems of oneness in 2.26b.30–3, and especially 43 (*isdem oris*), accentuates by contrast the unilaterally adopted instrument of simultaneity in 2.8.26 *eodem ferro*. Another link is forged by the cross-reference between 2.8.27–8 and 2.26b.57–8. The couplets are conspicuously akin in that they spell out the ethics of their respective *Liebestod* by means of the same term which is underlined either through repetition (*inhonesta* 27 and 28) or pointed litotes (*non inhonestus* 2.26b.58). It will also be noted that 2.26b.57 (*quod mihi si ponenda tuo sit corpore vita*) visualises the terminal posture in which the lover's act in 2.8.25–6, as well as that of Haemon in 22–3, must naturally result, and which is left to the reader's imagination in 27–8. In a word, structural analogies as well as pictorial and verbal links all go to show that the death fantasy of 2.8 may be thought of as corresponding to that of 2.26b. The criminal activity of 2.8.21–6, which on the face of it seems to carry the emotional agitation to its logical conclusion, demonstrates by virtue of its position within the poem's structure a theorem of erotic sensibility which in 2.13 was put to the test by means of the funeral, in 2.26b by means of the shipwreck imagery. 2.8.27–8 is the rider which confirms that what we have here is just another instance of *in amore mori* – without *laus*. This, to be sure, makes 2.8 the 'moral' antithesis of 2.26b. Shall we, then, accordingly, allow 'ravishment' its full semantic range and see in the mutinous female of 2.8 a 'victim', as we have seen in the compliant one of 2.26b a 'beneficiary'? How far and on what grounds is it possible to make a case for the potential suggestiveness of 2.8.21ff.?

The ancients could readily recognise the sexual symbolism of weapons.[57] It would be otiose to enlarge here upon a habit of thought that indulged in all sorts of innuendos, *double entendres* and *risqué* jokes, as J. N. Adams has recently documented in his very systematic study of the Latin sexual vocabulary. A couple of examples, however, may be allowed to pave the way to my main point. Propertius uses the word *arma* at least once as an unmistakable sexual metaphor in 4.8.88 *et toto solvimus arma toro* 'and we revolved and resolved our quarrel all over the bed' to mark in this particular way both the end of hostilities between himself and Cynthia and the consummation of their reunion.[58] Expressly pointed weapons and

---

[57] See Adams (1982) 19ff., upon which I have throughout this paragraph freely drawn.
[58] Cf. Edwards (1961) 138.

objects offered opportunities for more poignant and sustained ambiguity. Leucippe's mother in Achil. Tat. 2.23.5 dreams that ληστὴν μάχαιραν ἔχοντα γυμνὴν ἄγειν ἁρπασάμενον αὐτῆς τὴν θυγατέρα 'a robber carrying an unsheathed sword dragged away her daughter'. This is not a demanding piece of oneirology, although the novelist feels a clue, given in the course of the dream, to be in order: μέσην ἀνατεμεῖν τῇ μαχαίρᾳ τὴν γαστέρα κάτωθεν ἀρξάμενον ἀπὸ τῆς αἰδοῦς 'that with the knife he ripped the belly open starting below from the pudenda'. It is a short step from this to the duel that Apuleius described in *Met.* 2.17: Lucius stands by in priapic preparedness when Photis commands him to kill and be killed: *occide moriturus*. The whole thing is described as *proelium*, whereas in Apuleius' Greek source, Pseudo-Lucian, *Asinus* 9–10, the corresponding encounter is presented as a wrestling match, a κλινοπάλη. Apuleius betrays a predilection which may well have afforded the votaries of Romanness the small satisfaction of *militia amoris tota nostra est*, but he seems eventually unwilling to face up to the ultimate implications of his metaphor. These can be seen in Ausonius, *Cent. Nupt.* 131, where the male having discharged his duty collapses bloodless: *labitur exsanguis*. But this blood-as-semen metaphor had long ago been given the sanction of Lucretius in a section of the *D.R.N.* with which Propertius has already been seen (p. 45 above) to be creatively familiar.

Lucretius compares love-making to a single combat:

> irritata tument loca semine fitque voluntas
> eicere id quo se contendit dira libido,
> idque petit corpus, mens unde est saucia amore.
> namque omnes plerumque cadunt in vulnus et illam
> emicat in partem sanguis unde icimur ictu,
> et si comminus est, hostem ruber occupat umor.   (4.1045–51)

these places are stirred and swell with seed and there arises the desire to expel the seed towards the object to which fierce passion is moved and the body seeks that body, by which the mind is smitten with love. For as a rule all men fall towards the wound, and the blood spirts out in that direction, whence we are struck by the blow, and, if it is near at hand, the red stream reaches our foe.

The passage bursts with physical energy, its visual effect being almost that of a human geyser gushing out alternative streams of white and red. Lucretius' sharp sensuous imagination is as much a matter of Hellenistic *ars* as it is of individual *ingenium*, and E. J. Kenney has well shown that at least as far as his pronouncements on love are concerned he was operating with distinctly Hellenistic imagery and concepts.[59] In our

[59] Kenney (1970) 38ff.

passage, moreover, the chromatic counterpoint recalls that master stroke of the Hellenistic brush over which we paused in 2.13 (see p. 66 above). Propertius must have found a great deal that was to his taste here; and it is not inconceivable that he wrote 2.8.21ff. with a keen eye on Lucretius' image. For when Haemon/Propertius turns upon Antigone/*puella* he seeks that body whence his love wound comes, *mens unde est saucia amore*. Sexual connotations cannot be ruled out for the *permiscuit* of l. 23,[60] especially if we recall 4.7.94 *mecum eris, et mixtis ossibus ossa teram* 'You'll be with me, and bone on mingled bone I'll grind.' In *mecum moriaris* of l. 25 chance may have tessellated the sound of Lucretius' *umor*, vital throughout the quoted passage and explicit in l. 1051. If chance was again active in *quidem, tu moriere* (28), we have been deprived of a phallic cryptogram that would have given shape to the vague arousal of *irritata tument loca semine* in 1045. Perhaps one should not give in to fancy and see these meaning-producing, random collisions of letters as something right up Lucretius' street;[61] but then it is not irrelevant to remember that the game itself is by no means un-Roman and that Cicero was capable of a similar legerdemain, but with far more obscene particularities in mind: *hance culpam maiorem an illam dicam* (*Fam.* 9.22.2).[62] And even as one prepares to give Propertius the benefit of the doubt, suspicion creeps up that *cruor* in l. 26 may be flowing under false colours, for a few lines before the passage quoted from Lucretius *vestemque cruentent* (1036) describes the effects of nocturnal emission.[63] It is a delightful surprise to find S. Commager ending a footnote with the words: 'The scene in 2.8.21–6 may owe something to Lucr. 4.1048ff.';[64] but it is also a tantalising one, for he leaves it at just that. I hope that the preceding discussion has gone some way towards showing that such debt cannot be ruled out on aprioristic grounds. Nor is it to be thought that the Lucretian passage

---

[60] See *TLL s.v. misceo* 1081.46ff. and Adams (1982) 180–1.

[61] But 'fancy' may be far too strong a word to use in this connexion. More than once Lucretius makes a point of drawing the analogy between letters as elements of words and atoms as elements of the world: 1.196–8, 1.823–27, 1.912–14, 2.688–99. In all these passages *elementa* is used of both the letters and the atoms. Now, this idea, which Lucr. had probably taken over from the earlier atomists, Leucippus and Democritus, seems to have been singled out for ridicule by non-epicureans. The stoic Lucilius, for example, in Cic. *Nat. D.* 2.37.93 wryly observes that he who can ascribe the genesis of the world to the collision of atoms should have no difficulty in believing that if innumerable casts of the twenty-one letters of the alphabet were jumbled up and flung on the ground, they would result in a readable text of Ennius' *Annals*. Is it, then, too fanciful to think that in *this* context Prop. may once again be creaming off the fun of the philosophical issue? See esp. Snyder's (1980) 31–51 chapter 'Lucretius' analogy of the *Elementa*', but cf. also Friedländer (1941) 16–17; Bailey (1947) 1 158–9 and his note on 1.196.

[62] See Adams (1982) 97–8 on *landica*.

[63] *cruor* in 2.8.26 begins to look even more tendentious when one learns from the *TLL* that a similar use of *cruento* is hard to come by outside Lucretius.

[64] Commager (1974) 19 n. 41.

shows 2.8.21ff. in an inappropriately scabrous light. Lucretius' comparison of the sexual act to a single combat and of blood to semen is racy, not bawdy, it accords well with a Roman habit of thought and is meant to engage, not titillate, the reader. Propertius' 2.8 is a quite different, more disinterested enterprise with a strong ironical and humorous side (see below), but the ambiguities of 21ff., whether associated with Lucretius or not, besides diluting the gory literalness (the slaughter is carried out in a Donnesque 'gentle way') also appeal to the same habit of thought and taste. Adams is right to warn against 'the current mania for discovering obscene double entendres in unlikely places',[65] but to pronounce 2.8 an unlikely place or regard the physical suggestiveness of 21ff. as merely obscene is to fail to acknowledge the 'estetico-decadente' flavour brought out by the conjunction of death and sensuality. If a 'ravishment' does take place in this poem we can by no means speak of it as if it were a smutty wart on the face of a picaresque novel; but if it does take place the notion of a tragic passion would not be admissible either. This has been so far my assumption and I think that the final section of the poem can be relied upon to clinch the argument.

After pleading guilty in ll. 27–8 the poet now casts about for extenuating circumstances. Genre consciousness will bring out savoury ironies in 29ff. Achilles' refusal to carry out his epic mission is a unique example of a *recusatio* translated into military practice. His conception of the *Iliad* is of a piece with Propertius' as expounded in 2.1.13–14. As a matter of fact, he is the most compelling precedent the lover of 2.8 can wheel out, as the concept of an *Achilles eroticus* authorises a combination of violence (Achilles is, directly or indirectly, responsible for the slaughter of 29–38) and eroticism. At the same time ll. 29ff. with their lucid reasoning following hard upon what purports to be a turbid delirium contribute to the poem's tonal complexity. And their tonal function brings with it a sense of formal control and symmetry. Within individual lines nouns and adjectives fall into patterns and the patterns themselves are rhythmically spaced out:

29:	a	b	A	B
32:	a	b	B	A
33:	a	b	A	B
36:	a	b	B	A

'Such stylistic exquisiteness', remarks Lyne, 'suggests control'. No doubt, only I am not quite sure that the passage conveys 'the gravity, relent-

---

[65] Adams (1982) vii.

lessness, monumentality of grief';[66] or, perhaps, one may grant that it does on condition that Achilles' grief is exclusively calculated on the basis of his Hellenistic susceptibilities. In the *Iliad* poor Briseis is incidental to the bruising of Achilles' ego; she is simply not good enough for Achilles to barter his pride for. Here holocaust (31–2), death of those dear and near (33–4), indeed the gist of the whole epic is fastened on beautiful Briseis: *omnia formosam propter Briseida passus* 'All this he bore for beautiful Briseis' sake' (35). In Propertius the epithet is never inert, here it has a very special point as well, for ll. 31–5 substitute Briseis (as 2.3.39–40 substitute Cynthia: *digna quidem facies, pro qua vel obiret Achilles*; | *vel Priamo belli causa probanda fuit*) for Helen in a syllogism that goes right back to Hom. *Il.* 3.156–7: οὐ νέμεσις Τρῶας καὶ ἐϋκνήμιδας Ἀχαιοὺς | τοιῆδ᾽ ἀμφὶ γυναικὶ πολὺν χρόνον ἄλγεα πάσχειν 'Neither Trojans nor well-greaved Achaeans are to blame for suffering long woes over a woman like this.' In 2.8 ll. 29ff. reveal female *forma* both as *casus belli* and as war's casualty. Cause and effect are set in the same *sedes* and into relief by an almost perfect parallelism of rhythm and word volume between 33 and 35:

> viderat *informem* multa Patroclon harena
> > porrectum et sparsas caede iacere comas,
> omnia *formosam* propter Briseida passus. (2.8.33–5)

> *He saw Patroclus' mutilated body sprawled*
> *In the dust, his hair matted with blood;*
> *All this he bore for beautiful Briseis' sake.*

Achilles grieves as a lover of beauty. If his grief sounds monumental it is probably because these lines partake of the quality of a visual monument. A well-known painting may have contributed subtle visual touches in 2.9.9–16; 'on peut trouver la même recherche de couleur et de forme en ii.8.33–4'.[67] 29ff. are no less well-wrought than 21ff. and they hold, between the lines, an equally piquant, if less visible, secret.

Prop. 2.22a.29–34 divulge the momentous event that took place in Achilles' tent between 2.8.37 *at postquam sera captiva est reddita poena* 'But after late amends restored the captive to him' and 2.8.38 *fortem illum Haemoniis Hectora traxit equis* 'He dragged brave Hector behind Thessalian steeds.' They must be quoted in full:

> quid? cum e complexu Briseidos iret Achilles,
> > num fugere minus Thessala tela Phryges?
> quid? ferus Andromachae lecto cum surgeret Hector,
> > bella Mycenaeae non timuere rates?
> ille vel hic classis poterant vel perdere muros:
> > hic ego Pelides, hic ferus Hector ego. (2.22a.29–34)

---

[66] Lyne (1980) 146.   [67] Boucher (1965) 265.

What of Achilles when he left Briseis' arms?
Did the Phrygians stop running from Thessalian spears?
Or when fierce Hector rose from Andromache's bed
Didn't Mycenae's ships fear battle?
Both heroes could demolish barricades and fleets.
In my field I'm fierce Hector and Achilles.

A fine instance of *post hoc, ergo propter hoc.* Ovid took the point, as *Am.* 1.9.33ff. clearly show:

ardet in abducta Briseide maestus Achilles
  (dum licet, Argeas frangite, Troes, opes);
Hector ab Andromaches conplexibus ibat ad arma[68]

Achilles was chagrined when Briseis, the girl he loved passionately, was taken
away from him (bash the Greeks, Trojans, while you can!); Hector went
to war straight from Andromache's arms

I think that the same principle holds good for 2.8.37–8 as well. To link directly Achilles' culminating feat with his post-coital euphoria is devastating humour, but it is humour for which 2.8, as we have read it so far, is not an unlikely home.[69] This the last couplet does much to confirm:

inferior multo cum sim vel matre vel armis,
  mirum, si de me iure triumphat Amor?   (2.8.39–40)

As I am far inferior, both in birth and battle,
No wonder Love can triumph over me!

Here Propertius shows a gamesome hand that wears cold-blooded calculation on its sleeve. Jacoby was the first to emphasise that in Propertius' elegies it is often the case that the message of the poem first becomes clear in the light of the last couplet.[70] Building upon this Lefèvre postulated a special class of final couplets which in a manner of superior irony call retrospectively in question the 'validity' of the whole poem.[71] To the cases instanced by Lefèvre 2.8.39–40, and perhaps 2.32.61–2,

---

[68] If indeed there was a 'deeply ingrained and primitive belief that love (or, more specifically, the ejaculation of sperm) induces unmanly sloth' (Green (1982) on *Am.* 1.9.33–40), then Ovid's as well as Propertius' 'overkill' ('love is by no means detrimental, indeed it is conducive to manly prowess') is all the more understandable. Also, if the notion of *post coitum triste* (fathered at some time on Aristotle) had an equivalent in antiquity, a conscious counter-suggestion, on the part of the two elegists, of *post coitum forte* could easily be on the cards.

[69] Ovid was no doubt keen on trivialising Propertius, but in certain cases (and I think 2.8.29ff. is one of them) he must have been aware of adding the finishing, and more obvious, touches to an already spicy passage.   [70] Jacoby (1914) 398.

[71] Lefèvre (1966) 145ff. He also finds in some concluding lines an 'illusion-shattering function' which seems peculiar to Prop. That this poet delegates special powers to his final distichs we have already had the opportunity to see in the discussion of 2.26b. See pp. 90–1 above.

should be added. In the latter poem, after deploring at length (1–24) the unfavourable gossip that annotates Cynthia's regular excursions, the poet modulates into resignation (25ff.) but withholds the *carte blanche* until the very end:

> quod si tu Graias es tuque imitata Latinas,
>   semper vive meo libera iudicio.   (2.32.61–2)

> *So if you've done the same as Greek and Latin ladies*
> *My verdict is* Long life to you – and freedom.

The couplet delivers the *coup de grâce* to an ever weakening prudishness, just as the rhetorical question of ll. 39–40 deals the final blow to the illusion of tragic suffering and passion that 2.8 so deftly cultivates.[72] Butler and Barber's honest and understandable complaint that Propertius concludes 2.8 with 'surprising coldness (after his threats of suicide)...'[73] should be received as an invitation to look back over the poem and think again.

So 2.8, a 'monologo interno' on a less than tragic note, represents the triumph of erotic motivation. With 2.13 and 2.26b it shares a peculiarly Propertian fantasy of death and sensuality built up from mainly Hellenistic materials. And it is, moreover, a piece of factitious truculence fraught with irony, humour and sharp sexual innuendo.

---

[72] La Penna (1977) 56, who does not doubt the seriousness of 2.8.21ff., is converted to a brighter view by 29ff., where he finds the mythological example light-hearted, almost playful, and responsible for reducing the tragic tensions of the preceding lines – 'Achilles drives back the grim picture of Haemon'. This amounts to an indirect admission of tonal incongruity (of which our reading of the elegy found the poet not guilty) but still is preferable to Wiggers's (1972) 70ff. resolution not to trifle with the elegy, as a result of which the Achilles example is thought to provide an epic standard against which Prop. earnestly 'measures himself and finds himself lacking'.   [73] See their introd. note, 203.

7

IN AMORE MORI:
MINOR INSTANCES IN BOOK 2

A word must be spared in this chapter for poems 9, 17, 20 and 24b of Book 2. Two points can be immediately made about them. First, although by comparison with the poems dealt with so far the interaction within them of the themes of love and death is rather low-key and conventional, it can still be seen to entail the conceptual and pictorial ingredients of, and constitute the major precondition for the far more original enterprises of, poems 8, 13 and 26b in particular. Secondly, despite the textual and interpretational problems that beset all but one (20), their thematic organisation and structural pattern clearly allies them with the same group of poems. No detailed treatment of all the issues involved is possible within the limits of this work, so I shall confine myself to a brief discussion of the interrelated questions of their structure and *Liebestod* in much the same way as I have done with the poems of the previous chapters. The discussion will permit some final remarks on the form of the poems of both groups and, I hope, will also warrant one or two points concerning the structure and unity of Book 2 as a whole.

In 2.9.1–36 Propertius contrasts his fickle mistress with the proverbially faithful Penelope (3–8) and – in a passage that betrays the influence both of a later sentimental tale and of a painting inspired by it (p. 130 above) – with Briseis dutifully tending the corpse of Achilles (9–16). The source of the trouble is identified in the very first couplet as a rival enjoying temporary favours soon to be withdrawn and transferred to another. This is pretty general, but ll. 19–28 add what seems to be circumstantial detail. Propertius' girl has been thrown over on a previous occasion by the very same womaniser of ll. 1–2, she is being foolish enough to take up with him again and she forgets that when illness had brought her to death's threshold it was the poet, not her current lover, who kept praying for her recovery with vows. This sounds like true-to-life dramatic specificity, until of course one recalls Tibullus 1.5 which, some pastoral day-dreaming apart, presents almost the same scenario with salient parallels in ll. 9–18, 59–62 and 67–76. That more than one elegiac mistress was illness-prone in real life is not all that unlikely, but the primary message one should receive here is that both elegists rearrange the data of a more or less standardised erotic situation in which a rival threatens the elegiac ideal, which means – whether this is made explicit or not – both elegiac love and poetry. This standardisation is typical of Roman love elegy and one reason for it is not far to seek.

Callimachus took exception to the ποίημα τὸ κυκλικόν and, in the same breath, to the περίφοιτον ἐρώμενον; suffered defeat at the hands of a wealthy rival despite his poetic talent; and fulminated against purely generic opponents.[1] The Anticallimachus in Rome grew thus into a versatile figure: the poet dealing in epic subjects, the soldier/politician, the merchant/*dives amator*. All these are people from the walks of real Roman life but the way they stand to the elegiac *puella* and her poet-lover points to the literary manifesto as much as it points to *Lebensanschauung*. Give or take a number of topoi, allow for situational variations and differences in dramatic immediacy, and the same antagonism underlies 1.6, 1.7, 2.1, 2.8, 2.13, 2.26b; and also 2.9, 2.17, 2.20, 2.24b. We have seen how thoughts of death supervene on this antagonism in the elegies of the first group. We can observe analogous developments in those of the second as well.

2.9

The infidelity and ingratitude denounced in 2.9.1–36 prompt thoughts of death, but ll. 37–40 point to epigrammatic conceit rather than to elegiac tragedy.[2] We are given something more substantial in ll. 49–52, where the poet addresses his rival and throws down the gauntlet:

> non ob regna magis diris cecidere sub armis
> Thebani media non sine matre duces,
> quam, mihi si media liceat pugnare puella,
> mortem ego non fugiam morte subire tua.

> *The Theban princes, with their mother as spectator,*
> *Did not die for a throne beneath more ruthless weapons*
> *Than I, if I could fight, with my girl as spectator,*
> *Would not refuse death at the price of your death.*

No dramatic play could have actually represented the combat between Eteocles and Polynices on the stage, and Propertius may have had his eyes, as Boucher suggests, on a picture.[3] There is also a discrepancy between the roles of Jocasta, who tried to mediate between her sons, and

---

[1] See *A.P.* 12.43 (= 1041–6 Gow–Page); *Iambus* 3; and *Aet.* fr. 1 Pfeiffer.

[2] Commentaries compare *A.P.* 12.45 by Posidippus (= 3070–3 Gow–Page, where see notes).

[3] Boucher (1965) 258–9; cf. Rothstein on 2.9.49.

the woman of 2.9, who can only be the prize awaiting the winner, but the conception of the *mise-en-scène* will take this detail in its stride; and besides, the trio of the last couplet may owe something to a love story such as the one summarised in Parthenius 19, where two brothers, Scellis and Agassamenus, kill each other in a fight for the heart of Pancrato. This is not death as a result of cruelty and unfaithfulness, as is that of ll. 37-40, but death as the most valid vehicle for the assertion of love, and I think that Propertius chose what he felt to be the more interesting idea in order to bring his poem to an effective conclusion. Whether a lacuna exists between 48 and 49 or not, ll. 49-52 must be an integral part of the thought movement of this poem.[4] And although they do not permit suggestive interaction of the sensuous aspects of love and death, they certainly presuppose something of the forceful interpenetration between the concepts of *fides* and *mors*, of which poems 2.17 and 2.20 offer further illustration.

2.17 AND 2.20

The order of the lines within Barber's 2.17 is not a settled matter, nor is there agreement as to the poem's boundaries – solutions ranging from simple annexation to 2.17.1-18 of the two couplets marked as 18a to long-distance transplant.[5] The last line of the nine couplets Barber allots to the poem reads:

[4] Rothstein, Enk, Richardson, Hanslik assume no lacuna. Giardina says about 49-52 'hic alieni esse videntur'; Camps prints them as a separate 'four-line growl' but does not seem to rule out the possibility of their being read 'as a conclusion to what has preceded, with a strong pause before and a change of apostrophe'. See also Enk's note *ad loc.* and cf. p. 137 below.

[5] Rothstein follows Scaliger in tacking 2.17.1-4 on to 2.16; then he makes one poem out of 2.17.5-18, 18a and 18b (see Enk's criticisms in his introd. note to 2.17). Richardson stitches together 2.22b.43-50 + 2.17.1-18 + 2.18a.1-4; the way he explains the medley on p. 275 demands imaginative co-operation.

Most other editors transpose, after Lachmann, ll. 13-14 to follow 16, others (e.g. Camps, Richardson) adopt Housman's transposition of them after l. 2, the reason being, according to Enk, that whether one reads *nec licet* or *nunc licet*, ll. 15 and 16 lack point after 13 and 14. But *nec licet* is not indefensible. Take, for example, 2.20.33 *nec tu supplicibus me sis venerata tabellis*. This is as loosely linked with the preceding as *nec licet* with 13-14; indeed, more so since the poet's assurance in 2.20.33 that entreaties are unnecessary follows quite abruptly on a clearly marked off series of solemn oaths. It is strange that editors who take exception to *nec* in 2.17.15 should pass over in silence *nec* in 2.20.33. Camps alone points out that 'the connective in *nec* seems to have no point here' and prints (*Fedeli* (1984) *probante*) *ne* instead; needlessly, not only in view of 2.17.15 but also because this poet can be manneristically lax in his employment of conjunctions and particles. In neither line has *nec* any real connective force. I would, then, punctuate strongly after 12 and 14 and neither rearrange the order of the lines nor tamper with *nec licet*. The thought sequence would present no problem (15-16 can be understood: 'as for lying...and speaking...this is not allowed to me any more') and *quod quamvis ita sit* (17) would now follow quite smoothly, as Helm (1934) 788 saw. Cairns (1975) 18-19, followed by Fedeli (1984), defends the MSS order of the lines on different grounds.

> quod quamvis ita sit, dominam mutare cavebo:
> tum flebit, cum in me senserit esse fidem.   (2.17.17–18)

> *And yet in spite of all I'll not disown my mistress;*
> *One day she'll see how true I am and weep.*

What has led up to this sounds very much like the tribulations of a locked-out lover, yet to infer from this a paraclausithyron does not seem necessary.[6] Should we wish to extrapolate one, a komastic setting is potentially there in most of the elegies where the poet seems left out in the cold; 2.9, for example, could be thus construed (cf. 2.9.1–2, 21ff. and, perhaps, 41ff.). In the absence, however, of specific pointers it is, I think, better simply to see in both 2.9 and 2.17 the standard scourge of a successful rival driving the elegiac lover to a monologue. It will be noted that as in 2.9.37–40 so too in 2.17.13–14 (*nunc iacere e duro corpus iuvat, impia, saxo, | sumere et in nostras trita venena manus* 'Traitress, I am tempted to hurl myself from some bare rock | And lay my hands on brayed poison') Propertius comes upon the idea of death (here it is suicide) immediately after complaining of infidelity and cruelty on the part of his mistress. And as in that poem, the couplet quoted above resorts to death language in order to make a culminating declaration of faithfulness. But death is not conspicuous in 2.17.17–18 nor have the commentators reckoned with it, so I hasten to clarify my position with the help of 2.20.

Unlike 2.17, it is the girl who suspects foul play in 2.20 but otherwise the two poems share basic motifs. Her suspicions are dismissed as ungrounded (2.20.9ff.), and from 19 onwards, under a lenient regime (2.20.20 *servitium mite*), the crossroads take on a more benevolent aspect (2.20.21–2, cf. 2.17.15), the door gives in (2.20.23 *ianua mollis*, cf. 2.17.12 *nunc decimo admittor vix ego quoque die*), the bed serves two (2.20.24 *lecti copia facta tui*, cf. 2.17.3–4 *desertus amaras | explevi noctes, fractus utroque toro*). In ll. 15–16 a solemn oath is taken to the effect that:

> me tibi ad extremas mansurum, vita, tenebras:
> ambos una fides auferet, una dies.   (2.20.17–18)

> *Yours I shall remain, my life, till the final dark:*
> *One faith, one day, shall carry us both off.*

Dies abstulit may have been bandied about in funerary contexts,[7] but *fides auferet* is an exceptional phrase. Shackleton Bailey, following Hertzberg, explains that the expression 'belongs to the usage whereby the ac-

---

[6] This is suggested by Cairns (1975); his term for the 'genre' is *komos*.
[7] See, for example, Enk on 2.20.18.

companiment of an action is presented as its agent'.[8] This is the grammatical rationalisation (and as such it can hardly be bettered) of the alchemy by which this poet contrives to amalgamate the ideas of love/faithfulness and death. I think that Propertius here puts *fides* as a metonymy for *mors*, death being the expression *par excellence* of faithfulness. In this pentameter the two ideas aspire to the condition of conflation, *fides* and *dies* (sc. *mortis*) grow synonymous and the whole effect is one of hendiadys. Thought is more supple than 'death *in* love' would suggest; 'death *as* love' would capture something of that suppleness. We will also notice that thought is not as sensuously apprehended here as in other pieces we have studied. Propertius manipulates concepts rather than sensations. In one sense, the notion of *in amore mori* wins on the roundabouts what it loses on the swings, for the trenchant economy of 2.20.18 is hard to parallel elsewhere.

So what does 2.17.18 *tum flebit, cum in me senserit esse fidem* mean? This is a moot point in the commentaries, but they all encourage the idea of a woman breaking into tears when her lover's fidelity comes home to her.[9] This surely lacks the point it would have had, were it possible to see *fidem* as pointing by some sort of metonymy to the idea of death. One may certainly apply here the experience of the just-discussed *ambos una fides auferet, una dies*, and 2.24b.35–6 lend, I think, further support. Here Propertius is again the victim of infidelity, in the face of which he swears unswerving devotion. Sadly, his mistress is slow to realise this: *tu mea compones et dices 'Ossa, Properti, | haec tua sunt? eheu tu mihi certus eras'* 'You'll say as you lay mine to rest "Are these bones yours, Propertius? Alas, you were faithful to me"' (35–6). Regret is more poignant when the wronged party is no longer there to make amends to, and Propertius, apart from and beyond the widespread topos, seems genuinely fond of the idea of posthumous vindication as 1.7 (on which see p. 25 above), among other pieces, attests: *maius ab exsequiis nomen in ora venit* – as with the poet's fame so with the lover's loyalty, and so with 2.17.18 into which the sob of 2.24b.35–6 can be safely read. Thus 2.17 can be seen to exhibit, just like 2.9, a movement from the unexceptional idea of death as the end-product of unhappy love (13–14, cf. 2.9.37–40) to protestation of love in terms of death (17–18, cf. 2.9.49–52). A similar sequence may be traced in most of

---

[8] Shackleton-Bailey (1956) *ad loc.*

[9] Most reach out for Tib. 1.9.79–80 *tum flebis, cum me vinctum puer alter habebit | et geret in regno regna superba tuo.* Rothstein on 2.17.17 thinks of a more passive and patient lover: 'he will wait until her mood begins to change'. Likewise La Penna (1977) 236–7: 'it is not accusations that return here [i.e. in ll. 17–18] but the reaffirmation of his own *fides* which will perhaps succeed in touching the heart of the merciless woman'.

the poems that have so far come under discussion: at whatever point in them the theme of erotic death may first surface, it tends to reassert itself towards the close. This should perhaps make the continuity between 2.9.1–48 and 49–52 as well as the self-sufficiency of 2.17.1–18 less controversial than they currently seem to be.

But does 2.20 show a similar movement? One way to demonstrate that it does not is to interpret line 34 (*ultima talis erit quae mea prima fides* 'From first to last you'll find me faithful') so as to preclude considerations of death – which in view of *ultima* is not easy to do.[10] The associations of the adjective where the human condition is concerned are hard to escape, and a 'terminal' *fides* cannot be thought of as other than one displayed until, in or through death, especially where the noun has previously occurred in a pivotal couplet *exactly* half-way through the poem (l. 18) as a synonym for death. If 2.20.34 is a variation of 1.12.20 *Cynthia prima fuit, Cynthia finis erit* 'Cynthia was the first, Cynthia will be the last', it is perhaps worth noting that the pentameter from Book 2 promotes the idea of *Liebestod*, vaguely present but inert in the Monobiblos pentameter. 2.20.35–6

> hoc mihi perpetuo ius est, quod solus amator
> nec cito desisto nec temere incipio.

> *This is my prescriptive title – the only lover*
> *Not to start blindly or lightly end.*

may sound somewhat anticlimactic but one cannot help reading the pentameter in the penumbra, as it were, of 17–18 and, of course, 34.

2.24b

2.24b is a similarly structured poem, yet in terms of architecture it stands closer to the great specimens of Book 2 and in imagery it is more strongly reminiscent of one poem in that group (2.13) than any one of the three elegies we have just surveyed. There is general agreement that its thirty-six lines make up a self-contained poem, although the case for independence is stated rather than argued.[11] Yet argued it can be on the basis of its thought sequence and thematic structure. A rival is active again here, against whose alleged unreliability and philistinism (23–4) the poet sets a learned devotion while also stooping to an all but ludicrous muscle-flexing. This first thought paragraph (17–32) is then followed by

---

[10] The commentaries I know of seem hardly impressed by 2.20.34. When the pentameter as a whole is not altogether ignored, its *Liebestod* potential (like that of 2.17.18) *is*.

[11] See, for instance, Camps's introd. note. The MSS do not separate it from the previous poem.

a prolonged affirmation of love in the course of which death imagery is resorted to twice over (33–8 and 49–52). We need not enlarge upon this by now familiar picture but we can draw two instructive parallels, first between 2.24b.17–32 and 2.26b.21–8, and then between 2.24b.51–2 and 2.13.17ff. It is not hard to see that between the passages of the first pair the relation is one of reversal. In 2.26b.23–4 Propertius has indisputable sovereignty over the bed (*non... | dicat 'De nostro surge, poeta, toro'*) from which he had been cast out in 2.24b.20 (*et dicor lecto iam gravis esse tuo*); likewise, the *carmina* of 2.26b.25–6 have lost their grip on the girl of 2.24b.21 (*me modo laudabas et carmina nostra legebas*); we are also to infer that unlike 2.26b.25 (*nam mea cum recitat, dicit se odisse beatos*) mercenary prospects proved irresistible in 2.24b. Both poems deploy the same set of motifs but in order to build up antithetical dramatic situations. Moreover, at a certain point in both (line 33 in 2.24b, line 29 in 2.26b as it stands in the MSS) a strong thought-punctuation occurs, a sort of turning-point, after which the theme of death is developed. What happens here is true, to a greater or lesser degree, of most of our love-and-death elegies: if the variational principle before the main thought-punctuation is the ups and downs of an elegiac ideal invariably confronted with an 'opponent', what is notable after the punctuation is the variety of the postures of erotic death. I shall come back to this in a moment; first let me look briefly at the second of the parallels mentioned above.

The last two couplets of 2.24b read:

> noli nobilibus, noli conferre beatis:
> > vix venit, extremo qui legat ossa die.
> hic [hi *Barber*] tibi nos erimus: sed tu potius precor ut me
> > demissis plangas pectora nuda comis.

(2.24b.49–52)

> *Never have dealings with the rich or noble born:*
> *Scarce one will come to gather up your bones at last.*
> *I shall be he, but sooner be it you, I pray,*
> *Who loosen hair and beat bare breasts for me.*

For the mistress to die before her lover is preposterous, only aesthetically, not morally so. It will be noted that 51–2 pick up 35–8 and are practically the résumé of 2.13.17ff. Death imagery has been scaled down, but even by comparison with the roughly equal volume of 2.13.27–30 the image the two passages make up in 2.24b lags behind in sensory and sensual scope. In this respect 2.24b is fairly representative of the poems of the present section. This considerable difference between the two groups, however, should not obscure a fundamental similarity, for, in all poems of both, the dialectics of love and death, even when it operates at the conceptual level as in 2.17 and 2.20, gives expression to a highly individual sensibility. These poems are what they are because the moment he braces himself to celebrate erotic fulfilment, snatch love from the jaws of infidelity or pledge devotion against impossible odds, Propertius starts thinking – with a frequency and in a fashion unparalleled elsewhere in classical poetry – in terms of death. This obsession is served throughout Book 2 by a certain structural pattern, behind which lies a technique that we have come to understand better in recent years. Once it is recongised here, the common assumption of a severely muddled Book 2 can perhaps be examined from a different angle and in a cooler light.

Propertius rings the changes on the favourite Hellenistic theme of erotic death. The process involves imitation of himself, and the technique has sometimes been called self-imitation *cum* variation, e.g. by F. Cairns who in a series of discussions has done much to illustrate it both in Catullus and the elegists.[12] This is not the place to go into questions of origins or into the reasons for its popularity, and it will suffice to recall here that 'for Hellenistic Greek poets and their late Republican and Augustan successors it was a practice as important as the imitation of other literary sources'.[13] Whether the technique was always employed by the poet with conscious reference to a previous performance cannot, and need not, always be decided with certainty. Similarities of expression and imagery among Propertius' love-and-death elegies are sometimes so close that one cannot help thinking in terms of willed cross-reference, but of the same relationships a broader and more alert view also presents itself: 'Resemblances detected by critics may all be merely the repetitions which we would expect to find when the same mind with the same basic artistic language revisits, after some extra experience of literature and of life, a scene which it has already worked over.'[14] The structure and thematic sequence of poems 6 and 7 of the Monobiblos, and of poems 1, 13, 26b, 8, 9, 17, 20 and 24b of Book 2 has been approached in a similar spirit. I have argued that these poems can be seen as structural analogues. The unity of some of them, differences of interpretation notwithstanding, is no more a matter for dispute. Discussion, however, goes on in the case of others, with scholars all too often looking no further than the boundaries of the elegy exercising their mind at a given moment and rarely alive to the fact that 'the best evidence we can have for the unity

---

[12] See Cairns (1979a) 124–5.   [13] Cairns (1979a) 124.
[14] West and Woodman (1979) 196.

of an ancient poem is the existence of another which is both an analogue and indisputably a unity'.[15] This is a serious argument but liable to be overlooked when one works in disregard of the technique under discussion. Thus 2.13 can appear as two poems;[16] two couplets (if not more) may prolong the culminating funeral gesture of 2.17 into irrelevant feebleness;[17] the question of whether 2.24b and the sixteen lines preceding it in the MSS form one poem is swiftly pronounced open;[18] the continuity between 2.26a and 2.26b is still felt to be worth championing;[19] and excessive psychological ingenuity has been mobilised in the defence of the unity of 2.1 and 2.8.[20] What in all those cases has not been taken sufficiently into account is a degree of formal regimentation that must attend repeated self-variation. This is well reflected by the numerical facts to which attention has been drawn on more than one occasion, and the first sixteen-line paragraph of 2.24b contributes the final instalment to our series of observations on this structural feature of the discussed poems. It makes, I think, good sense to see here the poet taking pains with proportion. But it is equally important not to let the commendable pleasures derived from the sense of symmetry grow into a craving for computational phantasmagoria.

What Skutsch was able to do by following the thread of the Monobiblos addressees can hardly be emulated in the other books.[21] There is no room here for recording at length the brave and inconclusive attempts to force into order the recalcitrant material of Book 2 in particular, but even if universal agreement on a certain scheme or diagram were possible, it would still be a case, as I believe it is in the Monobiblos too, of the pattern of genuine congeners cutting across the formal correspondences established on the strength of external features, such as the addressee. It is probably more pragmatic to expect a book of love poetry to display not intricate numerological patterning but cycles of poems which would illustrate the inescapable vicissitudes of a love affair, but practice shows that even this approach keeps running into serious difficulties which often

---

[15] Cairns (1977) 345.   [16] In Barber and Fedeli (1984).

[17] For example, in Rothstein and Hanslik.

[18] See, for example, La Penna (1977) 239.

[19] Most recently by Wiggers (1980) 121 and Fedeli (1984).

[20] See the discussions of these poems, esp. pp. 20–1 and 113 above.

[21] Skutsch's (1963) 238–9 succinct article proved seminal. There is much in it that commands attention, but I find it hard to see the exact nature of the correspondences between his A panels and I do not feel any more enlightened after having consulted Otis (1965) 1–44. Nevertheless, attempts to trace a rigid symmetry apart, Otis's general conception of the Monobiblos elegies as an ensemble of conventional and 'detemporalized motifs and episodes' that lends itself to contrapuntal arrangement is quite helpful. Courtney (1968) 250–8 and King (1975–6) 108–24 come from the same stable. Skutsch was succinct and stated what facts he observed; some of his remarks were not built upon without a certain loss of pragmatism.

necessitate special – and rather feeble – pleading.[22] If poems of differing tones and moods enhance each other through being juxtaposed, in other words if some kind of *variatio* is at work throughout Book 2, its application does not seem to have been very strict.[23] All we can say with certainty is that Propertius chose to scatter throughout Book 2 versions of *Liebestod*, and that it is hard to discern any rigid principle according to which these kindred pieces have been organised. However unsatisfactory this may be as a comment on the precise architectonics of the book, it does, I believe, say something about another question which is still very much *sub iudice*.

I mean the question of whether Book 2 as presented by the MSS is not in fact a conflation of two separate books. Lachmann, brandishing in 1816 the *tres libelli* of 2.13.25, overawed Propertian editors away from the manuscript evidence, to which they eventually reverted nearly half a century later.[24] The case was reopened by Skutsch, but the skilful confidence of his arguments can by no means conceal the serious flaws of a theory that leaves the 'original' Book 2 either severely mutilated – for which no evidence exists whatsoever – or, since 2.10 is taken as the introductory poem to 'Book 3', with nine poems plus an unspecified number of others from among those that follow 2.10 in our MSS.[25] Full details would be out of place here, but when arguments from a single verse, in which it cannot be decided whether *tres* should be counted or discounted, or indeed, arguments from the habits of the grammarians have been advanced in support of Lachmann's proposal,[26] it is only fair

---

[22] From the more recent works of Juhnke (1971) 91–125, Wille (1980) 249–67 and King (1980) 61–84 it would seem to emerge that the less controversial structural feature of Book 2 is the arrangement of poems in pairs. But not all pairs suggested are as convincing as 8 and 9, 14 and 15 or 29a and b, and Wille (p. 264) finds himself under the obligation to thrust together such unlikely mates as 2.27 and 28 – the only pair, he says rather optimistically, which must for the time being remain uncertain. (On the so-called diptych arrangement and the pairing of poems in Prop. and Ovid see Jäger (1967) and Davis (1977).)

King (1980) 61ff. argues that poems 1–12 formed a separate book (on which see below) and wants to define their thematic unity and relationships. The categories of analysis she operates with are general enough to make a unity of any given number of Propertian elegies. Studies of this sort are also bedevilled by the erratic divisions of the poems in the MSS. Barsby (1974) 135 seeks a rather different solution in the assumption that the poet did not bother to repeat in Book 2 the careful organisation of Book 1.

When schemes, diagrams and tables – the hallmark of the sort of studies mentioned above – arrogate to themselves interpretative value grave reservations are in order; Williams (1968) 480 has voiced some, as did Luck (1973) 361–8.

[23] See Sullivan (1976) 127, Williams (1968) 480 and Luck (1969) 74, 157–8.

[24] On this see the lucid discussion in Butler and Barber's introd., xxixff.

[25] Skutsch (1975) 229–33.

[26] Skutsch (1975) 229–33 argues (after Lachmann and Birt) that since the ancient grammarians never quote from Prop. Book 1 (but see now on this Menes (1983) 137ff.), the Monobiblos must not have originally formed part of the *Corpus Propertianum*; 'at a comparatively late stage the Cynthia Book was prefixed to the *Corpus Propertianum*. The first book of the *Corpus*, which could now no longer be called *Liber primus*, was called *Liber secundus*, was telescoped with the second

that a broader consideration should be set beside them. Our group of love-and-death elegies spans the best part of Book 2 as we know it. Should we, then, following Lachmann's division, divide them between two poetic books written from about 28 to 25 B.C.? Well, this possibility cannot be brushed aside on aprioristic grounds *but* at this point the poet's habits, if those of the grammarians as well, must be taken into account. It is a highly visible fact that Propertius' style, technique, subject matter and even inspiration develop and vary considerably from book to book. Now in all these respects, I have argued, an elegy such as 2.9, which on this theory would have to be assigned to 'Book 2', stands close to 2.24b – which on the same theory belonged most probably to the original 'Book 3'; and the same would be true of the respective positions of the elegies 2.8 and 2.26b. Are we, therefore, to assume that the programmatic *in amore mori* of 2.1 was in fact implemented, in the same vein and by comparable means, not in the course of one but two books?[27] It seems to me that such an assumption does run counter to Propertian practice. Certainty is,

book, and the two together became *Liber secundus*... In order to fill up his putative Book II, which comprised only poems 1–9, Lachmann assumed that much had been lost; but the evidence for great textual loss is not compelling' (p. 233); Skutsch would have been more right to say 'non-existent', in view of which fact neither the allegedly inordinate length (1362 lines) of Book 2 nor the *tres libelli* of 2.13.25 should have taken on the paramount importance Lachmann first claimed for them. As regards the latter, Skutsch and those following him reject the possibility of a mystic or magic significance for the number three. Yet in Virg. *Ecl.* 8.73–5 the witch binds Daphnis' image with threads of *three* different colours and takes it *thrice* around the altar because uneven numbers please the god, *numero deus impare gaudet* (75). The god in question is, of course, Hecate, the same god that Prop. wants to please with *three* books in 2.13.25–6. The number three, as Gow on Theoc. *Id.* 2.43 remarks, *is* 'particularly appropriate to Hecate'.

Lachmann's theory created the need for an introductory poem to the putative Book 3. Lachmann himself opted for 2.19 (Skutsch does not find this objectionable), 2.12 was also considered for a time (by A. Marx and T. Birt) and now it is 2.13 that is tipped for the post by King (1980) 61–2, 82ff. and Heiden (1982) 156ff.

The idea of Book 2 consisting of two original books appeals to Hubbard (1974) 41ff, Sullivan (1976) 7 and Lyne (1980) 120. Menes (1983) 137ff. argues well that the neglect of the Monobiblos by the ancient grammarians is not unassailable proof of its separate publication.

[27] Here again we come up against the much-discussed problem of the publication of Propertius' poetry. Williams (1968) 480ff. has advanced the view that Prop. did not publish each of his four books separately but planned and composed the first three with a view to publishing them together, the fourth book being a later addition (but cf. on this theory Barsby (1974) 128–37 and Hubbard (1974) 41–2). Others (e.g. La Penna (1977) 69 n. 1) prefer to think that it was Books 2 and 3 that appeared simultaneously. Conjectures in this particular area can be neither confirmed nor refuted, but what seems quite clear to me is that, in the eyes of the poet's contemporaries as in ours, Book 2 would have clearly marked itself off by virtue of its thematic preoccupations. Even as part of a unitary publication it will have been felt to be, as it is today, a book beset by love and death. In the notion that it took Prop. two separate books to glean every love-and-death fantasy from his mind I admit to sensing an element of 'anomaly', even if, as Skutsch (1975) 233 thinks possible, the two original books represented by our present Book 2 were published together. Butler and Barber's (Introd. xxxiii–xxxiv) alternative of a publisher spreading, for reasons of convenience, the material of a *uniform* collection of poems over two rolls or *libelli* sounds a bit more acceptable and much more speculative.

needless to say, unattainable, yet Lachmann's followers would also have to contend with another potentially embarrassing detail.

Apart from the introductory, all the elegies of Book 2 relevant here fall between 4 and 27. A link between these two poems has been discussed on pp. 35–6 and another one can now be suggested. Besides 2.1, these are the only poems in the book where a *theoretical* statement is being made (in a somewhat *praeceptor amoris* mood) on the indissoluble connexion between love and death that poem after poem instances in between. 2.4 looks as much forward as it does backward to 2.1. Line 13 especially (*et subito mirantur funus amici*), with its versatile *funus* (see p. 47 above), rings anticipatory, while the preceding couplet, by giving short shrift to the conventional 'love-resulting-in-disease' fallacy, announces a very different analogy: neither *morbi* nor *militiae* but *mortis species amor est*. This is the shape of things to come, and 2.27, more theoretical and 'objective' in shunning any such personal reference as 2.4.5ff. admit, reads a bit like a Q.E.D. Should it, in fact, have been meant as one, it would be odd, although not inconceivable, if it was deferred – as the hypotheses of a new book beginning somewhere between 2.9 and 2.14 would have us believe – until the next session.

8

STRANGE BEAUTY:
A READING OF 4.7

'Of all melancholy topics, what, according to the *universal* understanding of mankind, is the *most* melancholy?' Death – was the
obvious reply. 'And when', I said, 'is this most melancholy of topics
most poetical?' From what I have already explained at some
length, the answer, here also, is obvious – 'When it most closely
allies itself to *Beauty*: the death, then, of a beautiful woman is,
unquestionably, the most poetical topic in the world – and equally
is it beyond doubt that the lips best suited for such topic are those
of a bereaved lover.'

Edgar Allan Poe, *The philosophy of composition*

We have been introduced in recent years to the various strands out of
which the opulent tapestry of 4.7 is woven; indeed, 'epic, tragedy, the
mime, the epigram have all been turned to account'.[1] Remarkable as this
may be, it should give little cause for surprise; we now have a better
understanding of the debt of Roman elegy to various generic sources. The
real challenge 4.7 poses for the reader is the interaction within its compass
of different styles and tonal levels. Opinions generally converge in the
process of identifying the poem's ingredients and diverge when it comes
to assessing its overall tone. It is rather ironical that the lush *Bildungserlebnis*
in this poem should have failed to warn against the fabrication of further
Urerlebnis-items: if 3.24 and 25 dismiss Cynthia, as they profess to do, the
hatchet must have been buried somewhere between those poems and 4.7;
Cynthia died after reconciliation and was summarily consigned to her
grave to re-emerge from it as a chiding apparition on the night following
her obsequies. Once we commit ourselves to the cross-currents of biographical reconstruction speculation grows apace:[2] Cynthia lays claim in
4.7 to better morals than she had been able to display in the course of
the first three books. Is it, then, a case of *de mortuis nil nisi bonum*? Has
Propertius really been as callous as the ghost would have us believe? If

[1] Hubbard (1974) 152.
[2] A survey of critical opinion may be found in Menes (1968) 263–8 and Warden (1980) 78–9.
The former rejects biography, takes Cynthia as the symbol of love poetry ('she will possess him
forever in the sense that his fame will depend on his reputation as a love poet', p. 271) but wants
to stop short of seeing 'allegory with Cynthia as Dame Elegy'.

so, why? The pendulum has also swung to a very different direction: Cynthia is alive and kicking, her posthumous performance only proving the immortality of her cantankerousness and, therefore, vindicating the decision of her long-suffering lover to cast her off at the end of Book 3.[3] This interpretation at least credits the poet with a sense of humour which others would rather brush aside in favour of a guilty conscience and an injured ghost.[4] Furthermore, while there are those who grant the poem unalloyed earnestness and profound pathos, others have been disturbed by an alleged aesthetic incongruity between the gravity of the opening scene and the frivolity of minor motifs within the poem.[5] Every single proposal put forward in connexion with 4.7 must be considered on its own merits, but it is, I think, not altogether uncharitable to mobilise scepticism mainly against those theories which have their premiss in inconclusively reconstructed biographies.

It is, perhaps, more reassuring to start, as for instance E. Lefèvre does, from assumptions of *Selbstvariation* and *Ironie*, which means paying closer attention to the rehandling of motifs and situations that occur elsewhere in Propertius, while watching out for such devices as may be thought to jeopardise the poem's emotional impact.[6]

Ever since Patroclus' querulous shadow in *Iliad* 23 was recognised as the major sponsor of Propertius' dream, it seems to have been felt imperative to read the elegy in terms of a stylistic–tonal antithesis, variously defined as one between serious vs. ironical, heroic-epic vs. contemporary-everyday or comic-realistic vs. heroic. But in what way, to what extent and how successfully do these two basic spheres of 4.7 harmonise? It seems to me that the answers returned to these questions leave much to be desired.

Lefèvre in his just-mentioned study is content with pointing out what he feels to be ironical undertones and comic effects that keep pathos at bay. But he has to meet the demands of his chosen title and spends too much time identifying the comic warts on the poem's façade; thus in practice he accepts the incongruity and builds upon it. A positive view of 'a disjunction in 4.7 between comedy and epic (or realism and the heroic)' is also taken by F. Muecke: they are 'vehicles for different aspects of Cynthia's character, ironically juxtaposed'.[7] This is an interesting suggestion and we shall come back to it in more detail later on. Hubbard notes the same duality of levels but assumes an interaction

---

[3] See Lake (1937) 53–5; Guillemin (1950) 182–93.
[4] See, for example, Helmbold (1949) 339, 342.
[5] La Penna (1951) 85 n. 1.   [6] Lefèvre (1966) 108ff.
[7] Muecke (1977) 129–30.

which eventually glamorises the actuality inhabited by the protagonists.[8] It would seem, then, that every genre laid under contribution here brings its own range of associations, and that the ultimate contrast between 'high' and 'low' which is thus brought about either generates humour or ironically reflects temperamental variations or elevates the quotidian. To have shelved the question of biographical accuracy and broached that of tonal complexity is sheer gain. What seems to emerge from analyses undertaken along these lines is that we have somehow outgrown La Penna's complaint about an 'aesthetic incongruity' in 4.7; still, there is a strong element of paradox at the heart of this poem, and the relationship of the modern reader with it – often one of fascination supervening on bewilderment – is something of a paradox itself. To see the widely disparate notes sounded by the apparition as a source of humour and satire, as mere characterological indications or as simply the concomitants of her shifting emotions is to fail to do justice to the intrinsic nature of the paradox, and ultimately to fail to appreciate it as such. In the following no systematic account is offered of all the issues raised by 4.7. The elegy has by no means been neglected and after J. Warden's recent and lemon-squeezing treatment there is a real risk of undue repetitiveness.[9] I will pause over those points of diction, sound, rhythm, motif-handling and literary background which seem to me to invite the reader of the poem away from biographical and moral riddles towards a more aesthetic response. I hope that in this way the elegy can be seen as the most consummate and wide-ranging expression of Propertius' 'aestheticism'. The use of the term may *still* be felt to require some apology, but at least I hope it by now needs no clarification. This is not the case with another term which nearly every scholar tackling the poem has made use of, namely realism.

Although sharp visual details are scattered throughout 4.7, the will for realistic particularisation is most evident in the haunting vignettes of the nocturnal debauchees wallowing in the squalor of Subura (15ff.), in the bizarre fiasco of the obsequies (23ff.) and in the scenes of domestic brutality (35ff.). The macabre in the second of these passages serves to compound the low realism which pervades all three – and low realism has

---

[8] Hubbard (1974) 150.

[9] Warden's analysis is sensitive and enlightening on sound effects, artistic word-arrangement and rhythm; with it I have more individual points of agreement than with any other single treatment of 4.7. It will nevertheless be evident that Warden's conception of the poem as a whole is quite different from that presented in the following pages. He generally finds Propertius much too ambivalent, and frequently assumes ambiguity and open-endedness (see pp. xi, 18, 20, 23, 33, 43, 76f.) on such evidence as seems to me to give away a very specific and unequivocal bias in the elegy. Scanning of Cynthia's emotional graph (on the whole quite plausible) is another concern which, for reasons that will be evident, I do not share with Warden.

very often been thought to minister to the poem's comic aspects, even by scholars who do not seem to be consciously aware of Auerbach's theories.

In his *Mimesis* the latter argues that the principal function of the realistic in the literatures of antiquity is the comic.[10] He stretches his definition to encompass occasional idyllic representation of everyday life but on the whole keeps the boundaries of ancient realism narrow: 'Everything commonly realistic, everything pertaining to everyday life, must not be treated on any level except the comic, which admits no problematic probing' and 'there could be no serious literary treatment of everyday occupations and social classes – merchants, artisans, peasants, slaves – of everyday scenes and places – home, shop, field, store...' (p. 31). Of course, Auerbach is anxious to show that such specimens of realistic writing as we come across lack the sociological probing of nineteenth-century realism. True in principle as this may be, it should not be allowed to confine every instance of ancient realism within the limits of the comic or, at best, of the playfully idyllic. Auerbach's theory is perhaps unassailable where it operates with the novel – surely, Petronius is no Balzac. But there is, outside the *Satyricon*, depiction of low everyday life which while not serio-problematic is not, in the accepted sense of the word at least, comic either.

Take Herodas, for example. To ask whether his *Mimiambi* are reflections *au grand sérieux* on the life of the urban proletariat *or* comic-satirical vignettes is to accept an unnecessary and misleading polarity. Auerbach begrudges the ancients a motive he himself acutely diagnosed in the moderns. When Edmond and Jules de Goncourt jointly published in 1864 their novel *Germinie Lacerteux*, they claimed in the preface to offer a comment on the condition of the lower classes. Auerbach saw through this: 'The thing that drew the Goncourts in the subject matter of *Germinie Lacerteux* was something quite different. It was the sensory fascination of the ugly, the repulsive, and the morbid'; he was a fine critic but in this case he could also produce extrinsic evidence from a diary entry, written seven years after the appearance of the novel, in which Edmond revealed how fascinatingly exotic and worth exploring he found the populace, *la canaille*.[11] One wonders whether Herodas was not subject to a similar temptation. This is, of course, not the place to expatiate on ancient realisms,[12] and, in any case, it matters little that the question whether

---

[10] Auerbach (1953) 24ff. especially.   [11] Auerbach (1953) 498–9.

[12] Auerbach is of course right to emphasise that the representation of reality in ancient literatures is impaired by linguistic stylisation; and in this sense it may be true that the plain, unstylised speech of some of the freedmen parvenus in Trimalchio's Banquet marks 'the ultimate limit of the advance of realism in antiquity' (p. 30). But although the language of Herodas' characters is no doubt more stylised than that of Seleucus, Phileros, Ganymede and Echion, it

aesthetic adventurism was the spur in the case of Herodas, as it seems to have been in that of the Goncourts, admits no certain answer; all I am saying is that it is important not to shrink on principle from asking it. I believe that once 'realistic' is given the benefit of such alertness to its potential function, the same question can and should be asked in connexion with 4.7. For though it teems with things ugly and morbid, low and vile, macabre and bizarre, no one on reading it has put on record spasms of disgust or unqualified horror. This brings us back to the paradox we have been talking about; we set out to explore it.

Over the elegy presides the spectre of Cynthia. Being the visual 'embodiment' as well as the exponent of the poem's aesthetics, her figure must be scrupulously scanned. She enters the poem in order to confirm the possibility envisaged in the opening couplet and takes her position on the borderline of Propertius' consciousness:

> Sunt aliquid Manes: letum non omnia finit,
>   luridaque evictos effugit umbra rogos.
> Cynthia namque meo visa est incumbere fulcro,
>   murmur ad extremae nuper humata viae,
> cum mihi somnus ab exsequiis penderet amoris,
>   et quererer lecti frigida regna mei.   (4.7.1–6)

> *The Blessed Dead exist. Death does not end it all;*
> *A pale shadow escapes, defeating the pyre.*
> *I have seen Cynthia, leaning over my bed's head*
> *Though lately buried by the busy roadside,*
> *While sleep for me was hung up on love's funeral*
> *And I grieved at my bed's cold kingdom.*

Nasals and *u*'s abound in these opening lines, sense and sound pointing to the crepuscular. In fact, ll. 1–5 seem to exist in the phonological as well as the semantic penumbra of the word *umbra* (2): *letum, omnia* (1); *namque, incumbere* (3); *extremae, humata* (4); *cum, somnus, amoris* (5).[13] *murmur* heralds the series of those sins of omission and commission that turned Cynthia's funeral into a macabre travesty. Cynthia was buried within earshot, or, perhaps, to the accompaniment (*ad murmur*), of the traffic rumble; the

is quite legitimate to apply here C. S. Lewis's (1961) 57ff. useful distinction between 'realism of presentation' and 'realism of content': 'the two realisms are quite independent. You can get that of presentation without that of content, as in medieval romance: or that of content without that of presentation, as in French (and some Greek) tragedy; or both together, as in *War and peace*; or neither, as in the *Furioso* or *Rasselas* or *Candide*.' We are going to see that in attempting the latter Propertius does not altogether neglect the former; and that a degree of stylisation is by no means prejudicial to the 'sensory fascination' of which Auerbach talks with regard to the Goncourts.   [13] Cf. Warden (1980) 16ff.

remarkable turn of phrase permits *murmur* as the first word of the pentameter to epitomise the circumstances of the burial: *post mortem tumuli sic infamantur amantum*. Propertius has done as he would not be done by (cf. 2.13 and 3.16), and one would like to believe that this is why he cannot quite compose himself to sleep in l. 5; for *somnus...penderet* can mean little else, whether in its conceptual ('sleep was holding off') or in its visual version ('sleep as a winged god hovering over the head'). One thing, however, is certain, that neither metre nor sleep are perfectly normal.[14] The 'after' which habitually renders the *ab* in *ab exsequiis* should not rule out the possibility that a temporal sequence here may have blended with a causal one; dreams operate like that sometimes. One may also notice how seasonably the metaphoric periphrasis *lecti frigida regna* is deployed in the presence of a visitor from a traditionally chilly realm. These first six lines submerge us in a twilit world from which we never really emerge. Cynthia's recollections wrench the reader from Propertius' dusky bedroom to Subura by night to the grimness of her funeral to the four walls within which those loyal to her memory are tormented to her niche in the caverns of Elysium. Her injunctions allow some moments of fresh air beside the banks of Anio (81–6), but her prophecy (93–4) renews with a vengeance the prospect of darkness. To and fro between underworld and Underworld, Cynthia the ghost recalls Cynthia the shady Subura demi-mondaine and presents Cynthia the Elysian shade. One remembers the sunny cynosure of Baiae and surmises that this is not so much how life transforms as how poetry metamorphoses.

Lines 7–12 bring Cynthia's figure into sharp focus:

> eosdem habuit secum quibus est elata capillos,
>   eosdem oculos: lateri vestis adusta fuit,
> et solitum digito beryllon adederat ignis,
>   summaque Lethaeus triverat ora liquor.
> spirantisque animos et vocem misit: at illi
>   pollicibus fragiles increpuere manus

> *She had the same hair as when borne to burial,*
> *The same eyes. But the dress she wore was scorched,*
> *And the fire had eaten into the beryl on her finger,*
> *And Lethe water had scoured her lips.*
> *She spoke, ominously sibilating her words –*
> *Her brittle fingers made a rattling sound*

The macabre and the ghastly are here the function of the minute and the selective; the necroscopy is at the same time accurate and significant:

---

[14] The line is non-caesural and has no second-foot diaeresis. See Platnauer (1951) 7.

hair-style, eyes, garment, lips and fingers. There is something to be said for Postgate's uncomfortable feeling that 'Cynthia's ghost was pieced together',[15] but then so was the lively and lovely muse of 2.1.7–14. We are offered the same items, but what the one passage presents as an erogenous zone becomes a funeral fetish in the other. Whereas *seu vidi ad frontem sparsos errare capillos* 'Suppose I spot an errant ringlet on her brow' (2.1.7) affirms love's and life's nimble and graceful variety, in 4.7.7 the terminal coiffure stiffens into a ritual embalmment. *seu cum poscentis somnum declinat ocellos* 'Or if she closes eyelids exigent for sleep' (2.1.11), with its interlacing of nasal lull, gliding *l*-sounds and dulcet diminutive, assimilates the languor of somnolence into that of desire; it is hard to mistake autopsy for endearment in *eosdem oculos* (8), especially when the phrase is assailed by a noticeable synizesis in *eosdem* and marked off by a strong break in the second foot of the pentameter – 'a gargle of surprise and shock', as Warden incisively put it.[16] The fiery lover in 2.1.13 (*seu nuda erepto mecum luctatur amictu* 'Or if, stripped of her dress, she wrestles with me naked') rips off what the funeral pyre chars: *lateri vestis adusta fuit* (4.7.8). Propertius knows of the habit of ghosts to appear as they were last seen by the living, but a comparison with, for instance, Hector's appearance in *Aen.* 2.270ff. (to say nothing of Tib. 2.6.40 where *sanguino-lenta* seems to suffice) shows that he is determined to go beyond the generically requisite to the realistically circumstantial. Virgil is vivid but not any more so than any description based on the traditional account of Hector's death would have been. The details he gives are harrowing, but epically not clinically so – to take it a bit further: the difference between the two is one between 'epic realism' and 'elegiac naturalism'. For in 8–9 Cynthia is less a visitor from the mythological Hades than a corpse awaiting identification in the mortuary. *ad-* in *adusta* as well as in *adederat* sums up the will for realism: a real-life accident, unlike cremation, rarely claims total or third-degree burns. It is also in a bid for imaginative realism that the rare *beryllon* is chosen. The word has an abstruse ring compounded by the Greek form of its accusative. It is precious in sound and material, and like *heroine* it smacks of neoteric aestheticism.[17] It has been sought out with 'Parnassian' fastidiousness and carefully weighed up for its evocative value; what it is calculated to evoke here is the urban gilded gutter with its jewellery-addict courtesans. This is *graecissare* – in

[15] Postgate (1881) lxix; cf. Warden (1980) 19.
[16] Warden (1980) 19.
[17] See Tränkle (1960) 26–7.
  It is a bit surprising not to find a beryl among Gautier's *Émaux et Camées*; the one so prominently featuring in D. G. Rossetti's ballad 'Rose Mary' (Rossetti 119ff.) is encrusted with the occult and the symbolical, but the fact that it was singled out for this role is significant in itself.

all senses of the word – inlaid in Cynthia's corrupt βήρυλλος, and Warden's 'a touch of urban sophistication in an *incongruous* context' misses half of the point.[18]

Classical poets in general duly keep Lethean water in a state of mythological evaporation; Propertius condenses it and exposes its acid properties: *summaque Lethaeus triverat ora liquor* (10).[19] He thus scores another ghastly-realistic point but also, I think, one of spacious irony: Cynthia's *perfide* three lines later (13), in view of the poet's single-minded infatuation, sounds unfair – or forgetful. Commentators go almost out of their way to ban the 'oblivion' associations of 10 when it would be more charitable to see the ghost as slightly (*summa ora*) amnesiac through no fault of its own, rather than as grossly unappreciative. If speculation was discouraged in 10, it came back with a vengeance in 11–12. An abortive greeting gesture reminiscent of 3.10.4 (*et manibus faustos ter crepuere sonos*) (Rothstein), a gesticulation indicating rebuke (Camps) or one intended to wake Propertius up have been suggested. But surely, what we are given here is not so much the accident as the very substance of a skeletal hand. The fingers (*pollicibus*, as Camps observes, need be no more specific) have been reduced to a sterile brittleness – a far cry from 2.1.9 *sive lyrae carmen digitis percussit eburnis* 'Suppose her ivory fingers strike a tune on the lyre.' What melodious use they could have been put to had death not intervened, we can also learn from Ovid, *Am.* 2.11.32 *Threiciam digitis increpuisse lyram.* Cynthia's fingers rattle (*fragiles increpuere* verges on the onomatopoeic) in a desolate and unmelodious manner – or should we say anti-melodious? Crepitation is, as it were, the poem's musical theme; dry, barren and lugubrious sounds echo throughout: the cloven cane in 25, the broken tile in 26, the broken jar in 34 and the grating engagement of the bones in 94. It is as if the aesthetics of this piece entailed a determination to explore the 'melody' of cacophony.

Lefèvre briefly surveys the quest for the ludicrous and the angry in the ghost's appearance – and takes a similar view himself.[20] Now it is only l. 11 that warrants an impression of anger, and even this is, in my view, not necessary. But to spot anything that may be termed 'comic' or 'jocular' is to treat a finely-wrought piece of macabre realism as amusing caricature – and it is also to miss the poetic potential in a woman's decay. This paradox, a kind of timeless *vulnus naturae* as M. Praz might have put it, has received high literary sanction by one aesthete after another. Poe

[18] Warden (1980) 19; my italics.
[19] Camps's remark 'There is no need to assign a strong value to *tero* in *triverat*' needs to be seen in the light of our observations in pp. 23–4 above and 190 below.
[20] Lefèvre (1966) 113–14.

celebrates the consumption of his heroines, Baudelaire extols the skeletal and the putrescent: *Ta carcasse a des agrèments | Et des grâces particulières*.[21] From Baudelaire Walter Pater learned as much as the Frenchman himself had absorbed from Poe. Here is a passage from the *Appreciations*:

> With a passionate care for beauty, the romantic spirit refuses to have it, unless the condition of strangeness be first fulfilled. Its desire is for a beauty born of unlikely elements, by a profound alchemy, by a difficult initiation, by the charm which wrings it even out of terrible things; and a trace of distortion, of the grotesque, may perhaps linger as an additional element of expression, about its ultimate grace[22].

One may well hesitate to allow this to account for Prop. 4.7.7–12. But Pater describes a whole syndrome, and if I am not wide of the mark the elegy will develop further symptoms to complement and confirm those of ll. 7–12.

In ll. 15ff. Cynthia conjures up her past life in terms of nightly Subura profligacy. Propertius is reminded of a complicity that makes his sleepiness all the more blameworthy. Subura stirs into life when respectable people are fast asleep; to those who can have no first-hand knowledge of the haunt, *vigilacis furta Suburae*|'the stolen joys in the wakeful Subura' is perhaps the most suggestive of its succinct descriptions. On this arena of sin Cynthia lands after giving the slip, through the window, to what seems to be an inadequate lover or careless pimp – the kind of thing that would have been at home in comedy or mime;[23] yet if its associations suggest the comic, its treatment and its context in 4.7 do not. Habitual nocturnal trickery has rubbed smooth Cynthia's windowsill, *et mea nocturnis trita fenestra dolis* 'Those tricky nights and my worn windowsill' (16). Friction is audible in the consonantal clusters with their *r*-ingredient, *dolis* sounds more bland. Cynthia is wily because she is lustful: *trita* could well be an interlinear comment on the effects of such regular escapades – a possibility guaranteed by 3.11.30 *et famulos inter femina trita suos* (of Cleopatra), see p. 23 above. Finally, with *dolis* in the close vicinity of *trita fenestra*, one is seduced with some reason into thinking of Pl. *Mil.* 938 *si...hunc dolum dolamus* 'if we turn out this trick'. Everything in the pentameter conspires to convey lubricity, in all senses of the word; there is subtle suggestiveness and mannerism but not situational humour. The submission to the pictorial detail established in 7–12 is kept up; Cynthia's

---

[21] Praz (1951) 42–3.

[22] From the *Appreciations* p. 250 in the 1889 edn; see p. 19 n. 33 above.

[23] Cf. McKeown (1979) 76: 'Entrances and exits through windows were probably a standard feature of amatory mimes.'

casement seems to open directly on Subura's perilous half-lights, we sense dark silhouettes and surreptitious movements, but the tiny spotlight shows a wayward partiality first for the rubbed section of the windowsill and then for the dexterous alternation of handgrips along the rope that lowers Cynthia on to the shoulders of her accomplice (17–18). To stress, as Lefèvre and Warden do, the comic in this couplet is to see it as a more or less light-hearted piece of acrobatic virtuosity.[24] I believe that this circumstantial detail is easily integrated into the atmosphere of dark, shared and relished villainy that ll. 13–22 exude. The comic potential of the manoeuvres described in 17–18 is hardly ever realised; besides, no sooner does it become a tempting possibility than the next couplet reasserts the keynote of Cynthia's reminiscing:

> saepe Venus trivio commissa est, pectore mixto
> fecerunt tepidas pallia nostra vias.   (19–20)

We often made love at the crossroads, breast to breast,
Our cloaks warming the pavement.

The engagement may or may not have produced the heat required by the notion of 20, but hyperbolic absurdity, which seems to be Lefèvre's verdict, is hardly the point here, and 'humour', if there were any at all, would have to be of the black variety, as his quasi-exclamatory footnote ('And all that at the crossroads') obliquely admits.[25] The implications of *trivio* are too important to be less than fully exploited. *trivium*, the crossroads, was a public place by day and, because associated with Diana/Hecate, potentially a centre of witchcraft and occult practices by night; and very often it was used to localise the ways of the gutter. That the latter should be connoted here is in the nature of the rendezvous, for after *vigilacis furta Suburae* in 15 the scene in the same thought-paragraph must be thought of as either Subura itself or Suburaesque. What is more, the lights are subdued enough to bring into play the fiends of the nocturnal crossroads. Line 19 strikes me as a masterly blend of the erotic, the squalid and the sinister. For this effect it relies on its own components as much as on its environment. Coupled with a goddess, *trivium* must have seemed orthodox in *Aen.* 4.609 *Hecate triviis*, but not quite so in *Venus trivio*; if Propertius is playing, as I think he does, with the theological expectations the noun arouses, he has not only allowed Venus to eroticise the uncanny but also Hecate to taint the erotic. The proceedings of 19–20 are thus ultimately placed under the auspices of both deities, a fact that may be

[24] Lefèvre (1966) 115 and Warden (1980) 24–5.
[25] Lefèvre (1966) 115 with n. 32.

reflected in *commissa est*: the dark commerce is perpetrated no less than enjoyed.

For the sights and sounds of the urban landscape to inspire poetry the city had to begin to look more like a congeries of people than a congregation of citizens. The 'poetic discovery of the city and its environs', as La Penna has entitled a brief chapter in his more recent book on Propertius, runs parallel with the widening streak of post-classical verism.[26] Theocritus, *Id.* 15 – virtually an urban mime – was by no means the only Greek Hellenistic specimen in this area, even if it is the most fascinating. Horace's leisurely perambulations through the motley crowds of the Circus and the Forum in *Sat.* 1.6.111ff. betray a powerful feeling for the hustle and bustle of city life. To the seamy side of the same picture belong crossroads, culs-de-sac and lanes as theatres of squalid eroticism. Catullus could effectively trumpet Lesbia's unspeakable degradation in just these terms: *nunc in quadriviis et angiportis | glubit magnanimi Remi nepotes* 'now at the crossroads and lanes she flays the descendants of noble Remus' (58.4–5). The aim here is *diffamatio*, so the sordid, underscored by the sardonic magniloquence of l. 5, is as straightforward as it is savage. It is a more complex and evocative kind of sordidness that we find in Horace, *Carm.* 1.25.9–12:

> invicem moechos anus arrogantis
> flebis in solo levis angiportu,
> Thracio bacchante magis sub inter-
> lunia vento

> *You in your turn, a paltry hag in a desolate alley, will weep for the haughty rakes when between the old and the new moon the fury of the Thracian wind becomes even greater*

I venture to think that had it not been for the remarkable snapshot in l. 10, Nisbet and Hubbard would hardly have credited the poet with 'a forceful realism of Alexandrian origin'; indeed, '*angiportus* is much more effective than any delineations of ῥυτίδες and πολίη', the stock features of the faded beauty, which is the central theme of the ode. But ll. 11–12 add mystique to realism: if Horace set out to depict a degraded whore, he came very near to suggesting a fallen Princess of Darkness (*sub interlunia*) in majestic isolation (*in solo*) amid Nature's ritual atrocity (*Thracio bacchante*). In a manner of speaking, this stanza constitutes a *hapax legomenon* of Horatian realism whose impact Propertius is not

---

[26] See La Penna (1977) 176–94, esp. 185–6, where he remarks that the new, 'Petronian' realism of Book 4 is closely related to Propertius' gradual poetic discovery of the city.

unlikely to have treasured. His own picture in 4.7.15–20, however, hinging as it does on the contingent and waywardly particular, achieves the compelling authenticity of red-light-district dealings; and it communicates the aura of the place and time with an almost Baudelairean involvement:

> Dans les plis sinueux des vieilles capitales
> Où tout, même l'horreur, tourne aux enchantements.[27]

That intimations of demonism and sensuality meet in 4.7.19–20 is neither fanciful nor unprecedented. This couplet is partly informed by the set of ideas explored with regard to 2.1.51–6 in particular (see pp. 30–1 and 40–1 above). Witch-hunting pays off in both places. The *femina* of 2.1.55 was credited with associations of harmfulness that attach to the sorceresses of 51–4, and the suspicion was thrown out that her name, no less than her virtual enrolment in the malignant troupe, made her a possible reincarnation of the Hecate of Theoc. *Id.* 2.12ff., a poem to which I believe 2.1 and 2.4 to be indebted, apart from and beyond mere verbal echoes, for their fusion of witchcraft and baneful eros. But although in both these instances Propertius borrowed 'atmosphere', he had little use for the idyll's dramatic details. Nor has he, strictly speaking, in the case of 4.7; and yet it may not be amiss to touch briefly on one or two points here. What Simaetha and Cynthia have in common is jealousy of rivals and determination to recapture their lovers. It is cold comfort to the Delphis of the idyll that unlike Propertius he can be recaptured alive, for the impeccable ̄professionalism of Simaetha's seance, if successful, forebodes nothing less than a haggard and woe-begone monogamy. Both women are injured only to threaten with irrevocable repossession, but whereas the one makes her claim by virtue of being herself a kind of chthonic demon, the other can only do so by invoking one. Simaetha practises through Selene/Hecate an act of necromancy in which Cynthia can afford to be her own medium. If *Id.* 2.163–6 represent, as Gow *ad loc.* notes, a ritual ἀπόλυσις (required by necromantic practice) of the summoned deity, following her – presumably beneficial – epiphany, then 4.7.89–94 could have a comparable function, with an enjoyable twist and an effective inversion: Cynthia has only herself to dismiss and

---

[27] 'In the winding nooks of old capitals where everything, even horror, acquires charm'; from 'Les petites vieilles' (see Pichois, I 89–91). Baudelaire's taste for the urban landscape is not unrelated to the Aesthete's well-attested preference for the artificial over the natural, as can be seen from his essay 'Le Peintre de la vie moderne'. In the light of other analogies the poetic discovery of the city by Hellenistic 'aestheticism' is certainly no coincidence. In this respect both Propertius and Ovid are more responsive than Tibullus; Horace's loyalties, despite *Epist.* 1.10.1–2 and other passages, seem to have been divided between city and countryside.

does so before, not after the prophecy of 93–4. Although none of these rather abstract parallels amounts to a positive proof of Theocritean influence, they may help back up certain other possibilities.[28]

Once the dream had been chosen as the narrative framework of 4.7, the highlights of Cynthia's affair with Propertius could only be presented by means of flashbacks. Simaetha must also travel back in time to explain why she resorts to sorcery (64–158). Both women reminisce, both describe the consummation of their liaison as a memorable experience. Simaetha recounts the crucial moment:

> μαλακῶν ἔκλιν' ἐπὶ λέκτρων·
> καὶ ταχὺ χρὼς ἐπὶ χρωτὶ πεπαίνετο, καὶ τὰ πρόσωπα
> θερμότερ' ἦς ἢ πρόσθε, καὶ ἐψιθυρίσδομες ἁδύ·
>
> (139–41)

and drew him down upon the soft couch. And quickly body warmed to body, and faces burned hotter than before, and sweetly we whispered.

Sweet nothings apart, sexual energy is estimated here in terms of the heat produced, which for all its suggestiveness seems hardly original. An instance of analogous thermogenesis is Meleager, *A.P.* 5.172.2 (= Gow–Page 4137) ἄρτι φίλας Δημοῦς χρωτὶ χλιαινομένῳ 'now that the body of my beloved Demo keeps me warm'; elsewhere, for instance in *A.P.* 5.165.3–4 (= Gow–Page 4256–7), Meleager crowns such snugness with a liberal cloak. It seems that we are dealing here with motifs of some currency and it would, therefore, be hazardous to allow *Id.* 2.140–1 specific influence on 4.7.19–20. The alchemy of reminiscence and cross-reference cannot be conclusively exposed, but there is some room here for speculating whether χρὼς ἐπὶ χρωτί could not have hardened into *ossibus ossa* in 4.7.94. This, it may be objected, could have been brought about

---

[28] Not only 4.7 as a whole, but the idea, in particular, of the repossession of the straying or oblivious lover is most probably the result of 'polygenesis'. Virgil, *Ecl.* 8.64ff. may have done no more than sharpen Propertius' interest in its model, but Dido's desperate attempts to keep her lover in Carthage in *Aen.* 4.296ff., and the magical practices described in 483ff. with the invocation of Hecate in 511 (repeated in 609), must have applied fresh stimuli (for the influence of the *Aeneid* on 4.7 see also below). Nor should one forget the abominable Canidia of Horace's fifth epode – indeed in going through 4.7 one should make a point of pondering over some of her words: *Nox et Diana, quae silentium regis,* | *arcana cum fiunt sacra* 'Night and Diana, queen of the silent hours, when secret rites are performed' (51–2); this is worthy of Subura's nocturnal revellers in 4.7.15ff. Her philandering Varus can sleep forgetful of his mistresses, nay, he walks unscathed *solutus...veneficae* | *scientioris carmine* 'released by the incantation of a more knowledgeable witch' (71–2). Cynthia has comparable grievances in 4.7.13–14 and suspicions in 4.7.72; and, of course, Canidia's *ad me recurres* 'you'll come back to me' (75) pales beside the words with which Cynthia expresses determination to get her own back (93–4). Last but not least, the dogs that bark in l. 58 of the epode are *Suburanae.* It has been suggested that Horace is here indebted to Theocritus' Φαρμακεύτρια; not unlikely. It is equally likely that Prop. was indebted to both Theocritus and Horace.

under the pressure of the Homeric ὀστέα in *Il.* 23.91, but it should also be remembered that Delphis' ὀστία are emphatically at stake in Simaetha's sympathetic magic (*Id.* 2.21). *pectore mixto* in 4.7.19 looks forward to *mixtis ossibus* in 4.7.94; the predicted mixture is by no means unrelated to the recalled one, and their joint evidence (*tepidas, ossibus ossa*), along with other possible indications of Theocritean contribution, should be cautiously assessed. A final point: the domestic cabal and cruel slapstick of 4.7.35–48 are arguably redolent of the mime (see pp. 169–70 below); further, there can be little doubt that Theocritus draws on one of Sophron's mimes, at least as far as Simaetha's magic is concerned – a fact which makes it reasonable to point out the logicality (though, admittedly, not the logical necessity) of a relationship between the elegy and the idyll by virtue of shared interests. But general reflections on such a relationship were occasioned by 4.7.19–20, and to this couplet we must now go back.

Compared to 4.7.19 such a line as 3.20.6 *forsitan ille alio pectus amore terat* 'perhaps, he is being consumed by passion in another's embrace' suggests that in Propertius' erotic jargon no meaningful line may be drawn between *terere* and *miscere*; 4.7.94, moreover, blurs the line between *pectora* and *ossa*. It is as though any one member of this verbal cluster cried out to be complemented by some other, and as though whenever one occurred we should broaden its conceptual spectrum by means of all others. Ezra Pound might have seen this as a variety of Propertian logopoeia, only here love and death, or, to be more accurate, love as death, dances among the words along with the intellect. Thus it comes about that neither is 4.7.94 free of erotic overtones nor 4.7.19 of funereal ones; also in the latter line, *trivio* localises the cross between metaphysical fear and physical passion, death and debauchery: *La Débauche et la Mort sont deux aimables filles*...It is important to remember that the Cynthia of 4.7 is a lustful incubus who stands half-way between Subura lewdness and sepulchral libido. Propertius' interim love life, caught up between two crucial assignations, is dwarfed to irrelevance – it is not even expressed as such. He is no active lover but the victim of the reshuffle in his ménage; no more than the seven words of l. 93 suffice to dismiss his transient (*mox*) aberration. It is almost as if the moment he embraced this woman at the nocturnal *trivium* he committed an act of erotic *devotio* of whose inescapable fulfilment he needs to be reminded rather than warned.[29] So if throughout the poem he does not get a word in edgeways,

---

[29] Yardley (1977) 85 reminds us that in ancient ghost stories an apparition was normally believed to forebode the addressee's death; I am inclined to believe that this rule is operative in 4.7.

it is probably because he has little remorse about their shared past and takes no objection to their projected future:

> Tombeaux et lupanars montrent sous leurs charmilles
> Un lit que le remords n'a jamais fréquenté.[30]

There is a pseudo-enjambement between 19 and 20: *pectore mixto* drifts towards the pentameter, yet it is also an inalienable part of the hexameter's conceptual complex. It seems to escape notice, or mention, that *pallia* can mean both garments and bed-covers. At any rate, these lovers need both meanings for they have made *vias* their couch. Through doing so they turn upside down the normal situation exemplified by, among others, Meleager, *A.P.* 5.165.3–4, which has been referred to above, p. 157.[31] Propertius has something analogous in 3.13.35–6:

> hinnulei pellis totos operibat amantis,
> altaque nativo creverat herba toro

> *A roebuck's pelt was the lovers' perfect cover and the grass grew high to give them a natural couch.*

– an idyllic picture of Golden-Age comfort supported, as the pentameter shows, by a most comfortable bed. One cannot help being directed back to the lovers' *Ur*-couch in *Iliad*, 14.347–51: it consists of lush vegetation which apparently helps to cushion the bruising effects of Jupiter's sexual improvisation... ἀπὸ χθονὸς ὑψόσ' ἔεργε. I do not know that it is fanciful to suppose that reminiscence of such elevated love nests would set off the *terre à terre* quality of 4.7.19–20. Quiet humour may be smouldering beneath the 'downing' of the motif, but audible laughter there is none. We are more likely to capture the tone if we realise that *vias*, whatever it may denote, certainly connotes uncleanliness, and the whole couplet celebrates direct contact with it. There is here – *scherzo ma non troppo* – nostalgia for the mud: *O fangeuse grandeur! sublime ignominie!*

As Cynthia rehearses the flaws of her funeral in ll. 23ff., the unclean shades off intermittently into the blasphemous. The aprioristic equation of the realistic with the comic-satiric must be counteracted by close attention to sound and diction no less than by constant appeal to general Propertian practice. The first complaint is registered in 23–4:

---

[30] 'Tombs and brothels show under their bowers a couch that remorse has never visited'; these verses and the one just quoted above come from Baudelaire's 'Les deux bonnes soeurs' (Pichois, I 114–15).

[31] Cf. Warden (1980) 25.

> at mihi non oculos quisquam inclamavit euntis:
> unum impetrassem te revocante diem

> *But no one keened for me as my eyes closed. Had you*
> *Called me back I'd have lived for one more day.*

Pronounced nasality monitors the couplet's lugubrious wistfulness. What actual funeral rites lie behind it (and *conclamatio*, the calling of the dying person's name, should be among them) must be retrieved, if they are worth retrieving at all, from evocative semantic and, probably, syntactic eccentricities. Propertius is unique in making the eyes the object of the act suggested by *inclamavit*; it would be an equally unique use if *euntis* were a genitive, as thinks Tränkle, who seeks a parallel for this remarkable shift from dative (*mihi*) to genitive in Hom. *Od.* 9.256–7 ἡμῖν δ' αὖτε κατεκλάσθη φίλον ἦτορ | δεισάντων and suggests that the construction was startling enough to attract Propertius.[32] But whether the latter experimented with the alluring involution or not, a suspicion of ambiguity seems to attach to the participle, whose effect may be vaguely felt as one of καθ' ὅλον καὶ μέρος, as genitive and accusative alternate in the reader's mind.[33] The slight alteration *eunti* (Reland), on the other hand, by appending the participle to the 'ethic' *mihi*, detracts from its corporeality – it makes it more grammatic than dramatic. But to substitute an altogether different word, such as *hiantes* or *hebentes*, for *euntis* is to ignore the attractive possibility that l. 23 may be fusing the *conclamatio*, the image of the failing eyes *and* the idea of *ire* or *iter*, as we find it in such expressions as Cat. 3.11 *qui nunc it per iter tenebricosum* (on the last journey of Lesbia's sparrow). Propertius, however, is his own best commentator. Note 2.27.15–16:

> si modo clamantis revocaverit aura puellae,
> concessum nulla lege redibit iter.

> *If only the breath of a cry from his girl should call him back*
> *He will return by the route no law allows.*

Clearly, the haunting *outre-tombe* conceit has been transferred to *in articulo mortis* circumstances in 4.7.23–4, and so Tränkle, in suggesting that *euntis* is a euphemism for *morientis* derived from the *Alltagssprache*, has probably miscalculated the pitch of the couplet.[34] Warden, who adduces K. Quinn

---

[32] Tränkle (1960) 75; he follows Löfstedt.

[33] *euntis* as a genitive is frowned upon on the ground that Latin, unlike Greek, has no genitive absolute construction. (See, for instance, Fedeli *ad loc.*) But to a reader fresh from *foederis heu taciti* (21) the Propertian construction may have seemed another bolder Graecism rather than an impossibility. [34] Tränkle (1960) 164–5.

on 2.27.15–16, attaches importance to the effect of hyperbole in 4.7.23–4. But where language is strained for poetic effect it would be highly inopportune to make much of the fact that our credulity is also strained. Warden's view is partly due to an assumption which the comparison of the two couplets in question renders all but untenable, namely, that we are meant to take 4.7.23 as a reflection of a precise and prescribed ritual act. But whatever such act may be, *conclamatio* or *condere oculos*, it lies too far beneath the poetic surface to ensure a gap between a 'perfectly normal everyday event' in 23 and the mythological miracle – *dead* Protesilaus' brief visit to Laodamia – at which 24 may be hinting.[35] Although in 23ff. Propertius is evidently reproducing the natural order of the stages of a Roman funeral, he is throughout evocative rather than descriptive, and factually accurate only in so far as this furthers his poetic aims – which means that the factual is at times subject to a cavalier treatment.

This one should bear in mind when approaching the next couplet:

> nec *c*repuit fissa me *p*ropter *h*arundine *c*ustos,
> laesit et obie*c*tum tegula *c*urta *c*aput.   (4.7.25–6)

> *No watchman rattled a split cane near me,*
> *And the crock against my head hurt.*

It is at least as enlightening to point out that these lines echo the bleak rattling of 12 (*crepuit* spawns a series of *c*'s and *r*'s) as it is to pin down the precise function of the split reed. One question that ought not to be asked here is whether Cynthia deplores the absence of the guard or his inadequate performance; it is enough that the custom (on which we know as much as Camps *ad loc.* notes) existed and could thus make its uncanny contribution. It looks, however, as if an instrument normally wielded to exorcise evil spirits[36] has here been brought in to magnetise them – and l. 19 is a reminder that this is by no means their debut. Not all poetry ought to be melodious, and cacophony in the pentameter has its place: Propertius has some harsh sounds (with the *c*'s the *t*'s are interlaced) for the jagged, broken tile; one remembers Homer's κόππ'· ἐκ δ' ἐγκέφαλος.[37] *curtus*, remarks Tränkle, does not quite belong to the elevated language;[38] to Propertius it seems to have been emblematic of unmitigated and terminal sordidness, for it also qualifies the vile amphora he would like to see on the bawd's tomb in 4.5.75 *sit tumulus lenae curto vetus amphora collo* 'let the bawd's tomb be marked by an old broken wine jar'. The word clearly outgrows its visual implications in at least one direction, that of

---

[35] Warden (1980) 28; but he says immediately afterwards: 'This must not be overstated.'
[36] Shackleton Bailey (1949) 28–9 rejects this, to my mind captiously and on very thin grounds.
[37] Wilkinson (1966) 43.   [38] Tränkle (1960) 130.

the sinister. If the broken wine jar can be seen as the symbolic relic of a hideous witch, the curtailed *tegula* is in contagious juxtaposition with the weird sisters that take advantage of the absent, or absent-minded, *custos*. It is in the nature of the elegiac couplet that the pentameter should be an extension of the hexameter, so the non-committal *et* may in fact be concealing a vague causal link; conceivably, in hexameter and pentameter alike human incompetence has conspired with evil interference. But if the undertaker of l. 26 intended to puzzle scholars he was singularly successful.

Beroaldus sensibly suggested that here the broken tile does duty for a pillow, Princess Teresa Uzeda *probante*.[39] Rothstein transposed the faulty tile to the roof of a ramshackle outbuilding which, naturally enough, did not shelter the laid-out body from inclement weather. The falling tile that accidentally struck Cynthia's head in Butler and Barber must have come off Rothstein's roof. Celentano suspects foul play on the part of the witches, who may have thrown the tile from the roof through the *inpluvium* in their effort to snatch the corpse.[40] Richardson replaced the fragment of terracotta on the bier but propped it *against* rather than *under* the head, explaining that it was inscribed with a curse meant to scare off evil spirits (something Prop. should have done himself); his solution involves transferring the force of *obiectum* to *tegula*. I believe it would be far less objectionable to understand from *tegula* a dative *tegulae* to go with the participle: *obiectum tegulae*. The head was thrown against, exposed, or given as prey to a jagged tile – and the tile chafed it. Since Propertius is here charged with negligence or recklessness rather than with violence, Caes. *Civ.* 1.64.3 *tantae magnitudini fluminis exercitum obicere* 'to expose the army to so strong a current' is a better parallel than Pl. *Cur.* 567 *priu' quam te huic meae machaerae obicio* 'before I throw you against this sword of mine', but both are good examples of a construction to which l. 26 easily accommodates itself.[41] On this interpretation the *tegula curta* can be

---

[39] See Muecke (1978) 242 but cf. Croce (1936) 149.

[40] Celentano (1956) 52 n. 50; she draws attention to a sepulchral bas-relief reproduced in Daremberg–Saglio *s.v. funus* with the help of which one may form a general idea of the setting implied by 4.7.25–6.

[41] See *OLD s.v. obicio* 6.

obiectum is strong, but a strong word is required here (a) to show the degree of negligence and (b) because the tile was angular and thus hurtful as well as mean. Laughton's (1958) 98–9 suggestion that *obiectum* may be alluding to the fact that 'the body was customarily laid with its feet towards the door' is an interesting piece of speculation, though one – if we must go into details – which will not quite explain how the globular can be said to point in a certain direction in the same sense as the longitudinal does, especially when the latter is affected by *rigor mortis*, as in Persius 3.105 *in portam rigidas calces extendit*. Unless it is by accident that *obicere* can nowhere else be found in this technical sense, Propertius' reader would certainly have interpreted *obiectum* as yet another count against the chief mourner.

nothing but a cheap and nasty substitute for the expected *pulvillum* – a brilliant piece of funeral travesty in perfect harmony with the rest of Propertius' omissions. *laesit* points in the same direction. It can, of course, mean 'strike' or 'hit', yet in its literal applications the verb mostly conveys injury caused by friction, attrition or prolonged contact as, for instance, in Ovid, *Her.* 4.21 *teneros laedunt iuga prima iuvencos* 'at first the yoke chafes the tender bullocks'. If the accidentally fallen tile is an argument for Propertius' innocence of at least this piece of callousness, then the argument must fail; *laesit* is an inculpatory word and, what is more, it may be pointing beyond grievous bodily harm to more insidious effects. For should the terracotta be as malignant as it is abrasive, *laesit...caput* will readily align itself with the devil; the prominent *numine laeso* in the *Aeneid* prologue and the *caput* as the *par excellence* recipient of curses suffice to ensure this. Lines 25–6 confront us once again with that exquisite amalgam of ruthless realism and brooding evil which was also in evidence in 19–20 – only the latter passage brings together the devil, death *and* the flesh.

The unholy trinity, as we have already seen in connexion with 2.1, is rampant in the pages of the Roman novel, obviously in emulation of Greek models and in accordance with the subliterary tradition of anecdotes and dinner-party stories (cf. p. 40 above). A man – goes one of these stories narrated in the presence of Lucius, the hero of Apuleius' *Metamorphoses* – was hired to stand guard by a corpse in the Thessalian town of Larissa, a traditional stronghold of sorcery. In the course of the story, which seems to be the result of a conflation on the part of Apuleius of two or three different anecdotes, there is a nocturnal witch raid; the *custos* falls fast asleep; the dead man's body is pillaged (although in Apuleius' version this does not become evident until later in the story); a *funeral procession* takes place the next day but is interrupted by the dead man's uncle who claims that his nephew has been *poisoned* by a wife bent on *adultery*; the corpse is *recalled to life* by a magician and confirms the accusations (*Met.* 2.21ff.). Heavily redolent of Milesian prurience, the story exhibits a blend of scheming lust and superstitious mumbo-jumbo;[42] and the italicised similarities with our poem make it more than probable that some details, or a particular combination of details, and much of the colour of Cynthia's speech were suggested by the subliterature that spiced the leisure of post-Classical society. Besides, some of this material may have been processed by the literary mime. Perry's suggestion that the

---

[42] Petronius' more famous widow in *Sat.* 111–12 will also be recalled: she entered her husband's sepulchral vault a chaste wife and left it a crafty mistress at the convenient cost of the corpse she so pathetically had refused to part company with.

custos incident in the story of Apuleius' *Metamorphoses* had already been performed on the Roman stage as a one-act mime has much to recommend it,[43] and with regard to 4.7 in particular it adds to the evidence – briefly touched upon on p. 153 above and to be assessed again later on – for marked overtures to mime in late Propertius.[44] Talk of mime elements in this case need mean no concession to Auerbach's thesis. The one-act mime Perry envisages must have had the audiences in stitches as the poor *custos* was being chucked out of the widow's house, his nose and ears chopped off; but one may be fairly certain that a good deal of spine chilling had gone before that. Addressed to a very different audience, the elegy neither appeals to crude, superstitious fear nor courts low-brow guffaw. It mixes the same ingredients to provide entertainment of a different order.

Back in the text Cynthia's lying-in-state is over, she has been carried – feet first, unless her lover failed to see to that too! – out of the house, and the funeral procession is under way. In lines 27–8 the oblique joins forces with the particular:

> denique quis nostro curvum te funere vidit,
> atram quis lacrimis incaluisse togam? (4.7.27–8)

> *Besides, who saw you bowed in grief above my body*
> *Or your black toga hot with tears?*

This is a masterly attempt to arrest the evanescent, and once again a crisp, strong adjective (*curvum*) is the centre of gravity; it 'says all that is needed', remarks Williams, who singles it out as an instance of Propertius' 'capacity to select a word which will create, by itself, a maximum appropriate effect in a given context'.[45] *vidit* will not strictly apply to 28 and yet a kind of synaesthesia transcends the formal zeugma: the eye captures the curve, absorbs the colour (*atram*) but also feels the moist (*lacrimis*) and the warm (*incaluisse*) penetrate (*incaluisse*) the fabric

[43] Perry (1967) 266–7 believes that 'it was bound to make a hit with any theatrical audience: Enter Thelyphron...boasting of his wakefulness...Thelyphron on guard, the gradual coming on of darkness and night...his rapidly mounting fear...Thelyphron falling suddenly into a deep sleep...enter the widow with her seven witnesses; the nose and ears of the dead man are found to be missing; Thelyphron's ears and nose are cut off to replace them, he is thrown out of the house...and down goes the curtain...'

[44] For the favour which mime enjoyed in Rome and its influence on elegy in general see McKeown (1979) 71–84 who argues that the elegiac love triangle may be partly indebted to the scenarios of the Adultery Mime. In that case one would have to reckon with mimic elements throughout Propertius, and indeed throughout the work of the other elegists too; but this does not alter the fact that situations which were immediately recognisable as peculiar to that genre are nowhere so sharply outlined as in the closely interrelated seventh and eighth elegies of Propertius' last poetic book. (See also p. 197 below.)

[45] Williams (1968) 781; cf. also pp. 22–3 above.

of the garment; the *toga* drinks the tears much as in 4.11.6 the deaf shore does: *nempe tuas lacrimas litora surda bibent* 'no doubt, the deaf shore will drink up your tears'. But 4.7.28 invites a more intricate sensory response, and Postgate selected the whole couplet in order to put, in the manner of some decades ago, 'the higher poetical qualities of Propertius beyond the reach of cavil'.[46] In ll. 29–30, however, detail is abandoned for a perspective of the whole:

> si piguit portas ultra procedere, at illuc
> iussisses lectum lentius ire meum.   (4.7.29–30)

> *If it bored you to go further, you could at least have slowed*
> *The bearer's pace to the city gates.*

Propertius would not proceed further than the city gates, nor does the clause conveying this proceed further than the fifth foot. But Cynthia proceeds to tax him, in 31–4, with neglecting the culminating rites, which could only have taken place outside the city walls. The inconsistency (never exposed so far as I know) is neither here nor there but serves as a reminder that this plaintiff shares with the defendant a proclivity to sacrifice credibility to visual completeness; neither reports an event, both wax eloquent over what has never, or not yet, happened. Comparison with 2.13 will show what this means; what is more important, it will point to a context within which the funeral proceedings of 4.7 must be set, and a perspective from which they can be better appreciated. Never had a single funeral developed so many hitches; what is more, never had a mourner so meticulously begrudged what in his own testament he had so fastidiously prescribed. The ghost might have allusively started: *accipe quae non servasti funeris acta mei*, and could have gone on to make the obvious contrast between the sumptuous Adonis-like posture that masqueraded as plebeian contentedness in 2.13 and the strident squalor that put her pauper's *funus* on a par with that of the abominable bawd-witch of 4.5 (see below). This triad chronicles Propertius' susceptibility to the ambivalent fascination of the funeral motif; it also answers Cynthia's queries in 4.7.25ff. If in 2.13 we have found *éclat, solidité, couleur*, the reversal of the *funus* aesthetics in 4.5 and 7 entails a stark realism and the far different qualities of the lack-lustre, the fragmentary and the grey; 'c'est un des privilèges prodigieux de l'Art que l'horrible, artistement exprimé, devienne beauté'. This principle[47] holds good for the description of Cynthia's funeral no less than for her appearance in 7–12. Some more points about the former will be taken up presently; I have just paused

---

[46] Postgate (1881) lxxxiii.   [47] See Pichois, I 181.

to stress the illuminative value of obvious but as a rule inadequately explored cross-references, and to renew my suggestion that 'extraire la beauté du mal' is most probably what the poet is after in these lines.

The last of Propertius' cardinal omissions was that no *broken* jar poured wine on Cynthia's ashes, *et fracto busta piare cado* (34). The use of wine in such cases is well-known but the breaking of its vessel is unattested outside Propertius. But even if the gesture was customary, we should most probably reckon with some of the overtones considered with regard to *curta* in 26, namely sordidness and meanness. Besides reintroducing the fragmentation motif, *fracto* keeps up the dry, harsh sounds that punctuate the whole length of 4.7; 34 as a whole will hardly rank as a euphonious line. More importantly, this broken wine jar directs attention once again to the death rattle of the bawd-witch in 4.5:

> vidi ego rugoso tussim concrescere collo,
> sputaque per dentis ire cruenta cavos,
> atque animam in tegetes putrem exspirare paternas:
> horruit algenti pergula curva foco.
> exsequiae fuerant [fuerint *Barber*] rari furtiva capilli
> vincula et immundo pallida mitra situ,
> et canis, in nostros nimis experrecta dolores,
> cum fallenda meo pollice clatra forent.
> sit tumulus lenae curto vetus amphora collo:
> urgeat hunc supra vis, caprifice, tua.
> quisquis amas, scabris hoc bustum caedite saxis,
> mixtaque cum saxis addite verba mala!   (4.5.67–78)

I saw her wrinkled throat stiffen with cough and the bloody spittle trickle through her hollow teeth; she breathed out her foul soul on the mats her father bequeathed her. The sagging booth with its chill fireplace was a frigid mess. Her funeral cortège was made up of some swag headbands she used for her sparse hair, a faded and filthy bonnet long fallen into disuse and a dog which, much to my dismay, had proved too alert whenever my fingers were about to negotiate the latch. Let the bawd's tomb be marked by an old broken wine jar, with a fig tree on it to grow wild and break it up. Come, all you who love, pelt this grave with rough stones, and mingled with the stones add your curses.

These last twelve lines of the poem are an apotheosis of funereal squalor and sinister overtones, and have little in common with either Tib. 1.5.49ff., which, one or two new twists apart, try to make the best of commonplace material, or Ov. *Am.* 1.8.111–14, which after contemplating punitive manhandling resort to maledictions short of pungency.[48] As a piece of unflinching realism applied to the anile condition, Hor. *Epod.* 8 is more interesting. However, Horace's realism, underpinned by nauseating analogies from zoology, expends itself in jibes at the flaccidity that turns him off. Looked at from a phallocentric point of view, the miseries of female obsolescence will scarcely admit of the serious, and the treatment here bears Auerbach out. What is the place of Prop. 4.5.67–78 in relation to these passages? One should approach the question unprejudiced by the literary provenance of the harridan or by the distinctly Ovidian tone in which she holds forth. The fact alone that she was endemic to the low stage[49] is no justification for the notion that at the end of the elegy *Propertius ludibundus* mocks her funeral.[50] On close inspection one's response tends to be something more along the lines of Boucher's view that the brief description which evokes so powerfully the horror of Acanthis' death places Propertius among 'des plus grands artistes réalistes, peintres ou romanciers, Goya ou Zola';[51] and this is far less bold than it may at first blush seem.

The pointers to the stylistic elevation of the passage are many and unmistakable: 68 *dentis cavos*, 69 *tegetes*, *putrem*, 70 *algenti*, *pergula*, 71 *furtiva*, 75 *curto collo* and *amphora* make up a strong colloquial and unpoetic condiment.[52] Shabbiness, putrescence and ignominious misery are all called up through a barrage of sensory impressions. But the peculiar force of these lines resides in the complementary relationship they establish between figure and décor: the bawd can be deduced from her milieu as the milieu implies her physique and morals; all her appurtenances stand for either her bodily or her moral condition or both.[53] It is, I think, this combination of stylistic and atmospheric realism, of realistic presentation with realistic content, that brings the passage closer to modern conceptions of realism. This is clearly the splendidly audacious, late Propertius and in wanting to take 4.5 back to 28/27 B.C. Luck is very wide of the

[48] What sets Propertius' passage apart is the swooping on the random and significant detail and the hard-edged depiction of the low and ugly. The difference is pointed out neither by Morgan (1977) 59–68, nor by Courtney (1969) 80–7 – an otherwise intelligent discussion of several points raised by the comparison between Prop. and Ovid –, nor by Thill (1979) 320–7. On the chronological relationship between Prop. 4.5 and Ovid, *Am.* 1.8 see Courtney, pp. 8off.

[49] An unmistakable breath of comedy attaches to bibulous bawd-procuresses, like the one in Herodas' first *Mimiamb*. But such figures must be seen as an integral part of the 'gerontological' interests of Hellenistic poets and artists and placed in the wider context of Hellenistic realism, which is not invariably comic. One thinks of Callimachus' Hecale and of the decrepit Phineus in Apoll. *Argon.* 2.197ff. Cf. Webster (1964) 168.

[50] Krokowski (1926) 91.   [51] Boucher (1965) 78.

[52] See Tränkle (1960) 129, 81 and 127, 123 and 132, 131, 114, 110, respectively.

[53] Cf. La Penna (1977) 95–6.

mark.[54] Tränkle's analysis is the best corrective of this view: 'The concluding lines are among the poet's most splendid linguistic performances'. And there is a right feeling underlying his further remark that although individual words are often unpoetic, the language used as a whole would be inconceivable in prose.[55] For this is imaginative and selective realism, not photographic and scrupulous naturalism, the line of Balzac rather than of Boucher's Zola. The former's *Le Père Goriot* (1834) begins with the famous description of Madame Vauquer's lodging-house, the setting for most of the novel's action. Balzac writes: 'toute sa personne explique la pension, comme la pension implique sa personne' and Auerbach's authoritative analysis shows how the novelist contrives to convey just that.[56] Madame Vauquer lives in a filthy environment, is physically repulsive (she has ill-attached false hair, cf. Prop. 4.5.71), and has the expression of a bawd; she is no witch but is heralded by a cat that adds a 'touch of witchcraft' (cf. 4.5.73). 'What confronts us', writes Auerbach, 'is the unity of a particular milieu, felt as a total concept of a demonic-organic nature and presented entirely by suggestive and sensory means' (p. 472). The desolate squalor of the place comes powerfully alive when the central figure, old Goriot, dies: '...the body was placed on the bare sacking of the bedstead in that desolate room. A candle burned on either side, and a priest came to watch there.' Later the pauper's coffin could be seen 'barely covered by a scanty black cloth, standing on two chairs outside the wicket gate in the deserted street. A shabby sprinkler lay in a silver-plated copper bowl of holy water, but no one had stopped to sprinkle the coffin...The dead man was a pauper, and so there was no display of grief, no friend, no kinsman to follow him to the grave.' For all the double inconvenience of generic and epochal disparity, the funerals of Acanthis, Cynthia and Goriot are managed in the same spirit and belong to the same class with the odd and, as it were, merely technical difference.[57]

[54] Luck (1955) 428ff. argues for an early composition almost against his better judgement, for he has not missed the movement in 4.5 from the elevated to the realistic, and from 'melodious loveliness to sharp insults' (p. 430); on this as a feature of Propertius' late manner, see below.

[55] See Tränkle (1960) 175–8, esp. 177 and cf. Lefèvre (1966) 101: 'We should also notice that it is not by accident that the two most distinctive representatives of the grotesque, Horos and Acanthis, are to be found in Book 4, and that they fit its particular style.'

[56] Auerbach (1953) 468ff.

[57] In 1871 Vincenzo Padula was moved to pious tears by Cynthia's indecorous funeral, but then he was, as Benedetto Croce (1936) 147 described him, something of a priest, a provincial 'professore' with a great deal of Latin, some Hebrew, little Greek and no modern languages at all. (Cf. La Penna (1977) 300–13.) Yet his comparison of Cynthia's demise to that of *Dame aux camélias* was not bad at all; it reminded Croce (p. 150) of some 'femmes du second Empire' who lived glamorously and were buried unceremoniously, a contrast of high poetic potential, as Baudelaire's 'Les petites vieilles' magnificently shows.

At this point the rationale of what may strike as an adventurous juxtaposition can be restated. Auerbach's thesis that ancient realism is narrow inasmuch as it fails to probe the forces at work behind the social phenomena is no doubt sound; it is equally true that the avowed aspiration of the nineteenth-century realists was to reveal exactly those forces. Viewed from this standpoint, what realism has been claimed for the Propertian passages is manifestly static and ahistorical. But comic it is not. Unlike Hor. *Epod.* 8 or, for that matter, 12, Prop. 4.5.67–78 would be misleadingly classified under the head of 'vetula-Skoptik', and not only because sex is a more obvious joke than death. Again, the ersatz gear of Cynthia's funeral in 4.7.26 is no more prankish than the dog cortège of 4.5.73–4 is derisive cynicism just for the sake of it. One gains a better perspective for tabulating the funerals of 2.13, 4.5 and 4.7; but once this has been done, a thematically linked piece from modern realism can be allowed to shine helpful light, for despite obvious differences of scope there seems to be no reason why the aesthetic partiality for what one of the lodgers *chez* Vauquer wryly calls 'mortorama' should not be predicated of ancient dilettante and modern professional alike.

Her funeral over, Cynthia protests in ll. 35–48 that an ordinary ménage has been turned by her rival into nothing less than a pandemonium. From this sudden *crise de nerfs* there accrue to the poem motifs and images which once again land the reader on the low stage. What is being performed here is some sort of *comoedia 'vapularis'*, with the goodies already suffering in the hands of Propertius' new mistress, although both Petale and Lalage might be relieved to know that a less fortunate fellow slave was once actually crucified.[58] Slaves are ritually under duress in comedy and mime, and the rowdy scenes of their punishment seem to have been part and parcel of the show. And yet the cruel slapstick in which these particular slaves engage reflects the weird obsessions of a woman surrounded by an evil aura while lying in Subura and in state. Poison, we have already seen, is an essential topos in these stories of ghosts and adulterers, but the use Propertius makes of it and the challenge it presents to his expressive powers cannot be taken for granted. 4.7.36 *cum insidiis pallida vina bibi* 'when I drank that treacherous white wine' is a more densely suggestive variant of 2.27.10 *neu subeant labris pocula nigra tuis* 'Lest black potions pass your lips'.[59] Both 3.11.54 *et trahere occultum membra soporis iter* 'and [I saw] her limbs channel the stealthy course of slumber'

---

[58] Beare (1964) 314ff. quotes the Oxyrhynchus mime from a papyrus of the second century A.D., in which a woman wants her slave flogged to death (along with his girl-friend) for refusing to gratify her sexually. Cf. Walsh (1970) 26.

[59] See the discussions of Shackleton Bailey (1956) 250–1 and Warden (1980) 33 especially.

and 4.7.37 *aut Nomas – arcanas tollat versuta salivas* 'let artful Nomas hide away her secret juices' insinuate lethal insidiousness, but the latter compounds dark secrecy with subtle secretion; Nomas *secretes* her bane. Words awaken as many connotations and associations as are needed to thrust her upon the mind's eye as some sort of spitting snake, and to present Cynthia as the victim of a crime that can be revealed, not investigated. It is fascinating to see what Propertius can extract from a rather overripened motif, as it is important to appreciate the fitting suggestiveness with which it is employed in this poem, for one cannot help feeling that anything less than an arcane and uncanny death from poison ordered by some trollop would be more or less out of tune with the evil hazards of Cynthia's Subura rendezvous – or even with her demonstricken bier. In one sense, funny things are going on in the little 'mimic' inferno of Propertius' household; in another, ll. 35–48 are not particularly funny. The sinners and martyrs of these lines, at least in their present activities, have been purloined from the boisterous world of comedy and mime; the sinners and martyrs of the next section (49–70) are situated worlds apart. By swinging from the human to the divine comedy Propertius revisits a cherished and intensely personal world of which we have caught but a glimpse in 1.19, and on which we must now concentrate.

We enter Cynthia's Underworld by way of her oath-backed assertion of *fides* in 51–4. Between the solemnity of these and the rancour of the preceding lines, 49–50 stand as a buffer couplet. Cynthia modulates the tone of her speech (*non tamen insector* 'but I'm not hounding you') out of consideration for the troubadour rather than the lover: *longa mea in libris regna fuere tuis* 'in your books my reign was long' (50). At the same time she extricates herself from the mundane imbroglio of 35–48 in time for the 'eschatology' of 55ff. A literary pattern for the latter had long been established by the *Catalogue of Women* in the eleventh book of the *Odyssey* no less than by *Aeneid* 6. But Propertius, indebted as he may be for pictorial and conceptual rudiments to these accounts, is here indulging a vision which ultimately blurs both topography and ethics.

More than once the Propertian Beyond is the function of its female denizens; it exists for them and through them. Since, however, this is part and parcel of the poet's obsession with pageants of female figures, the argument must broaden to take account of those instances that can help put 4.7.55ff. in perspective. It has been noted apropos of 2.1 (p. 29 above) that whenever such pageants unfold it is their collective impact rather than the individual record of their members that really matters. It is, I think, an even more important point that, whether specified by name or synoptically presented as a chorus, these women are invariably linked by the fact that they are *beautiful* and *long gone*. This, so to say, syzygy, which can hardly be overemphasised, has not been emphasised enough. Had it been given its due, preoccupation with the moral and emotional implications of this poetic theme would have stood less in the way of pure enjoyment; in fact, one often feels tempted to stretch the point: the poet may be so far from such concerns as to be swayed by the sheer aural aestheticism of the voluminous Greek names normally borne by these women.[60] Let it be stressed again that Roman poets had an ear for the melody of Greek names and that Propertius was never more receptive in this respect than when it came to the names of legendary women. His coveted paradise of female comeliness is appropriately accentuated by Miltonic sound effects – but puritanical it is not. Boyancé displays discerning taste in expounding the enchanting Propertian world of Greek heroines; to be sure, beauty is its main characteristic, 'la beauté mais pas seulement la beauté: la vertu aussi et surtout...la fidélité'.[61] This view has become something of an orthodoxy, as Warden's more recent remark about the moral significance of the Dead Beauties parade confirms.[62] But *fides* may be less what the poet highlights than what he has inherited. Classical poets are not given to mythological revisionism; at most, if they are learned enough, they may adopt a different version. When Propertius draws in Hypermestra an inevitable load of associations, some of them moral, trail behind her. Yes, she proved faithful to her husband; Propertius knows that as well as his readers do. But if his readers seize on his use of *fida, fides* or the like, they should know better, for he has given them cause to surmise that Hypermestra would have entered Boyancé's 'monde' even if she had slaughtered single-handed forty-nine brothers-in-law and one husband. Indeed, had she done so she might even have improved her poetical cachet. 2.32 is in itself an extensive and clear hint to that effect.

We have already glanced at this poem with its spectacular about-face in ll. 25ff., where Propertius concentrates on the aesthetic potential and, by implication, the moral insignificance of mythological and literary promiscuity. The abortive moralising of the first part is exposed as transparent irony, and the irony is sealed by the last couplet, where the

---

[60] Ovid could do the same with the names of the Greek mountain peaks in *Met.* 2.217–26; see Wilkinson (1955) 235–6.

[61] Boyancé (1956) 184, 186.   [62] Warden (1980) 39.

poet seems perfectly reconciled to the fact that fair ladies will always set tongues wagging: *quod si tu Graias es tuque imitata Latinas,* | *semper vive meo libera iudicio!* (2.32.61–2).[63] Cynthia is in good company: Tyndaris (31–2), Venus herself (33–4), Oenone (35ff.), Lesbia (45), very significantly Pasiphae (57–8) and Danae (59–60) – a rather heterogeneous band only made possible by the fact that the bourgeois ethics of 21–4 stands no chance against the splendours of divine and upper-class vice. Poetic beauty is apt to be redoubled by that which impairs moral beauty. These women, romantically distanced by status and time, are grouped together because they allow the poet to make aesthetic capital out of moral lapse.[64] But although it is irony that slides the poem from 'resentment' to 'resignation', we should beware of foisting on Propertius the donjuanesque cynicism which Ovid often flaunts in glamorising urbane adultery. Adultery is also at issue in Catull. 68.135–6:

> quae tamen etsi uno non est contenta Catullo,
> rara verecundae furta feremus erae

Although she is not content with Catullus alone, I'll put up with the occasional escapades of my coy mistress

but though twofold (it affects a lover as well as a husband) it shows no trace of cynicism and leaves one very uncertain as to the possibility of irony. What is certain and important is that Catullus' permissive disposition stems from the contemplation of Lesbia's beauty (see 68.131–4). It is, I think, true to say that this is the only instance in which Catullus, normally interested in the overall personality (cf. the discussion of 1.19), is swayed by the purely sensuous aspects of his mistress to the point of declaring himself prepared to wink at one or two *furta*. It will certainly be no coincidence that 68 influenced Propertius as no other Catullan poem did; in 2.32 he promptly took up the Catullan 'deviation', though in a more ironical, worldly-wise vein. As for Ovid, he certainly knew a promising piece when he saw one: *rusticus est nimium, quem laedit adultera coniunx* 'it is a very boorish man who is offended by an adulterous wife' (*Am.* 3.4.37). We should allow the pimpish jauntiness of this to serve as a foil to the elegant irony that waits upon the amoral aestheticism of Prop. 2.32.[65] Indeed, the world from which the female chorus of this

---

[63] In much the same way the last couplet of 2.8 is the crowning and long-deferred pointer of the poem's tone; see pp. 131–2 above.

[64] Jacoby (1914) 448 finds 2.32 'highly ironical' and 'highly sophisticated'; cf. Lefèvre (1966) 75ff.

[65] Ovid makes great play with the theme of 'non-exclusive possession' in *Am.* 3.14: *non ego, ne pecces, cum sis formosa, recuso...*; out of the gossamer of this poem's rhetorical wit Luck (1969) 173ff. has spun rather too much.

poem comes 'enchante l'imagination de Properce', but, springing from what Baudelaire would call 'sensibilité de l'imagination' in contradistinction to 'sensibilité du coeur',[66] it is alien to strong emotion and *not* readily amenable to moral distinctions. It is, then, my suggestion that the Elysian segregation of Cynthia and her like in 4.7 ought to be played down as the sanctimonious and thin veneer of a vision shaped on the very same principles that in 2.32 bring the poet's mistress in direct line of descent from Helen and Pasiphae. The deeper we penetrate their world, the more evidence of this will be forthcoming.

In his survey of the relevant passages Boyancé drew attention to the distinctive usage of *herois* and *heroine*.[67] The first of these nouns, modelled on the Greek ἡρωΐς, must have been launched by the Neoteroi;[68] and in the discussion of 1.19 it has been noted that *heroine*, a transcription of the Hellenistic ἡρωΐνη, appears to be a Propertian coinage, although in the case of a word which in its stylistic preciosity and form is strongly reminiscent of *Cytaeines* in 1.1.24, I would think of Cornelius Gallus for a moment. In any case, its ample sonority, guaranteed by a sequence of long vowels and underscored by the spondaic rhythm, conveys, perhaps more effectively than its variant, stature, outstanding beauty and dreamy remoteness. 1.19.13 is, I think, the most majestic of the verses it graces: *illic formosae veniant chorus heroinae*. The encounter envisaged in this hexameter is localised in the Beyond, and it is normally some 'Beyond', whether *legendary, artistic* or *eschatological*, that these choruses inhabit. By specifying these three categories I do not mean that they remain always distinct from one another; in fact, they mostly tend to overlap, blur or identify in order to monumentalise the Propertian female. Death, *and art inextricably bound up with myth*, employed as a mount for female beauty – this is an ideal and (*sit venia verbo*) a ganglion of post-Romantic/Aesthetic sensibility. Beautiful women during this period are ecstatically and systematically desired when sculptured, painted or dead. Towards this ideal Propertius does not go only half-way. Since, however, the emphasis on death in this book seems to suggest just that (cf. p. 3 above), it is all the more important to be alert to the fascinating and largely uncharted complexity of the phenomenon. Awareness of such complexity is vital even when the setting appears to be unequivocally specified, as, for instance, in 1.19.13–16 and, especially, 2.28.29–30 and 49–54.

---

[66] See the essay on Gautier, Pichois, II 115 and '*L'Art philosophique*' II 604: 'Il ne faut pas confondre la sensibilité de l'imagination avec celle du coeur.'

[67] Boyancé (1956) 184ff.

[68] See Tränkle (1960) 60–1.

The first two couplets of this last passage are worth quoting:

> sunt apud infernos tot milia formosarum:
> pulchra sit in superis, si licet, una locis!
> vobiscum est Iope,[69] vobiscum candida Tyro,
> vobiscum Europe nec proba Pasiphae   (2.28.49–52)

> *There are among those below so many thousand beauties:*
> *If possible, allow one in the world above!*
> *With you is Iope, with you flaxen-haired Tyro,*
> *With you Europa and unchaste Pasiphäe*

The request is addressed to Persephone, and its disingenuousness can only be exposed by a full-scale analysis of this much-discussed poem. For our present purposes it will suffice to note the Beauties' abode, the haunting sublimity of the muster-roll with its steady spate of Greek names, and the appearance of Pasiphae. She is, by any standards, unchaste but this is of no moment and *nec proba* in this context hovers between formula and stopgap. She qualifies by virtue of being a beauty, and a dead one at that; and it is on this account alone that she can glide over the asphodels hand in hand with Europa, who had obviously approached the bull with fairly conventional expectations. As with Cleopatra in 3.11.29–30, so with Pasiphae here Propertius celebrates the marriage between royalty and lust: 'Impériales fantaisies, | Amour des somptuosités; | Voluptueuses frénésies, | Rêves d'impossibilités.' If the first two verses fit the Egyptian,[70] nothing could be more appropriate of the Cretan than the other two. It is tempting to say, especially as the Homeric *Catalogue of Women* suggests itself as their formal archetype, that such lines as 2.28.49ff. do no more than resent, in the way classical poetry often does, death's indiscriminate rapacity. The facile assumption, however, ought to be resisted on two accounts, both of which may be deduced from what has already been observed on the Beauties theme: (a) that Propertius' dead heroines are only an extension of other legendary female groups where transience and

---

[69] Of the two heroines of this name known to us one was the wife of Theseus, the other the wife of Cepheus, the King of the Ethiopians. If Propertius wrote *Iope* (and not *Iole* or *Antiope*) he must have meant the latter, 'the Ethiopian Iope to contrast with Tyro's brilliant whiteness'; (Hubbard (1974) 57, cf. Richardson *ad loc.*) That he was fond of this particular contrast seems to escape notice: *vidistis pleno teneram candore puellam,* | *vidistis fuscam, ducit uterque color* 'You see a pretty girl with fair skin and fair hair, | You see a brunette – both colours attract' (2.25.41–2).

[70] Pasiphae also appears in 3.19.11–12 (the question of how genuinely censorious this piece is cannot be taken up here). Ovid was no less fascinated by her story 'which he treats as an Alexandrian motif, a working out in psychopathic terms of "the feminine libido gone beyond all bounds"' (Green (1982) on *Ars Am.* 1.289ff.); the predilection of Hellenistic poets for the sort of thing she stands for had been also commented upon by Wilkinson (1955) 125. The French verses come from Gautier's 'Impéria', a poem from *Émaux et camées* and one that introduces Cleopatra in its very first stanza.

decay are not at issue, and (b) their frequent deployment is by no means unrelated to the *poésie des noms*, the aural exoticism of their nomenclature, which could scarcely have been the case with Greek poets. Furthermore, nowhere does Propertius betray genuine interest in the existential and eschatological implications of the fact of death; rather than that, he would explore its aesthetic potential. The dying Adonis of 2.13 implies as much. What the Underworld scenes of 4.7 put in sharper focus is the effects of death on womankind, 'unquestionably the most poetical topic in the world'. If it seems too distinctly modern to be attributed to the elegist, it is also persistent and articulated in his poetry to a degree that warrants further reflections.

'The fascination of beautiful women already dead, especially if they had been great courtesans, wanton queens, or famous sinners' was very much in the air when Baudelaire, Gautier, Swinburne and Pater were engaged in poetry and criticism. Prominent among them were Helen and Cleopatra. For Gautier the latter is 'a "reine sidérale" of irresistible charm ("chaque regard de ses yeux était un poème supérieur à ceux d'Homère ou de Mimnerme"), and the knowledge of her body is an end in itself, beyond which life has nothing to offer'.[71] It was certainly so for Mark Antony. Had she not been so recent, real and Antonian Propertius might have made more poetry of her. Helen was equally fascinating and less objectionable. So much so that Cynthia was pronounced second to none but her; indeed, she was hailed as her reincarnation: *post Helenam haec terris forma secunda redit* 'Helen's beauty here returns to the world' (2.3.32). Pasiphae appears among 'wanton Oriental queens with strange names' in Swinburne's 'Masque of Queen Bersabe'. The procession also features Herodias, Cleopatra, Semiramis, who makes a brief appearance along with Cleopatra in Prop. 3.11.21ff., Myrrha, Sappho, Messalina and a host of others.[72] Swinburne's females, to be sure, are so many versions of the cruel and often bloodthirsty Fatal Woman of Romanticism's frenetic outskirts, whereas none of the female figures introduced by the elegiac poet affects institutionalised sadism of the Swinburnian type. Nevertheless, the analogies that should not be sought in this respect ought to be pondered in the general fashion that the phrase with which this paragraph began points to; and it is surely noteworthy that the modern poet's sensuous exoticism is specifically oriented, for Propertius' legendary ladies roam as a rule the Eastern part of the empire and in the case of 4.7.61–2 are unequivocally orientalised: *qua numerosa fides, quaque aera*

[71] See Praz (1951) 214ff.
[72] Praz (1951) 240ff.; see Gosse and Wise, I 349ff., esp. 354ff.

rotunda Cybebes 'Where numerous lutes and where Cybebe's brazen cymbals' (61). This line describes the goings-on in the heart of Elysium. After the preceding observations it is to be hoped that *en route* to and upon entering it one will be willing, against conventional wisdom, to concentrate on what unites rather than on what separates the female population of these regions. Misplaced pity for the 'damned' and the wrong sort of admiration for the 'blessed' can thus be avoided – and the prospects for textual criticism may improve.

Certain features of Propertius' Underworld will not fail to draw attention. First, it has been taken over by lovers only; in this Tibullus had earlier shown the way, possibly encouraged by a Hellenistic precedent.[73] In any case, such eroticisation is very much in the Hellenistic vein. Secondly, unlike Tibullus' 'co-educational' state of affairs, Propertius' Elysium is set aside for ladies only. This, as we are going to see, is not the only difference between the two elegists. Another Propertian peculiarity emerges in ll. 55–6. The traditional eschatology requires a fundamental bifurcation; so the sheep and the goats part company, though in this case they do so not after having crossed the river of death (55 *amnem* – the poet does not bother to be more specific) but while still rowing. As a result the dead sail, rather than trek, straight to their destination. For all its refreshing originality this detail should not set us working out Propertius' infernal landscape; its contours are far too hazy for that. It is far more illuminating to recall 2.27.13ff. and 2.28.39–40 which feature the dead lover(s) aboard a craft bound for the nether regions. Such passages suggest that the notion of 4.7.55–6, far from being intended as mere topographical variation on the standard itinerary, results from an inveterate habit of imagination – inveterate and somewhat whimsical, for although the craft has obviously been borrowed from Charon, Propertius insists on keeping him unemployed by making the dead row for themselves. This is explicitly so in 2.27.13 and 4.7.56, a highly characteristic parallel which shows both conceits stemming from the same imaginative disposition. Again, the aquatic setting points to that complex of water–death–love to which reference has been occasioned by 2.26b (see pp. 91–2 above). Although the received picture of the classical Underworld is no doubt one of a fairly watery place, such poems as 1.20 and 2.26a, where the landscape, albeit spelling death for the beloved, is far from being chthonic in itself, caution against taking 4.7.55ff. as just another instance of age-old Hades imagery; as much as, perhaps even more than this, they represent a transposition beyond the

---

[73] See Solmsen (1961) 282–3 and Cairns (1979) 52ff.

grave of an aesthetic unit, just as the females of the following lines (57ff.) represent the localisation of an aesthetic ideal in the afterlife. Expectations of topographical reconstruction should accordingly be modest, if not minimal. In the next three lines such expectations must be held responsible for a critical mêlée which has largely raged in resolute distrust of the manuscript evidence.

A highly prestigious consensus gives:

> una Clytaemestrae stuprum vehit altera Cressae
> portat mentitae lignea monstra bovis.
> ecce coronato pars altera rapta phaselo   (4.7.57–9)
>
> *One carries Clytemnestra's foulness, another floats*
> *The Cretan's monstrous wooden cow.*
> *But see, another group is swept in a flower-crowned boat*

Camps is illuminatingly succinct: '*altera Cressae* . . . cannot stand with the preceding *una*, since Clytaemnestra and Pasiphae are grouped, not contrasted'; moreover, most have found the sequence *una* . . . *altera* . . . *altera* eschatologically and grammatically forbidding.[74] One wonders whether scandalised by the content we have not grown too puritanical about the form. More than a new textual solution what we badly need is a contextual reminder. Propertius, I have just been arguing, is unconcerned about topography. Although *gemina sedes* in 55 does establish the traditional division into Tartarus and Elysium, it is not easy, nor is it advisable, to be confident that *diversa aqua* in the next line stands for no more than two streams flowing in the opposite directions of Elysium and Tartarus; one might just as well think of watery ramifications, the unspecified river of 55 being, as it were, the aggregate of implicit tributaries. On this assumption 55–6 issue smoothly into the next couplet (whose connexion with *aqua* some critics unaccountably will not consider). By the time *una* in 57 picks up the already diversified *aqua*, it may have itself shaded semantically into the more specific 'current'.[75] Should that be the case, we do not even have to postulate individual streams for the sinners (Cl. and Pas. are carried along on different currents but are drifting in the same direction), a possibility hampered by Hertzberg's *unda*; also, in this mobile sense *una* (*aqua*) is a more appropriate subject

---

[74] The essential facts may be found in the critical apparatus of good editions. See also Shackleton Bailey (1956) 251–2. Rothstein and, more recently, Richardson stick to the MSS reading. If it were imperative to emend, Camps's *aut ea Cressae* (for *altera Cressae*) raises, I think, fewer hackles than most.

[75] Virgil's infernal hydrography, albeit more detailed, is hardly less impressionistic. Richardson notes on 4.7.55ff.: 'if we assume a number of streams, what follows gives little difficulty'. This is not the only case where enlightened resignation works better than pedantic perseverance.

for *vehit* and *portat*. The asyndeton which appears in Barber's OCT has been rightly frowned upon. Consequently, we should punctuate after *vehit* in 57, take *Cressae* as substantival and understand with it, provisionally and for grammar's sake, a noun in the line of the preceding *stuprum*, just before the *enjambement* carries us over into full view of the bestialism in the pentameter. Here, if the participle is taken as passive the phrase *mentitae lignea monstra bovis* is in apposition to the noun understood with *Cressae*; if it is active it goes with *Cressae* ('the wooden horror of the pretended cow' or '...the Cretan queen, whose fraud contrived the wooden horror of the cow', Camps). But whichever is preferred, a subtle interplay arises between the abstract *stuprum* in 57 and the overwhelming concreteness suggested by the sequence *lignea monstra bovis*; the effect is felt as a pictorial overcompensation for the barely-realised ellipsis of a grammatical object. The couplet as a whole has a shifty quality to it and the commentator's passing reference to the lesser possibility of a link between *Cressae* and *bovis* warns that at the end of 58 one may still be in the wood.[76] Warden remarks that 'the behaviour of the language is almost as grotesque as that of Pasiphae';[77] it is easy to see that it also equals her resourcefulness. As for the sequence *una...altera...altera*, it is far less offending than it has been made out to be. The vagueness of the landscape and the semantic shift of *aqua* over 56–8 contrive, as has been already suggested, to present the two adulteresses as drifting on different currents in the same direction. They are not contrasted but they are differentiated (after all Pasiphae's genetic experiment puts her in a class of her own) – but differentiated as species of the same genus. Together they may be thought of as the *pars una* to which the *pars altera* of 59 is now contrasted.[78] This is not slovenliness but purposeful licentiousness that draws the traditional dividing line while blurring it. The quasi-exclamatory *ecce* at the very beginning of 59 by shifting the focus of attention distances the deferred *altera* from its correlatives, but without alienating it and so without seriously disturbing the impression of an even, continuous flow of female figures; language strains itself a bit to reflect the catalogue-like drift of a central Propertian theme – a theme which, in the absence of the moral fiction spun and upheld throughout 4.7, is apt to string together Helen, Lesbia, Pasiphae, Tyro, Europa *et quot Troia tulit vetus et quot Achaia formas*... These are all *heroinae*, i.e. bygone and glamorous. In the last analysis, that is all we really know, and all we need to know. And I venture to suggest that this is why, unlike Tibullus who in 1.3.67ff. takes the

---

[76] See Camps *ad loc*.   [77] Warden (1980) 41.

[78] Rothstein's reference, in his note on 4.7.57, to Virg. *Aen.* 8.678–85 as a parallel instance has been undeservedly snubbed.

traditional hard line against love criminals, Propertius in 4.7.55–8 chooses for his queens a watery limbo in which far from being chastised they can drift aimlessly and splendidly vicious.

That anything in the landscape Propertius has created is possible ll. 59–60 show well: *rapta*, if that is what the corrupt *parta* ousted, defies both gravity and distance, an effect to which also contribute, as Warden has seen, the omission of *est* with the participle, the unanticipated *ubi* in 60, the sound and the tempo of the lines;[79] and somehow the pentameter makes the fragrance of the roses an inescapable inference. The garlanded skiff is of a piece with the festivities of 61–2. The oriental outfit has been smuggled into Elysium for no more specific an effect than exoticism. But as the garland heralds the fiesta so the exotic preludes the sprawling and outlandish names that hold sway over the next couplet:

> Andromedeque et Hypermestre sine fraude maritae
> narrant historiae tempora nota suae   (4.7.63–4)

> *Andromeda and Hypermnestra, guileless wives,*
> *Tell of the well-known perils in their story.*

tempora is Ayrmann's correction of the MSS *pectora*. This is not a unique instance of confusion between the two words in the manuscript tradition;[80] besides, *historiae tempora...suae* is perfect Latin for 'the perils of their story' and there are two momentous parallels from 2.28, that other concourse of Dead Beauties, which throw their weight behind it:

> narrabis Semelae, quo sit formosa *periclo*   (2.28.27)

> *You will tell Semele of beauty's peril*

> narrabitque sedens longa *pericla* sua[81]   (2.28.46)

> *And sitting will describe her long ordeal*

Ayrmann's solution is palaeographically plausible, avoids transposition, introduces a welcome variation on *pericla*, and therefore enjoyed deserved favour with such editors as Barber (OCT), Camps, Fedeli (1984) and Hanslik. But one cannot adopt it without feeling that the expressive plasticity of *pectora* as an apposition to Hypermestra and Andromeda is somehow forfeited. If it is kept, Markland's *historias suas* produces a gentle and elegant word pattern in 69 and should probably be preferred to

---

[79] Warden (1980) 42.

[80] See Tränkle (1960) 69 n. 4 and Willis (1972) 76–7: 'It was noted at first, I believe, by Markland, that dactylic words were confused with peculiar frequency in Latin poetry; he gives as examples the following words: munera, vulnera, nomina, limina, lumina...tempora.'

[81] Indeed, it is quite likely that Heimreich's proposal to read *nota pericla* in 4.7.64 was inspired by these lines.

preserving the MSS genitive *historiae...suae* on the grounds that it depends on *nota* (= known for their story); the latter suggestion also involves depriving *narrant* of its object,[82] and although this, as we are going to see presently, would provide formal support for the sort of 'narrative' the poet envisages in 63ff., it is rather unnecessary and, I think, at odds with the syntactical tenor of ll. 63–8.

It has been seen that Propertius in indulging one and the same obsession can alternate between here below scenery and hereafter background; such an alternation may also be observed within the compass of 2.28, where l. 27 *narrabis Semelae, quo sit formosa periclo*, addressed to Cynthia the prospective heroine, is taken up by 45–6

> ante tuosque pedes illa ipsa operata sedebit,
> narrabitque sedens longa pericla sua.
>
> *And she herself before thy feet will sit in worship*
> *And sitting will describe her long ordeal.*

which picture a convalescent Cynthia fulfilling the vows made by her lover to Jupiter during her illness. This latter couplet with its precise stage directions as to position (*ante...pedes...sedens*) suggests that what we are dealing here with is a distinct visual motif which like the amatory complex of 2.13.11ff. recalls similar tête-à-têtes in literature and, possibly, in art. Margaret Hubbard goes back to Thetis and Zeus in *Iliad* 1.500ff., but mentions also the posture of Iris at Hera's feet in Callimachus, *Hymn* 4.228–36.[83] This is a case, in which, to vary a remark of the same scholar, Propertius' imagination is evidently beholden to the painter and the sculptor. Whether either of these media had represented a similar scene is not certain, but it is well worth noting that in both passages from 2.28 Cynthia's position and disposition are akin to those of the Hellenistic *fanciulla abbandonata*, as we have seen her in 1.15.9–14 (p. 118 above). What Calypso grieves for in the latter passage is Ulysses' departure: *multos illa dies incomptis maesta capillis | sederat...* (11–12). 'It is relevant to recall', remarks Hubbard, 'that the *Seated Calypso* of the painter Nicias was probably to be seen in Rome itself.'[84] Had Pliny, to whom we owe this piece of information, referred to the Propertian Calypso of 1.15, he might have said *flens* rather than *sedens*; with the painting in mind the emphasis falls naturally and inevitably on the latter, on the figure of her who weeps, not on the act of, or the reason for weeping. I stress this because unlike

---

[82] Rothstein keeps the MSS reading and punctuates after *narrant*, explaining that the object, *historiam*, should be understood from *historiae*; but I think this is less easy than understanding *tegula* from *tegula* in 26.   [83] Hubbard (1974) 56.

[84] Hubbard (1974) 165; Rothstein had already made this point in his note on 1.15.11. See also p. 118 above.

most critics I am fairly confident that both in 2.28.27–8 and 45–6 pictorial Propertius accentuates the narrator, *not the narrative*.

And so he does in 4.7.63ff. As in 2.28.27–8, so here the narrative takes place in Elysium. In its pleasance leisure can have but a limited range of visual manifestations and the Propertian ladies can do little else besides affecting the same posture for all eternity recounting in statuesque immobility the highlights of their earthly adventure:

> haec sua maternis queritur livere catenis
> bracchia nec meritas frigida saxa manus;
> narrat Hypermestre magnum ausas esse sorores,
> in scelus hoc animum non valuisse suum.
> sic mortis lacrimis vitae sanamus [sancimus *Barber*] amores:
> celo ego perfidiae crimina multa tuae.   (4.7.65–70)

The first complains her arms were bruised by her mother's chains
And her hands did not deserve cold rocks.
Hypermnestra tells how her sisters dared an outrage
And how her own heart quailed at it.
In this way with death's tears we strive to heal life's loves;
I conceal your criminal bad faith.

Of the two heroines, Andromeda abandoned and weeping on the rocks before Perseus' intervention was a favourite subject of painting; the pictorial dimension overrules logic, and querulousness is carried into Elysium by way of the querulous *posture*. Prying pedantically into the details of the confabulations in 63ff. is almost as impertinent as wondering what exactly passes between the foreground female figures in Dante Gabriel Rossetti's painting entitled *The bower meadow*. And impertinence in this case will be rewarded with barren quandaries regarding the point of Hypermestra's and Andromeda's complaint as well as their right to perpetuate that complaint in view of the reported happy end of their love affairs. After a rigorous application of thought to the passage Housman decided that l. 69 is 'meaningless of Andromeda and Hypermestra and false of Cynthia'.[85] No doubt; but by such

---

[85] Housman (1934) 139 (= *Classical Papers* III 1237); but see Shackleton Bailey (1956) 252–3; from his and other commentaries it will be clear how succulent a morsel for the logician l. 69 is. Propertius would be the last poet to eschew the paradox *mortis lacrimis sanamus*, even if the tears had not been diluted out of significance, as I am arguing below; but it so happens that he may also have had good reasons for giving us this beautiful hexameter. The conceit of love wounds being *washed away* in death should call up 2.34.91–2 *et modo formosa quam multa Lycoride Gallus | mortuus inferna vulnera lavit aqua*, which, as we saw in p. 68 n. 46 above, draws us into an allusive sequence leading back through Gallus to Euphorion's Κώκυτος μοῦνος ἀφ᾽ ἕλκεα νίψεν Ἄδωνιν (fr. 43 Powell). The water of 2.34.92 must be that of an infernal river or lake; and yet the idea of tears may also be flickering here not only because *aqua* is capable of conveying it, as it does in 3.6.10 *illius ex oculis multa cadebat aqua?*, but also because Κώκυτος is the River of Wailing (κωκύειν). The degree of oblique and learned allusiveness in this case is neither higher

standards there is no Propertian bevy but must disband. Better, with Shackleton Bailey, to risk the very specific guess that 'as he writes of their sorrows (*lacrimae*) [Propertius] is reminded of Dido and the rest...most of whom like Cynthia herself had an unhappy love to heal'.[86] That it is the Dido of the *Lugentes Campi* that has induced Propertius to sully Elysium with tears is also F. Solmsen's thesis in a very interesting article. Chronology would certainly allow Propertius to have composed 4.7 some time before 16 B.C. and hence under the spell of the recently published *Aeneid*; and generally I think that Solmsen makes out his case for Virgilian influence.[87] Where I differ from him is in his suggestion that one should read the grave pathos of Virgil's *curae non ipsa in morte relinquunt* 'even in death they are anguished' (*Aen.* 6.444) into the narrative of the heroines of 4.7. It has not escaped Solmsen that such poems as 2.28 with its narrating ladies, and other passages in Propertius' first three books, show clearly that *Aeneid* 6 struck only a congenial chord which had always been there; Virgil must have rekindled an imagination which was wont to dwell on the Women of Yore. But to argue with Solmsen that *Aen.* 6.444 revealed 'the ideal solution...of a problem which had engaged Propertius himself more than once', namely, the problem of *traicit et fati litora magnus amor* – this is to misunderstand both the nature of Virgil's influence and of Propertius' *amor*.[88] The elegist has no use for the brooding and smothering emotion of the Fields of Sorrow. Phaedra, Eriphyle, Pasiphae and the rest foreshadow and lead up to the appearance of the most majestic and tragic female in the whole poem. The Propertian counterpart would have to be Cynthia – neither majestic nor tragic in the sense that Dido was meant to be. I would, therefore, suggest that for all the impact that the atmosphere evoked by Virgil may have had on the elegist, tragic pathos does not filter into 4.7 and serious moral reflection is outside its scope.

Whence and wherefore those tears, then? Solmsen says that it would be cruel to deny that Propertius knew their healing power. But tears come in many varieties and for all sorts of purposes, and it seems to me worth asking whether those of 4.7.63ff. instead of being a hangover from earthly suffering cannot actually be an aid to beauty.

nor lower than in other confirmed or surmised instances. On this assumption *mortis lacrimis* in 4.7.69 would be bringing out an inherent possibility of *inferna aqua*, with *lavit* and *sanamus* corresponding and describing almost identical sedatives. Euphorion's preserved scrap shows a lovely blend of love–water–death, to which Prop. has already been seen to be partial. On the whole question see Boucher (1965) 310, 318–19.   [86] Shackleton Bailey (1956) 253.

[87] Solmsen (1961) 281ff.; for Virgilian influence on Prop. Book 4 see also Becker (1971) esp. 453–7, 477–80.

[88] Celentano (1956) 51 also holds Virgil responsible, along with Cynthia's death, for a more profound attitude to the problems of life and death as well as for a 'new pensiveness' in 4.7.

> Que m'importe que tu sois sage?
> Sois belle! et sois triste! Les pleurs
> Ajoutent un charme au visage...[89]

These opening verses of the 'Madrigal triste' should be read in the light of Baudelaire's *Journaux intimes*: 'I have found the definition of the Beautiful – of my own Beautiful. It is something radiant and sad...A beautiful and seductive head, a woman's head that is, makes you dream – vaguely though – at once of pleasure and sadness; it conveys an idea of melancholy, of weariness, of glut even...Mystery and regret are also characteristics of the Beautiful.'[90] There is no place here for the grave accents of unrelieved passion. To take up a distinction already applied above, if in Virgil sensibility of heart vies with that of imagination, in Propertius the latter takes the upper hand. To take the grievances of 4.7.65-8 at face value is to credit the tears shed in 69 with a cathartic effect; if, on the other hand, these women are, as I have been arguing, an extension of the ubiquitous Beauties imagery, then there are good reasons for surmising that in the last analysis they are not canonised as saints and martyrs of marital faith but as the poet's *beau idéal*. In a sense, these women lack the energy even to hate; they just gather and narrate on and on, but their narrative and their melancholy fall short of taking on 'the somber colors appropriate to the *Lugentes Campi*';[91] they are mere visual mannerisms not unlike those projected by Baudelaire and very much like the mannerisms which express 'female passivity and repressed pain' in Pre-Raphaelite poetry, namely, 'turning away of face, moaning, silence, tears'; the ladies referred to here, especially those of the poet-painter D. G. Rossetti, are also prone to repetitions of emotive words such as 'pride', 'shame', 'sin', 'love'.[92] Proud of her abode and loyalty, Cynthia is ashamed on account of her lover's sins and chooses not to join the tearful moaning of the others. If her silence owes something to Dido's taciturnity in front of her ex-lover at *Aen.* 6.469-71, it is instructive to see how Propertius turns the ominously incommunicative into the gracefully reticent. There is, I think, a fine blend of the sensuous and the visionary in the figures of 4.7.63ff. and much the same is true of the Blessed Damozel in Rossetti's homonymous poem.[93]

[89] Pichois, I 137-8 'Why should I care if you are chaste? | Be fair! And be sad! Tears lend | charm to the face.

[90] Pichois, I 657.   [91] Solmsen (1961) 287.

[92] See Saunders Boos (1976) 122ff. on the 'Characteristics of the early Pre-Raphaelite idealized female'.

[93] Rossetti 3ff. Written in 1847, the poem was at first much admired and subsequently disparaged, even by Rossetti himself.

> Around her, lovers newly met
> 'Mid deathless love's acclaims,
> Spoke evermore among themselves
> Their heart-remembered names

She too, though in a more angelic mood, waits for her lover to join her in a place graced by the

> five sweet symphonies,
> Cecily, Gertrude, Magdalen,
> Margaret and Rosalys

How do these damsels while their time away?

> Circlewise sit they, with bound locks
> And foreheads garlanded

Unaccountably, in view of her bliss, the heroine eventually dissolves into tears. Her abode is definitely some sort of Christian Elysium, but it would be rash to conceive of her as a spirit; distinctly yellow hair (a peculiarly Pre-Raphaelite tint akin to Cynthia's *fulva coma* in 2.2.5) cascades down her back and, more pointedly, her bosom makes warm the celestial bar on which she leans. Her whole demeanour in heaven argues her to have been staunchly faithful to her lover on earth, but no one with an understanding of Rossetti's life-long quest of the ideal type of beauty in general, and of ideal female beauty in particular, will probably set much store by this. Very soon in his career Rossetti realised that 'much of that reverence which he had mistaken for faith had been no more than the worship of beauty'.[94] It is, I think, through a similar misunderstanding that in 4.7.63ff. one is liable to miss the beauty parlour under the thin veil of the eschatological compartment and forsake sheer pleasure in a bid to comprehend tears shed to spice rather than sour. The sustained moral fiction of this elegy abets the reader's pieties, and the best corrective is close attention to the way Propertius deploys the Beauties theme throughout his work. Only thus is it possible to see how precarious is the line between the demonology of ll. 57–8 and the hagiology of ll. 59–70 – which is one of the reasons why Tibullus' Underworld in 1.3.57ff. is so different a place.

His erotic Elysium is a kind of debonair Golden Age endowed with the amenities of the Isles of the Blessed;[95] and the effect of 1.3.57–64 as a whole is one of a *fête champêtre*. Nothing could be more Tibullan than this. The tenor of these lines makes the choruses of young men and tender girls

[94] Doughty (1957) xi.
[95] See Bright (1978) 29 and, especially, Cairns (1979) 52ff.

(*ac iuvenum series teneris immixta puellis* | *ludit*... 63–4) just another feature
of the miraculous landscape. By contrast, in Propertius there is, strictly
speaking, no landscape (l. 60 is only there to bring home its absence), the
Underworld is, as it were, coextensive with the voluminous nomenclature,
the aura of the place is also that of the inhabitants. Comparing the two
passages Tränkle observes that whereas in Tibullus' Elysium nature is
enthusiastically described, Propertius has no more than a hint at l. 60
but gives full details of human actions.[96] Quite so, but the difference will
not be fully understood without reference to the latter poet's preoccupation with the Beauties, to whom Tibullus nowhere seems to be
susceptible. This will also account for another difference noticed by
Tränkle, namely that, unlike Propertius, Tibullus in his balanced and
even picture allows no detail to stand out in relief. So his eschatology,
thoroughly eroticised as it is, remains rigidly *comme il faut*, Hell exceeding
Paradise by three couplets. Cairns suggests that by abbreviating the
Tartarus section Propertius makes an acknowledging, complimentary
variation on his fellow elegist.[97] But Propertius did it for the sake of
Clytaemestra and Pasiphae, not for Tibullus.

The *mandata mortuae* in 71ff. mark a resurgence of domestic realism. Thus
a mundane frame (35ff. and 71ff.) heightens the effect of a supramundane
picture. Yet one cannot help feeling that the Cynthia of 71ff. is rather
different from the vindictive shrew of 35ff. After her consecration in the
intervening scene it could hardly be otherwise. Not that she has turned
into an angel: ll. 72 and 76 are restrainedly bitter – a subtle touch that
substitutes quiet rankling for outburst. Also, after a flash of unalloyed
altruism in 73–4, it is in the balance whether 75–6 spare Latris an irksome
duty or afford Cynthia a jaundiced pleasure; and by the next couplet she
has relapsed into self-interest:

> et quoscumque meo fecisti nomine versus,
> ure mihi: laudes desine habere meas.   (4.7.77–8)

And all the verses you have made on my account –
Please burn them. Cease your boasts about me.

Obviously, she regards poetry composed in her name as something of a
personal effect, and custom demands that it now be burned as an offering
to her; thus *ure mihi*. But poets are an excitable lot and in moments of
personal crisis they are known to have contemplated literary self-
immolation. Propertius may be making Cynthia enjoin upon himself a
gesture which he found gorgeously sensational. 'Many of the poems

[96] Tränkle (1960) 99–101.   [97] Cairns (1979) 53–4.

published in 1870 Rossetti had buried in his wife's coffin at the time of her death in 1862, in a mood of exaggerated remorse and sentimental self-sacrifice'; it comes as no surprise to learn that 'seven years later, when the desire for publication returned with increased intensity, he recovered the buried manuscript'.[98]

Cynthia's next demand has also roused animated discussion. This is what the MSS offer:

pelle hederam tumulo, mihi quae pugnante [praegnante *Barber*] corymbo
mollia[99] contortis alligat ossa comis. (4.7.79–80)

Clear my tomb of the ivy whose burgeoning clusters constrict my brittle bones
with tangled tendrils.

Does Cynthia ask for ivy, in which case *pone* (Sandbach) is the most probable correction of *pelle*, or does she want her overgrown tomb to be cleared of it? One of the arguments advanced against the latter is that ivy is not in the habit of overgrowing tombs overnight; those who are seriously troubled by this may perhaps be further reassured that the alarming *adynaton* would be even less possible at the dusty and well-trodden wayside. It is an altogether more serious objection that ivy is thought of by the ancients as a sepulchral asset. There is strong evidence of this but if *A.P.* 7.22.1–2 (= Gow–Page 3286–7) by Simmias is the most cogent instance that can be adduced ('Ηρέμ' ὑπὲρ τύμβοιο Σοφοκλέος, ἠρέμα, κισσέ, | ἑρπύζοις...'gently creep over the tomb of Sophocles, gently creep, O ivy'), the possibility has been generally ignored that the emphatic repetition of the adverb may be anxiously implying an unwelcome κισσός constrictor. That antiquity recognised such a species is clear from Pliny, *HN* 16.144 *hedera...sepulcra muros rumpens* 'ivy which breaks up tombs and walls', which has been snubbed by supporters of *pone* but should have been mentioned at least by sticklers for natural history.[100] If Cynthia's bones are threatened by this plant, *pugnante*, which

---

[98] Doughty (1957) ix.   [99] On *mollia* see below.

[100] Both Rothstein and Fedeli (but not Fedeli (1984)) quote Pliny and keep *pelle*, as do Pasoli and Shackleton Bailey (1956) 254. Stroh's (1971) 182ff. defence of *pelle* is tied up with his wider assumptions about the Propertian elegies. Cynthia, he argues, has entered Elysium *because of* her real-life moral integrity and *despite* the false accusations of Propertius' previous poems. Thus her lover's mundane scribblings, *symbolised by the traditional ivy*, have sunk beneath her present dignity – and she dismisses them in 77–80. This is in effect Lefèvre's Propertius Ludibundus turned dead earnest (see p. 146 above). Now it should be clear from my reading of 4.7 why I cannot agree with this, but it is also worth noting that, as Camps in his introd. note to the poem, Pasoli p. 38 and Warden (1980) 79 have also emphasised, the Cynthia of 4.7 is not as a whole idealised, and Rothstein had already hinted in his note on 4.7.63 that the real cause of Cynthia's bliss was more to do with beauty than faithfulness. In one sense the *fides* motif in 4.7 is detachable: we would, I suppose, readily tune with an amoral Andromeda and Co.; but who would ever entertain the idea of the strait-laced Cornelia idly confabulating with any one

has also come under attack,[101] is forcefully conveying the situation that ἠρέμα is intended to forestall. *mollia* (crumbling, brittle), a correction of *molli* by the *deteriores*, would then be used proleptically to describe the result of this process. The tussle over whether this adjective may or may not mean 'feminea'[102] shows a tendency, rightly warned against by Hubbard, 'to avert our gaze from the physical contents of the funerary urn';[103] it also shows lack of appreciation for Propertius' keen interest in the sensory implications of human decomposition and 'pulverisation'. Lines like 2.9.14 *maximaque in parva sustulit ossa manu* 'And lifted in her little hands the huge bones', 2.13.58 *nam mea quid poterunt ossa minuta loqui?* 'For my dwindled bones will say nothing', and 4.11.14 *et sum, quod digitis quinque legatur, onus* 'five fingers may collect what has remained of me' possess a stark physiological, post-mortem quality, and they lie closer to John Donne's 'Funerals' and 'Relics' than to the conventional pathos of ancient sepulchral poetry.[104] Finally, the idea of 4.7.79–80 as a whole must be compared to that of 4.5.76 *urgeat hunc supra vis, caprifice, tua*. Both passages concur in showing only a slight regard for factual accuracy, given that the bawd has no monument for the wild fig to break up and the ivy has implausibly penetrated Cynthia's urn instead of creeping over it. If it is justifiable to insist that, coming after ll. 77–8 with their *versus* and *laudes*, *hederam* cannot be completely dissociated from its traditional poetic symbolism, it is also reasonable to point out that in this section of the poem, after the modulation of tone at l. 49 and the foregoing Elysian splendours, it would be gratuitously distorting to have Cynthia complaining that her tomb has been afflicted by an uncouth *caprificus* or the like. Propertius has allowed ivy to grow out of its associations and into a hostile vegetation, which is all the more likely to be common to 4.5 and 4.7

of the Propertian heroines? When morality did become, for better or for worse, an issue in 4.11, the Underworld took on a far different aspect.

Stroh's discussion of 4.7 practically concludes with the words: 'Cynthia's speech ends in the confident hope of a reunion after death' (p. 184). As a comment on 93–4 (and it can be nothing else) this will most certainly not pass muster. Apart from the fact that this is no hope, these words, the last of the speech, come from the *larva*, not from the angel – and this is a point one cannot afford to play down or neglect. But as a matter of fact Stroh's view of 4.7 is ultimately determined by his concept of a poetry in the service of wooing (*werbende Dichtung*). Thus in the first three books the woman, regardless of, indeed, as Stroh implies, contrary to what she may have been like in real life, has to be refractory in order that *werbende Dichtung* may be written. 4.7, on the other hand, is simply narrative, so the truth of the actual relationship can now break through. I hope I am not alone in finding this hard to come to terms with.

[101] Cornelissen's *praegnante* has found favour with those adopting *pone* (e.g. Barber, Camps, Hanslik). Richardson, who retains *pelle*, suggests *peragrante* instead.

[102] See, for example, Fedeli *ad loc.* and Shackleton Bailey (1956) 253–4.

[103] Hubbard (1974) 35–6.

[104] Cf. Warden (1980) 63: 'The poet is haunted by the contrast between the living person and the bones and ashes that remain after the pyre.'

inasmuch as both poems treat at some length and with realistic vividness the pauper's-funeral theme.

The subtleties of poetic language, 'etymology' and word-patterning in 81ff. need no rehearsing here.[105] As if to make amends for the mean affair of ll. 23ff., Propertius expends a great deal of artistry on Cynthia's Tiburtine monument. The beautiful hexameter *ramosis Anio qua pomifer incubat arvis* 'Where fruitful Anio broods over branchy fields' (81) introduces Cynthia's last injunction. She wants the picturesque bank of Anio graced by a columnar grave-stone bearing the inscription:

HIC TIBURTINA IACET AUREA CYNTHIA TERRA:
ACCESSIT RIPAE LAUS, ANIENE, TUAE.   (4.6.85–6)

Here in Tiburtine ground lies golden Cynthia, bringing
Glory to your banks, Father Anio.

The burial site is no less idyllic, even if it is less exclusive, than that of 3.16.23–8. *aurea* connotes glamour or, as Warden (p. 56) would have it, 'high visibility'. By a widespread convention of sepulchral epigrams the dead are allowed to draw attention to such things as they would like to be remembered by, and this woman has nowhere in her speech suggested that her qualities were other than skin-deep. Line 42 *garrula de facie si qua locuta mea est* 'To any girl who gabs about my beauty' is an oblique comment on the inferiority complex of a less glamorous successor; the grand golden gown, *aurata cyclade* (40), which appears to come from the same outfit as *beryllon*,[106] pours scorn on a saucy slut whose sartorial pretentiousness is not matched by her social status; and *imaginis aurum* (47), presumably the gold of a bust, sizzles with womanish vanity. And whom would narcissism, vanity and single-minded devotion to cosmetics befit better than a courtesan? This is what these lines quietly insinuate, and the Subura adventure tells much the same story. That *aurea* may also be specifically pointing in the same direction is an idea that *A.P.* 7.218 (= Gow–Page 320–33) by Antipater of Sidon strongly recommends. The epigram purports to be an inscription on the tomb of Lais, the distinguished Corinthian hetaera. Lines of special interest are:

Τὴν καὶ ἅμα χρυσῷ καὶ ἁλουργίδι καὶ σὺν ἔρωτι
θρυπτομένην, ἁπαλῆς Κύπριδος ἁβροτέρην,
Λαΐδ' ἔχω   (1–3)

ἧς καὶ ὑπ' εὐώδει τύμβος ὄδωδε κρόκῳ,
ἧς ἔτι κηώεντι μύρῳ τὸ διάβροχον ὀστεῦν
καὶ λιπαραὶ θυόεν ἆσθμα πνέουσι κόμαι   (8–10)

---

[105] On these see some fine remarks by Warden (1980) 54ff.
[106] Cf. Tränkle (1960) 118.

I contain her who indulged in amours and gold and purple, one more graceful than tender Cypris, Lais . . . even her tomb smells of fragrant saffron, her bones are still drenched with heady balm and her sleek locks give off a whiff of frankincense.

The 'coquetterie posthume', as Gautier might have put it, crowns a life in the course of which Lais plied an auriferous trade, wallowed in gold and purple, and had a soft spot for fragrances and, presumably, cosmetics. A Propertian pentameter nicely sums up this epigram: *illa sepulturae fata beata tuae* 'the blissful Fate that decrees your burial' (2.28.26). May one also venture the conjecture that its sepulchral luxury may have done something to mould Cynthia's desire in 79ff. for a better tomb as well as for a specific adjective?[107] After all, this is not the first time that the radiant hetaera catches Propertius' imagination; in 2.6 she heads a list of eminent colleagues: *Non ita complebant Ephyraeae Laidos aedis . . .* (1).[108]

In 87ff. Cynthia shows herself a conscientious parolee; at the crack of dawn she must report herself to the ferryman: *luce iubent leges Lethaea ad stagna reverti* 'At first light law demands return to Lethe lake' (91). Thus *Lethaeus . . . liquor* (Lethe water), the synechdochic identification of her residence in l. 10, and *Lethaea . . . stagna* here stand as the inexorable boundaries of the brief reality she has established during her nocturnal visit. If, as suggested in p. 152 above, the adjective is used not merely as a conventional shorthand for the Underworld but also in order to connote oblivion, the ghost seems acutely aware of the danger, for it delivers an emphatic 'adieu, remember me' in ll. 87–8 ('mind you, dreams issuing from the pious gates come true') which is then compounded by the prophecy of 93–4:

> nunc te possideant aliae: mox sola tenebo:
> mecum eris, et mixtis ossibus ossa teram.

> *Others can have you now. Soon I alone shall hold you.*
> *You'll be with me, and bone on mingled bone I'll grind.*

[107] There can be little doubt that *aurea* in Tib. 1.6.58 *aurea . . . anus* as well as in other passages refers principally to moral qualities. Rothstein believes that *aurea* in 4.7.85 is a term of admiration rather than of endearment but cf. Hor. *Carm.* 1.5.9 *qui nunc te fruitur credulus aurea* and see Nisbet–Hubbard *ad loc*. In particular, it may not be superfluous to note that Philodemus' sensual Calliston in *A.P.* 5.123.3 is χρυσέην – a common, it would seem, characterisation of desirable courtesans deriving from sources that were also available to Propertius. With Warden (1980) 56 and unlike Lefèvre (1966) 118–19 I can see no humorous extravagance in Cynthia's epitaph.

[108] I am not of course presuming to have decided what Cynthia's real marital or social status was. With regard to this I would rather quote J. C. McKeown (1979) 76: 'The elegist casts himself and his *puella* in roles familiar from the genres which are his models.' Thus in 4.7 no sooner does Cynthia step out of her prestigious Nekyia than she unequivocally becomes a mime, comedy or epigram hetaera; she almost makes a point of presenting herself as such, and a slight juggling about with the last eight letters of 85 would produce something like HETAIRRA – though this may be a less likely teaser than Callimachus' ναίχι καλός – ἄλλος ἔχει in *A.P.* 12.43.5–6 (= Gow–Page 1045–6, on which see their note).

The idea of mingling the bones, especially those of husband and wife, in a single funeral urn is anything but novel;[109] nor, in view of the Greek μείγνυμι, are the sexual overtones of *mixtis* much of a peculiarity; but *teram* is, and what has been said about it in the discussion of 2.1 should be applied in full measure to this couplet. Commentaries have been waging a war of attrition on this word, begrudging it its physicalness.[110] Camps is no exception, but he ends his comment on *mixtis ossibus ossa teram* (94) in a mood of significant compromise: 'But the primary meaning of the words composing it are hard to escape from.' The ultimate encounter with Cynthia is hard to escape from too. The eternity of the future indicatives supervenes on the concessive mood of the subjunctive. The syllabic crescendo after the strong pause in the hexameter is amplified in terms of sound and image by the pentameter. Warden, who notes the rhetorical antitheses (*nunc/mox, possideant/tenebo, aliae/sola*) treats the last couplet of the speech as a kind of Parthian shot which seems to be 'worlds away from the carefree passion of Subura days'.[111] Carefree or not, that passion was conceived for *Cynthia* and was consummated within the domain of *Hecate*. The attentive reader will pay tribute to the power of the couplet but will not be taken by surprise; for, as has been already observed, it represents but the subterranean repeat performance of the crossroads congress in 19–20.

What is alluded to in 4.7.87–8 is most probably the Homeric idea of the Gate of Horn and the Gate of Ivory. Thus the poem's Homeric framework reasserts itself towards the close of the speech to become manifest in the fruitless-embrace motif of the concluding couplet. Enclosed in this epic envelope is a remarkable generic promiscuity. It is this, it was noted in the beginning of the discussion of 4.7, that poses the intriguing problem of the poem's overall tone. Within the compass of a single elegy Cynthia moves from the bohemian recklessness of comedy and mime through the hieratic atmosphere of epic Nekyia to the epigrammatic pieties of her last instructions. Is it, perhaps, a case of *quot* γένη *tot Cynthiae*? Should the various tonal levels be identified with different aspects of Cynthia's character? This, as has been noted, is F. Muecke's solution and, since she chooses to operate with an antithesis between comic-realistic and epic-heroic (see p. 146 above), she argues that at the former level Cynthia is shown to fall short of, while at the latter she

---

[109] See, for instance, Fedeli on 4.7.94 and Allison (1980) 170–3.

[110] In view of his discerning 'la connotazione stilistico-semantica di *teram* è certo fisica' (p. 38), Pasoli's reluctance to accept the 'obscene meaning of *terere*' (on which see Tränkle (1960) 138) is rather more striking than Fedeli's.

[111] Warden (1980) 60.

matches up to the ideal status of mythical heroine against which the poet is fond of measuring her. Thus 'the incongruities...are undoubtedly present' but enlisted in the service of character portrayal. Although this approach might seem preferable to the wholesale satire diagnosed by A. K. Lake (p. 146 above), and although the emotional graph, as distinct from the 'factual' exaggerations and distortions, of Cynthia's speech is not implausible, character portrayal does not seem to be the poem's chief concern. As J. C. Yardley has pointed out, the ghost's behaviour is almost completely predetermined by the conventions of ancient ghost stories,[112] a fact which, in the judgement of the ancient reader at least, would have made for typicality rather than individuality. No less than her ghost, Cynthia's temper shows clear signs of having been pieced together; furthermore, if, again on Muecke's interpretation, the poem's dominant theme is 'the comparison of Cynthia to the heroines of myth or legend' (p. 129), one fears that the thirty-four lines (15–48) which sharply detail her in reduced circumstances do a disservice to the theme besides throwing out the reader. Seemingly Cynthia is the protagonist, but the poem's central paradox has little to do with her personality.

Death looms large in 4.7. Biographically inflected readings take death as an event *tout court* and go on to treat the poem as the lover's emotional response to it. I have instead assumed that death is applied here as an imaginative stimulant. This is by no means arbitrary; Propertius has been seen to experiment with shapes and modes of erotic death. To put it otherwise, erotic death is the Propertian fantasy *par excellence,* just as bucolic day-dreaming hallmarks some of Tibullus' most memorable poetry. This much is certain. Whether a woman called Cynthia had to pass away before 4.7 could be written is neither certain nor relevant. It is not only that even if Cynthia did surprise the slumbering poet she 'did not address him in the accents of Patroclus';[113] it would also be strange if her real funeral were both an analogue of 4.5.67ff. and an antithesis to 2.13.19ff. Nor in view of, for instance, 2.28.49ff. do we have to postulate the event of death in order to account for the Elysian congregation in 4.7.63ff. Baudelaire says that a great poem can be written as much on what has been simply imagined as on what has been experienced. Imaginative sensibility will not spare (quite the reverse!) the beloved one, whether mistress or sister. D. G. Rossetti's 'My sister's sleep' – a poem in which Rossetti achieves an unusual realism as the pervasive sense of death sharpens his sensory responses – was written at a time when the poet was bereft of neither of his two sisters.[114] Propertius' biographical data are less

[112] Yardley (1977) 84–5.   [113] Hubbard (1974) 150.
[114] Rossetti 165–6. See Masefield (1947) 48.

certain, but this is no reason why the bereaved lover should get the better of the aesthete in 4.7. The possibility, on the other hand, cannot be dismissed that Propertius cast in the mould of a popular Hellenistic literary motif the substance of a real-life nightmare; but once this possibility is admitted the real-life cause of the nightmare ceases to be important for the critic.

Generally speaking, 4.7 is a poem of love and death: dead Cynthia protests her faithfulness to her lover. And yet, it has been here maintained, its overall bias is towards an ideal of beauty – and also towards the fascination of its opposites. The cadaverous, the bizarre and the squalid are conspicuous in the elegy, though hard to separate from one another; they are more like the opalescent nuances of a tissue across which eros and death run like red threads. The love-making of 19–20 is both squalid and heavily redolent of evil possibilities; read, as it should be, in conjunction with 93–4 it also points towards the cadaverous. The sordid funeral of 23ff. does not lack intimations of the demonic, and in 35ff. sexual jealousy blends with insidious sorcery and filthiness. Such passages bristle with sharp visual details, the result of a vigorous realism often reinforced by sound expressiveness. Seen from this viewpoint, realism far from calling attention to the comic is instrumental in highlighting the charm of unlikely things.

Less unlikely charm springs from ll. 59–70. In fact, it is the other-worldly appeal of the Elysian section, more than the heroic narrative framework, which has been felt to stand in the sharpest contrast to the scenes in which Cynthia, living or awaiting burial, is involved. As far as moral stature is concerned, the gap between Subura and Elysium is considerable and to bridge it critics have naturally seized on Cynthia's solemn protestations of faithfulness. It is along this line of interpretation that high-pitched arguments to the effect that the sheer fact of death has purged this woman of her earthly impurity tend to appear;[115] but this is a burden that will weigh down and distort the poem. I have instead argued that what ultimately binds Cynthia, Andromeda and Hyper-mestra together is death and beauty, the Elysian scenery being the specification, required by the poem's fictional reality, of the general background against which Propertius marshals similar sisterhoods in other poems.[116] If this is right, the segregation of the sinners of 57–8 from

[115] See Warden's (1980) 79 survey and cf. Stroh's views, above p. 186 n. 100. Lieberg's (1969) 339 conclusions are in the same line: 'The voice we hear [i.e. Cynthia's voice in 4.7] is that of a beloved who has gone through and been cleansed by death.'

[116] Boucher (1965), who in his study of Propertius repeatedly stresses the purely aesthetic element, observes (p. 82) that the separation of the heroines in 4.7.55ff. is only 'an imaginative participation in the artistic and literary world of mythology...' This is a vantage point from

the righteous of 63ff. does little more than keep up appearances. Propertius has nothing of the disciplinarian wishfulness of Tib. 1.3.57–82, nor the grave pathos of *Aen.* 6.440ff. His Cornelia elegy shows that he could sketch in an austere afterlife, judges, sinners and all. But it is highly significant that he did so in a poem (made to order?) featuring a *matrona* of the Roman nobility, who at the time of her death had fully satisfied the ethics and economics of Roman upper-class family life – and of the philosophy scoffed at by Gautier in the preface to *Mademoiselle de Maupin*: 'What is the use of beauty in woman? Provided that a woman is fit, well-formed and capable of having children, she will always be good enough for economists.' A lady of this kind can expect Tantalus to find her *curriculum vitae* more important than his thirst, but will not fall in with Andromeda and Hypermestra. Cynthia does join them to highlight yet another variety – though a less startling one – of paradoxical beauty, viz. beauty thrown into relief by a quiet, languorous sadness. All this, however, is not to say that no incongruity is to be felt between pandemic lechery and pauper's funeral on the one hand and heavenly bliss on the other; it is simply that the incongruity must be reassessed in different terms.

My suggestion, then, is that Propertius brings together and boldly juxtaposes images embodying opposite tendencies of the sensuous imagination. A squalid funeral takes place in 4.5.71ff. but there is nothing in that poem to set off the realism of the concluding lines. Again, legendary beauties including Cynthia regularly appear but nowhere except in this poem are they set amid low-life realism and encounters of a starkly sexual/sinister kind. Because 4.7 suggests the fascination of things beautiful and non-beautiful alike, it can be read as a synthesis enacting

which one would expect him to have made light of the *fides* motif (which is apparently responsible for Cynthia's afterlife reward) in 4.7. In the event he did not. Some of La Penna's most subtle thinking is prompted by the Propertian heroines, especially those of Elysium: 'The bliss of Elysium cannot be reduced either to Platonic idealism or to sublimation in the Freudian sense of the word, since it cannot be separated from an almost fierce sensuality which lives on in the grave' (p. 155); indeed Propertius' heroines, no less than his *Liebestod*, are firmly anchored in the sensuous/sensual: 'The comparison of Cynthia with the dead heroines...is made with reference to *forma*' (p. 210). To this La Penna sees one great *exception*: dead Cynthia in Elysium, no longer touched by the miseries of her life as courtesan, can now be seen as a loyal woman on a par with loyal heroines. But this is the scholar's palinode, not the poet's exception. (At this point Lieberg's (1969) highly stimulating article comes to mind, in which Cynthia's idealisation is discussed in the context of the Platonic Idea of Beauty (pp. 344–5); but if Lieberg means that 'Idealisierung' partakes of the veneration of a disembodied Idea, then talk of Platonic idealism – as La Penna, who may have had Lieberg in mind, has instructed – is better left aside.)

Weeber (1977) 150–69 knows only of Cynthia's sanctity, and he entertains no doubts whatsoever that 4.7 is solid testimony of (a) Propertius' feelings of shame about his behaviour at Cynthia's funeral, (b) his eventual realisation that despite everything he is inextricably attached to her (p. 168).

the ambivalence of beauty and affirming the complementary relationship between apparently incongruous sets of images, styles and tones. Cynthia rides astride the rift; by appointing her as his mouthpiece Propertius did something that was as necessary as it was ingenious. To run through the existential gamut, and thus through its sensory concomitant, you need someone experienced in the ways of both worlds – but not only that. You need the easy virtue of Subura and the more austere kind required by Elysium; a poor devil in a shabby coffin and a celestial seraph. In short, you need a connected account similar to that given by Cynthia. This is a selective, tendentious account, and on close examination it is revealed as a reworking, in the form of a brief biography, of motifs (the funeral, the burial place, the dead Beauties) to which the poet's imaginative sensibility responds powerfully throughout his work. Thus the less reliable it is as a speech reflecting upon the speaker's character the more credible it becomes as a vehicle for aesthetic meditation.

4.7 is no mean achievement. It has been executed with uninhibited verve, in a spirit of stylistic adventurousness; Propertius has brought to it a new sense of presentational realism often running into the grotesque. It vigorously exemplifies those changes in stylistic elevation and that rich tonality which, although traceable in the previous books, give evidence in the fourth of greater mastery of the poetic medium as well as of renewed aesthetic enterprise.[117] Widening of the literary scope and *poikilia* will also be found in other elegies of this book,[118] but it is the seventh that displays so vigorously *poikilia cum* incongruity; and even if incongruity can be felt elsewhere, it is only this piece which manipulates it so superbly for its aesthetic ends. The result is a well-calibrated paradox which transposes and modernises not only archaic Homer,[119] but also, I think, Hellenistic Callimachus. Talking of the latter's *Hecale*, fr. 260.63ff. Pfeiffer, Williams remarks on the variety of details which create the feeling of the dawn that finds Theseus in Hecale's humble abode; 'the technique differs from that of Virgil and Homer in their epics in the minuteness of the observation and the variety of the senses to which the poet appeals...The difference is underlined by that interest in realism and low life that characterizes much Hellenistic literature and art.'[120] The minutiae and the trivia of low life have a field day in 4.7 but the verism of the elegist appears on the whole more hard-edged and

---

[117] See Tränkle (1960) 172–4 esp., but the whole chapter on 'Wechsel in der Stilhöhe' (pp. 172–83) is essential reading.

[118] The new departures in Book 4 have been frequently commented upon by Propertian scholars; see, for example, La Penna (1951) 73–88 and (1977) 93–9, Weeber (1977) 274–83, not forgetting Tränkle (see preceding note).

[119] See Hubbard (1974) 150.   [120] Williams (1968) 657.

compelling. The difference is part of a more complex matter and their is room here for a brief consideration only.

If Callimachus substituted the subtle touch for the grand epic stroke, his subtle touch was also more likely than not to come with the self-conscious artificiality of phonetic and morphological cross-breeding which was made possible by a dazzling variety of prestigious literary dialects. To compound this incalculably was the fact that words and turns of phrase ennobled in the service of elevated subject matter were now applied to the humble and everyday; as a result the humble and the everyday were drawn into a pretty and esoteric literary game; part of the same procedure was the distinctly Callimachean juxtaposition 'of the highfalutin and the deflating colloquial'.[121] In Callimachus realism of content is seriously, though not unintentionally, compromised by the poetic idiom. By comparison with the vocabulary of the Alexandrian, Propertius' was both more limited and less diversified, but whatever handicaps this meant in other respects, it could certainly prove a blessing in disguise when it came to the imitation of reality, the mimesis in Auerbach's sense of the word; for although Propertius cannot be said to have consistently aimed at realism of presentation (4.5.61–78 is perhaps the nearest he gets to it), he was by virtue of his poetic medium closer to reality and was encouraged by language itself (the interaction is very important) to go more resolutely outwards and downwards to reality. The technique of successive pictorial flashes in 4.7 owes a great deal to the Callimachean school but the scenes and gestures they project have nothing of that museum-like Callimachean patina; and the poem's mimetic drive as a whole is far stronger than that of, say, Theocr. *Id.* 15. Again, and this is far more important, the juxtaposition in the elegy of the elevated and the everyday is not unrelated to Callimachean practice, but Propertius does not allow the sharp corners of reality to be smoothed away by the literary pumice; in fact, the juxtaposition is subtly designed to allow reality in its undiluted ugliness and grotesquerie to suggest its own fascination. Had he not done that, the paradox at the heart of the poem would have forfeited much of its appeal to modern taste.[122] It is, I believe, in this sense that 4.7 transposes and modernises Callimachus.

---

[121] Hubbard (1974) 11–12.

[122] Goethe's enthusiasm is attested by his elegy 'Euphrosyne', composed on the death of a young actress. Among the similarities pointed out by Tränkle (1979) 74–6 the encounter of the young girl with Underworld heroines and the interweaving of realistic with mythological elements are most noteworthy.

Wilamowitz valued 4.8 above 4.11; in a more apposite comparison Benedetto Croce (1936) 152 found dead Cynthia superior to dead Cornelia, and it was 4.7 that moved Robert Lowell to a superb 'translation'. See also Celentano (1956) 51–2.

One may wonder whether the latter would have approved of the criteria on which this piece was juxtaposed with 4.8.

Few Propertian issues have been so hotly debated. It is true that if 4.7 is a direct reflection of bereavement the arrangement that allowed the sex scandal of 4.8 to follow hard on its heels was not in the best humanitarian taste. And those who have put down the former poem convinced that Elysium rewarded Cynthia's *loyalty* understandably found her immediately following jaunt with the effeminate fop at least unpalatable. Whitewashers thought that a posthumous editor rather than the poet himself was responsible for this lapse of taste and there has also been some speculation that 4.8 is a considerably earlier piece than 4.7.[123] This line of thought has, I believe, been effectively scouted by Tränkle's stylistic analysis of the poem which shows that, in its verbal exuberance and rich tonality, in its use of elevated epic language to describe an undignified fracas and in its broad realism, it belongs, no less than 4.7, to Propertius' late manner.[124] It should be added here that whatever similarities in structure and plot there may be between these two poems, their affinity can also be assessed on the evidence of their generic orientation. It has been plausibly suggested that if Cynthia in 4.7 recalls a famous Iliadic

---

[123] To Warden's (1980) 80–1 list of the various views concerning the juxtaposition of 4.7 and 8 one may add Celentano (1956) 35–6, Jäger (1967) 95–8, who emphasises the points of contact which show the poems to form a pair, Hubbard's (1974) 153 elegant suggestion that 'the tragic heightening that his relation with Cynthia sustained in 4.7 is in 4.8 displaced when the same relation is displayed on the level of a "kind of comedy of manners"', (although I wouldn't quite agree with this assessment of 4.7) and Weeber (1977) 264–5, who suggests that 7 and 8 are no 'occasional poems' (*Gelegenheitsgedichte*) but written *sub specie aeternitatis* to make it clear that Propertius, as we know him, is inconceivable without Cynthia.

Of course, the problems of the relationship between 4.7 and 8 cannot be separated from the no less controversial question of the structural plan of Book 4 as a whole. Grimal's (1952) is the most resolute attempt to establish a clear-cut arrangement based on the supposedly central concept of *Fides* and manifesting itself as a pyramid in which 4.1 corresponds to 4.11, 4.2 to 4.10, 4.3 to 4.9 and so on, with 4.6 standing at the top (pp. 445ff.). His scheme, which is bound up with a politico-spiritual interpretation of the poems, has generally been received with scepticism, although it has found an unreserved supporter in Nethercut (1968). Burck (1966) argues, after A. Dieterich, that the book is organised around three cardinal elegies, namely, 1, 6 and 11 (cf. Camps, pp. 2–3) but he also seeks the manifold thematic analogies and cross-references that run across the whole book. Thus a poem like 7, besides showing affinity with 5 and 8, is 'multilayered' and 'many-voiced' enough to be in league with the axial poems 1, 6 and 11 (pp. 415–19). It is hard to quarrel with an analysis like this; the *societas omnium cum omnibus* for which it ultimately argues is after all of the essence of that highly organised form of discourse which is poetry. The trouble is that in structure studies of this kind the quest for a principle of arrangement (*Anordnungsprinzip*) extends far beyond the legitimate field of the external, formal arrangement. Butler and Barber (p. xxviii) suggest no definite scheme, Luck (1955) 428 denies its existence and so does Celentano (1956) 34, 68. Some favour the idea of alternating aetiological and erotic pieces (where 4.11 is sometimes assigned to the latter!) at least as far as poems 2–7 are concerned, with the principle of parallelism also at work in the case of 7 and 8. For a survey of the question see Burck (1966) 405–9 and Weeber (1977) 25–60.

[124] Tränkle (1960) 178–83.

apparition, her invasion of Propertius' ill-fated party in 4.8 is calculated to put one in mind of Ulysses' vengeful return to his home.[125] Even more distinctive is the debt of the two poems to the mime, especially the Adultery mime (cf. Cynthia's elopement through the window in 4.7), whose influence on 4.8 is all too evident.[126] I should, then, think that their juxtaposition reflects the artistic will of an increasingly learned elegist, bent on *poikilia*, anxious to broaden the scope of his chosen genre, and eager, at this stage of his poetic ambition, to present his reader with a diptych which demonstrates what he can *now* do (a) with a dead Cynthia, (b) with a Cynthia alive and kicking.[127] In this sense one could perhaps agree with Warden that the two poems are 'symphonies in two different keys'.[128]

'It is the addition of strangeness to beauty that constitutes the romantic character in art.'[129] This notion is central to the aesthetic outlook of Poe, Gautier, Baudelaire, Swinburne and Rossetti, all of whom have appeared at one point or another in the analysis of 4.7 as well as of other elegies. It is by reason of this shared attitude that the most recent anthology of their aesthetic writings rallies them under the title 'Strangeness and beauty'.[130] To describe the same antinomy Praz speaks more graphically of 'Medusean beauty' associated with satanism, death, horror, in short, 'beauty enhanced by exactly those qualities which seem to deny it'. In respect of this paradox Late Romanticism or Aestheticism/Decadence (or whatever label one may choose to apply) do not so much mark off an area outside which there is total lack as one within which there is remarkable plethora of instances. Praz traces kindred phenomena back to Torquato Tasso; even Shakespeare and other Elizabethans seem to have understood well that 'beauty and poetry...can be extracted from materials that are generally considered to be base and repugnant... though they did not theorise about it'.[131]

Nor did, as far as we can tell, Propertius or any other ancient poet or critic – a fact, however, which means very little, as anyone should admit when comparing the insights into classical creative writing that modern critical thinking has first made possible with what the rigidly rhetorical categories of ancient literary criticism made of the same material. Postgate understood this much, over a century ago:

[125] See Evans (1971) 51–3, esp. 53 and cf. Hubbard (1974) 152–3.
[126] See McKeown (1979) 74–5.
[127] It was as a result of a discussion with Professor Kenney that this view of the relationship between the two poems suggested itself.   [128] Warden (1980) 81.
[129] From W. Pater's *Appreciations* (see p. 19 n. 33 above) p. 248.
[130] Warner and Hough (1983).   [131] Praz (1951) 27–8.

The truth is that the literary criticism of the Romans was essentially superficial. They had not at their disposal the keen scalpel and the polymath terminology of modern analysis...Their rhetorical bias, the narrow limits and concrete character of their vocabulary and their practical habits of mind all worked in the same direction. And if the Roman critical resources were thus limited, Propertius must have taxed them severely.[132]

Postgate may be a little severe but unfair he is not. It is doubtful whether this sort of criticism, with its static character, could assess the artistic process that led from the Monobiblos to the rich and confident artistry of Book 4, let alone fully appreciate the peculiarity of its seventh elegy. This elegy gives full and sustained expression to trends, strains and tendencies which surface throughout Propertius' poetry. It may well be the case that in tackling it I have – by a reaction of, so to speak, interpretative overcompensation – all but 'dehumanised' what in some quarters has been proclaimed to be an eminently human poem. But then, to adapt one of the wildest aesthetes, 4.7 by fulfilling the conditions of beauty seems to me to have fulfilled its most important condition.

[132] Postgate (1881) lviii.

9

CONCLUDING THOUGHTS

Concentration on *Liebestod* must not obscure the fact that it is not only in the company of love that death stalks the Propertian *oeuvre*. This distinction is of importance, for by directing attention to the more general question of the poet's preoccupation with death it may point to *some* of the reasons for which the latter came to be so intimately involved in the language of love. Now the psychoanalyst tempted to step in at this point will soon find that he has simply not enough information to reconstruct a case history. We may well imagine the impact the death of a kinsman in the Perusine War of 41 B.C. (see 1.21 and 22) as well as that of his father (see 4.1.127–8) must have had on an impressionable child, but this is not much to go on. It is, perhaps, the historian who can make a better case, for the scars on the national psyche are amply documented. Boucher has given the historical and social background to the poet's 'sentiment de la mort' with economy and precision that cannot be bettered here: 'Ce sentiment apparaît alors chez les contemporains de Lucrèce, de Cicéron et de Virgile comme un sentiment italien profondément ressenti'; such were the effects of uninterrupted internecine strife from the Gracchi to Actium.[1] There may also be truth in the suggestion that it was this feeling against which Epicurean philosophy was mobilised at about the same time.[2] Once established, which according to Boucher cannot have happened until after Plautus and Ennius, the anxiety refused to go away, the dance of death was prolonged well beyond the dawn of the Empire, and Stoics like Seneca the Younger and Lucan joined in. It is hard to see the bloody horrors of Senecan tragedy in isolation from some of the ideas expressed in his other works, in one of which (*Ep.* 24.25) the striking phrase occurs: *affectus qui multos occupavit, libido moriendi* 'the ignoble passion which has assailed many, the lust, that is, for death'. It has been argued that the ubiquitousness of the *Todesgedanke* in Seneca must be linked as much with the social and political situation under the Principate as with his Stoicism.[3] It is likewise with Lucan. W. Rutz observes that the *amor mortis* in the *Pharsalia* is marked by the lack of any positive

[1] See Boucher (1965) 71–4.
[2] Boucher (1965) 71 mentions Philodemus' Περὶ Θανάτου, Lucretius' poem and the *De Morte* of Varius.   [3] Regenbogen (1961) 442–62, esp. 446–7, 454–8.

purpose, the condition of death being an end desirable in itself. This kind of death wish or, as Rutz puts it, *Todesfanatismus* represents a step beyond Seneca and the Stoic doctrines.[4] In fact, Lucan's position is so vanguard and absolute that one may well feel that the mortal dangers attending political vicissitudes, and even philosophical allegiance, offer too narrow a basis on which to place the problem of the attitude of all those writers to death. J. P. Poe, for example, while accepting Regenbogen's conclusions concerning the death theme in Senecan tragedy, also goes beyond him in considering a fascination with horror that 'indicates a new dimension of understanding'; in this state of mind one sees 'in the abomination a beauty to which other states of mind may be blind; or, if not its beauty, at least its *vertu*'.[5] Should there be truth in this, the classical Greeks fell, on the whole, short of such awareness, which, one suspects, may have something to do with their preference for ethos over pathos. Although the latter was clearly in the ascendant during the Hellenistic period (some at least of the roots of the *frisson nouveau* should be sought in this area), it none the less seems generally true to say that the Romans from their earliest literary enterprises favoured the *affectus* against the *mores*. Starting from E. Norden's remark that wherever the comparison is possible we can see that in his tragedies Ennius substitutes pathos for the ethos of his models, A. Traina contrasts the romantic and sentimental subjectivity of the Romans with the 'contemplative objectivity of the Greeks'.[6] There was surely more to the Roman character than *tu regere imperio populos, Romane, memento* suggests. That this people had a fairly developed 'sens du mystère' is no less true than that the Greeks had an irrational side as well.[7] Neglect of 'unorthodox' aspects, besides making refreshing surprises possible, fosters disabling

---

[4] Rutz (1960) draws his conclusions mainly from the evidence of Luc. 6.140–262 (the well-known Scaeva episode) and 4.448–581. These passages depict besieged soldiers seeking death but 'the interpretation of the freely chosen death as the besieged soldiers' act of despair...is explicitly rejected'; the soldier simply equates *virtus* and *mors*. One is tempted to think of those passages in Prop. where death grows almost autonomous and rather than representing the outcome of erotic despair is simply tantamount to an assertion of erotic virtue.

[5] Poe (1969) 359–60.

[6] Traina (1970) 65–7; all the papers collected in the book touch on this difference, but see esp. 65–70 and 161–5. On this extremely interesting question cf. Rostagni (1956) 75: 'compared with their Hellenic and Hellenistic predecessors all Romans in general were more spiritual, reflective and sentimental, in a word, they were more modern'; in his discussion on pp. 71–6 there is generalisation as well as truth, and also a slight underestimation of the Hellenistic 'pathos'. Cf. Stroh's (1971) 5ff. cautious remarks.

[7] See Bardon (1959) 7–14.
Propertius' native Umbria had been Etruscanised by the beginning of the fifth century B.C., and such poems as 1.21 and 22 show him thinking of Perusia as Etruscan. There is abundant archaeological evidence of the Etruscans' preoccupation with the Underworld, and Guy Lee suggests to me that the possibility of the poet's racy penchant for the funereal could perhaps do with a bit more *couleur locale*.

prejudices and narrows our field of vision. To ask why the aforementioned Roman writers allowed death so large a part is to raise at once all the issues briefly sketched in this paragraph. But the question must be asked in full awareness of the fact that literature is as much a reflection of the life of individuals and nations as it is an artefact under the spell of previous artefacts.

All too often, however, the intertwinement of life and art *laudatur et alget*. What one-sided approaches are apt to miss will be evident from J. Griffin's eloquent and amply documented remarks on the close relationship of Augustan poetry to contemporary life.[8] This general picture Griffin followed with a stimulating illustration. M. Antonius' relationship with Cleopatra is in the same mould as other stories concerning famous figures alternating between glorious action and glamorous debauchery; if the blend in such stories of sensational invention and historical truth put the ambitious womaniser on his mettle, it seems just possible that he himself, in his turn, supplied Propertius the poet-lover with patterns of un- or anti-Augustan *nequitia*; and even Propertius' sensibility for death, in particular his *Liebestod*, may owe something to the συναποθανούμενοι of Alexandria.[9] This skilfully promoted and elegant possibility is then judiciously qualified: 'And quite apart from this sort of source [i.e. Antonius' career], Propertius draws on other types of model: on contemporary experience, on his Latin predecessors, on Hellenistic poetry'.[10] If in the main body of this study I have tried to see love and death mainly against the Hellenistic literary background, it is because I believe that over and above the undeniable contributions of contemporary experience and individual life, the artistic formulation those themes receive and their patterns of *rapprochement* are due to, and *can best be discussed* in terms of, the techniques and thematic emphases of Hellenistic poetry in general. Propertius is another Hellenistic poet at Rome. His allegiance largely accounts both for the form the *Liebestod* takes and the spirit in which it is envisaged. But as a preliminary to a final consideration of this particular point, let me try to sum up here the evidence for the Hellenistic mode, some of which may not seem to be directly related to our main concern.

[8] Griffin (1976) 87–104.
[9] Griffin (1977) 19–26, esp. 25: '...in their last few days Antony and Cleopatra dissolved their society of Inimitable Livers "and founded another, not at all inferior in daintiness and luxury and extravagance, which they called the Partners in Death", συναποθανούμενοι. Antony died in her arms...' This is how (glamorised) life may have contributed, along with art and literature, to the posture of 2.13.11ff. (pp. 52ff. above).
[10] Griffin (1977) 26; after all, the Roman elegy is the 'genre ouvert' *par excellence*, on which see Boyancé (1956) 169–72.

A thumb-nail sketch of Hellenistic literary physiognomy is apt to arouse scepticism, and it may well bring to mind K. J. Dover's cautionary tale.[11] But well-informed diffidence need not preclude valid and useful distinctions. While conceding to Dover that some of the features associated with Hellenistic poetry can be found in earlier, even archaic, Greek writers, Cairns remarks that 'what is peculiar to Hellenistic as opposed to earlier literature is the conscious combination and concentration of those characteristics of earlier writers which Hellenistic poets found particularly effective and admirable and therefore imitated'.[12] Propertius displays quite a few of them.[13] We need not labour his *doctrina*, or his pretensions to it. All sorts of genres, themes and motifs have gone to make up the poems we have looked at. In 2.1 *recusatio*, Theocritean idyll, Lucretius' diatribe against love and sepulchral poetry have all contributed. Again in 2.13, along with the Callimachean affirmation of a slender Muse, a good case can be made for a Lucretian/Gallan/Tibullan posture in 11–16, for Bion's formative presence behind 17ff. and, perhaps, for Dioscorides' playful epigram. 2.26b warrants similar conclusions, while 4.7 (along with its companion 4.8), composed in the poet's late manner, registers the widest opening of the literary spectrum in Propertius' erotic poetry.

Antiquarian interest does not fall within the scope of this study but there is surely no lack of it in Book 4. In 2.1.47 (*in amore mori*) we have come across a major instance of linguistic interest, in the form of *etymological/semantic speculation* – another type of learning affected by Hellenistic poets. If the attractions of the countryside became a favourite topic with these poets, *the attractions of the urban centres* were equally acknowledged, and 4.7 was seen to evince partiality for the more shady aspects of their landscape – a partiality that can be discussed in terms of the new realistic trends in Book 4 as well as of Hellenistic realism in general. No less Hellenistic is *the preoccupation with magic in connexion with love*. This theme may be one of the specific debts of Roman elegy to New Comedy, but I have tried to show that in Propertius' hands it becomes something of a parable bringing home the deadliness of love. It is powerfully deployed in 2.4 as well as in 2.1, and is much in evidence in 4.7, where it also links up with low realism to cast over the elegy shadows of demonism temporarily lifted by the Elysian interlude. Significantly enough, all three elegies incorporate something of the evil atmosphere of

[11] Dover (1971) lxvi–lxvii.   [12] Cairns (1979) 10–11.
[13] In the following I have in the main followed the order in which Cairns (1979) 11ff. expounds the Hellenistic literary features; his footnotes provide further bibliographical information.

Theocritus' Φαρμακεύτρια (and 4.7, I have argued, may be more substantially indebted to this idyll), almost a *locus classicus* of Hellenistic fascination with erotic witchcraft.[14]

Self-imitation with variation, on which I have on several occasions commented, is another characteristically Hellenistic, Greek and Roman, practice. A fair number of the elegies dealt with display it, I think, with a neatness that is hard to parallel in other poets. Within the framework of this technique *abrupt transitions, heavy and angular paragraphing signalled by tenuous and vague linkage* are all there – and they can all be traced in Hellenistic masters and disciples alike.[15] I have argued for continuity between 2.1.43–6 and 47ff., 2.13.11–16 and 17ff., 2.26b.21–8 and 29ff., but this is continuity that coexists in fascinating harmony with the desultory, the spasmodic and the explosive. Of none is this more true than 2.8, which, smoothly conformist as it may ultimately prove when put alongside the other pieces, shows off its seams in order to create the illusion of exceptional agitation. Apart from 4.7, which affects the 'objective', narrative mode of Book 4, the poems we have looked at display another common feature in the *narrowness, even insubstantiality, of their dramatic and narrative basis*. Through anticipation of the future 2.13 develops from slender dramatic origins (in fact, a mere posture) into a resounding fantasy. The same is true of 2.26b and 2.8, where the main body of the poem is a mental event in the course of which erotic death is reached from antithetical emotional starting-points. The strong jerk forward in all these poems is reminiscent of *the projection into* the future which has been particularly associated with Hellenistic technique.[16] So has another device belonging to the other end of the time-scale, namely, *flashback*, a notable instance of which we have seen in 4.7.15ff. In the same poem Propertius relates a dream, and a Hellenistic vogue for *the dream motif* is perfectly understandable in the light of the Callimachean *Aetia*. Besides, this feature interlocks with the already mentioned penchant for the fantastic, and there is only a shade of difference between the proper dreaming of 4.7 and the day-dreaming of 2.26b and 2.13.

A great deal in this latter poem goes to show that the poet is casting his mistress and himself in the roles of the mourning Venus and the dying Adonis respectively. This is perfectly in line with the Hellenistic poet's

---

[14] On the influence of this idyll see most recently Wiseman (1985) 193–4 and p. 37 with n. 43 above. Cf. Pliny, *HN* 28.19 (no. 100 in Wiseman's Appendix).

[15] Cf. Cairns's (1979) 111ff. chapter on 'Exposition'. See also Boucher (1965) 374ff.

[16] See Cairns (1979) 129–30.

Irregular, fitful exposition and vivid forays into fantasy are surely part of the Hellenistic unorthodoxy in the matter of poetic narrative; both Lyne (1978) 180ff. and Cairns (1979) esp. 111–43 emphasise Callimachus' primary role in it.

readiness *to humanise heroic and divine figures*.[17] One of the points made by Dover with regard to the limitations of the term 'Hellenistic' is relevant here. He points out that mythological frivolity with regard to gods can be traced as far back as *Il.* 14.292ff., where Zeus reminds his consort of their wild oats;[18] quite, but here a distinction must be drawn which Dover seems to have missed. The humanisation of Artemis as a mischievous child in the Callimachean *Hymn*, to take a well-known example, cannot simply be seen in direct line of descent from the untrammelled levity of Homer's aloof immortals. The frivolity of *Hymn* 3.26–32 and 66–79 stems from a post-classical blend of urbane, sophisticated irreverence and intellectual play, and it is intimately related to the Hellenistic drive for more realism, as a result of which previously underrepresented or neglected characters, such as old people and children, came in for sympathetic portrayal. In Callimachus Jupiter's smile (l. 28) remains a strictly domestic occurrence with a strong flavour of bourgeois pride; it can never broaden into universal sunshine. This is humanisation of a quite different order, and it betokens a profound change in taste, sense and sensibility. Yet by far the best evidence for such change comes from our own thematic area: love and death.

When Aristophanes' Aeschylus (*Ran.* 1078ff.) took Euripides to task for introducing into his plays the incest theme, he could little imagine the worse that was to follow. Most of the Ten Commandments are flouted in the thirty-six stories of Parthenius' Περὶ Ἐρωτικῶν Παθημάτων and in no less than twenty-four of them erotic passion is, directly or indirectly, responsible for heavy casualties. What we have is bare outlines but it is enough to suggest the sensationalism, morbidity and grotesquerie that must have informed the treatment of the stories.[19] Parthenius was Gallus' mentor and, as W. Clausen suggests, he may also have put Cinna up to treating the story of *Zmyrna*.[20] Euphorion, no less important a figure for the Roman modernists, may have 'popularised the criminal love-story'.[21]

---

[17] See Fraser (1972) I 640–1; Cairns (1979) 9, 121.
[18] Dover (1971) lxvii.
[19] See, for instance, Crump (1931) 99–100, 108, 113.
[20] Clausen (1964) 190.
[21] A. M. Duff's suggestion, quoted by Clausen (1964) 191; cf. Crowther (1970) 325–6 and van Groningen, p. 123 n. 49 above. On Euphorion, apart from van Groningen, see Webster (1964) 221ff., Lyne (1978) 174, 185; on Parthenius, Crowther (1976); see also Crump (1931) 92–114 on both.
    This is the last place in which to press for fine distinctions among Callimacheans, νεώτεροι and *cantores Euphorionis* (for a distinction between the latter two groups see Crowther (1970)). 'A neoteric's Callimacheanism should or could have endeared him to Euphorion' synthesises Lyne (1978) 185. Puelma Piwonka once thought of Propertius and Tibullus as 'Neoteriker'.

I have pointed out the importance of Rohde's great work for the understanding of the post-Euripidean trends that fostered this 'decadent' taste. I hope that by now this term sounds less gratuitous. An informed anthologist of the Decadent Nineties will not fail to rally a number of poems under the rubric of 'Love and death'. R. K. R. Thornton does so; from his introduction one learns how Lionel Johnson, a critic who also happened to be a classicist, summed up in 1891 the essence of this literary fashion: '*Fin de siècle! Fin de siècle!* Literature is a thing of beauty, blood, and nerves.'[22] W. B. Yeats, himself no stranger to this school, also gave thought to the matter: 'Yet is it not most important to explore especially what has been long forbidden, and to do this not only "with the highest moral purpose"... but gaily, out of sheer mischief, or sheer delight in that play of the mind.'[23] Yeats and Lionel Johnson had in mind (the latter with satiric purposes) poets who set great store by sensation, pursued verbal poetry, colour and nuance, and often explored the unusual aspects of eros and beauty; they stood under the spell of Gautier, Baudelaire and W. Pater, so they revered the artificial and the artistic, and liked to put a poem side by side with a work of visual art. Not all the things that can be said of them are strictly relevant to the 'aesthetes and decadents' of the Hellenistic period but in attempting to assess what remains, or can be plausibly hypothesised, of the latter we cannot help being constantly reminded of the former. One is tempted to draw the parallel when going through Parthenius' résumés, and at least in one case one is irresistibly drawn to the parallel: a man was 'turned on' by the corpse of a beautiful woman which he found washed ashore, but unable to glut his desire because of incipient corruption he made a tomb for the body and, devoured by passion, killed himself by it (see p. 102 above). Here love and death pass (as they definitely pass for the nineteenth-century Aesthetes and Decadents) from static opposition to dialectic mobility. Today our deductive basis is broad enough to allow us to reconstruct with some confidence the way in which Parthenius would have expected Gallus to handle this material. He had admired in his predecessors, wrote himself with, and expected from others careful craftsmanship, a good ear for verbal poetry, a keen eye for colour and form, and when appropriate, a flair for sophisticated and morbid sensationalism. This is to all intents and purposes art for art's sake unconcerned 'to penetrate below a certain phenomenological level'.[24] Propertius' love-and-death poems have not

---

[22] Thornton (1970) 22. [23] Quoted by Hough (1949) 207–8.
[24] Dover (1971) lxix. His dissatisfaction with a conception of poetry that abdicated social and moral concerns should call to mind the charges of 'shallowness', 'immorality' and so on ritually hurled at the nineteenth-century Aesthetes.

been read as attempts at further penetration. What we sought in them was the seriousness of sensuousness, not that of morality or emotional involvement, for seriousness of the latter kind was not quite the way of his Hellenistic masters.[25] Apprenticeship to them, cultural environment and his own temperament are the main, interdependent and mutually reinforcing, factors one has to take account of. Although she failed to consider their combination, A. K. Michels made intelligent comments on the last of them in an article published some thirty years ago. This poet, she argues, does not generalise about death; his references to it lack the austerity of Horace's picture of the Underworld, and unlike Horace he does not think of death in the abstract.

> Perhaps one is wrong to use the word 'thought' at all to describe Propertius' relation to death, for in itself it presents no problems to him. He accepts it as a simple physical fact, the end of all the sensuous beauty that meant so much to him, but not of his own personality, which he could not imagine ceasing to exist . . . to a very marked degree he apprehends the world in which he moves primarily through his senses and only secondarily by his mind.[26]

Michels grasped a cardinal trait of Propertius' make-up, one that we cannot afford to forget when studying his treatment of love and death; nor is it possible to put the whole question in perspective without constant reference to the remarkable sensory performance of the Hellenistic literary school and to the proliferation of works of visual art in first-century B.C. Rome. A brief survey will help provide a wider context for some of the remarks occasioned by individual elegies.

Theocritus, *Id.* 1.29–56 is a fine example of ecphrasis, the kind of digression that demanded exceptional pictorial performance. The sensory abundance of *Id.* 7.135–46 is almost cloying; the chromatic flurry in *Id.* 15.123–5 is typical of Hellenistic interest in colour contrasts, a fancy avidly indulged, as we have seen, in Bion's *Adonis*. Related to this is an intense feeling for the effects of light. A virtuoso here is Apollonius

---

[25] Tiberius' dilettantism (Suet. *Tib.* 70) could grasp that Euphorion, Rhianos and Parthenius were birds of the same feather; and we can tell that the first was the most important poet. Some remarks on his art by van Groningen (pp. 267–71) are worth comparing with points already made and to be made about Propertius: 'Tout d'abord, fait-il un appel au raisonnement du lecteur? Non'; his poetry is not 'religieuse ou philosophique'; 'Il n'exprime aucune idée destinée à enrichir l'esprit du lecteur . . . à approfondir sa conception du monde, de la vie, de l'homme'; 'Euphorion est un adepte de cette forme de poésie que j'ai qualifiée de "verbale"'; 'il a sans doute voulu réaliser la beauté, la "poésie pure"'.

[26] Michels (1955) 171–9, esp. 178–9. When she writes that in Prop. poetry 'there is an awareness of sight, sound, and touch more immediate and more intimate than in any other Roman poet' she more or less describes the temperamental apparatus of the 'Aesthete'; but Michels was either unaware of, or unconcerned to draw the parallel.

Rhodius, and such passages of his *Argonautica* as 1.219–23, 3.755–9 and 4.125–6 suggest that he 'saw with the eye of the contemporary painter'.[27] Interest in the effects of light takes us smoothly over to the Roman side, where Lucretius displays similar felicities, as D. West's chapter on 'Light and fire and fluidity of imagery' has cogently shown.[28] R. Jenkyns has recently expounded the sensuous excellences of Catullus 64, a *tour de force* in the best traditions of Alexandrian aestheticism.[29] G. Williams's chapter on 'Observation, description and imagination' is important as a general framework within which the visual powers, and their limitations, of Lucretius, Propertius, Horace and Virgil can be assessed.[30] What emerges clearly is that the period encompassed by all the above poets could boast by comparison with any other previous period the greatest number of accomplished εὐφαντασίωτοι, poets endowed with the virtue of ἐνάργεια, which could bring the things described right before the eyes of their listeners and readers. ἐνάργεια could be applied to elevated subject matter in order to arouse pathos, but it could also be brought to bear on the contingent, the random and the minute of everyday life, as Hellenistic poets in pursuit of more realism came to know. This is the technique of Callimachus fr. 260.63ff. Pfeiffer (see p. 194 above), and G. Williams can show convincingly that Horace was a master of it too.[31] I believe that 4.7, where we have seen random and suggestive details reinforcing the sensory impact of humble and macabre realism, shows well that in his mature period Propertius, probably learning from both Callimachus and Horace, was capable of combining firm mastery with fertile enterprise.

Constant incentive and inspiration must also have been provided by works of visual art, and it will be no coincidence that during the period under discussion they were increasingly visible both in public places and as private decoration. If this is true of the great Hellenistic cities, it is even more true of first-century B.C. Rome.[32] It is against this background that J. André writes that the taste of Hellenistic poets for colour was further developed by Latin poets.[33] Scholars have been peering through Prop. 2.26a to catch a glimpse of a painting just as they have been measuring 1.3.1ff. against the contours of some sculpture. Similar influences have been claimed for Ovid. If it was landscape painting of the kind we see

---

[27] See Webster (1964) 72, 160.

[28] West (1969) 79–93; 1–22 are no less interesting.

[29] Jenkyns (1982) 98ff.; cf. Wiseman (1985) 129.

[30] Williams (1968) 634–81, esp. 669–70; cf. André (1949) 323–4 for a good comparison between older (epic and lyric) Greek and Hellenistic poets in respect of their visual interests, and see below on ἐνάργεια. [31] Williams (1968) 657ff.

[32] See Boucher (1965) 41ff., Luck (1969) 124 and Griffin (1976) 91: 'An aesthete lived amid images derived from Greece and its mythology...' [33] André (1949) 381.

at Pompei that especially caught his eye, then the difference from Propertius, who would be detained by the human figure rather than the scenery, is significant enough.[34] Tibullus, on the other hand, less visual to my mind than Ovid, betrays none of Propertius' ocular avidity.[35] 'Both Ovid and Propertius', remarks Luck, 'share an interest in works of art (statues, painting) which is hardly noticeable in Tibullus.'[36] Moreover, our discussion of Propertius' poems suggested that his was an all-round ἐνάργεια, not just one of sight; as Cicero puts it in *Part. Or.* 6.20 *is enim maxime sensus attingitur, sed et ceteri tamen* 'for it is this sense that is most affected, although the rest are affected too'. If G. Zanker is right in a recent paper, this term, ἐνάργεια, broke into the consciousness of Hellenistic literary critics as a result of their acquaintance with the writings of the Epicureans.[37] I do not wish to suggest here that Propertius' sensuousness, or that of any other poet for that matter, was directly indebted to Epicurus' privileging of sensory perception, but the connexion Zanker suggests is a convenient reminder that we should give brief thought to Propertius' philosophical outlook, in the broadest sense of the word.

It is a plausible inference from 3.5.23ff. that Propertius postpones serious philosophical studies for the Greek Kalends. Aristophanes in the Platonic *Symposium* (189d–193d) gave a charming, if somewhat grotesque, version of the myth of erotic oneness, but when this motif surfaces in erotic verse, as, for instance, in Prop. 2.28.42 *vivam, si vivet; si cadet illa, cadam* 'I live if she lives; if she falls I fall' (apropos of Cynthia's illness), it is already a hackneyed cliché.[38] Renowned thinkers on love are likely to become part of the love poet's conceptual arsenal through a process of excerption and *haute vulgarisation*. Propertius might have known that the idea of dying for the beloved, or that of an erotic reunion in the hereafter, were to be found in Plato without having ever read or pondered *Symp.* 179e or *Phd.* 68a (see p. 110 above). But it is, I think, a fair guess that if he knew more about Plato he must have found in him little to be genuinely excited about. Epicurus was different. Supposing for a moment that Propertius undertook a trip to Athens similar to that projected in 3.21, it makes good sense to imagine him skimming the precincts of the

[34] For the influence of contemporary painting on Ovid see Wilkinson (1955) 172 and further literature cited in n. 93.

[35] He gives Cairns (1979) 134, 140–1 precious little to comment upon.

[36] Luck (1969) 124; see also 125–6. His remarks should not lead one to put Ovid on a par with Prop. Comparing Prop. 3.9.9ff. with Ovid, *Pont.* 4.1.29ff. (both passages list artists and their work) Keyssner (1975) 267 rightly observes that in contrast to Ovid Propertius manages to convey a more immediate and vivid pictorial impression. Cf. also his remarks on pp. 276–7.

[37] Zanker (1981) 308–10.   [38] Cf. Bréguet (1960) 205–14.

Platonic Academy while taking a certain interest in some of the things asserted in Epicurus' gardens, especially if he chanced upon an exegesis of the master's 'Περὶ Τέλους': οὐ γὰρ ἔγωγε ἔχω τί νοήσω τἀγαθόν, ἀφαιρῶν μὲν τὰς διὰ χυλῶν ἡδονάς, ἀφαιρῶν δὲ τὰς δι' ἀφροδισίων καὶ τὰς δι' ἀκροαμάτων καὶ τὰς διὰ μορφῆς 'For my part, I cannot conceive the good without the pleasures of taste, sexual pleasures, the pleasures of listening to, and the pleasures of looking upon something beautiful.'[39] And he might have been particularly impressed by the Epicurean ἐνάργεια with its special relevance to sight. What the next step, and the most likely one, would have been is clear from the following:

> illic vel stadiis animum emendare Platonis
> incipiam aut hortis, docte Epicure, tuis   (3.21.25–6)

There I'll begin to reform myself in Plato's academy or in your gardens, learned Epicurus.

> *aut certe* tabulae *capient mea lumina* pictae
> sive ebore exactae, seu magis aere, manus.   (3.21.29–30)

Or else painted pictures will certainly capture my eyes, or works of art fashioned in ivory and bronze.

3.21.25–30 sound like the traditional project of a Roman poised for a postgraduate course in Athens, but they are also a piece of accurate self-analysis. Line 29 ensures the primacy of the eyes, but in point of fact all senses are intensely active. We have seen this in 1.19 and we can see it again in 2.15.

The besetting sin of the poem is *concupiscentia oculorum: non iuvat...in caeco* 'there is no point...in darkness' (11), *oculi sunt duces* 'the eyes lead the way' (12), *oculos satiemus* 'let us glut our eyes' (23), *dum lucet* 'while there is still light' (49 *pace* Housman). *amor* in this, perhaps more than in any other poem, is circumscribed by sensory perception; *oculos satiemus amore* (23) is incomprehensible on any other hypothesis. 2.15 also resolves into the *carpe diem* of the last three couplets but like 1.19 it does not do so until it has achieved its moments of heightened sensuous awareness under the stimulus of prospective darkness and extinction – 'the desire of beauty quickened by the sense of death'. Pater's words, quoted on p. 19, read as if they were meant to feel and follow the pulse of this poem; and one of the Decadent pieces Thornton culled under 'Love and death' reads like its replica. No wonder, for the poem, Ernest Dowson's 'Cease smiling, dear! A little while be sad', written in 1896, is heralded by: *Dum*

---

[39] Fr. 67 Usener; cf. Ath. 12.546e and Diog. Laert. 10.6.

nos fata sinunt oculos satiemus amore.[40] The flaunted voguish *fin-de-siècle* pessimism not withstanding, Dowson's 'love' is similar in texture and depth to Propertius', and it nowhere seems to be more than the aggregate of the woman's 'sweet eyes', 'lips', 'breast' and 'red pomegranate of her perfect mouth'. 'E. Dowson loved his Propertius'[41] – and understood him. This is love as sensuous beauty and as sensuous excitement, death enhancing the former and exacerbating the latter – the common aesthetic matrix of the *erotic death* and the *dead Beauties*. In this sense, Prop. 4.7 differs from the other poems only in so far as it wants also to sound the sensuous charm of unlikely things.

'Fear is upon me and the memory | Of what is all men's share.' Dowson makes the same exquisite capital out of his fear as Propertius does in 1.19 and 2.15. Catullus, Tibullus, Horace and Ovid, all shared the fear (who doesn't?) but none made quite the same capital out of it.

Poems 1.19 and 2.15 define a sensibility which can see the co-operative potential beneath the surface antagonism of love and death, and which can, therefore, see the one in terms of the other. I think it is this that gives the Propertian utterances on love and death their unique quality – and their essential unity. For the apparent divergence between *love as an incurable disease, nay, the one irreversible kind of death* in 2.1 and *love as luxurious and easeful death* in 2.13 is a matter of dramatic fiction and inherited theme, and has very little to do with some grave ambivalence in the poet's attitude to erotic death. Sensuous Propertius thrills to bring together two forces that can generate climactic and ultimate sensations; the *rapprochement* takes place *within* and *through* a variety of traditional poetic fictions but *beyond* the good and evil, so to speak. I have argued that aestheticism of this sort cannot be denied him. Not that it will explain everything; the Paterian formula quoted on pp. 19–20 seems more germane to the full-blown *Liebestod* of our first group than it does to the conceptual equations of the second. Yet even the lesser pieces are

---

[40] Longaker, 90–1; also Thornton (1970) 147–8. I feel that more than one poem bears testimony to Propertius' impact on Dowson. The latter's most famous, and perhaps most original, poem is titled 'Non sum qualis eram bonae sub regno Cynarae', but whenever I read it I fail to descry the genuine Horatian connexion; indeed, I think that Dowson just relished the sound of the proper name (elsewhere he goes for *Lalage*) and now I learn from Longaker's note on the poem (p. 208) that in a book published in 1914 Victor Plarr, himself a poet and Dowson's friend, reports: 'Horace suggested, but Propertius inspired' (cf. Thornton (1983) 94 and note Longaker's remark in *Explicator* 9 (1951) 48 that '"Cynara" is essentially a sensation poem'). R. Fowler's paper on 'Ernest Dowson and the classics' in *Yearbook of English Studies* 3 (1973) 243–52 draws attention to a fascinating and largely uncharted area; she writes on p. 247: 'Propertius, who was a favourite of the poets of the nineties, was a figure with whom Dowson could feel a greater personal sympathy.' This is a claim that can be substantiated, though some of Fowler's own comments on pp. 247ff. are not quite helpful or relevant.

[41] Victor Plarr's remark in connexion with this poem; see Longaker, 227.

revealing in their own way in that they broaden the sensuous basis of interaction into an all-round conception of equivalence. Perhaps here resides that part of the mystery that must remain inviolate. After all, Propertius is a sensuous poet, not a mere sensation collector. Writing on love and death he ultimately sets out from, and contributes something to the eternal enigma of the syzygy Eros–Thanatos. La Penna forbears to pry into it and quotes instead Leopardi confessing that no sooner does love surge in his heart than he desires death: 'come, non so: ma tale | d'amor vero e possente è il primo effeto'.[42] We cannot presume to know more, but Keats writing on 25 July 1819 to Fanny Brawne comes to mind: 'I have two luxuries to brood over in my walks, your Loveliness and the hour of my death. O that I could have possession of them both in the same minute!'[43]

Are we, then, in view of the above, entitled to speak of death as a metaphor for love? It is, perhaps, economical to do so, but not without being uncomfortably aware of the disparity between this kind of metaphor and, say, the metaphor of love as soldiering. For in the latter case the areas of experience brought into metaphorical relation (or, to use two well-known technical terms, the tenor (love) and the vehicle (soldiering)) remain fixed and far apart, the intellect shuttling between the two (a process, incidentally, well-suited to Ovid's genius). No one will ever be tempted to think of the lover as actually soldiering, but consider the reluctance of the commentator on Prop. 2.4.13 to commit himself: 'It *need not* be meant that the man literally dies of love: sudden death here *may be* a metaphor for his being suddenly knocked over by love' (my italics).[44] Faced with a similar question, namely, Catullus' adaptation of the vocabulary of Roman social commitment to love poetry, Lyne comes down against metaphor: 'Catullus did actually conceive of love or part of love as a form of *amicitia*.'[45] So, we have seen, does Propertius conceive of love or part of love as a kind of dying, although the 'dying' of 2.26b may be felt to rely less on conscious metaphorical thinking than that of 2.8. Lyne is, I think, fundamentally right, perhaps in the sense that some metaphors are less 'metaphorical' than others. A first-rate poet of sensation rather than of thought will both 'make' and 'mar' his metaphors, and we have come across instances where Propertius allows physicalness to shake up a blunted metaphor and imperil its identity. In describing, however, such phenomena the critic may on balance find 'metaphor' a quite serviceable and economical term. To use it in the case of the elegies discussed in the present work, and under the *caveat* suggested

[42] La Penna (1977) 166.
[43] Rollins, II 133.
[44] Camps, *ad loc.*
[45] Lyne (1980) 25.

by the preceding remarks, is perhaps all the more legitimate since, in one sense, the love-as-death novelty is an outgrowth on recognised and well-known tropes of erotic language such as the lover's funeral in 2.13 and 2.24b, the love magic in 2.1 and 2.4, the *navigium amoris* in 2.26b and the weapon symbolism in 2.8. And besides, one may appeal to the more liberal and imaginative application of 'metaphor' in modern criticism which is guided not so much by the Aristotelian definition (speaking of *A* in words that pertain to *B*) as by the Romantic preference for the metaphor's non-verbal aspects. 'More typical of modern attitudes is the non-verbal, even anti-verbal, emphasis apparent in, for instance, Lorca's somewhat extreme manifesto, "la métaphore unit deux mondes antago-nistes dans le saut équestre de l'imagination", or in I. A. Richards's more restrained comment, "fundamentally it is a borrowing between and intercourse of thoughts".'[46]

A substantial part of Propertius' work boasts the unique distinction of having struck older scholars as textually corrupt before it fascinated recent ones as surprisingly modernist. 'There is something in the Umbrian poet that appeals to the modern mind', wrote G. Luck some years ago,[47] and this has been variously sought in his Laforguesque irony, imagistic tendencies and abrupt openings and transitions.[48] Bold imagery and abruptness, suggests Luck, 'may be partly the result of an inadequate application of Alexandrian technique'.[49] It seems more likely that they represent its *reductio ad extremum*, an escalated Hellenistic desire to renew the poetic manner by avoiding at all costs the *iam vulgatum*.[50] It has long been recognised that some of the forces at work here are comparable to those that shaped the 'pure' and 'absolute' poetry of the Decadence and Aestheticism. Since in approaching the Hellenistic Propertius I have often referred to the writings of this period, let me fill in some more general information on the background against which some of the parallels suggested must be seen, by way of outlining in this concluding

[46] See Silk (1974) 6–7.   [47] Luck (1969) 121.

[48] Some of the most perceptive comments on Propertius' singularity of expression were made by Postgate (1881) lviiff. more than a hundred years ago. His subheadings show him putting a finger on such well-known Propertian issues as 'vagueness', 'stress on single words', 'violent transitions', 'boldness of imagery' and *modernity of spirit* – a spirit which he finds 'modern and even romantic'. Although Propertius' poetry is not romantic in the sense that Postgate in 1881 understood the word, it is modern in other respects that struck a responsive chord in modernists like Ezra Pound. Dilettantes like Cyril Connolly in *Ideas and places* (1933) sensed rightly ('this antique Baudelaire') even if they explained superficially ('they had several quarrels and we are inevitably reminded of the relationship between Jeanne Duval and Baudelaire').

[49] Luck (1969) 120.

[50] Cf. White's (1958) 20–1 remarks on the abruptness of Propertius' transitions.

section of the book, and in juxtaposition, the efforts of two scholars who have, in my opinion, made clear the merits, if also the hazards, of putting the poetics of Alexandria side by side with that of late nineteenth-century Europe.

In 1948 E. Howald published a slim volume in which he sought access to the essence of Augustan poetry by way of the tenets of *Absolute Dichtung*, as they had been foreshadowed by E. A. Poe and crystallised by his French progeny.[51] Baudelaire, Mallarmé and Valéry, all set great store by self-conscious craftsmanship at the expense of 'fine frenzy', counselled painstaking elaboration, cultivated the individual word, dreaded banality of diction, excluded didacticism and the immediate communication of feeling and passion, strove after the 'rhythmical creation of Beauty' and consciously addressed themselves to an appreciative coterie.[52] It is difficult not to think of Callimachus here, and yet it is something of a methodological oddity that Howald does not mention him until the last couple of pages. Even when allowance has been made for the fact that a complex question is tackled here in an uncomfortably brief compass, the reader cannot help noticing that at certain points Howald's nets are gross enough for essential distinctions to escape, whereas at other times dubious, to say the least, parallels between nineteenth-century *Absolute Dichtung* and especially Horace are rather unconvincingly enlarged upon. The theory of composition in more or less 'independent blocks' (*Einzel-blöcke*), for example, (which, incidentally, may be of some relevance to Propertius' methods of composition) is given only superficial attention.[53] Further, when the Horatian use of personified abstracts in *Carm.* 1.24.6-7 and *Carm. Saec.* 57ff. is treated as 'propensity to the abstract' (*Neigung zum Abstraktum*) comparable to the Mallarmean practice (pp. 43 and 76-7), one finds it hard to assent. In projects like this, however, one should be prepared to take the rough with the smooth, and there are, on the other hand, genuine similarities which are discussed here for the first time by a scholar convinced of the validity of the comparison and able to pursue it within a theoretical framework. Features of 'pure' or 'absolute' poetry, as Howald himself knows, can be found in all periods of poetic activity, but it was after Poe that they were cultivated to the exclusion of other poetic means and functions; and they were enshrined in critical theory because it was during this period that writer and reader alike became highly conscious of them (pp. 24-5 and 52). Similar developments in ancient literature command attention. The fact that Mallarmé's *Hérodiade*

---

[51] Howald (1948).　　　　[52] Howald (1948) 15ff.

[53] Howald (1948) 49-51, 6off.; the argument, in particular, for looking at some Horatian Odes from this viewpoint seems to me feeble.

was gestated almost as long and painfully as Cinna's *Zmyrna* (p. 29) might in itself mean nothing were it not that both poets had imbibed similar aesthetic lessons. Howald makes a number of other interesting points which have unfortunately received less attention than they deserve and, surprisingly enough, there is, as far as I can see, no mention of his work in Bonelli's more recent book on 'Decadentismo antico e moderno'.[54]

Bonelli's title is a good reminder of the terminological laxity which characterises the study of nineteenth-century literary trends in particular, for it is abundantly clear that he uses 'Decadentismo' in exactly the same sense as Howald used *Absolute Dichtung*. It is also to be noticed that his subtitle features 'estetismo' as an explicative synonym. It seems to me that through sensitive discussion of individual passages Bonelli makes a more cogent case for Alexandrian aestheticism than Howald does for Augustan *Absolute Dichtung*, but whereas he can thus lavish credit on the Greek Hellenistic masters he all but grudges their Roman followers that detachment of the aesthete which he rightly claims for the Alexandrian 'Decadents'. Propertius bears, I think, the brunt of a cavalier reading of Roman elegy on the part of Bonelli. I have maintained that the human suffering and pessimism which would forbid aesthetic detachment are not to be found in his love-and-death poems, but since attention has already been drawn to the unsound premiss of Bonelli's views in the discussion of 2.13, I would rather not repeat the same arguments here (see pp. 69–70 above). To avoid further repetition we must also dispense with giving an *aperçu* of his pages on the Callimachean poetics and its relation to the aesthetic doctrines of Poe, Baudelaire and others, since, stimulating reading as they are, they make by and large the same points about the same parallels between 'antico' and 'moderno' as Howald's study;[55] instead we may sample some enterprising remarks Bonelli offers on the question of the social and cultural background to the Decadence, ancient and modern.

Bonelli, like others before him, calls attention to the dismantling of the classical polis towards the end of the fourth century B.C., a development with far-reaching consequences: 'l'uomo diventa da "polita" "cosmopolita"', the city no longer ensures a communal participation in matters cultural and spiritual, culture is taken over by sophisticated and unconventional individuals with little respect for traditional values (pp. 5–9). All areas of intellectual activity were affected by the change of *Weltanschauung*, and Epicurus recast philosophy on a purely individual basis, which in turn led to an intense cultivation of individual sensibility. In the literary field the attitude to epic material undergoes significant changes.

[54] Bonelli (1979).   [55] See Bonelli (1979) 5–23, 69–102.

CONCLUDING THOUGHTS

The Alexandrians view the Homeric world from a distance, reflect on it, write learnedly about it (pp. 9ff.). It is exactly this state of affairs which allows 'the aesthetic process'. Hence the Callimachean manifesto with its injunctions and implications of erudition, brevity, poetic *labor*, stylistic fastidiousness and 'Parnassian' relish for the carefully chosen word (pp. 15–23). From this poetics emotion was not excluded, but purged of its dross and more effusive elements it came to be embodied in the form; Callimachus' 'stylistic rarefaction pursues the Parnassian programme of art for art's sake, and the Baudelairean-Poesque programme of pure poetry' (p. 22). The question must now arise: to what extent does the cultural and social situation that fostered the modern Decadence tally with the picture of fourth-century B.C. developments?

The answer Bonelli returns involves some pretty bold strokes. He sees the Greek fifth century B.C. as broadly equivalent to the first half of the European nineteenth century inasmuch as both periods, by comparison with their Alexandrian and post-Romantic sequels respectively, show a spiritual vigour which is the result of cultural homogeneity. Thus, Decadence stems from the impossibility of identifying oneself with ideas widely accepted in the previous period, just as the Alexandrian Hellenism stems from inability to uphold the ideas of the disintegrating polis. The 'borghesia liberale', which imposed and maintained cultural homogeneity, is in decline in both periods, and becomes increasingly apolitical. Translated into intellectual terms, the political crisis of the nineteenth-century bourgeoisie appears as the 'crisi dell' Io romantico', which from idealistic and universal becomes self-indulgent, introvert and solipsistic, in other words 'Io individuale' (pp. 58–60). From this bird's-eye view Bonelli seems to derive confidence where others might develop vertigo symptoms, but the model he proposes is well worth pondering. To attempt this is beyond my powers and outside the scope of the present work. Nevertheless, two points can be modestly and safely made. First, Bonelli's account, with its socio-historical determinism, is certain to appeal to Marxist literary historians; in fact, one of them has postulated similar causes for the Hellenistic literary movement.[56] Secondly, in surveying the socio-historical breeding-ground of an artistic revolution a thought must be spared for the vagaries of extraordinary individuals.[57]

[56] This is S. I. Radtsig (*Istoriya drevnegrecheskoy literatury*, Moscow 1959) quoted by Newman (1967) 44. Radtsig argues that the environment of Hellenistic cities was conducive to extreme individualism on which alone 'pure art' or 'art for art's sake' could thrive.

[57] Newman (1967) 44–5 takes a hard line against Radtsig's approach (see preceding note): 'it seems to assume that in real life we start with the state or society first and that personal individuality is a secondary discovery. Surely the concrete historical situation is encountered in the reverse order.' The situation is never as black and white as it may seem from such disputes.

The best poets may mark 'the growing points of a culture and...bear witness to its sensibility',[58] but they must also set fashions that cannot be completely, or exclusively, accounted for in socio-historical terms. There must be an internal history of artistic temperament that partly eludes the historical mould; one need only remember the displaced European who gave Baudelaire his lead from across the Atlantic.

'Propertius was admittedly not in the least like Poe...he was not like any other nineteenth-century romantic, either.' Thus Hubbard in an understandable reaction to a 'hysterical' Postgate who took a profoundly gloomy and crudely biographical view of 4.7.[59] And yet in dealing with Propertius' love and death it is at least as rewarding to be hysterical with Postgate as it is advisable to be sober with Hubbard. For what does 'in the least' mean and how is a 'nineteenth-century romantic' to be defined? I have suggested answers to such questions by making distinctions which are normally lost sight of. Admittedly, Propertius does not sound in the least like Wordsworth, but he does occasionally sound like Keats, the most aesthetic–decadent among the early nineteenth-century Romantics. He is alien to the Romantic concept of organic form or uncontrollable inspiration; indeed, his craftsmanship is self-conscious and deliberate, as W. Pater would have expected it to be – and Pater was not alien to the romantic spirit. This book did not primarily set out to substantiate the claim of a 'Decadent–Aesthete', and to that extent 'late Romantic', Propertius *avant la lettre*; but in the course of tackling the *Hellenistic* Propertius on love and death it has found the parallel illuminating. Types of sensibility are limited across history; history is likely to repeat itself in the aesthetic sphere, 'and where this happens', writes L. P. Wilkinson, 'to any marked extent, comparisons may help us to better appreciation and understanding'.[60] To better understand and appreciate the sensibility that shapes the poems discussed in the preceding pages is, I believe, a vital task. 'It is Ovid's intelligence that is individual, not his sensibility (if one can separate the two).'[61] If the two can be separated, then it must be the other way round with Propertius, for it was a highly individual sensibility that Hellenistic education could galvanise into fascinating modernity.

[58] Sullivan (1976) 81, perhaps with Ezra Pound's aphorism (from the *ABC of reading*) in his mind: 'Artists are the antennae of the race.'
[59] Hubbard (1974) 117–18.   [60] Wilkinson (1950) 4.
[61] Lee (1962) 173–4.

BIBLIOGRAPHY

I TEXTS AND COMMENTARIES

Barber, E. A. (1960). *Sexti Properti Carmina*. 2nd edn. Oxford.

Butler, H. E. and Barber, E. A. (1933). *The elegies of Propertius*. Oxford (repr. Hildesheim 1969).

Camps, W. A. (1961). *Propertius. Elegies, Book I*. Cambridge.

    (1967). *Propertius. Elegies, Book II*. Cambridge.

    (1966). *Propertius. Elegies, Book III*. Cambridge.

    (1965). *Propertius. Elegies, Book IV*. Cambridge.

Enk, P. J. (1946). *Sex. Propertii Elegiarum Liber I (Monobiblos)*. Two Parts. Leiden.

    (1962). *Sex. Propertii Elegiarum Liber Secundus*. Two Parts. Leiden.

Fedeli, P. (1980). *Sesto Properzio. Il primo libro delle elegie*. Florence.

    (1965). *Properzio. Elegie, Libro IV*. Bari.

    (1984). *Sexti Properti Elegiarum Libri IV*. Bibl. Teubn. Stuttgart.

Giardina, I. C. (1977). *Sex. Properti Elegiarum Liber II*. Corpus Scriptorum Latinorum Paravianum. Turin.

Hanslik, R. (1979). *Sex. Propertii Elegiarum libri IV*. Bibl. Teubn. Leipzig.

Luck, G. (1964). *Properz und Tibull: Liebeselegien*. Zurich–Stuttgart.

Pasoli, E. (1967). *Sesto Properzio. Il libro quarto delle elegie*. Bolognia.

Richardson, L., Jr (1977). *Propertius. Elegies I–IV*. Univ. of Oklahoma Press, Norman.

Rothstein, M. (1920). *Die Elegien des Sex. Propertius*. 2nd edn. Berlin (repr. Dublin–Zurich 1966).

Note. Unless further indication seems essential, the above works are referred to by author's name only, with the exception of Fedeli's Teubner edition which, to avoid confusion with his 1980 Monobiblos and 1965 Book IV editions, is throughout cited as: Fedeli (1984).

    Discussion of Propertian poems and passages is based on Barber's 1960 Oxford Classical Text with Arabic numerals normally substituted for Roman ones in the numbering of the elegies. Departures from the text of this edition should be clear from individual discussions.

Quotations from the text of other ancient authors are based on the following.

R. A. B. Mynors 1958 OCT for Catullus.

A. S. F. Gow and D. L. Page 1965 Cambridge edn of the *Greek Anthology* for the Hellenistic epigrammatists.

E. C. Wickham OCT, rev. 1912 by H. W. Garrod, for Horace.

BIBLIOGRAPHY

C. Bailey 1947 Oxford edn for Lucretius.
K. Kost 1971 Bonn edn for Musaeus.
E. J. Kenney 1961 OCT for Ovid, *Amores* and *Ars Amatoria*.
H. Dörrie 1971 Berlin and New York (Texte und Kommentare, 6) edn for Ovid, *Heroides*.
W. S. Anderson 1977 Bibl. Teubn. edn for Ovid, *Metamorphoses*.
E. Martini 1902 Leipzig (*Mythographi Graeci*, Vol. II, Fasc. I Suppl.) edn for Parthenius.
A. S. F. Gow 1952 OCT (*Bucolici Graeci*) for Theocritus, *Idylls* and Bion, Ἐπιτάφιος Ἀδώνιδος.
J. P. Postgate 1915 OCT for Tibullus.

II EDITIONS OF MODERN AUTHORS

Note. The following works are referred to by editor(s)' name, volume (when appropriate) and page number only.

Behler, E. *Kritische Friedrich-Schlegel-Ausgabe* (unter Mitwirkung von Jean-Jacques Anstett und Hans Eichner). Munich 1958– .
Beutler, E. *Johann Wolfgang Goethe. Gedenkausgabe der Werke, Briefe und Gespräche.* 24 vols. Zurich 1948–54.
Garrod, H. W. *Keats. Poetical works.* Oxford 1956 (frequently reprinted).
Gosse, E. and Wise, T. J. *The complete works of Algernon Charles Swinburne.* 20 vols. London and New York 1925–7 (The Bonchurch edn).
Longaker, M. *The poems of Ernest Dowson.* Philadelphia, Univ. of Pennsylvania Press 1962.
Mabbott, T. O. *Collected works of Edgar Allan Poe.* Cambridge, Mass.–London 1969– .
Pichois, C. *Baudelaire, Oeuvres complètes.* 2 vols. Bibliothèque de la Pléiade, Paris 1975–6.
Rollins, H. E. *The letters of John Keats, 1814–1821.* 2 vols. Cambridge, Mass. 1958.
Ross, R. *The first collected edition of the works of Oscar Wilde.* 15 vols. London 1908 (repr. 1969).
Rossetti, W. M. *The works of Dante Gabriel Rossetti.* Revised and enlarged edn. London 1911.

III OTHER PUBLICATIONS CITED

Note. The following works are referred to by author's name, date and page number only.

Abel, W. (1930). *Die Anredeformen bei den römischen Elegikern.* Diss. Berlin.
Adams, J. N. (1982). *The Latin sexual vocabulary.* London.
Alfonsi, L. (1945). *L'elegia di Properzio.* Milan (repr. in the Garland Libr. of Latin Poetry, New York and London 1979).
   (1960). 'Topica Erotico-Elegiaca in Petronio', *Aevum* 34:254–5.
   (1973). 'Propertiana', *Aevum* 47:302–4.

218

Allen, A. W. (1950). 'Elegy and the classical attitude toward love: Propertius 1.1', *YClS* 11:255–77.

(1962). 'Sunt qui Propertium malint' in *Critical essays on Roman literature. Elegy and lyric* (ed. J. P. Sullivan) 107–48. London.

Allison, J. W. (1980). 'Propertius 4.7.94', *AJPh* 101:170–3.

André, J. (1949). *Étude sur les termes de couleur dans la langue latine*. Paris.

Arrowsmith, L. (1966). 'Luxury and death in the *Satyricon*', *Arion* 5:304–31.

Auerbach, E. (1953). *Mimesis. The representation of reality in Western literature* (transl. W. R. Trask). Princeton.

Bailey, C. (1947). *Titi Lucreti Cari De Rerum Natura libri sex*, 3 vols. with prolegomena, critical text, translation and commentary. Oxford.

Baker, R. J. (1970). '*Laus in amore mori*: love and death in Propertius', *Latomus* 29:670–98.

Bardon, H. (1959). 'Un aspect méconnu du génie latin: le sens du mystère', *RCCM* 1:7–14.

Barsby, J. A. (1974). 'The composition and publication of the first three books of Propertius', *G&R* 21:128–37.

Bartoletti, V. (1965) in 'Euforione e i poeti latini' *Maia* 17:158–76 (discussions by F. Della Corte, P. Treves, A. Barigazzi, V. Bartoletti (pp. 165–8), L. Alfonsi).

Beare, W. (1964). *The Roman stage*. 3rd edn. London.

Becker, C. (1971). 'Die späten Elegien des Properz', *Hermes* 99:449–80.

Berthet, J. F. (1980). 'Properce et Homère' in *L'Élégie romaine. Enracinement, thèmes, diffusion*. (Bulletin de la Faculté des lettres de Mulhouse, Fascicule x, 141–55.) Paris.

Birt, T. (1895). 'Die vaticanische Ariadne und die dritte Elegie des Properz', *RhM* 50:31–65, 161–90.

Bömer, F. (1980). *P. Ovidius Naso. Metamorphosen. Buch X–XI*. Heidelberg.

Bonelli, G. (1979). *Decadentismo antico e moderno. Un confronto fra l'estetismo alessandrino e l'esperienza poetica contemporanea*. Turin.

Boucher, J.-P. (1965). *Études sur Properce*. Paris.

(1966). *Caius Cornelius Gallus*. (Bibliothèque de la Faculté des Lettres de Lyon, 11.) Paris.

(1974). 'Place et rôle de la religion dans les élégies de Properce' in *Mélanges offerts à P. Boyancé* (Collection de l'École Française de Rome, 22) 79–102. Rome.

(1977). 'Properce et ses amis' in *Colloquium Propertianum* (ed. M. Bigaroni and F. Santucci) 53–71. Assisi.

Boyancé, P. (1956). 'Properce' in 'L'influence grecque sur la poésie latine de Catulle à Ovide' (*Entretiens sur l'antiquité classique*, 2.169–220). Fondation Hardt, Geneva.

Boyle, A. J. (1974). 'Propertius 1.19: a critical study', *Latomus* 33:895–911.

Bradbury, M. and Palmer, D. (1979) (eds.). *Decadence and the 1890s*. (Stratford-upon-Avon Studies, 17.) London.

Bréguet, E. (1960). 'In una parce duobus' in *Hommages Herrmann*. (Collection *Latomus*, 44) 205–14. Brussels.

Bright, D. F. (1978). *Haec mihi fingebam: Tibullus in his world*. Leiden.

Burck, E. (1952). 'Römische Wesenszüge der augusteischen Liebeselegie', *Hermes* 80:163–200.

(1966). 'Zur Komposition des vierten Buches des Properz', *WS* 79:405–27.

Cairns, F. J. (1969). 'Propertius 1.18 and Callimachus' *Acontius and Cydippe*', *CR* N.S. 19:131–4.

(1972). *Generic composition in Greek and Roman poetry*. Edinburgh.

(1975). *Further adventures of a locked-out lover*. Inaugural Lecture series, University of Liverpool.

(1977). 'Two unidentified komoi of Propertius': 1 3 and 11 29', *Emerita* 45:325–53.

(1979). *Tibullus: a Hellenistic poet at Rome*. Cambridge.

(1979a). 'Self-imitation within a generic framework' in *Creative imitation and Latin literature* (ed. D. West and T. Woodman) 121–41. Cambridge.

Calder, W. M. III (1960). 'Was Antigone murdered?', *GRBS* 3:31–5.

Carey, J. (1981). *John Donne. Life, mind and art*. London.

Carter, A. E. (1958). *The idea of decadence in French literature 1830–1900*. Toronto.

Celentano, L. (1956). 'Significato e valore del iv libro di Properzio', *Annali della Facoltà di Lettere della Università di Napoli* 6:33–68.

Clausen, W. V. (1964). 'Callimachus and Latin poetry', *GRBS* 5:181–96.

Coleman, R. (1977). *Vergil: Eclogues*. Cambridge.

Commager, S. (1974). *A prolegomenon to Propertius*. Cincinnati.

Courtney, E. (1962). 'Parody and literary allusion in Menippean satire', *Philologus* 106:82–100.

(1968). 'The structure of Propertius Book 1 and some textual consequences', *Phoenix* 22:250–8.

(1969). 'Three poems of Propertius', *BICS* 16:70–87.

Croce, B. (1936). 'Intorno a Properzio, a un suo vecchio interprete italiano e all' elegia dell' ombra di Cinzia', *La Critica* 34:146–55.

Crowther, N. B. (1970). 'Οἱ νεώτεροι, poetae novi, and cantores Euphorionis', *CQ* N.S. 20:322–7.

(1976). 'Parthenius and Roman poetry', *Mnemosyne* 29:65–71.

Crump, M. M. (1931). *The epyllion from Theocritus to Ovid*. Oxford.

Curran, L. C. (1968). 'Propertius 4.11: Greek heroines and death', *CPh* 63:134–9.

Curtius, E. R. (1953). *European literature and the Latin Middle Ages* (transl. W. R. Trask). London (repr. 1979).

Dalzell, A. (1980). 'Homeric themes in Propertius', *Hermathena* 129:29–36.

Damon, P. W. and Helmbold, W. C. (1952). 'The structure of Propertius Book 11', *Univ. of California Publ. in Class. Philol.* 14:215–53.

Davis, J. T. (1977). *Dramatic pairings in the elegies of Propertius and Ovid*. (Noctes Romanae, 15.) Bern and Stuttgart.

Dawson, C. M. (1944). *Romano-Campanian mythological landscape painting. YClS* 9.

Day, A. A. (1938). *The origins of Latin love-elegy*. Oxford.

Delatte, L. (1967). 'Key-words and poetic themes in Propertius and Tibullus', *RELO* 3:31–80.

Doughty, O. (1957). *Dante Gabriel Rossetti. Poems*. London.

Dover, K. J. (1971). *Theocritus: select poems*. London and Basingstoke.

Drews, H. (1952). 'Der Todesgedanke bei den römischen Elegikern'. Diss. (typescript) Kiel.

Edwards, M. W. (1961). 'Intensification of meaning in Propertius and others', *TAPhA* 92:128–44.

Eitrem, S. (1941). 'La magie comme motif littéraire', *SO* 21:39–83.

Enk, P. J. (1956). 'The unity of some elegies of Propertius', *Latomus* 15:181–92.

Evans, S. (1971). 'Odyssean echoes in Prop. 4.8', *G&R* 18:51–3.

Falkner, T. M. (1975). *Critical studies of select elegies of Propertius*. Diss. State Univ. of New York at Buffalo.

Fedeli, P. (1977). 'Properzio 1.15: Arte allusiva e interpretazione' in *Colloquium Propertianum* (see under Boucher (1977)) 73–99.

Fletcher, I. (1973). *Swinburne*. Longman.

Follett, N. E. (1973). 'Studies in Propertius and the Roman elegists'. Diss. (typescript) Univ. of London.

Fraser, P. M. (1972). *Ptolemaic Alexandria*. 3 vols. Oxford.

Friedländer, P. (1941). 'Pattern of sound and atomistic theory in Lucretius', *AJPh* 62:16–34 (= *Studien zur antiken Literatur und Kunst*, Berlin 1969, 337–53).

Friedrich, W.-H. (1956). 'Episches Unwetter' in *Festschrift Bruno Snell*, 77–87. Munich.

Gaunt, W. (1975). *The aesthetic adventure*. Rev. edn. London.

Gelzer, T. (1975). *Musaeus: Hero and Leander*. Loeb. London and Cambridge, Mass.

Green, P. (1982). *Ovid. The erotic poems* (transl. with introd. and notes). Harmondsworth.

Griffin, J. (1976). 'Augustan poetry and the life of luxury', *JRS* 66:87–104.
 (1977). 'Propertius and Antony', *JRS* 67:17–26.

Grimal, P. (1952). 'Les intentions de Properce et la composition du livre iv des "Élégies"', *Latomus* 11:183–97, 315–26, 437–50.

Guillemin, A. (1950). 'Properce. De Cynthie aux poèmes romains', *REL* 28:182–93.

Habinek, T. N. (1982). 'Propertius, Cynthia and the lunar year', *Latomus* 41:589–96.

Harmon, D. P. (1975). 'Myth and proverb in Propertius 2.8', *CW* 68:417–24.

Hartman, J. J. (1921). 'Propertiana', *Mnemosyne* N.S. 49:311–32, 337–51.

Heiden, B. A. (1982). 'Book-division within Propertius Book ii', *QUCC* N.S. 11:151–69.

Heinze, R. (1914). *Virgils epische Technik*. 3rd edn. Leipzig and Berlin (repr. Stuttgart 1957).
 (1938). 'Die Horazische Ode' in *Vom Geist des Römertums* (ed. E. Burck) 185–212. Leipzig and Berlin.

Helm, R. (1934). Review of H. E. Butler and E. A. Barber, *The elegies of Propertius*, Oxford 1933, *Philologische Wochenschrift* 54:783–93.

Helmbold, W. C. (1949). 'Propertius IV.7. Prolegomena to an interpretation', *Univ. of California Publ. in Class. Philol.* 13.9:333–43.

Herz, W. (1955). 'Vergänglichkeit und Tod in der römischen Elegie'. Diss. (typescript) Freiburg.

Hodge, R. I. V. and Buttimore, R. A. (1977). *The 'Monobiblos', Propertius Bk 1* (text, transl. and critical analysis of each poem). Cambridge and Ipswich.

Hough, G. (1949). *The last Romantics.* London (repr. 1983).

Housman, A. E. (1888). 'Emendationes Propertianae', *JPh* 16:1–35 (= *The Classical papers of A. E. Housman* (ed. J. Diggle and F. R. D. Goodyear, 3 vols. Cambridge 1972) 1 29–54).

  (1934). 'Butler and Barber's Propertius', *CR* 48:136–9 (= *The Classical papers* III 1234–38).

Howald, E. (1948). *Das Wesen der lateinischen Dichtung.* Erlenbach–Zurich.

Hubbard, M. (1974). *Propertius.* London.

Jacoby, F. (1909). 'Tibulls erste Elegie', *RhM* 64:601–32 (= *Kleine philol. Schriften* (ed. H. J. Mette, 2 vols. Berlin 1961) II 122–49).

  (1910). 'Tibulls erste Elegie', *RhM* 65:22–87 (= *Kl. phil. Schr.* (see Jacoby 1909) II 149–205).

  (1914). '3 Gedichte des Properz', *RhM* 69:393–413, 427–63 (= *Kl. phil. Schr.* (see Jacoby 1909) II 216–65).

Jäger, K. (1967). *Zweigliedrige Gedichte und Gedichtpaare bei Properz und in Ovids Amores.* Tübingen.

Jenkyns, R. (1982). *Three classical poets: Sappho, Catullus and Juvenal.* London.

Juhnke, H. (1971). 'Zum Aufbau des zweiten und dritten Buches des Properz', *Hermes* 99:91–125.

Kenney, E. J. (1970). 'Doctus Lucretius', *Mnemosyne* 4.23:366–92.

  (1979). 'Two disputed passages in the *Heroides*' *CQ* N.S. 29:394–431.

  (1983). 'Virgil and the elegiac sensibility', *ICS* 8:44–59.

Keyssner, K. (1975). 'Die bildende Kunst bei Properz' in *Properz* (ed. W. Eisenhut), *Wege der Forschung* 237:264–86. Darmstadt.

King, J. (1975–6). 'Propertius' programmatic poetry and the unity of the Monobiblos', *CJ* 71:108–24.

  (1980). 'Propertius 2.1–12: his Callimachean Second Libellus', *WJA* N.F. 6b:61–84.

Klingner, F. (1956). *Catulls Peleus-Epos.* Bayer. Akademie der Wissenschaften, Phil.-Hist. Klasse, Heft 6. Munich (= *Studien zur griechischen und römischen Literatur* (ed. K. Bartels, Zurich and Stuttgart 1964) 156–224).

Kölmel, B. W. (1957). 'Die Funktion des Mythologischen in der Dichtung des Properz'. Diss. (typescript) Heidelberg.

Kost, K. (1971). *Musaios, Hero und Leander.* Bonn.

Krokowski, G. (1926). 'De Propertio Ludibundo', *Eos* 29:81–100.

Kroll, W. (1924). *Studien zum Verständnis der römischen Literatur.* Stuttgart (repr. 1964).

Kröner, H. O. (1970). 'Elegisches Unwetter', *Poetica* 3:388–408.

Kühn, J.-H. (1961). 'Die Prooimion-Elegie des zweiten Properz-Buches', *Hermes* 89:84–105.

BIBLIOGRAPHY

Lake, A. K. (1937). 'An interpretation of Propertius 4.7', *CR* 51:53–5.

La Penna, A. (1950). 'Properzio e i poeti latini dell' età aurea', *Maia* 3:209–36, continued in La Penna (1951a).

(1951). *Properzio. Saggio critico seguito da due ricerche filologiche.* Florence.

(1951a). *Maia* 4:43–69.

(1951b). 'Note sul linguaggio dell' elegia erotica latina', *Maia* 4:187–209.

(1977). *L'integrazione difficile. Un profilo di Properzio.* Turin.

Lattimore, R. (1962). *Themes in Greek and Latin epitaphs.* Urbana.

Laughton, E. (1958). 'Propertius 4.7.26', *CQ* n.s. 8:98–9.

Lausberg, H. (1960). *Handbuch der literarischen Rhetorik.* Munich.

Leach, E. W. (1966). 'Propertius 1.17: the experimental voyage', *YClS* 19:211–32.

Lee, A. G. (1960). Review of G. Luck, *The Latin love elegy*, London 1959, *Gnomon* 32:515–19.

(1962). 'Tenerorum lusor amorum' in *Critical essays on Roman literature* (ed. J. P. Sullivan) 149–79. London.

Lefèvre, E. (1966). *Propertius ludibundus. Elemente des Humors in seinen Elegien.* Heidelberg.

(1977). 'L'unità dell'elegia Properziana' in *Colloquium Propertianum* (see under Boucher (1977)) 25–51.

Lesky, A. (1966). *A history of Greek literature* (transl. J. Willis and Cornelis de Heer). London.

Lewis, C. S. (1961). *An experiment in criticism* (repr. 1969). Cambridge.

Lieberg, G. (1962). *Puella divina: Die Gestalt der göttlichen Geliebten bei Catull im Zusammenhang der antiken Dichtung.* Amsterdam.

(1969). 'Die Mythologie des Properz in der Forschung und die Idealisierung Cynthias', *RhM* 112:311–47.

Lier, B. (1903). 'Topica carminum sepulcralium latinorum', Part I, *Philologus* 62:445–77.

Lloyd-Jones, H. and Parsons, P. (1983). *Supplementum Hellenisticum.* Berlin and New York.

Luck, G. (1955). 'Das Acanthisgedicht des Properz', *Hermes* 83:428–38.

(1962). *Hexen und Zauberei in der römischen Dichtung.* Zurich.

(1969). *The Latin love elegy.* 2nd edn. London.

(1973). 'Probleme der römischen Liebeselegie in der neueren Forschung' in *Aufstieg und Niedergang der römischen Welt: Geschichte und Kultur Roms im Spiegel der neueren Forschung.* (ed. H. Temporini) 1.3, 361–8.

Lundström, S. (1967–8). 'Reminiszenzen an Properz bei Petron', Humanistiska Vetenskaps-Samfundet i Uppsala. Årsbok, 68–97. Uppsala.

Lyne, R. O. A. M. (1978). 'The Neoteric poets', *CQ* n.s. 28:167–87.

(1980). *The Latin love poets from Catullus to Horace.* Oxford.

Macleod, C. W. (1976). 'Propertius 2.26', *SO* 51:131–6 (= *Collected essays* (ed. O. Taplin, Oxford 1983) 196–201).

Maiuri, A. (1953). *Roman painting* (transl. S. Gilbert). Lausanne.

Masefield, J. (1947). *Thanks before going.* London.

McKeown, J. C. (1979). 'Augustan elegy and mime', *PCPhS* 25:71–84.

Menes, E. P. (1968). *Cynthia as symbol: love, patriotism, and poetry in the elegies of Propertius*. Diss. Princeton Univ.

(1983). 'The external evidence for the division of Propertius, Book 2', *CPh* 78:136–43.

Michels, A. K. (1955). 'Death and two poets', *TAPhA* 86:160–79.

Morgan, K. (1977). *Ovid's art of imitation. Propertius in the 'Amores'*. Mnemosyne Suppl. 47. Leiden.

Muecke, F. (1977). '*Nobilis historia?* Incongruity in Propertius 4.7', *BICS* 24:124–32.

(1978). 'Propertius 4.7.26', *CQ* n.s. 28:242.

Munro, J. M. (1970). *The decadent poetry of the eighteen-nineties*. Beirut.

Nakayama, T. (1963–4). 'Schönheitsbegriff bei Catull und Properz', *AIGC* 1:61–74.

Naumann, W. (1968). 'Staub, entbrannt in Liebe. Das Thema von Tod und Liebe bei Properz, Quevedo und Goethe', *Arcadia* 3:157–72.

Nethercut, W. R. (1968). 'Notes on the structure of Propertius Book 4', *AJPh* 89:449–64.

Newman, J. K. (1967). *Augustus and the new poetry*. (Collection Latomus, 88.) Brussels.

Olivares, J. (1983). *The love poetry of Francisco de Quevedo*. Cambridge.

O'Neil, E. N. (1958). 'Cynthia and the moon', *CPh* 53:1–8.

Osborne, H. (1972) (ed.). *Aesthetics*. Oxford.

Otis, B. (1965). 'Propertius' single book', *HSPh* 70:1–44.

Paduano, G. (1968). 'Le reminiscenze dell' *Alcesti* nell' Elegia 4.11 di Properzio', *Maia* 20:21–8.

Parca, M. (1982). '*Tardus Amor* and *Tardus Apollo* in Propertius' Monobiblos', *Latomus* 41:584–8.

Pasoli, E. (1977). 'Poesia d'amore e "metapoesia": aspetti della modernità di Properzio' in *Colloquium Propertianum* (see under Boucher (1977)) 101–21.

Paton, J. M. (1901). 'The *Antigone* of Euripides', *HSPh* 12:267–76.

Perry, B. E. (1967). *The ancient romances*. (Sather Classical Lectures, 37.) Berkeley and Los Angeles.

Pichon, R. (1902). *De sermone amatorio apud Latinos elegiarum scriptores*. Paris.

Platnauer, M. (1951). *Latin elegiac verse. A study of the metrical usages of Tibullus, Propertius and Ovid*. Cambridge.

Poe, J. P. (1969). 'An analysis of Seneca's *Thyestes*', *TAPhA* 100:355–76.

Pöschl, V. (1956). Discussion on A. Rostagni's 'L'elegia erotica latina' in *Entretiens sur l'antiquité classique* (see under Boyancé (1956)) 88–90.

Postgate, J. P. (1881). *Select elegies of Propertius*. London.

Praz, M. (1951). *The Romantic agony* (transl. A. Davidson). 2nd edn. Oxford. (repr. 1978).

Quinn, K. (1963). *Latin explorations. Critical studies in Roman literature*. London.

Regenbogen, O. (1961). 'Schmerz und Tod in den Tragödien Senecas' in *Kleine Schriften* (ed. F. Dirlmeier, Munich) 409–62. Repr. as monograph, Darmstadt 1963.

Reitzenstein, E. (1936). *Wirklichkeitsbild und Gefühlsentwicklung bei Properz. Philologus* Supplementband 29, Heft 2. Leipzig.

Reitzenstein, R. (1896). 'Properz-Studien', *Hermes* 31:185–220.

(1912). 'Noch einmal Tibulls erste Elegie', *Hermes* 47:60–116.

Roberts, L. (1968). *A concordance of Lucretius*. Supplement to ΑΓΩΝ.

Robertson, F. (1969). 'Lament for Paetus – Propertius 3.7', *TAPhA* 100:377–86.

Rohde, E. (1914). *Der griechische Roman und seine Vorläufer*. 3rd edn. Leipzig (repr. Hildesheim 1974).

Ross, D. O. (1975). *Backgrounds to Augustan poetry: Gallus, elegy and Rome.* Cambridge.

Rostagni, A. (1956). 'L'influenza greca sulla origine dell' elegia erotica latina', in *Entretiens sur l'antiquité classique* (see under Boyancé (1956)) 59–82.

Rudd, N. (1981). 'Romantic love in Classical times?', *Ramus* 10:140–58.

Rutz, W. (1960). '*Amor Mortis* bei Lucan', *Hermes* 88:462–75.

Saunders Boos, F. (1976). *The poetry of Dante G. Rossetti: a critical reading and source study.* (Studies in English Literature, 104.) The Hague–Paris.

Schöne, W. (1911). *De Propertii ratione fabulas adhibendi.* Diss. Leipzig.

Schulz-Vanheyden, E. (1969). *Properz und das griechische Epigramm.* Diss. Münster.

Sconocchia, S. (1972). 'L'*Antigona* di Accio e l'*Antigone* di Sofocle', *RFIC* serie terza 100:273–82.

Segal, C. P. (1969). *Landscape in Ovid's Metamorphoses. Hermes* Einzelschriften, 23. Wiesbaden.

Shackleton Bailey, D. R. (1949). 'Propertiana', *CQ* 43:22–9.

(1956). *Propertiana.* Cambridge (repr. Amsterdam 1967).

Silk, M. S. (1974). *Interaction in poetic imagery.* Cambridge.

Skutsch, F. (1901). *Aus Vergils Frühzeit.* Leipzig.

Skutsch, O. (1963). 'The structure of the Propertian *Monobiblos*', *CPh* 58: 238–9.

(1975). 'The second Book of Propertius', *HSPh* 79:229–33.

Smith, K. F. (1913). *The elegies of Albius Tibullus.* New York (repr. Darmstadt 1964).

Snell, R. (1982). *Théophile Gautier. A romantic critic of the visual arts.* Oxford.

Snyder, J. M. (1980). *Puns and poetry in Lucretius' 'De Rerum Natura'.* Amsterdam.

Solmsen, F. (1961). 'Propertius in his literary relations with Tibullus and Vergil', *Philologus* 105:273–89.

(1962). 'Three elegies of Propertius' First Book', *CPh* 57:73–88.

Starkie, E. M. (1962). *From Gautier to Eliot.* London.

Steidle, W. (1962). 'Das Motiv der Lebenswahl bei Tibull und Properz', *WS* 75:100–40.

Stroh, W. (1971). *Die römische Liebeselegie als werbende Dichtung.* Amsterdam.

Suits, T. A. (1965). 'Mythology, address and structure in Propertius 2.8', *TAPhA* 96:427–37.

Sullivan, J. P. (1976). *Propertius. A critical introduction.* Cambridge.

Temple, R. Z. (1974). 'Truth in labelling: pre-Raphaelitism, Aestheticism, Decadence, Fin de Siècle', *English literature in transition* 17:201–22.

Thill, A. (1979). *Alter ab illo. Recherches sur l'imitation dans la poésie personnelle à l'époque augustéenne.* (Collection d'études anciennes.) Paris.

Thornton, R. K. R. (1970). *Poetry of the nineties.* Harmondsworth.

——— (1979). '"Decadence" in later nineteenth-century England' in Bradbury and Palmer (1979) (*q.v.*) 15–29.

——— (1983). *The decadent dilemma.* London.

Traina, A. (1970). *Vortit barbare. Le traduzioni poetiche da Livio Andronico a Cicerone.* Rome.

Tränkle, H. (1960). *Die Sprachkunst des Properz und die Tradition der lateinischen Dichtersprache. Hermes* Einzelschriften, 15. Wiesbaden.

——— (1979). 'Das römische Vorbild für Goethes "Euphrosyne" (Properz IV.7)', *Acta Philologica Aenipontana* 4:74–6.

Tupet, A.-M. (1976). *La Magie dans la poésie latine: I Des origines à la fin du règne d'Auguste.* Paris.

Verstraete, B. C. (1980). 'Propertius' use of myth in Book Two', Collection *Latomus* 168:259–68.

Walsh, P. G. (1970). *The Roman novel.* Cambridge.

Warden, J. (1980). *Fallax opus: poet and reader in the elegies of Propertius. Phoenix* Supplementary Vol. 14. Toronto–Buffalo–London.

Warner, E. and Hough, G. (1983). *Strangeness and beauty. An anthology of aesthetic criticism.* 2 vols. Cambridge.

Webster, T. B. L. (1954). 'Fourth century Tragedy and Poetics', *Hermes* 82:294–308.

——— (1964). *Hellenistic poetry and art.* London.

Wecklein (1878). 'Über drei verlorene Tragödien des Euripides', *Sitzungsberichte der königl. Bayer. Akademie der Wissenschaften zu München.* Philos.-Philol. und Histor. Classe, Band 2, 170–223.

Weeber, K.-W. (1977). *Das 4. Properz-Buch. Interpretationen zu seiner Eigenart und seiner Stellung im Gesamtwerk.* Diss. Bochum.

Welcker, F. G. (1839–41). *Die griechischen Tragödien mit Rücksicht auf den epischen Cyclus. Rheinisches Museum für Philologie,* 2nd Supplementband. Bonn.

Wenzel, U. (1969). *Properz. Hauptmotive seiner Dichtung (Lebenswahl, Tod, Ruhm und Unsterblichkeit, Kaiser und Rom).* Diss. Bamberg.

West, D. (1969). *The imagery and poetry of Lucretius.* Edinburgh.

West, D. and Woodman, T. (1979). *Creative imitation and Latin literature.* Cambridge.

Whitaker, R. (1983). *Myth and personal experience in Roman love-elegy. A study in poetic technique. Hypomnemata,* 76. Göttingen.

White, R. E. (1958). *Some techniques of development in Propertius and their bearing on poem division.* Diss. (microfilm) Univ. of North Carolina.

Wiggers, N. E. P. (1972). *Heroic love: a study of Propertius' adaptation of erotic tradition to personal poetry.* Diss. Brown Univ.

——— (1980). 'Variations on a theme: nightmare and daydream in Propertius 2.26', *Latomus* 39:121–8.

Wilamowitz-Moellendorff, U. von (1900). *Bion von Smyrna: Adonis.* Berlin.

Wilkinson, L. P. (1950). 'The baroque spirit in ancient art and literature' in *Essays by divers hands*, vol. 25, 2–11.

(1955). *Ovid recalled*. Cambridge.

(1966). *Golden Latin artistry*. Cambridge.

(1966a). 'The continuity of Propertius II.13', *CR* N.S. 16:141–4.

Wille, G. (1980). 'Zum Aufbau des zweiten Buches des Properz', *WJA* N.F. 6a:249–67.

Williams, G. (1968). *Tradition and originality in Roman poetry*. Oxford.

(1980). *Figures of thought in Roman poetry*. New Haven and London.

Willis, J. (1972). *Latin textual criticism*. (Illinois Studies in Language and Literature, 61.) Urbana–Chicago–London.

Wimmel, W. (1960). *Kallimachos in Rom. Die Nachfolge seines apologetischen Dichtens in der Augusteerzeit. Hermes* Einzelschriften, 16. Wiesbaden.

(1976). *Tibull und Delia. Erster Teil. Tibulls Elegie 1.1. Hermes* Einzelschriften 37. Wiesbaden.

Wiseman, T. P. (1985). *Catullus and his world. A reappraisal*. Cambridge.

Woodman, T. (1984). 'Horace's first Roman ode' in *Poetry and politics in the age of Augustus* (ed. T. Woodman and D. West) 83–94. Cambridge.

Wright, J. R. G. (1983). 'Virgil's pastoral programme: Theocritus, Callimachus and Eclogue 1', *PCPhS* N.S. 29:107–60.

Yardley, J. C. (1977). 'Cynthia's ghost: Propertius 4.7 again', *BICS* 24:83–7.

Zanker, G. (1981). 'Enargeia in the ancient criticism of poetry', *RhM* 124:297–311.

INDEXES